T. W. Brents

Gospel Sermons

T. W. Brents

Gospel Sermons

ISBN/EAN: 9783337266028

Printed in Europe, USA, Canada, Australia, Japan

Cover: Foto ©Lupo / pixelio.de

More available books at **www.hansebooks.com**

GOSPEL ⊙ SERMONS,

A Series of Discourses on Induction into Christ,
one each on Church Organization and the
Origin and Ministry of Angels,
the Millennium, etc.

―――BY―――

DR. T. W. BRENTS.

NASHVILLE, TENN.:
GOSPEL ADVOCATE PUBLISHING CO.,
1891.

PREFACE.

On the subject of the Christian religion, the Bible is the only infallible authority in the universe. Good, wise, and great men have met in councils, assemblies, presbyteries, conferences, and associations, and have formulated creeds, confessions of faith, and disciplines, which have been adopted by religious bodies; but, like all things of human origin, they are imperfect. That *they are often wrong* is seen in the fact that it is necessary to change, alter, or amend them. *Translations* of the Bible may need revision, but the *Bible*, as it came from the inspiring Spirit of God, needs no alteration. Being perfect, it is not susceptible of improvement. Perfection cannot be improved. *Science* is progressive. Improvements are frequently made. New discoveries are often developed. But *Christianity* was perfect when it came from its author, and cannot be improved. Man may grow in a knowledge of the divine will, so as to more perfectly teach and practice it, but to *improve* it would be to improve perfection itself. This cannot be done, and it is unwise to attempt it.

When we wrote our book on the *Gospel Plan of Salvation* we did not expect that we would ever write another; hence we sought to make it an exhaustive work of its kind. We have found it not a little difficult, therefore, in writing this book, to keep entirely clear of thoughts presented in that one. In a few places, where such thoughts seemed necessary in treating subjects discussed in this book, we have referred the reader to that work, without transferring them to this one. In this book, however, will be found a number of subjects not treated in that work at all. Quite a number of sermons, which we have been accustomed to preach, are omitted in this book, because the subjects are fully treated in the former work.

We cannot promise that the sermons presented in the following pages are exactly as we have been accustomed to preach them. We never wrote out a sermon until we wrote it for this book. Nor did we ever memorize a sermon in life; hence the impossibility of writing a sermon just as we preached it. We are quite sure that we never preached the same sermon twice in the same words. We could not have done so had we attempted it, and we never tried. We have preached *substantially* the same sermon often, but not in the same words. We have always *prepared our thoughts*, but trusted to the occasion to furnish the verbiage in which to present them.

Whether or not the *written* sermons will be an improvement on the *oral*, we cannot say. We have yet to see a living speaker who could put himself on paper. The sparkling eye—the earnest face—the intonations of voice—the impressive gesture, and other things which give force to the living orator, cannot be seen in what he writes, however well he may write what was spoken. While this is all true, yet book sermons have some advantages over the oral. If the hearer fails to catch a thought as it is spoken, it is gone; but if he fails to understand what he reads, he can turn back and read again, and again, until he does understand it. If he hears a good sermon he may wish his neighbor to have the benefit of it; but he cannot always call it up so as to tell it to him; but if he reads it in a book he can lend his book to his neighbor, until he gets the benefit of it. The afflicted may read a good sermon, and be edified by it when unable to go to preaching at all. Others may live remote from any place where they can hear preaching at all, and a book of good sermons is a good substitute for a preacher to them. Indeed it matters not how much preaching a man hears, he wants something for himself and family to read at home.

But he says: "I have the Bible to read, and that is better than any book of sermons." If you will show us a man who reads nothing but the Bible, we will show you one who reads and understands very little of that. He who is anxious to understand the Bible will want to read, not only the Bible, but every thing else he can get that will help him to understand it.

Of course no one is responsible for anything in this book but the writer, nor does he expect any one to believe it, unless it be in harmony with what the reader conceives the Bible to teach on the subjects treated. We have written for the purpose of aiding the reader in coming to a knowledge of what is taught in the Bible. We believe the Bible to be a revelation from God, and therefore true. It contains all we know of God or the devil—heaven or hell—angels or spirits—eternal life or eternal death. We may misconstrue its teachings, but we are ever willing to be taught it more perfectly. Nor have we any inclination to *figure or symbolize* it all away either. Some construe its language quite literally, until it comes in conflict with their peculiar hobbies, then it must be symbolic or figurative. Unquestionably there are figures and symbols in it, but where they occur the context will clearly show them to be such; otherwise we accept the plain literal construction *without an "if" or a "but."* Plain literal constructions cannot be set aside for no better reason than the *preservation of a theory*. If we may take such liberties as this, then there can be no certainty as to what the Bible teaches about any thing. One man will figure it to suit him; another will figure it to suit him; and so there will be no end to such figuring. Surely a theory must be *doubtful* that requires such *symbolizing* and *figuring* to support it. It occurs to us that he who is truly loyal to the Master, is always willing to accept his teaching without straining it to fit theories. *We propose to form theories by the Bible, rather than construe the Bible to fit theories already formed.* If there is any thing in this book that cannot survive this treatment let it die; the sooner it is dead and forgotten the better. But, kind reader, if you find that what we have written is supported by the plainest teaching of Holy Writ, then let not your *prejudice* keep you from receiving it. *If it is not true*, you should reject it, but *if it is true*, you cannot afford to reject it. To this test we most cheerfully submit our work. T. W. BRENTS.

Lewisburg, Tenn., Aug. 1, 1891.

CONTENTS.

	PAGE
CHAPTER I.	
The Mission of John the Baptist	7– 21
CHAPTER II.	
The Sonship of Christ	22– 45
CHAPTER III.	
The Commission	46– 61
CHAPTER IV.	
The Conversion of the Jailer	62– 75
CHAPTER V.	
Types and Antitypes, Shadows and Substances	76– 90
CHAPTER VI.	
Salvation of the Hebrews from Bondage	91–108
CHAPTER VII.	
The Tabernacle	109–130
CHAPTER VIII.	
Freedom From Sin	131–145
CHAPTER IX.	
Justification	146–176
CHAPTER X.	
Regeneration	177–190
CHAPTER XI.	
The Transfiguration	191–204
CHAPTER XII.	
Paul's Charge to Timothy	205–220
CHAPTER XIII.	
A Reason for the Christian's Hope	221–236

CONTENTS.

CHAPTER XIV.
Zeal Without Knowledge..................................237–250

CHAPTER XV.
Paul's Natural Man..251–266

CHAPTER XVI.
The Divine Nature in the Christian........................267–281

CHAPTER XVII.
Excuses...282–298

CHAPTER XVIII.
The Origin, Mission, and Destiny of Angels................299–323

CHAPTER XIX.
The Millennium..324–352

CHAPTER XX.
Church Organization.......................................353–410

CHAPTER XXI.
Conditional Salvation.....................................411–440

GOSPEL SERMONS.

CHAPTER I.

THE MISSION OF JOHN THE BAPTIST.

"And thou, child, shalt be called the prophet of the Highest; for thou shalt go before the face of the Lord to prepare his ways; to give knowledge of salvation unto his people by the remission of their sins." Luke i: 76, 77.

THIS is the language of Zacharias as he prophesied by the Spirit when John was born. He was to go before the Lord to prepare a people for His reception. There was perhaps never a time in the world's history when the world was farther gone in wickedness than at the time when Jesus came. There was not a crime known to the whole dark list of wickedness and sin that was not practiced by the Jews in those days. The heart grows sick in contemplating the picture drawn by Paul in his letter to the church at Rome. Had Jesus come without some one going before him to prepare public sentiment and reform the people, it is more than probable that he would have been murdered before his preparatory work was complete. Even as it was He often had to get away from the rabble privately to keep them from killing Him before the time for His crucifixion came. Hence the wisdom of God in sending John before the Lord to prepare the way before Him.

The church of God having begun on the day of Pentecost, and since the days of John the Baptist, our scribes and preachers have passed by John's work and mission, perhaps without giving them that attention and study which their importance demands; and as a result we think it possible that their *connection* with the establishment of the great spiritual temple has not been as clearly seen by every one as may be desirable.

The conception and birth of John were as purely miraculous as were those of Isaac or of Jesus the Christ. He was given to his parents when his father was an "old man, and his wife well stricken in years;" (Luke i: 18,) and the angel Gabriel was sent from the presence of God to announce the glad tidings of his birth, the character of his life, and the object of his mission. He was to be filled with the Holy Spirit from his mother's womb, (Luke i: 15) and was to go before the Lord in the spirit and power of Elias, to turn the hearts of the fathers to the children, and the disobedient to the wisdom of the just; *to make ready a people prepared for the Lord.* Luke i: 17. As it was John's God-appointed work to make ready a people prepared for the Lord, did he perform the work assigned him? If so, how did he prepare them? Whom did he prepare? What position, if any, did they occupy in the spiritual Temple when it was erected? Our first question is answered by answering the second, how did John make ready a people prepared for the Lord? Well, how did he prepare them? He gave them knowledge of salvation. How did he give them knowledge of salvation? By the remission of their sins. Luke i: 77. Did they have "a *feeling sense of pardon?*" Well, yes, they had *knowledge of salvation* by the remission of their sins, and we guess they felt like they were pardoned.

But how did they get *knowledge* of salvation? We suppose they got it by compliance with the conditions upon which God authorized John to offer it to them.

What were the conditions of salvation imposed by John? Let us see. "There was a man sent from God whose name was John. The same came for a witness to bear witness of the Light, that all men through him might believe." John i: 7. Then it was necessary that men *believe*, in the days of John. Yes, but what were they required to believe? "John verily baptized with the baptism of repentance, saying unto the people that they should believe on him which should come after him, that is, on Christ Jesus." Acts xix: 4. Thus we see they believed on a *Christ to come*—we believe in a Christ already come; this difference in their faith and ours—no more. Christ was the *object* of their faith then, and he is the *object* of our faith to-day.

But the theory of salvation by faith alone had not been discovered in John's day. "In those days came John the Baptist, preaching in the wilderness of Judea, and saying, *Repent ye:* for the kingdom of heaven is at hand." Matt. iii: 1, 2.

In preparing a people for the Lord in John's day it was necessary that the wicked should be reformed—turned in heart from disobedience to the law of God under which, as Jews, they had always lived, to the wisdom of the just; hence John commanded the people to repent, and he preached the baptism of repentance; that is, a baptism which belonged to or grew out of repentance; a sorrow for the past, with a determination to amend the life; and he baptised with water *unto* repentance. Matt. iii: 2. Thus we see that John's baptism was both preceded and followed by repentance. The former the emotion and resolve of a moment, the latter a life in harmony with that resolve. But their repentance was toward God in whom, as Jews, they had faith, and against whom they had sinned; and having repented for violating God's law under which they had lived, they were admonished to believe in him who was to come.

It may be well to remark here, that while John's mission was confined to the Jews, it was no part of Judaism. His mission was a special one—he was sent from God. John i: 6. He lived under the law of Moses and complied with it as any other Jew, but his preaching and baptizing were done, not in obedience to that law, but by direct authority from God. Said he: "I knew him not: but he that sent me to baptize with water, the same said unto me, Upon whom thou shalt see the Spirit descending and remaining on him, the same is he," etc. John i: 33.

Then God sent John to baptize clothed with special authority; and it is idle to talk of John baptizing in obedience to Jewish law. Let him who so affirms tell us the chapter and verse in the law of Moses under which John preached and baptized.

But what was the result of John's preaching? "And there went out unto him all the land of Judea, and they of Jerusalem, and were all baptized of him in the river of Jordan, confessing their sins." Mark i: 5.

But for what did John baptize? He "preached the baptism of repentance for the remission of sins." Mark i: 4; Luke iii: 3. What did he preach for remission of sins? Certainly *that baptism that belonged to repentance.* However important faith may be there is nothing affirmed of it here; nor is there anything affirmed of repentance, only that it was connected with *the baptism preached by John for remission of sins.* Suppose I say "the coat of my friend kept me warm?" What do I say kept me warm? Certainly the coat that belonged to my friend kept me warm. Again: "The house of my friend gave me shelter for the night." What do I say gave me shelter? Certainly the house that belonged to my friend gave me shelter. Very well —the baptism of repentance for remission of sins—what is for the remission of sins? Certainly the baptism that followed or belonged to repentance. If this is not plain and conclusive then human language can make nothing so.

But what have we found now? Let us post up a little.

John's mission was a preparatory one—he came to make ready a people prepared for the Lord. He came from God to bear witness of the Light. Said he, "I saw and bear record that this is the Son of God." Again, "Behold the Lamb of God that taketh away the sin of the world." The object of his testimony was that all men through him might believe—believe in him who was to come after him. Then faith was necessary and John preached it. Repentance was necessary and John preached that also. Baptism for the remission of sins was necessary and John preached and practiced this; and thus he gave knowledge of salvation to his people by the remission of their sins. Every one who accepted the terms was made ready for the Lord, but every one who refused to obey, rejected the counsel of God against themselves not being baptized with the baptism of John. Luke vii: 30.

"Now, when Jesus had heard that John was cast into prison, he departed into Galilee; and leaving Nazareth he came and dwelt in Capernaum." Matt. iv: 12, 13. "From that time Jesus began to preach, and to say,

Repent: for the kingdom of heaven is at hand." Matt. iv: 17.

Jesus seems to have been in Judea when he heard that John was cast into prison, and when he heard it he departed into Galilee. Nazareth had been the home of his childhood, but he now left it and went to dwell in Capernaum and from that time he began to preach the same thing in Galilee that John had preached in the wilderness of Judea, "Repent for the kingdom of heaven is at hand." Matt. iii: 1.

When John's preparatory work was ended and the fullness of time came for Jesus to enter upon, and continue the proclamation of the approaching kingdom it was necessary that his apostles be selected to carry forward this preparatory work, hence Jesus "came to his own, and his own received him not; but as many as received him, to them gave he power to become the sons of God, even to them that believe on his name." John i: 11, 12.

Jesus came to his own, who? His own, the Jews, says every one at once. It is an old maxim, that "what everybody says must be true," and we freely admit that a construction put upon a Scripture, by everybody, for a long time, should be abandoned only after very careful examination; but when so examined and found erroneous it should be given up, however hoary with years or honorable of parentage. This has been the universally received construction put upon this passage for so long that it will be almost if not quite impossible to get a faithful re-hearing on the subject. Many are publicly committed, and they must not be expected to go back on themselves. We once accepted the common theory without examination, but it does not hurt us at all to say we were wrong, for we are most thoroughly convinced that it is not the thought, and we have been so convinced for several years.

John came to make ready a people prepared for the Lord; did he prepare them? Yes. Did he prepare the Jewish nation? No, only a part of it. How did John prepare those he made ready? He gave them knowledge of salvation by the remission of their sins. Were these the Lord's people? Yes, for it is said he (John,) gave knowledge of salvation to his (the Lord's) people. Here those that John prepared are called the Lord's people. To whom did Jesus come? He came to his own. Well, what is the difference between his own to whom he came—the people John made ready, prepared for him, and his people to whom he gave knowledge of salvation by the remission of their sins?

When Jesus came to select his apostles did he come to those made ready for him by John? He did, and we know that some of his apostles were John's disciples, and there is strong reason for believing that all of the twelve were, and perhaps the seventy also. When Jesus came to his own did he come to the Jews? No, he did not need to come to them, for his mother was a Jewess, and he had been among them all his life. Had the inspired writer been seeking to guard us against this very thought, we see not how he could have selected language better calculated to protect us than the language employed. Let us look at it a little. He tells us that *his own* to whom Jesus came *were born* (past tense equivalent to had been born) "not of blood, nor of the will of the flesh, nor of the will of man, but of God," (verse 13.) Bear in mind these *were born* when Jesus came to them, not of blood; had not every Jew been born of blood? If not, who had? Not born of the will of the flesh—had not every Jew been born of the will of the flesh just like other people? Not of the will of man—had not all Jews been born of the will of man just as other men. But *his own* to whom Jesus came had been born in a different sense—how? Born of God. Yes, but born of God, how? By being born of, or complying with that system of means which God sent John to preach to them. We are, if Christians, children of God to-day, begotten of him. Begotten of him through the gospel. The gospel presents a system of means by compliance with which we become God's children, then why is it not true that John's disciples had all been born of God when Jesus came to them as his own, by having been born of that system of means which God sent John to preach to them, and with which they had complied? They had believed, repented, confessed their sins, and had been baptized by John in the river of Jordan for the remission of sins, and thus had knowledge of salvation by the remission of their sins, hence were "his people" "his own" to whom he came.

They all obligated themselves to believe on Christ when he should come, but when he did come many of them did not receive him or believe on him and hence were condemned already because they believed not in the name of the only begotten Son of God, but had forfeited the obligation they assumed when John baptized them, by not believing on Jesus when he came.

But to those who kept the obligation assumed when baptized by John, and believed on Christ when he came, as they covenanted to do, Jesus gave *power* or *privilege* to become sons of God when the family should be organized on the day of Pentecost without anything more. They had believed, repented, been baptized for remission of sins and had knowledge of salvation, what need had they of anything more, unless they, in some way, forfeited the privileges they had?

The disciples, made by John, were ready for companionship with Jesus, and when they saw him, they followed him, and became his disciples without anything more. "Again, the next day after, John stood and two of his disciples, and looking upon Jesus as he walked, he said, Behold the Lamb of God! And the two disciples heard him speak, and they followed Jesus. . . . . One of the two which heard John speak and followed him was Andrew, Simon Peter's brother." John i: 35–40.

Thus we see that those made ready by John were his people to whom Jesus came, of whom his apostles were selected; and, if they were faithful, had power or privilege of becoming sons of God when the family should be organized. These, and those made by Jesus after John's death, became the "charter members" of the church on the day of Pentecost. One hundred and twenty of them were, with one accord, in one place, but they were restrained from operating until endowed with power from on high. When the Spirit came and took up its abode in the body, the church or spiritual temple stood forth. Then Peter preached, made converts, and they were added to the church daily. The church was established on the day of Pentecost, but it was a church before Peter began to preach on that occasion. Adam was a man in all his members, before God breathed into his nostrils the breath of life, but until then there were no vital manifestations; so the church existed in its material before the day of Pentecost; but, until the Spirit came to give it *power* and *life*, neither power nor life was manifested. When Jesus became King in Zion —head over all things to the church and the spirit vitalized the body, it went to work, before a convert was made, on the birthday of the church.

The temple of Solomon was typical of the church (see 1 Cor. iii: 16, 17,) and the temple was built of prepared stones, made ready for position before it was brought from the quarry, so that there was neither hammer, nor ax, nor tool of iron heard in the house while it was in building. 1 Kings vi: 7. So the spiritual temple was made of prepared material, *not a piece had to be worked over* before it was ready for position in the temple or spiritual family organized on that day. It needed nothing, but the Holy Spirit.

The very fact that John gave the approach of the kingdom as a reason why the people should repent shows that the *reformation enjoined by him had reference to citizenship in the coming kingdom.*

But if the disciples of John had to be baptized on or after Pentecost to enter the church or family of God, then the power or privilege of becoming the sons of God given to those who kept their obligation by believing on him when he came, was mere sounding brass and tinkling cymbal. The promise was meaningless to them, for they were not a whit in advance of the murderers of Jesus, for, even *they* could come into the church in that way, on the day of Pentecost and afterward. If this theory be true, then *John's ministry was a failure;* and notwithstanding all the miracles attending it, his *mission* seems to us a most ridiculous farce; therefore true it cannot be.

But was not some of John's disciples baptized after Pentecost? We answer, not one. Let him who so affirms show *who, when* and *where.* Were not the disciples found by Paul at Ephesus rebaptized? Yes, but it remains to be shown that they were John's disciples. Let us see. "And a certain Jew called Apollos, born at Alexandria, an eloquent man, and mighty in the Scriptures, came to Ephesus. This man was instructed in the way of the Lord, and being fervent in the spirit he spake and taught diligently the things of the Lord knowing only the baptism of John. And he began to speak boldly in the synagogue, whom when Aquila and Priscilla had heard, they took him unto them, and expounded unto him the way of God more perfectly." Acts xviii: 24–26. Now, were the *disciples made by Apollos* the disciples of John? Surely not. We may well imagine the correction given by Aquila and Priscilla: "John's baptism was valid in its day, but John obligated those baptized by him to believe in a Savior to come, for then he had not come; but since he has come, died for the sins of the world, entered the grave and brought about a resurrection from the dead for all the race, and having all authority in heaven and on earth, commands penitent believers to be baptized into the sublime names of the Father, and of the Son, and of the Holy Spirit. *This baptism has superceded all others* and is in force now, why be baptizing with John's baptism setting aside that ordained by Christ?"

The moment they said they had not so much as heard whether there be any Holy Spirit, Paul knew there was something wrong with their baptism, for the name Holy Spirit was a part of the formula into which they would have been baptized, if it had been correctly done; hence his question "unto what then were you baptized? And they said, unto John's baptism." This explains the whole matter. John's baptism was valid until superceded, since that of course it is not. Were a man baptized with it to-day it would be just as good, and no better, than the baptism of those disciples found by

Paul at Ephesus, but *he would surely not be a disciple of John, neither were they.*

But it is said John's baptism was simply that Christ should be made manifest to Israel. Well, if this was its only object, then it was not necessary to baptize any others but Jesus. The passage reads, "And I knew him not: but that he should be made manifest to Israel, therefore am I come baptizing with water. And John bare record, saying, I saw the Spirit descending from heaven like a dove, and it abode upon him. And I knew him not; but he that sent me to baptize with water, the same said unto me, upon whom thou shalt see the Spirit descending and remaining on him, the same is he which baptizeth with the Holy Ghost. And I saw and bare record that this is the Son of God." John i: 31-34. *At his baptism* he was made manifest to Israel, because the Spirit abode upon him, and God acknowledged him as his Son; *but was it necessary to baptize the multitudes for this purpose?* Nay verily, they were baptized for the remission of sins to fit them for position in the kingdom, with those who might come into it on the day of Pentecost and after that time. What they were commanded to do by John *was to be done because the kingdom was at hand,* and what bearing could its coming have on what they were required to do unless they were doing it to prepare them for position in the kingdom when it should come?

But as John's disciples were baptized by him for the remission of sins, and as Peter commanded the Pentecostians to be baptized *for the remission of sins*, for what should John's disciples be baptized who had been baptized for remission already? O, they had to be baptized to get into the kingdom, into which they could not enter when baptized by John because it did not exist. This goes upon the presumption that all the material used in the construction of a house must go in at the same door through which the house is entered after its construction. In short, this theory ignores John's mission entirely, hence his miraculous conception, birth, and fullness with the Holy Spirit from birth, and the multitudes flocking to him to be baptized of him, was all much ado about nothing, for he was indeed but *a reed shaken by the wind*.

We must bear in mind that the teaching of John and Jesus was chiefly preparatory, prospective, hence in parables and figures which gave place in due time to literal realities; but if we undertake to make *literals out of figures* we are likely to get into trouble.

We are sometimes told that there was not time enough to have immersed the three thousand baptized on the day of Pentecost, hence they were not immersed.

By mathematical calculation it can be shown that there was ample time to have baptized twice the number; but before making this objection it might be well for those making it to prove that *three thousand were baptized on that day.* "Does not the Bible say that three thousand were baptized the same day?" No, it says no such thing. Well what does it say? It says that as many as gladly received his word were baptized. Yes, just that many—no more. And we remark in passing, that infants could not have gladly received the word, and as none were baptized that could not so receive it, it follows that not an infant was baptized on that occasion. Is it not a little strange, that among so many there was not one dear little babe baptized?

But to return. As many as gladly received his word were baptized—how many did thus receive it? We do not know—does any one?

But three thousand were added unto them the same

day; were they added without baptism? No, none were added without being baptized, unless they had been baptized before. But if there were any there who had been baptized by John, or by the disciples of Jesus under their first commission, they were ready to be added without baptism. Were any such there? Most likely there were. We can scarcely conclude that, of all the multitudes so baptized, only one hundred and twenty were in that city and country. In arguing the resurrection of Jesus, Paul says, "He was seen of Cephas, then of the twelve; after that he was seen of more than five hundred brethren at once, of whom the greater part remain unto this present, but some are fallen asleep." 1 Cor. xv: 5, 6. Here are more than five hundred brethren who saw the Lord after His resurrection; and how many there were that did not see Him, we have no means of knowing. Would not these have been as likely to be brought together by the things noised abroad on that occasion, as the rabble? These were doubtless expecting remarkable events; and would have been, we think, even more likely to come to the scene than others. Then they were ready to be added without baptism; and these five hundred would have reduced the number to twenty-five hundred. And how many more of that class there were, no one can tell. Hence no man can tell how many were baptized that day.

We insist that the construction of the language raises a presumption that *not all* of those added were baptized that day. Why not say, "Three thousand gladly received his word, and were baptized, and added to them the same day." This would have stated the case without ambiguity, and we conclude that the only reason it was not so expressed, was, that the *fact was not that way*.

"As many as gladly received his word were baptized."

This is a complete affirmation in itself. Then follows another. "The same day there were added unto them about three thousand souls." This is a full and complete affirmation. Now why make the two affirmations while one would have been so much shorter and more clear. As stated before, the presumption is that the fact was not that way.

But our object in introducing this thought here is to call attention to the fact that those previously baptized by John, or the disciples in preparing material for the Kingdom were ready for position in the church without a second baptism. How many were baptized that day, we do not know; and we are quite sure that no one else knows.

Other minor matters might be mentioned, but we think we have struck the most important. We are not vain enough to suppose that our positions will all be accepted without criticism, but we are sure we have Christian love and patience enough to enable us to meekly hear anything that may come.

CHAPTER II.

THE SONSHIP OF CHRIST.

"What think ye of Christ? Whose son is he?"
Matt. xxii: 42.

THE faith of man seems to be like the vibrating pendulum of a clock; when it goes in one direction as far as it can, and turns back, it goes just as far in the other direction; and thus it seems ever swinging from one extreme to another. When the pendulum ceases to move it seeks a perpendicular, midway between the two extremes; but then the clock no longer keeps the time, and becomes worthless. The truth is generally to be found, like the perpendicular, between the two extremes; but men seem to think that if they stop there they will be as worthless as the clock; and hence they are rarely content until they swing off into one extreme or the other.

These extremes are clearly seen in the faith of men concerning Jesus Christ. *Trinitarians* insist that He is the *very and eternal God;* and if you deny this they set you down as denying the *divinity* of Jesus Christ. The *Unitarian* believes that He was entirely human—a very good man, but simply, and only man. We think the truth is unquestionably between these extremes. Neither Trinitarianism nor Unitarianism is true. No one is commanded to believe either; nor is he promised any thing for believing either; nor is he threatened with any punishment if he fails to believe either. On the contrary, he who fails to believe that Jesus Christ is the *son of God* will be lost—forever lost. Jesus said to the unbelieving Jews: "If ye believe not that I am he, ye shall die in your sins." John viii: 24.

Men believe this they tell us, but at the same time they believe that "Jesus Christ was, is, and ever will be the only true God." We once debated this proposition, worded just this way. How any one can believe it, is more than we can understand. He was both Father and Son; the sender and the sent; the mediator and one party to the mediation; equal to the Father, and the Father greater than the Son; seated at the right hand of the Father, and was the Father. Lord Bacon said, "A Christian is one who believes three to be one, and one to be three; a father not to be older than his son, a son to be equal to his father, and one proceeding from both to be equal to both; a virgin to be the mother of a son, and that very son to be her maker. The more incredible and absurd a divine mystery is, the more do we honor God in believing it, and so much the nobler is the victory of faith." God is never honored by believing any such incredible and absurd thing, because He is not the *author* of any such thing; nor did He ever command any one to believe any such thing; and fortunate it is that He did not; for it must have filled the world with infidels if He had required any such faith as this.

When a man reaches the point that the more incredible and absurd a thing is the stronger he believes it; and feels that he is all the more honoring God in believing it, he will reject every thing *that is not incredible and absurd;* and he will reject it *because he can understand it.* He concludes that whatever is *not incomprehensible,* is not in harmony with his ideas of God, and therefore is unworthy of belief. Is it possible that any one can work himself into such condition as this? Don't deceive yourself. Their name is legion. How much better was

Lord Bacon's theory? But we are not expecting to benefit such.

JESUS CHRIST IS THE SON OF GOD.

This is the grand central truth of the Christian religion. It is that around which revolves every thing connected with the scheme of human redemption; hence there is more and stronger proof establishing it than any one proposition of which the Bible treats. John says: "If we receive the witness of men, the witness of God is greater; for this is the witness of God which he hath testified of his Son. He that believeth on the Son of God hath the witness in himself; he that believeth not God hath made him a liar; because he believeth not the record that God gave of his Son. And this is the record that God hath given to us eternal life, and this life is in his Son. He that hath the Son, hath life; and he that hath not the Son of God hath not life. These things have I written unto you, that believe on the name of the Son of God; that ye may know that ye have eternal life, and that ye may believe on the name of the Son of God." 1 John v: 9–13.

This is the testimony that God has given of His Son; and he that does not believe it makes God a liar. We have not room for all the testimony given us on this subject, but we will examine some of it—enough to show that it is nothing less than a contradiction of God Himself to refuse to believe it.

GOD'S TESTIMONY.

"And Jesus, when he was baptized, went up straightway out of the water; and lo, the heavens were opened unto him, and he saw the Spirit of God descending like a dove, and lighting upon him; and lo, a voice from heaven, saying, This is my beloved Son, in whom I am well pleased." Matt. iii : 16, 17. John said: "And I knew him not; but that he should be made manifest to Israel, therefore am I come baptizing with water." John i : 31. Thus Jesus was made manifest. God spake from heaven to the assembled multitude, in plain and unmistakable terms, " This is my beloved Son." This testimony came from heaven, when Jesus was coming up out of the water. Surely no one will say that the water, out of which Jesus came, was heaven from which the voice came. The Spirit descended—Jesus came up.

Once more: On the mount of transfiguration, " a bright cloud overshadowed them ; and behold, a voice out of the cloud, which said, This is my beloved Son, in whom I am well pleased; hear ye him." Matt. xvii : 5. Peter says : " This voice which came from heaven we heard, when we were with him in the Holy mount." 2 Pet. i : 18.

To every one who believes the Bible, this testimony is sufficient to show that *Trinitarianism* and *Unitarianism* are both false, if there was not another word in the Bible on the subject. The voice came from God in heaven to where Jesus was on the earth ; and He acknowledged Jesus as His Son ; hence He was not the very and eternal God ; and as He was the Son of God, He was more than man. No man is the Son of God in this sense. Thus we see that when any one denies that Jesus Christ is the Son of God he makes God a liar, for God says, " This is my beloved son." This is true, or it is false. This is not very well calculated to prove that He was very and eternal God. Did God mean that Jesus was the son of himself; and the father of himself?

THE TESTIMONY OF JOHN THE BAPTIST.

"And John bear record, saying, I saw the Spirit

descending from heaven like a dove, and it abode upon him. And I knew him not: but he that sent me to baptize with water, the same said unto me, Upon whom thou shalt see the Spirit descending, and remaining on him, the same is he which baptizeth with the Holy Ghost. And I saw, and bear record that this is the Son of God." John i : 32–34. This is virtually the testimony of God and John together. God told John how he would be able to know the Son, and John gives the testimony. John heard the Father say, "this is my beloved Son" at His baptism, hence he was fully competent to testify that Jesus was the Son of God; but he never testified that He was the very and eternal God.

JESUS BORE WITNESS OF HIMSELF.

"I am one that bear witness of myself, and the Father that sent me beareth witness of me." John viii : 18. If Jesus was the only true God, then the Father and the Son were the same witness. He was the Father of Himself, and the Son of Himself; and sent Himself. This is not respectable nonsense.

When Jesus restored the blind man to sight, the enraged Jews cast him out. "Jesus heard that they had cast him out; and when he had found him, he said unto him, Dost thou believe on the Son of God? He answered and said, Who is he, Lord, that I might believe on him? And Jesus said unto him, Thou hast both seen him, and it is he that talketh with thee." John ix . 35–37.

Again : "Say ye of him, whom the Father hath sanctified, and sent into the world, Thou blasphemest; because I said, I am the Son of God? If I do not the works of my Father, believe me not; but if I do, though ye believe not me, believe the works; that ye may know, and believe, that the Father is in me and I in him." John x: 36–38.

Once more: "Again the high priest asked him, and said unto him, Art thou the Christ, the Son of the Blessed? And Jesus said, I am." Mark xiv: 61, 62. It is said that Jesus never claimed to be the Son of God; but this honor was thrust upon Him by His followers. We leave these quotations to speak for themselves. Many others might be added but these are enough, and plain enough. He never claimed to be the very and eternal God; but He did claim to be the Son of God in divers places.

THE APOSTLES' TESTIMONY

"When Jesus came into the coasts of Cæsarea Philippi, he asked his disciples, saying, Whom do men say that I the Son of man am? And they said, Some say that thou art John the Baptist; some, Elias; and others, Jeremias, or one of the prophets. He saith unto them, But whom say ye that I am? And Simon Peter answered and said, Thou art the Christ, the Son of the living God. And Jesus answered and said unto him, Blessed art thou, Simon Barjona; for flesh and blood hath not revealed it unto thee, but my Father which is in heaven." Mat. xvi: 13–17.

This question was propounded to all the apostles and answered by Peter in their presence; hence may be regarded as the answer of all of them. And as Peter's answer was made known or revealed to him by the Father it was the testimony of the Father. And as Jesus blessed Peter for making it, He is fully committed to it. So in this quotation we have the combined testimony of the Father, the Son, and all the apostles to the fact that Jesus was the Christ the Son of the living God.

When Jesus walked upon the water, to the ship in which the apostles were being tossed by the angry waves in a howling storm, after saving the doubting Peter from a watery grave, He went up into the ship and the wind ceased. "They that were in the ship came and worshipped him, saying, Of a truth thou art the Son of God." Matt. xiv: 33. Thus testify the twelve.

Paul's testimony is in every epistle he wrote. We can only give a few samples with which his letters abound. His salutations in his letters clearly show that the Father and Jesus were a plurality of persons. "Grace to you, and peace, from God our Father, and the Lord Jesus Christ." Rom. i: 6; 1 Cor. i: 3; 2 Cor. i: 2; Gal. i: 3; Ephes. i: 2; Phil. i: 2; Col. i: 2; 1 Thess. i: 1; 2 Thess. i. 2; 1 Tim. i: 2; 2 Tim. i: 2; Tit. i: 4. Why make such distinctions between God our Father and the Lord Jesus Christ if they were the same person? But he says: "God is faithful, by whom ye were called unto the fellowship of his Son Jesus Christ our Lord." 1 Cor. i: 9. This shows not only a plurality of persons, but that Jesus Christ our Lord was God's Son.

THE TESTIMONY OF DEVILS.

"And unclean spirits, when they saw him, fell down before him, and cried, saying, Thou art the Son of God." Mark iii: 11. "And devils also came out of many, crying out, and saying. Thou art Christ the Son of God. And he rebuking them suffered them not to speak: for they knew that he was Christ." Luke iv: 41.

THE TESTIMONY OF THE WICKED.

"Now when the centurion, and they that were with him, watching Jesus, saw the earthquake, and those things that were done, they feared greatly, saying, Truly this was the Son of God." Matt. xxvii. 54. Thus we have the testimony of God, the Father; John the Baptist; Jesus Christ; all the apostles; devils; and wicked men to the fact that Jesus Christ was, and is the *Son of God*, not one of them testifies that he was the very and eternal God.

THE TESTIMONY OF MIRACLES.

"Then came the Jews round about him, and said unto him, How long dost thou make us to doubt? If thou be the Christ, tell us plainly. Jesus answered them, I told you, and ye believed not; the works that I do in my Father's name, they bear witness of me." John x: 24, 25.

"Believest thou not that I am in the Father, and the Father in me? The words that I speak unto you I speak not of myself: but the Father that dwelleth in me, he doeth the works. Believe me that I am in the Father and the Father in me; or else believe me for the very works' sake." John xiv: 10, 11.

Jesus here intimates that the works wrought by him were done by the Father through him. These were stronger, or more convincing testimony than even what he had told them, though his words were given him by the Father. They might not believe what he said, but how could they disregard what he did before their eyes. These they saw, and were bound to know that unaided human power could not do them. Who could see him hush to silence the howling storm; calm the surging waves of the sea of Galilee, and walk upon them as a pavement beneath his feet; open the eyes of those who had been born blind; unstop the ears of the deaf; cure all manner of disease, even the loathsome leprosy; cast out devils by the legion; and raise the dead to life and health, without being convinced as was Nicodemus: "No man can do these miracles that thou doest except God be with him." John iii: 2. God would not have aided an impostor to do these things, nor could an impostor have done them himself; hence that he was what he claimed to be his miracles abundantly show. "And many other signs truly did Jesus in the presence of his disciples which are not written in this book; but these are written that ye might believe that Jesus is the Christ, the Son of God, and that believing ye might have life through his name." John xx: 31.

The miracles which Jesus did are recorded to prove that he is the Son of God; so that sinners, in need of salvation, may have an intelligent faith in him; and yield a hearty obedience to him; that they may have eternal life through him. "Not every one that saith unto me, Lord, Lord, shall enter into the kingdom of heaven; but he that doeth the will of my Father which is in heaven." Matt. vii: 21. But suppose a man believes that He is the *very and eternal God*, will that secure the same blessings that were intended for him who believes that He is the Son of God? Why not? If these propositions are the same why not as well believe one as the other?

This is the faith that must be confessed in order that God may dwell in us, and we in him. "Whosoever shall confess that Jesus is the Son of God, God dwelleth in him and he in God." 1 John iv: 15. Surely there can be no more sacred relationship than this. Will it do just as well to confess that Jesus is the only true God as to confess what is required of us—that he is the Son of God?

"That which we have heard and seen declare we unto you, that ye also may have fellowship with us; and truly our fellowship is with the Father, and with his Son Jesus Christ." 1 John i: 3. Here are two persons with whom the saints have fellowship—the Father and his Son Jesus Christ. That they are distinct persons is as clear as language can make anything.

If Jesus Christ was the only true God, then it occurs to us that during the three days in which he was dead the world was without a God. And we insist that the fact that he rose from the dead is conclusive proof that he was not the only true God; for there must have been a living power equal to the task of raising to life that which was dead, otherwise a resurrection never could have been; and He would have remained dead forever.

But the Trinitarian smiles at this difficulty when it is presented; saying: "It was only *humanity* that died. As God He did not die. As man, He wept, suffered and died; as God, He rose from the dead." Plausible as this theory may appear, it is both contradictory and unreasonable. How could He, as God, rise from the dead, if, as God, He did not die? Only that which died could be raised from the dead. If only humanity died, then only humanity was raised from the dead. It matters not by what power that which was dead, was made alive, only that which was dead could be raised from the dead. If that which was raised did not die, then there was no resurrection of the dead at all. The whole theory of a resurrection of the dead was a sham, a fraud, a deception, and all our hopes of a resurrection of the dead through Christ are delusions. "And if Christ be not risen, then is our preaching vain, and your faith is also vain. Yea, and we are found false witnesses of God; because we have testified of God that he raised up Christ; whom he raised not up, if so be that the dead rise not; for if the dead rise not, then is not Christ raised: and if Christ be not raised, your faith is vain; ye are yet in your sins. Then they also which are fallen asleep in Christ are perished. If in this life only we have hope in Christ, we are of all men most miserable." 1 Cor. xv: 14-19.

It was the fact that Jesus Christ was the Son of God that gave efficacy to the blood of the atonement. "But if we walk in the light, as he is in the light, we have fellowship one with another, and the blood of Jesus Christ his Son cleanseth us from all sin." 1 John i: 7. It occurs to us that if nothing more than humanity died when Jesus died, the blood of any other man would have been as efficacious in cleansing from sin as would the blood of Jesus. "For God so loved the world, that he gave his only begotten Son, that whosoever believeth on him should not perish, but have everlasting life. For God sent not his Son into the world to condemn the world; but that the world through him might be saved." John iii; 16, 17. Thus we see that it took richer blood than that of mere humanity to secure the world's redemption. It took nothing less than the *blood of God's own Son* to magnify his law and make it possible for him to be just and pardon those who violated his law.

John says. "In this was manifested the love of God toward us, because that God sent his only begotten Son into the world, that we might live through him. Herein is love, not that we loved God, but that he loved us, and sent his Son to be the propitiation for our sins." 1 John iv: 9, 10. Now if nothing but humanity suffered, as *Jesus derived all that from his mother*, then there was nothing sent from God that suffered at all. And it looks a little like God sent himself to earth, and placed himself in a human body, made of a woman; and submitted that body to be crucified, while he. the Divinity, suffered not at all, and then claimed to have so loved the world as to give his only Son to suffer and to die for it. This claim was unjust according to this theory; for it was only the Mary part of Jesus that suffered and died; for the divine part was God himself and he never suffered at all. We cannot very well understand such a sending as this. In place of sending any one or any thing, he came himself, and did not suffer any when he came. Mary made all the sacrifice—God made none. Such a theory is a slander upon God and his Son, both.

It really seems to us that there was quite a useless commotion in the material universe when Jesus died if only humanity suffered. The sun, "the bright orb of day," that had never refused to give his light from the time God swung him in the heavens until then, refused to light up a scene like that, and the earth was mantled in darkness for three long hours. The earth trembled as a leaf, until the rocks about Jerusalem were broken: and the veil of the temple, that had stood for ages, was rent from top to bottom. Why all this? Humanity is suffering on the cross. Humanity had suffered in the death of men every hour of every day for a thousand years; but nothing like these things had ever occurred before. Then again we ask, why all this? The truth is, *the Son of God is dying;* and the heavens and the earth are in commotion. We say, as did those who stood by: "Truly this was the Son of God." Matt. xxvii: 54.

"Wherefore when he cometh into the world, he saith, sacrifice and offering thou wouldst not, but a body hast thou prepared me: In burnt offerings and sacrifices for sin thou hast had no pleasure." Heb. x: 5, 6. If the body of Jesus Christ was *wholly human*, it was an exception to all law known to us. It is a fact well known, even by common observation, to say nothing of any thing else, that physical appearance and general temperament are derived from the father as well as from the mother. Indeed it is within the observation of every man that has given attention to the subject that *complexion* is derived even more from the father than from the mother; so much so that in the course of many generations the color of the mother is lost in that of the father. We predicate nothing of this, however; the idea to which we object is that the body and blood of Jesus Christ is *entirely human*, like his mother, and partook not of the nature of the Father at all. This absurdity is assumed to justify the theory that nothing but *humanity* suffered on the cross. A body that did not partake of the nature of Father and mother both, has never been seen on this earth—never.

It is all a myth too, that the divinity that was in Jesus Christ was the power by which he arose from the dead. Paul says: "That if thou shalt confess with thy mouth the Lord Jesus, and shalt believe in thine heart that God hath raised him from the dead, thou shalt be saved." Rom. x: 9. We have already quoted him saying: "Yea, and we are found false witnesses of God; because we have testified of God that he raised up Christ; whom he raised not up, if so be that the dead rise not." 1 Cor. xv: 15.

Peter said: "This Jesus hath God raised up, whereof we all are witnesses." Acts ii: 32. "Be it known unto you all, and to all the people of Israel, that by the name of Jesus Christ of Nazareth, whom ye crucified, whom God raised from the dead, even by him doth this man stand here before you whole." Acts iv: 10. "But God raised him from the dead." Acts xiii: 30. It was by the power of God that Jesus was raised from the dead—

not by any inherent quality in Him, either human or divine.

But we must further notice a quotation made some time ago: " Believest thou not that I am in the Father, and the Father in me. The words that I speak unto you I speak not of myself; but the Father that dwelleth in me, he doeth the works. Believe me that I am in the Father, and the Father in me.' 'John xiv: 10, 11. We are told that as the Father was in the Son, and the Son in the Father they were necessarily the same person. Well, in the 20th verse of the same chapter He says: " At that day ye shall know that I am in my Father, and ye in me and I in you." Did the Savior intend to teach that the disciples and he were, or ever would be the same persons because they should know that they were in him and he in them? Hardly, we suppose, yet the form of expression is the same, and if it does not prove that Christ and the apostles were one in person, neither does it prove that God and his Son were the same person.

Again: "Whosoever shall confess that Jesus is the Son of God, God dwelleth in him and he in God." 1 John iv: 15. Are we to understand that those who make this confession and God, himself, are, or ever will be one in person? We suppose not, yet the same style is used with reference to their dwelling in God, and God in them, that is used with reference to the Father being in the Son, and the Son in the Father. If the same language cannot prove one proposition it cannot prove the other. All the fullness of the Godhead dwelt in Jesus Christ. The nature, attributes, and purposes of God were in his Son, and hence they were said to be in each other.

But Jesus said: "I and my Father are one." John

x: 30. Yes, and he said a man and his wife were one, but he expected them to remain two persons—a man and a woman as before. They were one in purpose and sympathy, (Matt. xix: 5, 6) but not one person, surely.

Jesus prayed: "Holy Father, keep through thine own name those whom thou hast given me, that they may be one as we are." John xvii: 11. Verse 22, "And the glory which thou gavest me I have given them: that they may be one even as we are one." Did Jesus pray that the apostles might become one person? Surely not. But he did pray that the apostles might be one in the same sense that he and his Father were one. Then if the apostles were different persons, and would so remain, it is certain that He and His Father were different persons. From this conclusion there is no escape. Then as God and his Son were one in spirit, object and work, so He prayed that His apostles might be perfectly harmonious in all their labors for the salvation of man. Paul admonished the brethren at Corinth to this unity. "Now I beseech you, brethren, by the name of our Lord Jesus Christ, that ye all speak the same thing, and that there be no divisions among you; but that ye be perfectly joined together in the same mind and in the same judgment." 1 Cor. i: 10. Christ prayed for this unity among the apostles and he prayed for them to be one as he and his Father were one.

"For the Father himself loveth you, because ye have loved me, and have believed that I came out from God. I came forth from the Father, and am come into the world; again, I leave the world, and go to the Father." John xvi: 27, 28. If this does not show that while Jesus was on the earth he and his Father were, in some sense, in different localities, and were different persons, then we may as well pronounce the New Testament a riddle and beyond human comprehension, on this subject at least.

"Ye have heard how I said unto you, I go away, and come again unto you. If ye loved me, ye would rejoice, because I said, I go unto the Father: for my Father is greater than I." John xiv: 28.

Jesus said: "I am the true vine and my Father is the husbandman." John xv: 1. This expression was taken from real life. In horticulture there are the vine, the branches, and the husbandman, or dresser of the vine. Then in order that the figure may fit that which is illustrated the husbandman cannot be the vine dressed by Him. Then Jesus Christ, the vine, could not have been the Father, or dresser of the vine.

Jesus prayed to the Father. John xvii. Matt. xxvi: 39–44. Mark i: 35; xiv: 35–39. Luke i: 35; xxii: 41. Prayer suggests two persons—one to pray, and another to pray to. The prayers of Jesus were senseless if Trinitarianism be true. But they tell us it was the humanity praying to the divinity. When did the humanity of Jesus begin? Not until he was conceived by the Virgin Mary. Very well, then, we will hear him pray to his Father: "O Father, glorify thou me with the glory which I had with thee before the world was." John 17: 5. Jesus then had a glory with the Father before the world was. As his humanity began at the conception this could not have been the *humanity with the Father* before the world was. This effectually disposes of that quibble—that wherever a plurality of persons are shown, one was the humanity and the other the divinity.

John says: "In the beginning was the Word, and the Word was with God, and the Word was God. The same was in the beginning with God." John i: 1, 2.

The preposition *with*, twice occurring in this quotation, clearly shows *companionship, association of two or more parties*, agreeing with the expression, "The glory I had with thee before the world was," as seen above.

But He was God. Yes, but let us be careful not to add any thing to that which is written. It does not say He was the *only* God; nor does it say He was the very and eternal God. He was the manifestation of God's power in creation as seen in the next verse; and He was called God because He inherited the name of His Father. "Being made so much better than the angels, as he hath by inheritance obtained a more excellent name than they." Heb. i: 4.

Stephen saw Him at the right hand of God. "But he, being full of the Holy Ghost, looked up steadfastly into heaven, and saw the glory of God, and Jesus standing on the right hand of God, and said, Behold, I see the heavens opened, and the Son of Man standing on the right hand of God." Acts vii: 55, 56.

" So then after the Lord had spoken unto them, he was received up into heaven, and sat on the right hand of God. Mark xvi: 19. We suppose that it will not be contended that it was the *humanity* which Stephen saw at the *right hand of the Divinity* in heaven.

Jesus is our mediator. "For there is one God, and mediator between God and men, the man Christ Jesus; who gave himself a ransom for all, to be testified in due time." 1 Tim. ii: 5, 6. The idea of mediation suggests at least three parties, a mediator and two parties between which the mediation is had. God was one party, man another, and Jesus Christ the mediator between God and man. Surely Jesus did not mediate between himself and the people. A mediator, to be competent must be entirely disconnected from both parties, or equally related to both, so that no charge of partiality can be brought against him. Jesus was just such a character. He was divine and he was human. He was Son of God and Son of man. His father was divine, his mother was human. He was as nearly related to man as to God. In him humanity and divinity met—pre-eminently fitting him to be mediator between God and men.

Just to *what extent*, or even *how* humanity and divinity were blended in Jesus Christ we may never perfectly comprehend; but we do know that he was born of a woman, that he hungered, thirsted, wept with those in distress, and sympathized with suffering humanity; that he was tempted—sorely tempted as we are, yet without sin; that he was touched with the feeling of our infirmity; that he took not on him the nature of angels but the seed of Abraham; hence we know that if we sin we have an advocate with the Father, even Jesus Christ the righteous; and we gladly trust our cause to the care of such an advocate. He says: "I am the way, the truth, and the life. No man cometh unto the Father but by me." All our approaches to the Father are made through our advocate—our mediator—our high priest. We have no worth or merit in ourselves to commend us to the favor of God. Our confidence is in Jesus, who as our advocate will order our cause aright—in our mediator who will intercede for us—in our high priest who will present all our offerings before the mercy-seat.

> "What a friend we have in Jesus,
> All our sins and griefs to bear;
> What a privilege to carry
> Every thing to God in prayer."

That Jesus Christ is the Son of God has already been fully shown. His divine character may be further seen in his sinless life. Never did man pass through such trials, and persecutions as he, and yet remain undefiled by sin. He did no sin, neither was guile found in his mouth. When he was reviled, he reviled not again; when he suffered, he threatened not; but committed himself to him that judgeth righteously. Such purity was never seen in any one wholly human.

But in nothing is the divinity of Christ more clearly seen than in his own resurrection from the dead. Paul said: "Because he hath appointed a day, in the which he will judge the world in righteousness by that man whom he hath ordained; whereof he hath given assurance unto all men, in that he hath raised him from the dead." Acts xvii: 31. The fact that God raised his Son from the dead gives assurance unto all men that he was what he claimed to be; and that he would judge the world in righteousness by him. God would not have raised an impostor, nor could an impostor have raised himself; hence, in his resurrection, we have the strongest assurance of his divine character.

That he did rise from the dead is as certain as it is that the Bible is true. We have seen a number of passages saying, in the plainest terms possible, that God raised him from the dead. Not that he raised himself by the divinity that was in him, but that *God raised him*. This being true, we have the strongest possible assurance of his divinity that could be given. The testimony is *direct*, and as certainly true as it is that God cannot lie.

What is the probable reliability of the testimony of the apostles? They all say he arose from the dead and that they saw him, and that he was seen by many others

—more than five hundred at once. They could not have been mistaken in his identity, for they knew him well before his death. They had associated with him intimately for three years and a half. They ate with him, talked with him, and probably slept with him almost continuously; hence that they knew him is simply certain. They could not have been mistaken. They either saw him alive after his crucifixion or they fabricated a stupendous falsehood. Men generally act from motive—what motive could have induced them to fabricate and tell such a lie as this? They did not do it for money for Jesus told them he was so poor that he had no place to lay his weary head; and as the soldiers were paid to testify falsely it is quite probable that they could have made a fortune by giving up the false testimony and telling the truth if Jesus did not rise. Their testimony to the resurrection was false if Jesus did not rise, hence they could have exchanged the falsehood for the truth and been well paid for it beside. Why did they not do it? What else? They could not have expected to gain popularity by the story of the resurrection, for he told them that they would be persecuted and despised of all men for his sake; and they found this quite true. They were put to death for Jesus' sake, every one of them but John; and tradition tells us that he was thrown into a caldron of boiling oil, and was only saved from a martyr's death by a miracle. Whether this be true or false, one thing is certain: he did not escape the fire of persecution; for he was banished to the isle of Patmos for the word of God, and for the testimony of Jesus Christ. This we have from his own pen (Rev. i: 9). Then they did not hatch up, agree upon, and tell their story for *popularity*. *Why did they tell it?* The persecutions to which they were subjected separated them, and they were martyred in different countries; where, the probabilities are, they did not hear from each other. One could not know that the others had not given up the falsehood so as to make it folly for him to adhere to it; and yet they all stuck to it, and died on account of it; when they could have saved their lives by giving it up and telling the truth. Can any sane man believe that they did it? Is there a parallel to it in the world's history anywhere? We venture to affirm that not one case can be found, where twelve men, or more, agreed upon a falsehood, and told it, and every one adhered to it, until it brought death upon all of them, when they could have saved their lives by giving up the falsehood and telling the truth; and all without any reward of any kind—with nothing to gain, but everything to lose by it. Is it reasonable? Do you think twelve men could be found on the earth to-day who would be guilty of such stupendous folly? Surely not. The testimony of the apostles was true. Jesus rose from the dead, and they saw, and knew him. They gave up their lives rather than bear false witness against his resurrection. This one fact establishes his divine character forever.

My dear friend, have you pursued and considered the testimony here presented? If so are you not convinced that Jesus was more than human? Nay, are you not convinced that he was, and is none other than the Son of God? If so, we ask you as he asked the Jews: "Why call me Lord, Lord, and do not the things which I say?" If you believe him to be the Son of God you are under obligations high as heaven, deep as hell, vast as the universe to believe every word that fell from his lips, to trust every promise he made; and obey every command he gave which applies to such as you. Your faith in him will do you no good unless it moves you to love, trust and obey him. Come, then my brother, let us renew our devotions to him—love him more and serve him better; and let us cultivate this determination, and act upon it, to the last moment of life. God help us to do it.

Friendly sinner, have you no place in your heart's deepest affections for love of a Savior like this? Can you look with indifference on the suffering Son of God, as he hangs bleeding and dying on the cross for you. God loves you. Jesus died for you. Angels are concerned for you. The church invites you, begs you, pleads with you. Your mother weeps over you; but you, the one most interested, are still indifferent and unconcerned. The sun refused to shine on the crucifixion of Jesus, but you can look upon it without a blush. The earth trembled when the Son of God died, but you can contemplate it without the tremor of a nerve. The solid rocks were shivered, but your heart remains unbroken.

This is an abnormal condition of the human mind. No one is so, naturally. He has to educate himself up to it. At first he felt deeply when he heard the story of the cross. It cost him a desperate struggle to refuse obedience to the gospel when first he learned the Master's will. But every successful resistance hardened him a little, and enabled him to resist with less effort the next invitation until he reached his present condition. Once he could feel, now he cannot. Once he could weep on account of his sins and in sympathy with the sufferings of Jesus; now the fountain of his tears is dried up, and he can resist the most heart-stirring appeals which human tongues can make with the most perfect indifference. When he reaches this condition he is gone. He has passed beyond all the appliances and means by which God proposes to save men and he *will never return*. Resistance to the devil is right—resistance to God is vain and dangerous. O do not start in that direction. You may soon get so far as to make it difficult to turn back.

Here we remember an incident of the late war, an account of which we read in a paper called " The Children's Quarterly," then published in Lexington, Ky. We did not memorize the report, nor did we preserve the paper, hence we can only give the substance, as we now remember it.

A man, having a wife and three small children, was compelled to go into the army—on which side we do not know, nor does it matter. The day of rendezvous was authoritatively appointed; and he made all necessary preparation for starting. The day came, and with it his neighbors to bid him farewell, and pray God's protection upon him. First, he bade his neighbors goodbye, then one by one he took up his children, and imprinted a father's kiss upon each. Then came the parting from his wife. The scene beggars description—it was like tearing soul and body asunder. All hearts felt, and all eyes wept. In all probability they would never meet again. From that dreadful war many never returned, hence the parting was severe. Among those present was a boy who was too young to be compelled into military service. He bravely stepped forward and took the man by the hand and said: " Sir, let me go in your place. I have no family to leave. If I fall there will be no widow left; nor orphan children to suffer for a father's care. Let me go and you stay with your family." The proposition was accepted—the boy went and the man stayed at home. It is unnecessary to say that that boy made a brave soldier—that he went under the circumstances assures that fact. On the bloody field of Chickamauga in the van of his host he fell and never breathed again. When the battle was over his friends buried him, as best they could, and placed a board at the head of the grave with his name and place of address inscribed upon it. They wrote to the man in whose place he had gone that the brave boy had fallen, and how his grave could be found. The man made his way to that grave, disinterred the body, took it home and buried it with all the honor he could bestow upon it. Over the grave he placed a costly marble monument with suitable inscription upon it. Among other things inscribed were these impressive words: "HE DIED FOR ME."

This shows that that man appreciated and loved that boy. Jesus died for you—have you done as much for him? If not, is it not ungrateful in you not to do it? Will you not begin it now? Blessed Jesus hast thou died for me? And shall we not live and labor for thee?

"See from His head, His hands, His feet,
  Sorrow and love flow mingled down,
Did e'r such love and sorrow meet?
  Or thorns compose so rich a crown?

"Were the whole realm of nature mine,
  That were a present far too small;
Love so amazing, so divine,
  Demands my soul, my life, my all."

Amen and amen.

CHAPTER III.

THE COMMISSION.

THE first religion ever given by God to man after his expulsion from the garden of Eden was a *family* religion. Nothing more was needed at that time. The race of man consisted of a few families, hence the system of worship then given was conducted by the father as the head of each family. For this reason it was called the Patriarchal dispensation; and it continued until succeeded by the Jewish religion instituted at Mount Sinai, the law for which was there given by God to Moses.

This was a *national* religion and was given to Moses for the Jewish nation, and continued until it was abrogated by the death of Christ. It was called the Jewish dispensation, and began with the giving of the law at Sinai, and continued until Christ took it away. This was succeeded by the Christian religion co-extensive with the race of man. This period is called the Christian dispensation, which was fully inaugurated on the day of Pentecost, and is destined to continue until Jesus comes again, or until time shall be no more.

God promised Abraham that in him and his seed all the families of the earth should be blessed. When, in the course of events the time drew near to carry this promise into effect, God sent a harbinger before the Lord, the promised seed of Abraham, to make ready a people for his reception. Jesus came to this prepared people, and of them selected his apostles and sent them out to further perfect arrangements for the establishment of a kingdom or system of government for those who might desire to become the beneficiaries of this new order of things. When the Lord sent these agents on this preparatory mission he gave them a restricted commission, forbidding them to go into any city of the Samaritans, or among the Gentiles; but confining their labors, strictly, to the lost sheep of the house of Israel. When this preparatory work was completed, and the time had come for the consummation of God's promise to Abraham, Jesus gave these chosen apostles a commission co-extensive with the human race. As the promise was to all the families of the earth, so the commission extended to *all nations*—to *every creature* in all the world. In all lands and countries where man might live, there the gospel, as God's power unto salvation would be needed, and there the apostles were authorized to go and preach it. In the word of God we have three reports of this commission, one each by Matthew, Mark, and Luke, as follow:

"Go ye therefore, and teach all nations, baptizing them in the name of the Father, and of the Son, and of the Holy Ghost: teaching them to observe all things whatsoever I have commanded you: and, lo, I am with you alway, *even* unto the end of the world." Matt. xxviii: 19, 20.

"Go ye into all the world, and preach the gospel to every creature. He that believeth and is baptized shall be saved; but he that believeth not shall be damned." Mark xvi: 15, 16.

"Thus it is written, and thus it behooved Christ to suffer, and to rise from the dead the third day: And that repentance and remission of sins should be preached in his name among all nations, beginning at Jerusalem. And ye are witnesses of these things." Luke xxiv: 46-48.

Before giving this commission Jesus said: "All power is given unto me in heaven and in earth." Matt. xxviii: 18. There was no power in heaven above that he did not have, nor was there any power on the earth beneath that had not been delegated to Him; hence He makes this authority the basis of the authority embodied in the commission given to them. *Go ye therefore.* As the Father had thus delegated all authority to the Son, he was fully clothed with power to enlarge the area of their operations to the ends of the earth, and perpetuate the proclamation of the gospel under this commission to the end of all time. This we think he certainly intended to do.

In Matthew's report of this commission there are two lessons taught, one each to two classes of persons. The first: "Teach all nations, baptizing them in the name of the Father, and of the Son, and of the Holy Spirit," was a charge to to the apostles to teach aliens how to become Christians—children of God. The second: "Teaching them to observe all things whatsoever I have commanded you," had reference to the duties of the Christian life and was applicable to those who had become obedient disciples under the first part of the commission. With that part of it applicable to the alien we have to do at present.

That this commission is in full force *now*, and is applicable to all who would honor God's authority to-day, is admitted by all who believe the Bible to be an inspired book, and have given any thought to the subject. This is evident from the fact that all who administer baptism at all use the formula here laid down; for they could not so use it if they did not believe the commission containing it to be in force. This formula, used by all, is found no where else.

This commission is the *great organic law* of the Christian dispensation. The constitution of the State is the organic law of the State. All laws made by legislative authority must be in harmony with this constitution, otherwise the supreme court will declare them void. So had any apostle given any law, either oral or written, not in harmony with this great commission, it would have been a usurpation, for it was the sum of their authority—they could not go beyond it or come in contact with it. Yea, had an angel from heaven preached another gospel than that authorized by this commission the curse of God would have rested upon him. This being true, it becomes a matter of very great importance to know what is taught in this commission, that we may know what we are required to do, and to what we must submit.

If we would understand all that is contained in it we must examine all the reports we have of it. If a jury would correctly understand a case in court upon which they are to render a verdict, they must hear all the testimony and collate all the facts set out by all the witnesses brought before them. They cannot make up their verdict from the testimony of one witness, ignoring the testimony of other witnesses equally entitled to credit. So we must treat the commission if we would come to correct conclusions concerning it. We cannot take any one report of it and get all there is in it.

In order that our eyes may assist our ears in seeing more clearly the contents of the commission we will *formulate* it, somewhat after the style of an example in addition of compound numbers. To do this we write down the several items clearly expressed, and make marks of omission for items not expressed though implied in some reports, but expressed in others, being careful to write items of like significance under each other so that the sum of all the items found may appear in a connected summary at the bottom of the formula. As Matthew comes first in the books of the New Testament we will begin with his report.

His first item is *teach*, so we write down *Teach*, as the first item found in the commission. But if the apostles were required to *teach* there must be some one or more to teach. *Teach whom?* Matthew answers, *all nations*. Very well, we put all nations as the second item reported by him. But if the apostles were required to teach, there must not only be persons to teach, but there must be something to teach. *Teach what?* Matthew does not tell us, so we make a *sign of omission* and pass on. But if the apostles were required to teach, there must not only be persons to be taught and something to teach them, but they must *believe* what is taught. Matthew says nothing about believing, so we make a sign of omission here and pass on again. A God-approved belief or faith always *produces repentance*, and the necessity of repentance is clearly taught elsewhere; but Matthew says nothing about repentance, so we make another mark of omission and pass on. As John and the disciples of Jesus have been baptizing all who became submissive to the Lord's will, and as Jesus said except a man be born of water and of the Spirit he cannot enter into the kingdom of God, we may expect the commission to say something about baptism, hence Matthew clearly states that the taught are to be baptized—then we write down *baptizing*. But no formula has been given yet, so if any formula is to be used we may expect it to be found in the commission, and Matthew records it, so we write it down. But what is all this for? Surely all this is not required without an object in view. No, but Matthew says nothing about the *design* of it, so we make another sign of omission and pass on. This procedure must have a *beginning* somewhere. Matthew says nothing about a place to *begin*, so we make another sign of omission and close his report.

Next in order comes Mark's report. Corresponding to Matthew's *teach* Mark gives *preach*. All preaching should be teaching, but unfortunately this is not always so. We place preach under teach. Corresponding to Matthew's *all nations*, Mark gives us every creature in all the world, and we put it down accordingly. Matthew tells us nothing of what is to be taught, but Mark says *the gospel* is to be preached, hence we are able to fill Matthew's first blank with *the gospel* of Mark's report. Matthew says nothing of the necessity of faith, but Mark says we must *believe*, hence with this we supply Matthew's second omission. Mark, like Matthew, says nothing of repentance, leaving it to be inferred as a *result* of faith. We make our marks of omission and pass to *baptism*, which he mentions as well as Matthew. Mark does not give the *formula*, hence we leave a sign of omission here. Mark enables us to supply another blank in Matthew's report by giving *salvation* as the blessing promised to those who comply with the stipulated conditions. But neither Matthew nor Mark tells us *where* operations under this commission are to *begin*, we therefore insert our mark of omission for this, and close his report.

Luke changes the order of the items mentioned in the record given by him, but the same order given by the others may be followed without at all changing the sense. He gives *preaching*, and we put it under the preaching in Mark's report. He gives *all nations*, among which the preaching is to be done. He speaks of the suffering and resurrection of Christ, implying burial, which are included in the gospel mentioned by Mark. He says nothing of belief, but he enables us to fill a blank in both the preceding reports with the mention of *repentance*. What Mark calls salvation Luke calls *remission of sins*, hence we place this under the word *saved* in Mark's report, having placed marks of omission where baptism is placed in both the preceding reports. He gives us Jerusalem as the place where the preaching is to begin under this commission.

By thus placing together the three reports left recorded, as we would the testimony of any three witnesses testifying in court or elsewhere concerning any fact to be established by testimony, we certainly get the entire contents of this very important portion of Holy Writ. Now let us put this formula before our eyes, and examine it carefully, comparing it with the reports of the inspired historians who have recorded it. Will any one say that any thing found in this summary is not found in the inspired reports examined? Is there an item which we may rub out? If so, which one is it? And by what authority shall we take it away? Surely there must be some important changes made if ever this commission is made to fit some of the orthodox theories of modern times. Some of the items must be canceled, and others transposed. And worse still, the same changes will not fit all the theories. To fit infant baptism, the commission must begin with baptism and every thing else must be canceled; but when the same persons baptize adults, they begin with teaching, and put baptism after salvation.

THE COMMISSION.

Matthew xxviii: 19, 20.   Mark xvi: 15, 16.   Luke xxiv: 46, 47.

TEACH	All Nations,	....	....	Baptizing,	Formula,
PREACH	{ Every Creature, In all the world,	The Gospel,	Believe,	Baptized,	Saved,
PREACH	All Nations,	....	Repent,	....	Remission of Sins, Begin. at Jeru'lem
TEACH OR PREACH	{ To all Nations, Every Creature in all the world.	The Gospel,	Believe, Repent,	Baptism, Formula,	Saved or Remission of Sins, Begin. at Jeru'lem

Let us carefully examine this summary and see if it contains any thing which we may safely take away. Shall we take away teaching or preaching? Before persons can believe on Christ they must have the testimony concerning him, for how can they believe in him of whom they have not heard; and how can they hear without a preacher. Before any one can obey the gospel he must know what the gospel requires of him. We cannot, therefore, take away the preaching, for it pleased God by the foolishness of *preaching* to save them that believe.

Can we take away the words, *all nations, every creature, in all the world?* No, for then the preacher would not know where to go, or to whom he should preach. The Jews might wish to confine the preaching to them; or the Calvinist might conclude that there was no use to preach to any but those elected in Christ to salvation before the world began. I guess the Lord fixed that item about right and it is best to let it alone.

Shall we take out the *gospel?* The preacher might not know what to preach. He might get to preaching Mormonism, Calvinism, Universalism or something else. I guess we can hardly take that item out—it is hard enough to keep them straight now. It is the power of God to salvation; and it is that by which Paul said the Corinthians had been saved; and if it saved them it might be necessary to save us. We will let that item remain surely.

Shall we take out belief? Must not the gospel be believed when preached? It is only the power of God to the salvation of him who believes it. Jesus said, he that believeth not shall be damned. It occurs to us that this would be rather a dangerous place to use the amputating knife.

Shall we take away repentance? All say no. But why not? If we are justified by faith only, or if faith is the only condition of pardon what is the use of repentance, or where is any place for it? "O but repentance comes before faith." Well, suppose we were to grant this; if it is a condition coming after faith, without which all must perish, will it cease to be a condition if placed before faith? *Changing places* with faith and repentance does not make either one cease to be a condition of pardon. Though placing the *cart before the horse* might put things in quite an awkward shape, yet *cart* and *horse* are both there all the same. So placing *repentance before faith* brings no relief to the doctrine of justification or salvation by faith alone. If it is by faith only or alone, then repentance has nothing to do with it, and hence it may be *rubbed out* of the commission. But Jesus had not learned the doctrine of justification by faith only when he put repentance into the commission, nor has he learned it yet so far as heard from, so we will let repentance stay just where he placed it.

But does the fact that repentance is mentioned in a few places before faith settle the order in which these conditions come in the plan of salvation? Peter said: "The God of our fathers raised up Jesus, whom ye slew and hanged on a tree." Acts v: 30. Again: "And we are witnesses of all these things which he did both in the land of the Jews, and in Jerusalem; whom they slew and hanged on a tree." Acts x: 39. Did the Jews slay Jesus and then hang him on the tree of the cross? Yes, if the order of mention is always the order of occurrence. Once more: "If thou shalt confess with thy mouth the Lord Jesus, and shalt believe in thine heart that God hath raised him from the dead, thou shalt be saved." Rom. x: 9. Are persons to confess with the mouth before they believe with the heart? The very next verse in the same connection reverses this order. "For with the heart man believeth unto righteousness; and with the mouth confession is made unto salvation." Rom. x. 10. On the day of Pentecost the people heard Peter preach Jesus as the then crowned King, Lord and Christ. They believed and were cut to the heart by faith in Jesus. When they asked what they should do the first thing required of them was to repent. This example should forever settle the order in which faith and repentance come. But having discussed this subject elsewhere I only present a thought or two here, not presented there.

But now comes the trouble. There is *baptism*; it must come out of the commission surely. Well, Jesus put it there; who has a right to revise his work? If I had made the commission I might have put a mourners' bench right where Jesus put baptism. I am quite sure that I would have made a bungle of it in some way. Fortunately it was made by Him who had all power in heaven and on the earth, and our duty is to accept it as He gave it.

Shall we take out the *formula?* No, all use it and I suppose none want it taken out. If removed from the commission it is forever gone, for it can be found nowhere else.

Shall we take out salvation, or remission of sins as the blessing promised to those who would honor the Master? Some might want to change the position it occupies, but I suppose none would like to have it taken out entirely. But it is just where Jesus placed it—who has a right to change it? He did not say, he that believeth and is saved may or should be baptized; but He did say, he that believeth and is baptized shall be saved.

He promised salvation to him who would believe and be baptized; and surely the blessing promised cannot be reached before compliance with the conditions on which it is promised. Such language could not be misunderstood concerning the ordinary affairs of every day business.

Suppose I engage a laborer to plant me a crop of corn; and cultivate it to maturity: for which I agree to give him a specified horse. The proposition is accepted, the details are all understood and reduced to writing. The man goes to work and plants the crop, but does nothing more to it. The crop is choked out by weeds and is wholly worthless. But he demands of me the horse specified in the contract, as though he had done all the work agreed upon, when no one was to blame in any way for his failure but himself. Of course I refuse to deliver the horse, and he sues me. Is there a court on earth that would say he is entitled to the horse? Surely not. Very well, he that believeth and is baptized shall be saved. The man believes, has not been baptized—is he saved? Though perhaps many have been the opportunities offered, yet he allowed the lust of the flesh, and the deceitfulness of riches to choke out the word. His faith is *dead*, and wholly worthless. Now where is the difference? One is business—the other pertains to religion—the principle is precisely the same.

But if we could still be in doubt as to the import of the commission as operations were to begin under it at Jerusalem, we have only to go there and see what the apostles, to whom it was given, did in carrying it out. What did they do in obedience to it?

The first requisition made of the apostles in the commission was to preach. They were to begin at Jerusalem and here they are. " Peter, standing up with the eleven, lifted up his voice, and said unto them, Ye men of Judæa, and all *ye* that dwell at Jerusalem, be this known unto you, and hearken to my words." Acts ii : 14. Thus began the first discourse ever preached under the commission given by Christ to the apostles for the conversion of the world.

They were required to preach to, or teach all nations, and there were dwelling at Jerusalem Jews, devout men from every nation under heaven, which gave favorable opportunity for the work to begin; and it was extended as, in the providence of God, they had opportunity to extend it.

The gospel was to be the subject matter of their preaching, and every prominent fact connected with the gospel was embraced in Peter's discourse on that occasion.

The people were to believe the gospel, and they did believe what Peter preached, and as Jesus, the crowned King, Lord and Christ was the central theme of his discourse, when they believed what he preached they *believed on Christ;* and *believing*, they were cut to the heart—mightily wrought upon and affected by the Holy Spirit, who dictated the words spoken by him to them.

The commission required *repentance* to be preached in the name of Jesus, so when the people were cut to the heart, and anxiously inquired what to do, the first thing commanded in the name of Jesus was that they should repent.

But the commission required believing penitents to be baptized, hence Peter not only commanded these believers to repent, but in the name of Jesus Christ, he told them to *repent and be baptized;* and he told them to do *both* for the *remission of sins*, the very thing which, in connection with repentance was to be preached in the name of Jesus. *

Thus we see that every item of the commission was present in the events of Pentecost. This was indeed an *inspired commentary* on the commission, *showing what it meant by showing what inspired men did in obeying it.*

One more thought and we close our examination of the commission for the present. In all God's dealings with man in every age of the world, when he promised a blessing to any person, or number of persons, on compliance with a specified number of conditions, the blessing could only be reached on compliance with all the conditions standing between the party and the blessing promised. When Naaman was commanded to wash himself seven times in Jordan in order to be cured of his leprosy, he did not reach the cure until he dipped the seventh time. When the Israelites were commanded to march around the city of Jericho once a day for six days, and seven times on the seventh day, the walls of the city were not thrown down until the completion of the seventh circuit on the seventh day. Other examples might be given, but these are sufficient to illustrate the principle. Now, if the language of Jesus can establish any thing, it is certain that he has placed *faith, repentance and baptism* in the commission as conditions of *salvation* or the *remission* of sins. Can we reach the blessing promised until we comply with *all the conditions?* If we can, then this ever-present principle in God's dealings with man has been overcome, or set aside in some way. For what did Jesus put these conditions in the commission if they are not to be regarded

---

* For a critical examination of this subject see Gospel Plan of Salvation, pages 505 to 510 inclusive.

in order to reach the *salvation,* or remission of sins promised? If the blessing promised may be obtained without compliance with *all the conditions, why not without compliance with any?*

Now, friendly sinner, is there any possibility of a mistake in this matter? We confess our inability to see a chance for mistake; but suppose we are wrong, and it should be true that we are pardoned the moment we believe, will God damn us for going on and obeying him in baptism? We think not. Surely he would not condemn us for obeying him in baptism after commanding it. Hence we are safe even on that theory.

Again, we are told that whatever a man believes to be right is right to him. Well, if this be so, we cannot be wrong, for it will surely be conceded that we honestly believe what we teach; and this being so, we will be saved in our honest belief if any are thus saved.

But we occupy safe ground all along the line. Some tell us that the commission authorizes the baptism of infants. Suppose this is true; it is admitted on all hands that if we were not baptized in infancy it was no fault of our own, but simply the neglect of our parents; and that we ought to be baptized as adults if we were not as infants. Very well, then, when we are baptized as believers we are doing right; and we will surely not be lost for doing right.

Some think that sprinkling or pouring will do for baptism. Suppose this is true, the same persons will admit that immersion is valid baptism; hence when we are immersed we are Scripturally baptized beyond the shadow of a doubt, and cannot be wrong. So we occupy safe ground in any aspect of the case. Others *may be right,* yet may be wrong. We are right and cannot be wrong.

Then the question for your decision is, do you want to be saved? If so, what hinders you from being saved? God is willing to save you—are you willing to be saved? O yes, you are willing that God may save you if he will save you in your own way. My dear friend, you have no right to dictate to God as to how he shall save you. You must accept salvation on his terms or be lost. And if you are not willing to be saved on any terms which may be pleasing to him, you are not in a fit frame of mind to be saved at all.

But you say you are not good enough to obey God yet. How long will it take you to get to be good enough in serving the devil? Will you ever make much improvement in that direction?

Well, but you intend to do better some day. But suppose you die before that some day comes, what then? And if you should live a thousand years you could never repay God for what he has done for you. You owe all to him.

Men act more consistently on every other subject than on the subject of their soul's salvation. They will move in the direction of their interests in other matters. Convince them that they will lose a few hundred dollars if they do not immediately secure it and they will move at once. But when their eternal destiny is at stake they seem perfectly indifferent and unconcerned.

It is not necessary for a man to become a liar, a thief, or a murderer, in order to be lost. He can be lost without becoming that bad. Paul said: "How shall we escape if we neglect so great salvation." *Neglect* is the word. Did you ever think of the fact that *neglect* of duty will damn you forever? Arise and come to Jesus now. Now is all the time you can claim. To-morrow to you may never come.

CHAPTER IV.

THE CONVERSION OF THE JAILER.

"Sirs, what must I do to be saved? And they said, Believe on the Lord Jesus Christ, and thou shalt be saved, and thy house." Acts xvi: 30, 31.

WE propose an examination of the jailer's conversion because it is supposed to teach the doctrine of salvation by faith only. As the jailer was told to believe on the Lord Jesus Christ, and he should be saved and nothing more is contained in the direct answer to the question asked by him, it is assumed that nothing else was necessary to his salvation but to believe.

Before entering upon an examination of the real merits of this case of conversion, there are a few preliminary considerations to which we invite attention for a few moments.

When we ask a person, demanding baptism, if he believes with all the heart that Jesus Christ is the Son of God, our religious neighbors tell us that *belief is not faith;* yet when these same persons wish to preach a discourse, setting forth the doctrine of justification by faith only, the answer of Paul to the jailer is a favorite text from which to preach it. Why use a command to *believe*, to teach the necessity of *faith*, if belief is not faith? Surely there is a want of fitness of *text* and *sermon* in such efforts as these. It occurs to us that if *belief* is not *faith*, they should select a text having the *word faith* in it at least.

Again, if from the fact that belief is the only thing

mentioned in the direct answer of Paul to the Jailer, we are authorized to conclude that nothing else is necessary; then why may we not select other examples where neither faith nor belief is mentioned directly, in answer to substantially the same question, and conclude that faith is not necessary at all because it is not mentioned? Is not one conclusion just as logical and Scriptural as the other? But if we treat the Bible in this way we may soon have as many *theories* of conversion as there are cases of conversion recorded.

One man may take this example, and construct him a theory of salvation on faith alone, because nothing but belief is mentioned in the direct answer. He will have neither repentance nor baptism in his theory; for we must remember that there is as little said about *repentance* as about *baptism*; and hence they must *both* go out together. If baptism is to be rejected because not mentioned directly in the answer, then *repentance* must be rejected for the same reason. But we may be answered that repentance is *implied*. Implied indeed! Then why may not baptism be implied as well? If we may *imply* one why not the other? If you open that door you must take in both or neither. As neither is mentioned they must stand or fall together.

When Saul said, Lord what wilt thou have me to do? he was told to go into the city and there he should be told what he must do. Not to be tedious in unnecessary details, Ananias was sent by the Lord to tell him; and he told him to arise and be baptized and wash away his sins, calling on the name of the Lord. Nothing was said about *faith* and just as little was said about *repentance*. Therefore the reasoning adopted in the jailer's case forces the conclusion that neither of them is necesary. Then on this example we may construct a theory of salvation on baptism alone. Is there not just the same authority for it that is claimed to build a theory of salvation by faith only on the jailer's case?

But another man comes upon the arena, and he is not pleased with faith alone, nor with baptism alone—indeed he has no use for either; and he begins turning the leaves of his New Testament in search of an example by which he can exclude both. He turns to the 3rd chapter of Acts and reads the 19th verse: "Repent ye, therefore, and be converted that your sins may be blotted out." Here it is. No faith, no baptism mentioned here, and he constructs him a theory of conversion on *repentance* alone. Has he not the same authority to do it that any one has to construct a theory of salvation on the jailer's case by faith alone because nothing else but belief is mentioned in the answer?

Still another man appears who is not pleased with faith alone, repentance alone, or baptism alone, and he looks up an example that suits his taste better. He opens at Acts ii: 37, 38. He finds that substantially the same is asked by the Pentecostians that was asked by the jailer: "Men and brethren what shall we do?" It was answered by an inspired man who spake as the Spirit gave him utterance: "Repent and be baptized, every one of you, in the name of Jesus Christ, for the remission of sins." Here there is nothing said about faith; and the reasoning applied to the jailer's case forces the conclusion that that which is not specifically mentioned is unnecessary, and he, therefore, builds him a theory on *repentance and baptism* without any faith at all. Has he not a right to come to such conclusion from the theory adopted in the jailer's case?

And so we might go on, multiplying theories to any extent desirable. Is it possible that God has no *system* at all; but just pardons or saves one man in this way, another in that way, and still another in some other way, as may chance to happen? Surely this cannot be. If we look at the material universe, where God controls every thing by natural law, we find day and night, summer and winter, seed time and harvest, have succeeded each other in regular order, without a single failure, from the dawn of creation until now. Planets roll in regular cycles around the sun, as they have ever done, since God's almighty hand hung them in space upon nothing save the law by which, from the beginning, he has held them in position subservient to his will. In all directions we see every thing subordinate to law, conceived in infinite wisdom; and no discordant note is heard, or want of harmony seen in any department of his dominion. Can we conclude, then, that in the salvation of man, whom he so loved as to give the life of his Son to consummate it, there is no system, harmony, or order; but every thing left in confusion, and subject to the mere happenings of chance. Surely such utter want of *system*, in a matter so important, is wholly unlike God; and nothing of the kind ever emanated from him. The plan of salvation, understood as God gave it, is the grandest exhibition of harmony and order on which the mind of man was ever permitted to dwell; and when we see and appreciate its *perfection* these conflicting theories will have passed into the darkness of eternal night.

One other matter of general application demands attention before entering upon an examination of the jailer's conversion.

Circumstances connected with different cases of conversion, and *conditions* on which conversion depends are not the same. *Circumstances* connected with cases of conversion have differed, do differ, and will continue to differ, as long as man lives in a tenement of clay; but *conditions* of conversion, or salvation under the Christian dispensation, always have been, are now, and will continue to be the same in all cases. We know nothing of exceptions to this position. If exceptions there be, they are not connected with any case of conversion recorded, and hence we can know nothing about them.

It was a circumstance connected with the conversion of the Pentecostians that they had gone to Jerusalem, fifty days before, to attend the annual feast of the passover; and were awaiting the feast of Pentecost; and hence were dwelling there during the fifty days between those two festivals. Thus they were present, and heard Peter's preaching on that memorable occasion, by which they were converted. Must this circumstance attend every case of conversion? If so no one could be converted until he made a pilgrimage to Jerusalem; and not then until the other events of the day were repeated.

It was a circumstance connected with the conversion of Cornelius that he saw and talked with an angel, by whom he was told where to find a man who would tell him what to do to be saved. Must every one see and talk with an angel before he can be converted now? Such agencies are not necessary now as they were then. The New Testament was not then written, from which Cornelius could learn his duty, as we can now. Why should we want an angel to tell us that which we may plainly read in the word of God?

It was a *circumstance* connected with Saul's conversion that he saw the Lord, and talked with him in person. Another *circumstance* was that he saw a light above the brightness of the sun. It was still another *circumstance* that he was made physically blind, and had to have his friends to lead him by the hand. Do these *circumstances* have to be reproduced in the conversion of any one to-day? If so, we suppose there is not a man living who has been converted, or ever will be.

It was a *circumstance* connected with the conversion of the jailer, that he was the keeper of that prison; and as such, had charge of those holy men, of whom he learned what to do to be saved. It was another *circumstance* that there was an earthquake there, the prison doors were opened, and the fetters of the prisoners were taken off. Must these *circumstances* be present in conversion to-day? Thus we dispose of all the *miracles* connected with the conversions recorded. They were *circumstances*, not *conditions*; and were not the same in any two cases recorded. And to-day we cannot find any two cases of conversion the *circumstances* connected with which are the same throughout. We could easily demonstrate this by an examination of cases, but cannot spare space to do so. Any one can satisfy himself by an examination of the *circumstances* connected with such cases as may be personally known to him. If he will make the search he will soon be convinced that in no two cases are the *circumstances* precisely the same.

We are now ready to look for the *conditions* upon which the jailer was saved; and if we will allow the inspired teachers that common sense, to say nothing of their inspiration, that other men exercise in the ordinary affairs of life, we will have no difficulty in harmonizing his conversion with all others recorded for our inspection.

It is twenty-one miles from Lewisburg, where I am now writing, to the town of Shelbyville. Suppose a man wishing to go from here to Shelbyville, and not knowing the distance, inquires of me, " how far to Shelbyville?" Of course I reply it is twenty-one miles. He starts on the road, and after traveling seven miles, he meets another man and makes the same inquiry of him: "How far to Shelbyville?" Now, will this man give him the same answer given him before starting? No; it would not be true if he were to so answer him; and any man governed by the plainest dictates of common sense would adapt his answer to the position of the traveler when he made the inquiry; and the answer would be, "it is fourteen miles, sir." He moves on another seven miles, and meets another man of whom he makes the same inquiry: "How far to Shelbyville?" Will he reply as did either of those of whom he inquired before? No; it is not twenty-one miles from where he now is, nor is it fourteen miles, but it is seven miles; and the man exercising reasonable common sense so answers him. Here are three different answers, given to the same question, about a very plain matter; and though the answers were different they were all true; and had the same answer been given every time it would have been false two out of the three times, because of the different position of the man making the inquiry. This is only an illustration, but it is a very plain one, and if we keep it in mind it may help us to understand the jailer's conversion, and not only his but others as well.

Now what was the jailer's inquiry? It was: "Sirs, what must I do to be saved?" This was a very important question, and we would expect intelligent men (to say nothing of inspired men) to adapt their answer to the condition of the party at the time he asked it. Then what was his condition at that time? He was a heathen jailer, and had these holy men in his keeping for casting a spirit of divination out of a damsel in the name of Jesus, of whom, as yet, he knew nothing. He doubtless regarded Jesus as an impostor, and his followers as disturbers of the peace, and worthy of the punishment they had received. Then surely we would expect just such an answer as was given: " Believe on the Lord Jesus Christ and thou shalt be saved." Not that he would be saved at the moment he believed on Him; but when he believed on him he would be ready to accept terms of salvation coming from him. It would not be reasonable to command him to do *any thing* in obedience to him in whom he did not believe. When he be-believed in Jesus as the Son of God and Savior of man, then, and not until then, would he be inclined to accept his teaching, and respect his authority. Then the plan of salvation might be taught him, with a reasonable prospect of compliance with it. This was just the order observed. After telling him to believe on the Lord Jesus Christ, they spake unto him the word of the Lord and to all that were in his house. In the *word of the Lord* spoken to him was included all the conditions of pardon. That the necessity of baptism was preached to him, in the word of the Lord, is evident from the fact that he took them the same hour of the night, and was baptized he and all his, straightway. Surely he did not so promptly attend to that about which nothing had been said, and of which he knew nothing; and he could have known nothing about it until they preached the word of the Lord to him. Like the man in our illustration, before he started the jailer had the entire distance before him—he had to begin at the beginning; and he was instructed accordingly. Thus we see that these inspired teachers adapted their instruction to the condition of the party desiring salvation, and all preachers should do the same thing now.

But the same question, in substance, was asked by the

Pentecostians, and it was answered differently. Here again the inspired teachers adapted their instructions to the condition of those wanting the information. They had believed Jesus an impostor, and with wicked hands had crucified him. Peter corrected their mistake by assuring them that God had raised him from the dead and had made him both Lord and Christ. When they believed on Christ as Peter preached him to them they were cut to the heart, and cried out, men and brethren, what shall we do? Now would any reasonable man have given these the same answer given to the jailer? I suppose not. These *are believers*, the jailer was not. Why should they be told to believe when they had already believed? Please read Peter's discourse to them, see what he had preached to them, what they believed, and the effect it had on them; and you will be able to see why they were not told to believe. To use our illustration again, they had already traveled one-third of the distance, and needed only to go the remaining two-thirds. So they were not told to do that which they had done, but that which remained to be done: Repent and be be baptized in the name of Jesus Christ for the remission of sins.

This is plain practical common sense, and better still, it was instruction given by one who spake as the Spirit gave him utterance. The words were borne by the Holy Spirit, fresh from the eternal throne, and put into his mouth as he used them, and were surely appropriate. *Do you know any people who believe and preach that way now?* Do you know any preacher who would answer such a question, coming from persons just in such condition, just in the same way to-day? If an angel from heaven were to give a different answer it would surely be wrong. Then if persons in such condition cry to us, "what shall we do?" we will not tell them to kneel down that we and our brethren may pray for them, but we will tell them to repent and be-baptized, in the name of Jesus Christ, for the remission of sins: and if they receive this instruction we will baptize them, feeling perfectly sure that we have followed the teaching of God—not the tradition of men.

But we have, substantially, the same question asked on another occasion, and still a different answer is given—why was this? Come and see.

When the Lord appeared to the persecuting Saul on his way to Damascus, and convinced him that he was not an impostor as he had believed him to be, he, like the others, was cut to the heart, and cried out, "Lord, what wilt thou have me to do?" The Lord having delegated the preaching of the gospel to human agency, did not answer Saul's question directly, but told him to go into the city and there he should be told what to do. He went into the city, and there continued praying in deepest agony for three days and nights. The New Testament was not written then, so that Saul could go to it and learn his duty as we can now; hence the Lord sent a man to tell him what to do in answer to his question, "Lord, what wilt thou have me to do?" Here the whole doctrine of justification by faith alone breaks down. In this question is a clear and public expression of Paul's faith in Christ, and a willingness to do any thing required of him, by him in whom he now believes; and yet it is conceded, on all hands, that he did not yet know what to do that he might be pardoned, and hence was not pardoned until Ananias went to him and told him how to wash away his sins. *Here were three days and nights between his faith and pardon*, beyond the possibility of a respectable quibble. Then pardon does not take place the moment a man believes. This is settled if a plain Scriptural example can settle any thing.

But the Lord sent Ananias to tell him what to do. He said: "Why tarriest thou? Arise and be baptized and wash away thy sins calling on the name of the Lord." Acts xxii: 16.

Here again the answer is varied to suit the condition of the man wanting the information. He was not told to *believe*, as was the jailer, for he had believed. He was not told to repent, as were the Pentecostians, for he was as truly penitent as he could ever get to be. To use our illustration again, he had already traveled two-thirds of the distance and only one-third remained before him. It was not necessary that he should go back and start again; but to go on from where he then was. So Saul was not told to do that which he had done; but he was told to do that which remained to be done—*arise and be baptized*. When he did this he had complied with all the conditions required in the commission—he had believed, repented and been baptized; and in order to salvation, pardon or remission of sins, he needed nothing more. This instruction came by inspiration and cannot be wrong. Will you accept it? Why not?

But do you know any modern preacher who would so instruct a man in his condition to-day? ' Remember, he was down praying when Ananias went to him, why not tell him something like the following: "Pray on, Brother Saul; you will get through after awhile if you persevere. You are on the right road now; I have been along there, and that is the way I got through. A little more faith, believe in Jesus, trust in the Lord, etc., etc." Did you never hear anything like this? But is this the way Saul was instructed by the man of God?

Not a word like it. We respectfully suggest that Saul's condition was very much like that of modern *mourners*. He was a *believer*—so are they. If they did not believe on Christ they would not leave their seats and go forward to seek salvation through Him. Suppose you ask an infidel to go to the mourner's bench to seek salvation through Christ in whom he does not believe—would he go, do you think? No, indeed; he would laugh at you. But Saul was penitent—so are they. See their faces all bathed in tears of bitterest grief on account of past sins and anxious to live a new life, and tell me if such are not penitent. Then why not give them the same instructions that were given to Saul? "Arise and be baptized and wash away your sins." But are they ever so instructed? If not, why not?

We think it likely that these three cases cover every conceivable condition in which sinners may be found to-day. They are believers, or they are in unbelief. If they are in unbelief the instructions given to the jailer would apply to them. He was in unbelief, and if they are as he was, they should be instructed as was he.

If they have believed and have not repented, the instructions given to the Pentecostians would apply to them, "Repent and be baptized, every one of you, in the name of Jesus Christ for the remission of sins," would surely apply to such. If they have *believed* and *repented*, but have not been baptized, then the instructions given by Ananias to Saul would apply to them. "Arise and be baptized and wash away your sins calling on the name of the Lord." Can you think of any other condition in which sinners may be found? If not, then we have covered the whole ground with these three cases. You are in one of these three conditions

—will you apply the instructions to your own case and act upon it? Why not?

In conclusion we propose to show that the same thing was preached to the jailer that Peter preached in Jerusalem on the day of Pentecost. Paul said to the jailer: "Believe on the Lord Jesus Christ, and thou shalt be saved, and thy house. And they spake unto him the word of the Lord, and to all that were in his house." Acts xvi: 31, 32. Now please notice that the *word of the Lord* was spoken to the jailer, and if we can learn what was included in the *word of the Lord*, we may feel sure that we have found what was required of him. The prophets Isaiah and Micah both said: "Out of Zion shall go forth the law and the word of the Lord from Jerusalem." Is. ii: 3; Mic. iv: 2. Here we see that the word of the Lord spoken to the jailer was to go forth from Jerusalem. The Lord said: "Repentance and remission of sins should be preached in his name among all nations beginning at Jerusalem." Luke xxiv: 47. Perhaps repentance and remission of sins that were to begin to be preached at Jerusalem constituted the word of the Lord that was to go forth from there. Peter said: "Repent and be baptized, every one of you in the name of Jesus Christ for the remission of sins." Did this constitute the *word of the Lord* at Jerusalem, that the prophets said should go forth from there? We suppose it did. Then as the word of the Lord was what was spoken to the jailer, it is certain that the same thing was preached to him that Peter preached in Jerusalem on Pentecost. Nor is this all—they understood and obeyed it in the same way at both places. On Pentecost they that gladly received his word were baptized, and the same day there were added unto them about three thousand souls. Yes, they that gladly received what Peter preached were baptized the same day. What was the result at the Philippian jail? He took them the same hour of the night and washed their stripes and was baptized he and all his straightway. Thus we see that not only the same thing was preached at both places, but it was understood and obeyed in the same way at both places.

As to whether or not the jailer was baptized in the house see Gospel Plan of Salvation, page 347.

As to whether or not infants were baptized with the jailer, see Gospel Plan of Salvation, page 459.

Thus we see that the jailer's conversion was in strict accord with the other cases of conversion recorded, and with the commission given by the Lord, as well. Every condition of the commission was complied with by him. He believed, repented, was baptized, and was saved. There is not a case of conversion recorded under the gospel of Christ where these conditions were not all present, either expressed or implied. He who has complied with all these conditions has the words of Jesus pledged for his pardon. "He that believeth and is baptized shall be saved." This was said by him who had all power in heaven and on the earth. Will you trust it? Who has power to revise and improve upon it?

CHAPTER V.

TYPES AND ANTITYPES, SHADOWS AND SUBSTANCES

THE symbols, parables, allegories, and figures of the Bible were all based on the imagery furnished in the places, times, and occupations familiar to the principal actors in the events recorded in this most wonderful Book. Printing was not known until about the middle of the fifteeth century—nearly fourteen hundred years after the last inspired sentence had been recorded; hence the word *type* does not occur in our English Bible at all. The Old Testament abounds in descriptions of persons, places, events, buildings, furniture and service connected with the patriarchal, and Jewish dispensations which more or less fully adumbrated persons and things analagous in the Christian dispensation.

In printing there is the metalic type, and the letter or character made by it, answering to it, or standing against it, hence comes our English word antitype. A Scripture *type*, then, is something in one age or dispensation exhibiting, at least in general outline, some person or thing appearing in some future period; and when it or they so appear, as typified, they or it may fitly be called the *antitype*.

In studying these types the Bible student may group them into two classes—viz : *Single* and *systematic*. The *single types* are such as set out or point to some particular feature in the *person* or *ministry* of Jesus Christ. The *systematic types* are such as more or less fully exhibit the whole system of salvation offered the world through Jesus Christ.

We do not propose an extensive examination of these single types; indeed they are so numerous that we cannot even mention them all; but we will mention enough of them to give an idea of what we mean by them.

Adam, the first man, was a type of Christ. Paul says: "Nevertheless death reigned from Adam to Moses, even over them that had not sinned after the similitude of Adam's transgression, who is the figure of him that was to come." Rom. v: 14. The word *figure* is here used in the sense of our word *type*; and by the word, or rather phrase, " him that was to come," is most certainly meant Jesus Christ.

"And so it is written, the first man Adam was made a living soul; the last Adam *was made* a quickening Spirit. Howbeit that *was* not first which is spiritual, but that which is natural; and afterward that which is spiritual. The first man *is* of the earth, earthy: The second man *is* the Lord from heaven." 1 Cor. xv: 45–47. Adam was the great head of the natural family of man. Jesus Christ is the head of the church, or Spiritual family on the earth.

Moses was a type of Christ. "The law was given by Moses, but grace and truth came by Jesus Christ." John i: 17. Or as some render this verse, "The grace and the *reality* came by Jesus Christ." Moses was the law-giver to the Jews, Jesus Christ was the Law-giver in his kingdom.

The law given by Moses was a type, or shadow of the gospel of Jesus Christ. "The law having a shadow of good things to come, and not the very image of the things." Heb. x: 1.

Aaron was the high priest of the Jews under the law,

and as such was a type of Christ, our High Priest under the gospel. Heb. ix: all.

The paschal lamb that was slain on the night of the departure of the children of Israel from Egypt was a type of Christ, who is our passover. 1 Cor. 5-7.

And without being further tedious we may say that every victim slain as a sin-offering under the law of Moses was a type of Jesus Christ, who was offered to bear the sins of many. Heb. ix: 9-14; 23-28.

The smitten rock that gave water to the famishing Israelites in the wilderness was a type of Christ, who was smitten for our offenses. 1 Cor. x: 4.

The right application of types and the interpretation of prophecies are fruitful fields of doubtful speculation without an *inspired interpreter;* but when an inspired apostle says, "This is that which was spoken by the prophet," then we feel that we have something solid beneath us—that our feet are upon a rock. In our application of the types and shadows of the Old Testament we have endeavored to follow the light cast on our pathway by inspired interpreters.

There are at least four systematic types in the Old Testament, each one symbolizing the plan of salvation revealed in the New Testament—viz: The salvation of Noah and family, the deliverance of the Israelites from Egyptian bondage, the tabernacle of the wilderness, and the temple of Jerusalem. To the first one of these we propose directing attention for the present.

THE SALVATION OF NOAH.

"Which sometimes were disobedient, when once the longsuffering of God waited in the days of Noah, while the ark was a preparing, wherein few, that is, eight souls were saved by water. The like figure whereunto *even* baptism doth also now save us (not the putting away of the filth of the flesh, but the answer of a good conscience toward God,) by the resurrection of Jesus Christ." 1 Peter iii: 20, 21.

We have the words "like figure" from the Greek word *anti-tupon*, which is as nearly the exact synonym of our English word *antitype* as two words ever are in different languages; and there is no good reason why it should not be so rendered here. Then we would have " The *antitype* whereof baptism doth also now save us." That this is a correct translation of the passage we think no unprejudiced scholar will deny. Then we are not guessing at the fact that the salvation of Noah was a type of our salvation, for the apostle Peter plainly says so.

In what sense are we to regard baptism as saving us? Surely there is no saving virtue or power in baptism to save us. God alone has the pardoning power. Then Peter must have meant that baptism was a *condition* on compliance with which God saved those to whom he wrote.

But did Peter mean that baptism *alone* saved them, or that baptism was the *only* condition necessary to their pardon? It was certainly the only thing mentioned in Peter's statement; and whenever we are said to be saved by faith, or justified by faith, or eternal life or remission of sins is said to depend on belief, and nothing else is mentioned, it is always assumed that nothing else is necessary but faith or belief. Then as baptism is the only thing mentioned by Peter, in this connection, by which we are saved why not assume that we are saved by *baptism alone?* There is not a word said here about faith, not a word about repentance. Suppose we conclude, therefore, that they are not necessary; would we not be adopting just the reasoning of those who claim to prove justification by faith alone?

But is this correct reasoning? We think not; for when Jesus put faith or belief, as a condition of salvation, into the commission he put it there to stay, and Peter had no right to take it out, and he certainly did not attempt it. When Jesus said, "He that believeth not shall be damned," he meant it; and Peter did not intend to contradict it. So when Jesus put baptism, as a condition of salvation, into the commission he put it there to stay, too; and we had better not attempt to take it out. When Peter said baptism saves us he meant such a baptism as Jesus authorized him to preach; and that was a baptism preceded by a hearty belief of the gospel. No other baptism was ever preached or taught by Peter or any other inspired man. It was not at all necessary that every condition of saltion should be mentioned every time the subject of salvation was referred to. As well might we expect the multiplication table to be repeated, or printed on every page of an arithmetic where an example is found requiring its use. It would indeed be a queer book. When the conditions of salvation were given in the commission they are all presumed to be present in every case of conversion whether mentioned or not. Any other reasoning would indefinitely multiply *theories* at the expense, and *utter destruction of all system.*

But were we to conclude that nothing but baptism was required because nothing else was mentioned in that connection, we would destroy all fitness between the type and antitype. Was Noah saved by water without faith? Surely not. Paul says: " By faith Noah, being warned of God of things not seen as yet, moved with fear, prepared an ark to the saving of his house;

by the which he condemned the world, and became heir of the righteousness which is by faith. Heb. xi: 7.

Here we find that by faith Noah prepared the ark in which he was saved by water; and as faith was in the type we must expect to find it in the antitype. Were a printer to set up the letters "G-o-d" to spell the word *God* in his type, he would be quite surprised to find only the letter "G" in the antitype. So when Jesus put faith, repentance, and baptism in the commission, as conditions of salvation, is it not a little strange to see justification by *faith only* in the teaching of those who believe the Bible? And would not the printer be even more surprised to find only the letter "d" in the impression made by his type? Would he stand around and expect the other two letters to change places and come out "o g" after a few years? This would be quite a transposition—"d-o-g." And yet is this not exactly what happens when those who say that the commission gives all the authority they have to baptize any one, and under it baptize a baby? They claim to baptize the babe, under the commission, in the formula it contains, and then reverse the order of faith and repentance and expect the child, when grown, to *repent* and *believe.*

But the commission is not the type. This makes the matter all the worse. The printer's type may get jostled about, but after the impression is made—the word printed, to see the letters *changing places,* or some of them *disappearing,* is unaccountable indeed. Now, is this a perversion? Is it not true to real life in the teaching of modern times? If it is not then we confess our inability to understand what we hear from the pulpits, and read from the highest standard works on these subjects. We do not *wish* to misrepresent any one, and have no interest in doing so. "But does not Paul say: Therefore being justified by faith, we have peace with God through our Lord Jesus Christ? Rom. v: 1. As there is nothing else mentioned, is not this equivalent to saying we are justified by faith only?"

We think not. That we are justified by *faith*, is most certainly true, but that we are justified by faith only is not true; for an inspired man has said: "Ye see then how that by works a man is justified, and not by faith only." James ii: 24.

Let us try this reasoning a little further. It is said: "By faith Noah, being warned of God of things not seen as yet, moved with fear, prepared an ark to the saving of his house." Heb. xi: 7. Now here it is said that by *faith* Noah prepared an ark, and there is nothing said of any thing else by which he did it, therefore according to the reasoning on justification *nothing else was used but faith* in building the ark. Can this be true?

God said to Noah: "make thee an ark of gopher wood; rooms shalt thou make in the ark, and shalt pitch it within and without with pitch. And this *is the fashion* which thou shalt make it of: The length of the ark *shall be* three hundred cubits, the breadth of it fifty cubits, and the height of it thirty cubits. A window shalt thou make to the ark, and in a cubit shalt thou finish it above; and the door of the ark shalt thou set in the side thereof; *with* lower, second, and third *stories* shalt thou make it. And, behold, I, even I, do bring a flood of waters upon the earth, to destroy all flesh, wherein *is* the breath of life, from under heaven; *and* every thing that *is* in the earth shall die. But with thee will I establish my covenant; and thou shalt come into the ark, thou, and thy sons, and thy wife, and thy sons' wives with thee. And of every living thing of all flesh, two of every *sort* shalt thou bring into the ark, to keep *them* alive with thee; they shall be male and female. Of fowls after their kind, and of cattle after their kind, of every creeping thing of the earth after his kind, two of every *sort* shall come unto thee, to keep *them* alive. And take thou unto thee of all food that is eaten, and thou shalt gather *it* to thee; and it shall be for food for thee, and for them. Thus did Noah, according to all that God commanded him, so did he." Gen. vi: 14–22.

Here we find that God made a revelation to Noah and Noah believed it—was he saved when he believed God? God revealed to him his purpose to destroy the wicked, and how he would do it. He told him how to build an ark; of what kind of wood he should make it; how long, wide, and high it should be; and how many stories should be in it, and where to put the door and window; and that he should pitch it within and without with pitch; and what, and who he should take into it with him; and how to provide food on which to subsist while the waters were upon the earth. All this God reavealed, and Noah believed it; but did *believing only, accomplish the work?* You will say such a question appears *foolish;* why so? It is said by *faith* Noah prepared an ark to the saving of his house, and nothing else is mentioned; therefore nothing else was used, or employed but faith. O, but this was a temporal salvation! True enough, indeed; but Peter says *it was a type* of our salvation by baptism; and the religious world with one voice agrees that it is a type of our salvation; and this being so, there must be a fitness of *type* and antitype. But let us have no dodging the issue. When it is said we are justified by faith, and nothing else is mentioned, that means by faith only; so when it is said *by faith* Noah built the ark and nothing else is mentioned, it must be admitted that by faith only he built the ark, or the reasoning on the subject of justification by *faith only* breaks down. The record says: "Thus did Noah; according to all that God commanded him, so did he." This is the way Noah built an ark by faith—he believed what God said to him, and he perfected his faith by doing what God commanded him to do. Had he trusted to faith alone he would have been drowned with the wicked. But he believed and obeyed God and was saved. He had as much faith before he built the ark as he had after it was done; indeed he had as much faith as any man can have to-day—*faith to do all God commanded him;* no man can have more; all must have as much. With all his faith he was *saved in the ark by water*, hence he was not saved when first he believed, but saved when he obeyed God. This is plain enough.

Now are we prepared to look at the *antitype?* Peter says baptism, the antitype of Noah's salvation in the ark by water, now saves us. We have seen that baptism is not the *power* that saves us, but it is a *condition*, on compliance with which, God saves us. We have seen that baptism alone, if there could be such a thing, saves no one. We have seen that baptism, that is not preceded by a hearty faith in Christ would be worth no more to a *man* than it would be worth to an *infant*; and we have seen that it is worth nothing to either. What, then, is the *salvation* to which Peter alludes as secured by baptism?

It is not salvation from persecution, insult, or personal injury, for the baptized man is just as subject to these as the unbaptized. It is not salvation from pain, sickness, or death, for these are the common lot of all men, whether baptized or not. It did not refer to final salvation in heaven, for Peter said, "baptism doth also

NOW save us." This clearly shows that it was a *present* salvation to which he referred. Then we repeat, to what salvation did Peter refer?

Peter was one of the apostles to whom Jesus gave the commission, saying: "He that believeth and is baptized shall be saved." Then when Peter said baptism doth also now save us, he certainly meant the same salvation to which Jesus referred in the commission. Then to what salvation did Jesus refer in the commission? Luke records the same commission, saying: "Thus it is written, and thus it behooved Christ to suffer and to rise from the dead the third day, and that repentance and remission of sins should be preached in his name among all nations, beginning at Jerusalem." What Mark calls *salvation* Luke calls *remission of sins*. When Peter first preached, under this commission, in Jerusalem on the day of Pentecost, he told believers to repent and be baptized in the name of Jesus Christ for the remission of sins. Here Peter gives *remission of sins* as the object for which persons were to be baptized, and hence *remission of sins* was the salvation to which Peter referred when he said, "baptism doth also now save us."

But Peter puts in parenthesis, ("not the putting away of the filth of the flesh, but the answer of a good conscience toward God;") and we are told that *filth of the flesh* here means *sin*, and hence this was intended to forbid the idea that baptism is for the remission of sins. It occurs to us that this is a very elastic construction of the words filth of the flesh Suppose you wished to say that baptism was not to wash dirt from the body, could you think of a better way of expressing it than to say, "it is not the putting away of the filth of the flesh?" The passage means exactly what it says. Baptism being an entire submersion of the body, like bathings for cleansing filth from the body, the apostle thought it necessary to guard his readers against the supposition that it was for any such purpose. But had baptism been only dropping a few drops of water on the head it is likely the apostle would hardly have found it necessary to guard his readers against supposing it was for putting away the filth of the flesh. Such caution would hardly have been necessary.

"But baptism is the answer of a good conscience, and the conscience must be good before baptism, or baptism could not be the answer of a good conscience." This is certainly true. The conscience must be good before baptism, or baptism will do the party no good. A good conscience just means that the party is *honest* in what he is doing; and if he is not honest, he is a *hypocrite*, and his baptism would be worth nothing. Baptism must be the response of a good conscience; but a good conscience by no means implies that he who has it is a pardoned man. Paul lived in all good conscience when he was killing Christians. Long after his conversion he said he had lived in all good conscience up to that day; and verily thought he ought to do many things contrary to the name of Jesus which things he did; but his good conscience did not prove him a Christian, or a pardoned man. He says he obtained forgiveness because he did it in ignorance and unbelief. The conscience is the result of faith, and faith is the result of testimony. If the testimony is correct the faith may be correct, and if the faith is correct the conscience will be correct. But if a man's teaching is wrong his faith will be wrong, and *he may have a good conscience in doing very bad things, because he believes them right.* The conscience of one man will approve that which another man's conscience condemns, simply because of *different faith* produced by different teaching. For example, one man's conscience will approve of what he calls the baptism of his children, while another's conscience would rebuke him sharply for doing the same thing; and both are honest, and living up to the conscientious discharge of duty as they understand it. A man should *never violate his conscience*, for were he to do so, he would do what he conscientiously believed to be wrong, and if he were to do right believing it wrong, he would be dishonest in doing it, and such service would not be *obedience from the heart*. There is only one thing safe, and that is to *study the word of God*, and be sure that our consciences are moulded by its teaching. If we prayerfully read and study the word of God, and use all the means and opportunities we have of coming to a knowledge of the truth, we will not be likely to go wrong—at least not very far wrong; and I cannot resist the conviction that such persons *will get right*, even though they start wrong. But we must not forget that a good conscience only proves a man to be *honest*. That is all.

Then the idea that baptism is the answer of a good conscience only means that it is the obedience of an honest man. From my very soul have I been sickened at the futile efforts of good men to switch around and evade the grand truths that sparkle on the very surface of this passage.

When Peter says baptism is not the putting away of the filth of the flesh *it is true, literally true*. There is no use running off into *ceremonial pollution*, or any thing of the kind. It just means that baptism was not for the purpose of removing *filth from the body*. That is what it says, and that is what it means—just that, exactly that. And we have seen the best kind of reason why this parenthetical clause was put in—to guard against a very natural mistake. Now do let the apostle's language mean what it implies. He meant what he said.

Again, when Peter says baptism is the answer of a good conscience, that is what he meant—just that, exactly that. It is plain and unambiguous, why not let it alone? He simply meant that it must be obedience *from the heart of an honest man*, for if not honest he is a *hypocrite*, and such a man could not be Scripturally baptized at all.

What is the use of all this talk about *seeking* of a good conscience? You are digging tunnels, my brother, that you may find treasures buried deep below, when they sparkle in the sunlight of Truth on the very surface; unseen, because you are hunting for something hidden and mysterious. It is right as it is—exactly right. The truth plain and simple. Will you receive it?

When Peter said baptism doth also now save us, he told the truth, or he told a falsehood. The statement is plain and unambiguous, and it is true, or it is not true. If this is not true, then nothing that he ever said or wrote is worthy of credit. A witness convicted of false testimony in one thing is unworthy of credit in any thing. This is true, or Peter's testimony must be set aside from beginning to end.

There is no evading this conclusion. Peter stands before us as a witness unimpeached, and his testimony must be accepted as true; hence *baptism doth also now save us*, for he said so. And if it saves us, it must *save us from something;* and if it does not save us from sin, *from what does it save us?* He does not say it *symbolically* saves us; or that it symbolizes a salvation previously secured by something else; but he says *it saves us*.

No one loyal to the will of the Master ever conjures up something to protect theories from the plain, obvious meaning of the word of God. He is ever ready to mould his theory by the Word, in place of warping the Word to fit his theory.

We repeat, what by this time must be quite apparent, that baptism is a *condition*, on compliance with which God saves us from the punishment due us in consequence of violating his law. If this is not true, then let him who can, tell us from what baptism does save us. It saves us from something—what is it?

"But Noah was a good man before he was saved in the ark by water, therefore we must be good—pardoned before we are baptized." Certainly Noah was a good man when he first appears in Bible history; but if this fact proves that we must be pardoned before we are baptized, it proves that we must be pardoned before we have faith, for he was just as good before he ever heard of the flood, or the ark; or had any faith in God's promise to save him, as he was when he landed upon Mount Ararat. Then if your reasoning be correct, and your objection to baptism be well-taken, it is worth just as much against faith as against baptism. You brush them both out with the same broom. Are you prepared for this? But your objection goes behind the beginning of the type to find fitness in the antitype. The type was a temporal salvation, and *begins with that salvation*. As to how, or when Noah became good we know nothing; and it has nothing to do with the type, or with the subject of our investigation. We must not go behind this or any other type to find fitness in the antitype; if we do we will destroy all types. We must always begin our application with the beginning of the type—not before it.

Now, my dear friends, are we sufficiently free from prejudice to allow us to accept the lesson taught in the type? We have no right to debate the terms of our salvation with God. As unworthy and helpless sinners we should gladly, humbly, and thankfully accept salvation on any terms upon which he is pleased to offer it to us. We have no worth or merit in ourselves to commend us to his favor. When we see ourselves as we are, we feel like covering our faces with a mantle of shame, and, like the lepers of old, crying unclean! unclean!! unclean!!! It is only through the grace and mercy of God that one of Adam's race can ever hope for salvation. The blood of Jesus is our only plea.

> "Sinner, hear the invitation
> Sent in mercy from above;
> Come, receive this great salvation,
> Purchased by redeeming love.
> Jesus calls in sweet compassion,
> Come, you weary souls, to me;
> Sinner, heed the invitation;
> Rise forthwith, he calleth thee."

CHAPTER VI.

SALVATION OF THE HEBREWS FROM BONDAGE.

AFTER the destruction of the wicked and the salvation of Noah and his family, the earth was again populated by their descendants. In view of the fact that an event so important as the flood was, most certainly, handed down, through tradition, from father to son through the ages following it, we would suppose that the sad fate of the wicked antediluvians would have been a lesson of warning to succeeding generations sufficient to have kept them sensible of their dependence upon God, and prevent them from rebellion against him for all time. But the lessons of experience are soon forgotten; so when the people became numerous and seemingly prosperous, they again became wicked, forgot God, and went into idolatry. They had learned the importance of worship, by tradition and observation, and having forgotten God, they made gods of their own, and worshiped them; as though the true God had never been.

After Noah came out of the ark God said: "I will establish my covenant with you; neither shall all flesh be cut off any more by the waters of a flood; neither shall there any more be a flood to destroy the earth." Gen. ix: 11.

Having thus entered into covenant with Noah that he would not again destroy the wicked by a flood, he determined to abandon them until they made the experiment of living without him—in the worsnip of gods of their own make. Finding one righteous man in Ur of the Chaldees, he determined to separate him from the idolaters by whom he was surrounded; and make him a great nation, which should be a nation devoted to Him. We suppose His motive for removing Abram from the land of his nativity was to prevent him and the nation he proposed making of him from being corrupted by idolatry. Be this as it may, "the Lord had said unto Abram, Get thee out of thy country, and from thy father's house, unto a land that I will show thee; and I will make of thee a great nation, and I will bless thee, and make thy name great; and thou shalt be a blessing." Gen. xii: 1, 2.

Accordingly Abram moved from Ur to Haran, and there remained until Terah, his father, was dead. After Terah's death he "took Sarai, his wife, and Lot, his brother's son, and all their substance that they had gathered; and the souls that they had gotten in Haran; and they went forth to go into the land of Canaan, and into the land of Canaan they came." Gen. xii: 5.

Abram was seventy-five years old when he left Haran; he was eighty-six years old when Ishmael, his son by Hagar, was born; he was ninety-nine years old when the covenant of circumcision was instituted, and he and Ishmael were circumcised; and he was one hundred years old when Isaac, the child of promise, was born to him of Sarah when she was ninety years old. To Isaac were born Jacob and Esau; to Jacob were born twelve sons, who became the heads of the twelve tribes of Israel.

The sale of Joseph by his brothers, his prosperity in Egypt, his appointment as governor, the famine in the land of Canaan, Joseph's introduction to his brothers, and the removal of Jacob and seventy-five souls down into Egypt are matters with which all Bible readers are familiar. These seventy-five persons were the children of Israel, Hebrews, or Jewish nation at that time.

We have not time to mention the events that made Joseph governor of Egypt. Sufficient it is to say that his influence with the king secured a favorable reception of his father, brothers, and their families; and their settlement in the land of Goshen, one of the richest portions of the land of Egypt.

While the then reigning Pharaoh, king of Egypt, lived the Hebrews were blessed with peace, rapid increase, and prosperity; but when another king arose who knew not Joseph, the Hebrews were made slaves to the Egyptians, by whom they were most grievously oppressed; and God heard their groanings and determined to deliver them. In this deliverance from slavery or bondage in Egypt our kind Father in heaven gave us a beautiful type of the delivery of the sinner from the guilt, slavery or bondage ot sin, by the gospel. This typical salvation and its antitype is the subject of our lesson for the present.

Please remember that the type was laid in the *delivery of the Isrælites from bondage*, and we cannot go *behind that delivery* for a fitness of things in the antitype. If we keep this well in mind it will greatly aid us in understanding the lesson taught in this most beautiful type. That the deliverance of the children of Israel from Egyptian bondage was a type of our deliverance from the guilt and bondage of sin under the gospel, is admitted by all theologians of note every where; but we will hear what Paul says about it:

"Moreover, brethren, I would not that ye should be

ignorant, how that all our fathers were under the cloud, and all passed through the sea; And were all baptized unto Moses in the cloud and in the sea; And did all eat the same spiritual meat; And did all drink the same spiritual drink: for they drank of that spiritual Rock that followed them: and that Rock was Christ. But with many of them God was not well pleased: for they were overthrown in the wilderness. Now these things were our examples, to the intent that we should not lust after evil things, as they also lusted. Neither be ye idolaters, as *were* some of them; as it is written, The people sat down to eat and drink, and rose up to play. Neither let us commit fornication, as some of them committed, and fell in one day three and twenty thousand. Neither let us tempt Christ, as some of them also tempted, and were destroyed of serpents. Neither murmur ye, as some of them also murmured, and were destroyed of the destroyer. Now all these things happened unto them for ensamples: and they are written for our admonition, upon whom the ends of the world are come. Wherefore let him that thinketh he standeth take heed lest he fall." 1 Cor. x: 1–12.

The argument of the apostle here is, that notwithstanding the baptism of the Israelites unto Moses, as their deliverer, in the cloud and in the sea, and their deliverance from bondage at the time of that baptism, yet they acted wickedly afterward and were lost; and these things were examples, that after our baptism and deliverance we are liable to be lost as they were, if we act wickedly as they did. This is the thought beyond the possibility of a doubt. Then we see that their deliverance through Moses was a part of the lesson left to us, and if we would understand the entire lesson we must examine the history of Moses, and trace his connection with the deliverance effected through him, as a type of our deliverance from sin.

"And the children of Israel were faithful, and increased abundantly, and multiplied, and waxed exceeding mighty; and the land was filled with them. Now there arose up a new king over Egypt, which knew not Joseph; and he said unto his people, Behold, the people of the children of Israel are mor eand mightier than we; come on, let us deal wisely with them; lest they multiply, and it come to pass, that, when there falleth out any war, they join also unto our enemies, and fight against us, and so get them up out of the land. Therefore they did set over them taskmasters to afflict them with their burdens. And they built for Pharaoh treasure cities, Pithom and Raamses. But the more they afflicted them the more they multiplied and grew. And they were grieved because of the children of Isræl; and the Egyptians made the children of Isræl to serve with rigour; and they made their lives bitter with hard bondage, in mortar, and in brick, and in all manner of service in the field; all their service wherein they made them serve, was with rigour." Ex· i: 7–14.

Notwithstanding all his efforts the king saw that the children of Israel increased, and he issued a decree that all male children born of Jewish mothers should be put to death as soon as born. But this decree was not carried out; so he charged all his people, saying: "Every son that is born ye shall cast into the river, and every daughter ye shall save alive." Ex. i: 22.

Pending this decree Moses was born. He was the son of Amram, by Jochebed, his wife, who was his aunt, or his father's sister. (See Ex. vi: 20.)

"When the mother of Moses saw that he *was a* goodly *child*, she hid him three months. And when she could no longer hide him, she took for him an ark of bulrushes, and daubed it with slime and with pitch, and put the child therein; and she laid *it* in the flags by the river's brink. And his sister stood afar off, to wit what would be done to him. And the daughter of Pharaoh came down to wash *herself* at the river; and her maidens walked along by the river's side; and when she saw the ark among the flags, she sent her maid to fetch it. And when she had opened *it*, she saw the child: and, behold, the babe wept. And she had compassion on him, and said, This is *one* of the Hebrews' children. Then said his sister to Pharaoh's daughter, Shall I go and call to thee a nurse of the Hebrew women, that she may nurse the child for thee? And Pharaoh's daughter said to her, Go. And the maid went and called the child's mother. And Pharaoh's daughter said unto her, Take this child away, and nurse it for me, and I will give *thee* thy wages. And the woman took the child, and nursed it. And the child grew, and she brought him unto Pharaoh's daughter, and he became her son." Ex. ii: 2–10.

Thus Moses was preserved from death by the King's decree, which he had issued in fear for the safety of his throne. When Moses was forty years old he went to visit his brethren, and when he found an Egyptian smiting one of them he slew him and hid him in the sand. The next day he found two of his brethren striving together; and he said to him who did the wrong, Wherefore smitest thou thy fellow? And he said, Who made thee a prince and a judge over us? intendest thou to kill me as thou killedst the Egyptian? And Moses feared, and said, Surely the thing is known. Now when Pharaoh heard this thing, he sought to slay Moses; but Moses fled from the face of Pharaoh, and dwelt in the land of Midian. Ex. ii : 11–15. Here he married Zipporah, the daughter of Jethro, and remained with his father-in-law, the priest of Midian, forty years. " And it came to pass in process of time, that the king of Egypt died: and the children of Israel sighed by reason of the bondage, and they cried, and their cry came unto God by reason of the bondage. And God heard their groaning, and God remembered his covenant with Abraham, with Isaac, and with Jacob. And God looked upon the children of Israel, and God had respect *unto* them." Ex. ii : 23–25.

When Moses led his father-in-law's flock to the mountain of God, even to Horeb, " The angel of the Lord appeared unto him in a flame of fire out of the midst of a bush ; and he looked, and behold, the bush burned with fire and the bush was not consumed. And Moses said, I will now turn aside, and see this great sight, why the bush is not burnt. * * * And the Lord said, I have surely seen the affliction of my people which are in Egypt, and have heard their cry by reason of their taskmasters ; for I know their sorrows ; and I am come down to deliver them out of the hand of the Egyptians, and to bring them up out of that land into a good land. * * * Come now, therefore, and I will send thee unto Pharaoh, that thou mayest bring forth my people, the children of Israel, out of Egypt." Ex. iii : 2–10.

And Moses answered and said, But, behold, they will not believe me, nor hearken unto my voice : for they will say, The Lord hath not appeared unto thee. And the Lord said unto Moses, What *is* that in thine hand? And he said, A rod. And he said, Cast it on the ground. And he cast it on the ground, and it became a serpent ; and Moses fled from before it. And the Lord said unto

Moses, Put forth thy hand, and take it by the tail. And he put forth his hand, and caught it, and it became a rod in his hand: * * * And the Lord said furthermore unto him, Put now thine hand into thy bosom. And he put his hand into his bosom: and when he took it out, behold, his hand *was* leprous as snow. And he said, Put thine hand into thy bosom again. And he put his hand into his bosom again; and plucked it out of his bosom, and, behold, it was turned again as his *other* flesh. And it shall come to pass, if they will not believe thee, neither hearken to the voice of the first sign, that they will believe the voice of the latter sign. And it shall come to pass, if they will not believe also these two signs, neither hearken unto thy voice, that thou shalt take of the water of the river, and pour *it* upon the dry *land:* and the water which thou takest out of the river shall become blood upon the dry *land.*" Ex. iv; 1–9.

Thus God revealed to Moses his purpose of delivering the children of Israel by him; and he enabled him to confirm the fact that God had sent him, by the performance of such miracles as unaided human power could not perform, that the people to whom he sent him might believe.

And I may here state, that in no age of the world, from the creation of Adam until now, did God ever *directly* call and send a man on any mission, that he did not enable him to do something to confirm his mission, and induce *faith* in those to whom he was sent that unaided human power could not perform. To this I know not an exception. I might *amplify* and *apply* this thought at great length; but it is said a hint to the wise is sufficient. Acting upon this maxim we must leave every one to apply it for himself.

But poor, frail humanity is always seeking excuses from the discharge of duty, and Moses was not an exception. "And Moses said unto the Lord, O my Lord, I *am* not eloquent, neither heretofore, nor since thou hast spoken unto thy servant: but I *am* slow of speech, and of a slow tongue. And the Lord said unto him, Who hath made man's mouth? or who maketh the dumb, or deaf, or the seeing, or the blind? have not I the Lord? Now therefore go, and I will be with thy mouth, and teach thee what thou shalt say. And he said, O my Lord, send, I pray thee, by the hand *of him whom* thou wilt send. And the anger of the Lord was kindled against Moses, and he said, *Is* not Aaron the Levite thy brother? I know that he can speak well. And also, behold, he cometh forth to meet thee: and when he seeth thee, he will be glad in his heart. And thou shalt speak unto him, and put words in his mouth: and I will be with thy mouth, and with his mouth, and will teach you what ye shall do. And he shall be thy spokesman unto the people: and he shall be, *even* he shall be to thee instead of a mouth, and thou shalt be to him instead of God." Ex. iv: 10–16.

"And Moses and Aaron went and gathered together all the elders of the children of Israel: And Aaron spake all the words which the Lord had spoken unto Moses, and did the signs in the sight of the people. And the people believed: and when they heard that the LORD had visited the children of Israel, and that he had looked upon their affliction, then they bowed their heads and worshiped." Ex. iv: 29–31.

Please *notice especially* that here is an account of the preaching, or presentation of the purpose of God to deliver the children of Israel, and its confirmation by the miracles done in the sight of the people, and the people "believed." Here is their faith—are they delivered yet? No, this is the first they had heard of God's purpose to deliver them. Don't forget this.

We need not speak of the ten plagues that God, by the hand of Moses brought upon Pharaoh and the Egyptians to make Pharaoh consent to the departure of the children of Israel; it is sufficient to say that they turned their backs upon their enemies, and under the lead of Moses " they took their journey from Succoth, and encamped in Etham, in the edge of the wilderness. And the Lord went before them by day in a pillar of a cloud, to lead them the way; and by night in a pillar of fire, to give them light; to go by day and night: He took not away the pillar of the cloud by day, nor the pillar of fire by night, *from* before the people." Ex. xiii : 20–22.

Now, they have believed, turned away from serving the Egyptians, and have started for Canaan under the lead of Moses, and are in camp at Etham. Are they delivered or saved yet? No, they are still in the land of Egypt, and liable to be captured and taken back at any moment.

" And the Lord spake unto Moses, saying, Speak unto the children of Israel, that they turn and encamp before Pi-hahiroth, between Migdol and the sea, over against Baal-zephon: before it shall ye encamp by the sea." Ex. xiv : 1, 2. Now, they are in camp by the sea—are they safe yet? " And when Pharaoh drew nigh, the children of Israel lifted up their eyes, and, behold, the Egyptians marched after them; and they were sore afraid: and the children of Israel cried out unto the Lord. And they said unto Moses, Because *there were* no graves in Egypt, hast thou taken us away to die in the wilderness? wherefore hast thou dealt with us, to carry us forth out of Egypt? *Is* not this the word that we did tell thee in Egypt, saying, Let us alone, that we may serve the Egyptians? For *it had been* better for us to serve the Egyptians, than that we should die in the wilderness." Ex. xiv: 10-12. This shows that they did not feel very safe, to say the least of it. "And Moses said unto the people, Fear ye not, stand still, and see the salvation of the Lord, which he will show to you to-day: for the Egyptians whom ye have seen to-day, ye shall see them again no more for ever." v. 13. See the salvation of the Lord which he *will show to you to-day*—not did show you when you believed.

"And Moses stretched out his hand over the sea; and the Lord caused the sea to go *back* by a strong east wind all that night, and made the sea dry *land*, and the waters were divided. And the children of Israel went into the midst of the sea on dry *ground;* and the waters *were* a wall unto them on their right hand, and on their left." vs. 21, 22.

The Egyptians pursued after them, "And Moses stretched forth his hand over the sea, and the sea returned to his strength when the morning appeared; and the Egyptians fled against it; and the Lord overthrew the Egyptians in the midst of the sea. And the waters returned and covered the chariots, and the horsemen, *and* all the host of Pharaoh that came into the sea after them; there remained not so much as one of them. But the children of Israel walked upon dry *land* in the midst of the sea; and the waters *were* a wall unto them on their right hand, and on their left. Thus the Lord saved Israel that day out of the hand of the Egyptians; and Israel saw the Egyptians dead upon the sea shore." vs. 27-30. Thus the Lord saved Israel *that day.* What day? The day they believed, when they were back in Egypt? No, but the day they were baptized unto Moses in the cloud and in the sea. *There* is where their enemies were drowned that they saw them no more; and they sung their song of rejoicing on the opposite shore from where they went in. Now they are delivered from *slavery* and *bondage* in Egypt, but not before. This surely is plain enough.

Though saved from their enemies, and from slavery and bondage in Egypt, they are not in Canaan yet. This is their objective point. This is their inheritance to which they have started—will they ever get there? This depends entirely upon their fidelity to God. Certain it is they have started right, and never could have reached Canaan by remaining in Egypt. If they are faithful to God he will lead them safely home.

But their fidelity must be tested, and God put them on a trial or probationary state, and they proved ungrateful and rebellious. So their probation was protracted until of the six hundred thousand men of war who crossed the Red sea only Caleb and Joshua were faithful. Under the lead of Joshua, after the death of Moses, those who were faithful crossed over Jordan and entered the land of Canaan, the home to which they all started when they left the land of Egypt.

The deliverance of the children of Israel is now sufficiently before us to enable us to see, with great clearness, its typical import; and it only remains for us to recapitulate its typical features, and apply them to their corresponding features of the antitype, in order to fully bring out the lesson contained in it. Before beginning our application we wish to call attention to certain facts upon which all religious teachers are agreed.

First, it is agreed that all men who would be saved must believe in Christ. Faith in Christ is indispensable to acceptance with God. Second, it is agreed, on all hands, that sinners must repent or perish. Third, it is agreed that believing penitents should be baptized. Where then is the real ground of difference? *It is as to the point in the process where pardon takes place.* The large majority believe that pardon takes place at the moment of belief, while we think it takes place at the time of baptism, the last condition standing between the sinner and pardon. We think all will agree that this is a correct statement of the real controversy; and we wish this thought kept in mind in the application of this type; that we may see exactly where pardon or deliverance takes place.

(1) The children of Israel became slaves in Egypt by their own wickedness—men become servants of sin by indulgence in sin. "Know ye not, that to whom ye yield yourselves servants to obey, his servants ye are to whom ye obey: whether of sin unto death, or of obedience unto righteousness?" Rom. vi: 16.

(2) God heard the groanings of his people in Egypt and provided for their deliverance. God so loved the world that he gave his Son to die to save them.

(3) Moses was the deliverer of the children of Israel —Jesus is our deliverer, whose blood cleanseth from all sin.

(4) Pharaoh feared for the safety of his throne on account of the rapid increase of the children of Israel, and ordered all male children born of Hebrew mothers to be put to death—after Jesus was born "King of the Jews," Herod fearing for the safety of his throne, "sent forth and slew all the children that were in Bethlehem, and in all the coasts thereof, from two years old and under." Matt. ii: 16.

(5) God preserved Moses from death by Pharaoh's

decree—God sent Joseph with the infant Jesus into Egypt, there to remain until Herod was dead, and thus saved him from death by Herod's decree.

(6) Moses was enabled to perform miracles in confirmation of his mission, that the people might believe in him as sent of God—" Many other signs truly did Jesus in the presence of his disciples which are not written in this book: but these are written that ye might believe that Jesus is the Christ, the Son of God, and that believing ye might have life through his name." John xx: 30, 31.

(7) Moses, through Aaron, made known to the Israelites the plan of their delivery, and they believed it. (Ex. iv: 29–31)—Jesus required his apostles to preach the gospel to every creature in all the world, that every one might believe it; for faith comes by hearing, and without faith it is impossible to please God. "He that believeth not shall be damned." Mark xvi: 16.

(8) The Israelites were required to quit serving the Egyptians and turn away from them—Jesus required the people every where to repent, turn away from the service of sin.

(9) The Israelites were baptized unto Moses in the cloud and in the sea—Peter commanded the people to be baptized in the name of Jesus Christ for the remission of sins; and he wrote to the scattered strangers that " baptism doth also now save us."

(10) The Egyptian task-masters of the Israelites were left just where the people were baptized unto Moses, and they saw them no more—those baptized in the name of Jesus Christ for the remission of sins leave their sins just where they are baptized; if they do not, this type is a false representation, and there is no fitness in

it. In baptism the Romans obeyed from the heart the form of doctrine delivered them and were *then* made free from sin.

(11) The Israelites rejoiced in their deliverance on the shore after their baptism. (Ex. xv: 1.)—as soon as the Eunuch was baptized he went on his way rejoicing. Acts viii: 39.

(12) The Israelites were not secure in Canaan as soon as they were baptized, but they had to be faithful to God or die short of the promised land—those baptized in the name of Jesus Christ for the remission of sins, though freed from past sins, are not in heaven, but must live lives of devotion to God or be lost at last. Paul records the sad fate of the Israelites as examples to us lest we should fall as they fell. 1 Cor. x: 5–12.

(13) The Israelites who remained faithful to God through their period of probation were conducted across the Jordan and into the land of Canaan, the inheritance promised to their fathers—those Christians who remain faithful to God through life will be conducted across the jordan of death into heaven, the everlasting Canaan which God has prepared for them that love him.

Now this type with its lesson is before us—could any thing be more plain? Can there be any possible mistake in its application? Can this whole matter be the result of accident? Can we not see the finger of God in it from beginning to end? Had not the apostle said that all these things happened to them as examples to us, would not such exact fitness have been conclusive in itself?

Moses specifically locates the time of their salvation. " Stand still and see the salvation of the Lord, which he will show to you to-day." " Thus the Lord saved Israel that day." Ex. xiv: 13–30. Language could not more definitely locate the time of their salvation at their baptism than it does here. Not only does the language itself show it, but all the facts connected with their delivery show it so clearly that we cannot fail to see it without closing our eyes.

All agree that the baptism of the Israelites in the cloud and in the sea was a type of our baptism; but some seek to evade the force of the lesson so plainly taught in it, by the fact that God recognized the Israelites as *his people* when he appeared to Moses in the burning bush; and as this was *before their baptism*, they assume that we must be God's people before we are baptized. But if this objection amounts to any thing against *baptism* for remission of sins, it amounts to just as much against *faith*, for the Lord had not *then* revealed the plan of their delivery, but had then appeared to Moses for the purpose of making it known to him. The Israelites knew nothing about it. So they were God's people before they had faith, as well as before they were baptized. Indeed, they were God's people before the birth of Moses; hence, if we must be God's people at the same time they were, it follows that we must have been God's people before Jesus, the antitype of Moses, was born. The objector forgets that *the type was in the salvation, or deliverance of the Israelites from bondage*, hence, we cannot *go behind the type* for impressions in the antitype. To do this would destroy the fitness of all types.

But we are told that the Hebrews were saved when the blood of the passover was shed, typical of Christ's blood which was shed for the remission of sins. Well, if they were saved at that time, and *that* was the salvation contemplated in *this type*, then it follows that there is no such thing as pardon or salvation *now* at all. The antitype must fit the type; and those saved under the antitype must be saved *at the time and place* indicated in the type. Then as the Israelites were saved when the blood of the passover was shed, so all persons saved through Christ, were saved or pardoned when his blood was shed, and there is no pardon of sin *now*, by faith or otherwise.

But from what were the Hebrews saved by the blood of the passover? From Egyptian bondage? Certainly not. They were saved from death by the angel that slew all the first born of the Egyptians. When this blood was seen on the door posts and lintels of a house, the inhabitants of that house were secure from death; but were they saved from bondage in Egypt at that time? No indeed. They were saved from bondage when baptized unto Moses in the cloud and sea; and the word of the Lord plainly says so: "Stand still, and see the salvation of the Lord, which he will show to you to-day." Not did show you back in Egypt when the blood of the passover was shed, but *to-day;* "for the Egyptians whom ye have seen to-day ye shall see them again no more for ever." Ex. xiv: 13. And after their baptism the record says: "Thus the Lord saved Israel that day." What day? When the blood of the passover was shed? No, but when they were baptized and their enemies were all drowned. Ex. xiv: 30. Could anything be more plain? And when Paul gives the type he associates it with their baptism, and the results following; and he draws the lesson acccordingly. 1 Cor. x: 1–12. It may not be out of place to remark here that *within the progress of one type* God may give quite a number of other types. While the deliverance of the Hebrews from bondage and their location in the land of Canaan was in progress, very many other types occurred; of which the passover was one, the tabernacle was another, and the animals slain as sin offerings were others; but these do not destroy the lesson taught in the deliverance of the Hebrews from bondage. Other types have their places in the scheme of redemption, and each one may be considered in its place; but as the Bible says, "Thus the Lord saved Israel that day," we may as well believe and accept it, without worrying ourselves to find something by which to evade the force of a truth so plainly spoken.

As to how the Israelites were baptized see Gospel Plan of Salvation, page 350. Infant baptism connected with the baptism of the Israelites see Gospel Plan of Salvation, page 476.

Our object in this discourse has been to see the time when pardon takes place, and we should feel thankful to God that he has made a matter of so much importance so very plain. God gave to man powers of thought and reason by which he can appreciate his will when clearly revealed to him; and he has given man a complete revelation adapted to the organization furnished him; and he expects man to exercise his God-given powers of thought in an intelligent submission to his will. Can we rise above our prejudices to an intelligent acceptance of the truth taught in this type? Surely we cannot mistake its import, and surely our responsibility will be great, if knowing the Master's will and our duty to him, we still fail to trustingly obey him.

> Lord Jesus, look down from thy throne in the skies,
> And help me to make a complete sacrifice;
> I give up myself, and whatever I know;
> Now, wash me, and I shall be whiter than snow.
> Lord Jesus, for this I most humbly entreat;
> I wait, blessed Lord, at thy crucified feet,
> By faith, for my cleansing, I see thy blood flow;
> Now, wash me, and I shall be whiter than snow.

CHAPTER VII.

THE TABERNACLE.

WHEN the children of Israel were safe from their enemies, and from their bondage and slavery in Egypt, they gave themselves up to a season of rejoicing in which they ascribed their deliverance to God, and from their expressions of gratitude we would suppose that they never would have forsaken or forgotten God, whose power had been so plainly seen in their deliverance. But alas, their songs of praise to God were soon lost in shouts of revelry, and dancing around a golden calf.

The cloud in which they were baptized did not forsake them when they were saved from bondage; but went with them in all their journeyings; and was a pillar of cloud by day, and a pillar of fire by night. By it God indicated their time, and route of travel; and their place of rest. When it was God's pleasure that they go forward the cloud began to move; and when it was God's pleasure that they go into camp the cloud ceased to move. Thus their movements and camping places were selected by God through this cloud, as clearly as though God had said when the cloud moved, "go forward," and when it stopped, "camp here."

Guided by this cloud they went to, and camped at the base of Mount Sinai, and there remained in camp forty days. Moses went up on the mountain and God gave him the ten commandments written on two tables of stone; and a description of a building and furniture; and a system of worship to be conducted in connection with it adapted to their condition in their nomadic state. In this system of worship God gave us another beautiful type of the system of worship offered the world through Jesus Christ in the gospel dispensation. The writer of the letter to the Hebrews, says:

"Then verily the first *covenant* had also ordinances of divine service, and a worldly sanctuary. For there was a tabernacle made; the first, wherein *was* the candlestick, and the table, and the shew-bread; which is called the sanctuary. And after the second vail, the tabernacle which is called the Holiest of all; which had the golden censer, and the ark of the covenant overlaid round about with gold, wherein *was* the golden pot that had manna, and Aaron's rod that budded, and the tables of the covenant; and over it the cherubims of glory shadowing the mercy seat; of which we cannot now speak particularly. Now when these things were thus ordained, the priests went always into the first tabnacle, accomplishing the service *of God*. But into the second *went* the high priest alone once every year, not without blood, which he offered for himself, and *for* the errors of the people: The Holy Ghost this signifying, that the way into the holiest of all was not yet made manifest, while as the first tabernacle was yet standing: which *was* a figure for the time then present, in which were offered both gifts and sacrifices, that could not make him that did the service perfect, as pertaining to the conscience; *which stood* only in meats and drinks, and divers washings, and carnal ordinances, imposed *on them* until the time of reformation. But Christ being come an high priest of good things to come, by a greater and more perfect tabernacle, not made with hands, that is to say, not of this building; neither by the blood of goats and calves, but by his own blood he entered in once into the holy place, having obtained eternal redemption *for us.*" Heb. ix: 1–12.

Here we learn that the building or tabernacle, a description of which God gave to Moses at Mount Sinai, was a figure of the greater and more perfect tabernacle, which all agree, is the church.

To understand the lesson taught in this type we must know something of the tabernacle of the wilderness, the furniture connected with it, and the system of worship conducted in it.

The word *tabernacle* literally means a *movable building.* It was so constructed that it could be taken down, and carried from one camping place to another, by the Levites in whose care it was placed, and put up wherever the cloud indicated that the Israelites should go into camp.

This building was thirty cubits long from east to west, and ten cubits broad from north to south. This equals about forty-five by fifteen feet. It was made of upright boards ten cubits long, and one and a half cubits broad. On the lower end of each board were two tenons set in sockets of silver. If these sockets were made of wood in our day they would be called mortises in blocks of wood. Of these upright boards there were twenty on each side, six in the west end and one at each corner, making fifty boards, and one hundred blocks of silver, each weighing a talent or about one hundred and fourteen pounds, or eleven thousand four hundred pounds of silver in these blocks that were the foundation of this building. The boards were overlaid with gold. In these were staples of gold through which passed bars of wood overlaid with gold. On the top of each board was a ring of gold through which passed a cord, so that when the blocks of silver were placed on the ground, the tenons on the boards put in the sockets, the bars put in position and the cords tightened around the top, it was quite a substantial building.

This building was divided by a vail, crossing from north to south, into two apartments. The first was called the holy place, and was twenty cubits long; and the other was called the most holy place, and was of course ten cubits square. I say *of course*, for the whole being thirty cubits by ten, and twenty cubits being cut off the eastern end, the part remaining would be ten cubits square. This vail was suspended upon four pillars, and was of fine-twined linen, colored blue, purple and scarlet; was made of exquisite workmanship, "with cherubim and cunning work." The entire building was lined and closed at the eastern end with the same material.

The first ply of the covering or roof was of the same material as the lining; the second ply was made of goat's hair; the third ply was of ram's skins, dyed red; and the fourth or outer ply was of badger's skins.

The building or tabernacle was surrounded by a fence made by suspending a curtain on pillars set in sockets of brass, and the space thus enclosed was one hundred cubits by fifty; the long way being from east to west, with an opening of twenty cubits in the eastern end; and I may here say, "once for all," that all the entrances were from the east. The outer court, or "court of the tabernacle" was entered from the east, the *holy place* was entered from the east, and the *most holy place* could be entered *only through the holy place*, hence from the east.

THE FURNITURE.

The *brazen altar* was so called because it was made of

durable wood, overlaid with brass sufficiently thick to protect the wood against the fire when the offerings were burned upon it. It was also called the *altar of burnt offerings*, because on it were burned all the offerings made during the time the tabernacle worship was continued. It was five cubits square and three cubits high. It had four horns, one on each corner; and four rings, two on each side, in the four corners; through these went a rod or staff on each side made of wood covered with brass. These were to bear the altar from one camping place to another. The pans to receive the ashes, the fire pans, shovels, basins, flesh hooks, and grate were all of brass.

The laver was made of brass. Its dimensions are not given, but it had a main sea, and a foot or rim. This contained water in which the priests washed at their consecration, and in their daily ministrations. In their consecration they washed the person, (Ex. xxix: 4) and in cleansing from defilement; "Then the priest shall wash his clothes, and he shall bathe his flesh in water." Num. xix: 7. But in their daily ministrations they washed their hands and feet only. Ex. xxx: 19; xl: 31–32.

The *table of shewbread* was made of durable wood overlaid with gold. It was two cubits long, one cubit in breadth, and a cubit and a half high. It had a border and a crown of gold. Its dishes, spoons, bowls and cover were of gold. There were two rings of gold on each side, through which passed two rods or staves, one on each side, to bear the table. These were made of wood covered with gold.

The candlestick was of solid beaten gold. It had a central stem and six branches, three coming out of its two sides. Its stem, branches, bowls, knops, flowers, seven lamps, snuffers, and snuff dishes, were all of beaten gold. It required a talent (about 114 pounds) of pure gold to make this candlestick and appendages.

The *golden altar, or altar of incense* was one cubit square and two cubits high. It was called the golden altar because it was made of wood and overlaid with gold sufficiently thick to protect it from damage by fire when incense was burned upon it. It was also called the *altar of incense* from the fact that on it the priests burned incense in their daily ministrations. Its horns and crown were of gold. It had four rings of gold, two on each side, through which passed two rods or staves, one on each side, made of wood overlaid with gold to bear the altar withal.

The ark of the covenant was made of wood and overlaid with gold. It was two and a half cubits long, a cubit and a half in width, and a cubit and a half high. Its crown was of gold. "And he cast for it four rings of gold, *to be set* by the four corners of it; even two rings upon the one side of it, and two rings upon the other side of it. And he made staves *of* shittim wood, and overlaid them with gold. And he put the staves into the rings by the sides of the ark, to bear the ark. And he made the mercy seat *of* pure gold: two cubits and a half *was* the length thereof, and one cubit and a half the breadth thereof. And he made two cherubims *of* gold, beaten out of one piece made he them, on the two ends of the mercy seat; one cherub on the end on this side, and another cherub on the *other* end on that side: out of the mercy seat made he the cherubims on the two ends thereof. And the cherubims spread out *their* wings on high, *and* covered with their wings over the mercy seat, with their faces one to another; *even* to the mercy seatward were the faces of the cherubims." Ex. xxxvii : 3–9.

Much of this description may be deemed more minute than is necessary to a development of the lesson contained in this type. This may be true, but it gives us clearer conceptions of the building and furniture; and it teaches us a lesson of liberality by which we might be benefitted if we would study it. This people were unsettled, and certainly had but little opportunity of making money or accumulating wealth; yet when Moses issued a proclamation calling for material of which to construct the tabernacle and things connected with it, the people brought it with such liberality that " all the wise men, that wrought all the work of the sanctuary, came every man from his work which they made; and they spake unto Moses, saying, The people bring much more than enough for the service of the work, which the Lord commanded to make. And Moses gave commandment, and they caused it to be proclaimed throughout the camp, saying, Let neither man nor woman make any more work for the offering of the sanctuary. So the people were restrained from bringing." Ex. xxxvi : 4–6.

Can a parallel to this be found in modern times? The mind is bewildered in calculating the value of the material used in constructing this tabernacle and appendages; and the eye is dimmed by its dazzling splendor as we attempt to call before us a conception of it. No work of man has ever eclipsed it except the temple that succeeded it; and yet the Jews, in their recent exit from slavery and bondage, brought free-will offerings to the Lord until they had to be restrained; and yet we, in an age of vast resources, when multiplied millions are rolling in wealth until they know not what to do with it, can with difficulty raise money enough to build a meeting house. If the tabernacle had to be built in this country to-day, would it be necessary to issue a proclamation restraining the people from giving material with which to build it? We have a better religion than they had; and have more light than they had—do we love the Lord less than they did? Why were they more liberal than we?

We now propose to set up the tabernacle and put the furniture in position. As this is a very important part of our lesson we have made a ground-plan drawing that will assist us in locating every part of it as directed in the bill of instructions given by Moses.

Let the attentive Bible student read carefully the last sixteen chapters of the book of Exodus for a description of the tabernacle and its furniture. In these chapters will be found a minute description of each piece in detail; and in the last or fortieth chapter will be found the *erection* of the tabernacle, and the location of each piece of furniture in its God-appointed position. As he reads the location of each piece let him look at the diagram and see whether or not it occupies just the place in the drawing that the word of the Lord commanded Moses to place it. Let us be specially careful at this point, for a mistake in the location of the furniture will be fatal to our study of this most beautiful of all types.

The exterior lines inclose the Outer Court, 50 cubits by 100. The Tabernacle was 30 cubits by 10, and was covered with a four-ply covering. *Vail* dividing the Tabernacle into Holy Place and Most Holy Place. A. C. Ark of Covenant. T. S. Table of Shew-bread. A. I. Altar of Incense. L. the Laver. B. A. Brazen Altar.

THE TABERNACLE.

WEST.

SOUTH. **NORTH.**

Outer Court.

EAST.

"Thus did Moses: according to all that the Lord commanded him, so did he. And it came to pass in the first month of the second year, on the first *day* of the month, *that* the tabernacle was reared up. And Moses reared up the tabernacle, and fastened his sockets, and set up the boards thereof, and put in the bars thereof, and reared up his pillars. And he spread abroad the tent over the tabernacle, and put the covering of the tent above upon it; as the Lord commanded Moses. And he took and put the testimony into the ark, and set the staves on the ark, and put the mercy seat above upon the ark: And he brought the ark into the tabernacle, and set up the vail of the covering, and covered the ark of the testimony; as the Lord commanded Moses. And he put the table in the tent of the congregation, upon the side of the tabernacle northward, without the vail. And he set the bread in order upon it before the Lord; as the Lord had commanded Moses. And he put the candlestick in the tent of the congregation, over against the table, on the side of the tabernacle southward. And he lighted the lamps before the Lord; as the Lord commanded Moses. And he put the golden altar in the tent of the congregation before the vail. And he burnt sweet incense thereon; as the Lord commanded Moses. And he set up the hanging *at* the door of the tabernacle. And he put the altar of burnt offering *by* the door of the tabernacle of the tent of the congregation, and offered upon it the burnt offering and the meat offering; as the Lord commanded Moses. And he set the laver between the tent of the congregation and the altar, and put water there, to wash *withal*. And Moses and Aaron and his sons washed their hands and their feet thereat: When they went into the tent of the congregation, and when they came near unto the altar, they washed; as the Lord commanded Moses. And he reared up the court round about the tabernacle and the altar, and set up the hanging of the court gate. So Moses finished the work." Ex. xl : 16–33.

This Scripture locates the furniture too plainly to admit of mistake. The mercy seat was placed upon the ark, and its contents put within it, and it was brought into the tabernacle and the vail put up, covering it from sight. Then the table was placed on the north side without the vail, and the candlestick was put on the south side over against, or opposite the table. The golden altar was placed before the vail. Then the hanging was set up at the door, closing the tabernacle; thus showing that nothing more was to be put within. Then the brazen altar or altar of burnt offering was placed by the door, and the laver was placed *between* the altar and the door. To this agrees the letter to the Hebrews, saying : "For there was a tabernacle made; the first, [that is in the first apartment] wherein *was* the candlestick, and the table, and the shew-bread; which is called the sanctuary. And after the second vail, [the first vail was at the door, the second vail divided the tabernacle into two rooms] the tabernacle which is called the Holiest of all [Most Holy place] ; which had the golden censer, and the ark of the covenant overlaid round about with gold, wherein *was* the golden pot that had manna, and Aaron's rod that budded, and the tables of the covenant; and over it the cherubims of glory shadowing the mercy seat; of which we cannot now speak particularly." Heb. ix : 2–5.

There is a remarkable emphasis given to the fact that this furniture was located as God commanded Moses. The Lord not only gave him specific directions for making every thing, but also for the location of every thing; hence whenever a piece was put in position it was by divine authority, "as the Lord commanded Moses." He had no discretion in the matter; and any departure from God's order was punishable with death. The priests' robe had on it " a golden bell and a pomegranate upon the hem of the robe round about. And it shall be upon Aaron to minister; and his sound shall be heard when he goeth in unto the holy place before the Lord and when he cometh out, that he die not." Ex. xxviii. 34, 35. "For Aaron and his sons shall wash their hands and their feet thereat; when they go into the tabernacle of the congregation, they shall wash with water, that they die not; or when they come near to the altar to minister, to burn offering made by fire unto the Lord; so they shall wash their hands and their feet, that they die not." Ex. xxx: 19–21.

THE PRIESTHOOD.

During the patriarchal dispensation the father was the priest of the family, and conducted the service for the family; and in his absence the first born son officiated in his stead. When the first born of the children of Israel were saved from death on the night of their departure from Egypt, God claimed them as his, and for a time settled the priesthood with them, but when the two sons of Joseph were made heads of separate tribes, making thirteen of the original twelve, God abandoned the first born as priests, and settled the priesthood in the tribe of Levi. "And I, behold, I have taken the Levites from among the children of Israel instead of all the first born that openeth the matrix among the children of Israel; therefore the Levites shall be mine." Num. iii: 12. From this time the family of Aaron, of the tribe of Levi, became the priests, and the other Levites were engaged in the service of the sanctuary.

But it was not enough to make a man a priest that he be a Levite, and have the blood of Aaron in his veins—he must be consecrated to that service in accordance with a ceremony given by God to Moses. And the ceremony was very lengthy and somewhat complicated; but only a few features of it were brought into the new dispensation, and these are all that are of practical value to us. There was a sin offering made at the brazen altar, or altar of burnt offerings where all sin offerings were made. This done he was taken to the laver at the door of the tabernacle and washed in or with water. Next he put on the priestly garments. And it is worthy of note that the same term "*flesh*" is used to indicate the extent of the washing that is used to indicate the parts on which the holy garments were to be worn. "Thus shall Aaron come into the holy *place:* with a young bullock for a sin offering, and a ram for a burnt offering. He shall put on the holy linen coat, and he shall have the linen breeches upon his flesh, and shall be girded with a linen girdle, and with the linen mitre shall he be attired: these *are* holy garments; therefore shall he wash his flesh in water, and *so* put them on." Lev. xvi: 3, 4.

Having accepted the sin offering, been washed in water, and clothed in the holy garments, he enters the tabernacle and officiates as a priest—is a priest. He can go to the candlestick and attend to the seven lamps on it, which give all the light there is in the holy place. He can go to the table and on the Sabbath day eat of the shew-bread kept on it. He can go to the golden altar, and there burn sweet incense before the Lord. This is close to the vail, and is the nearest approach that can be made to the mercy seat where God is, except by the high priest alone, and he only once a year.

The common priests dare not even lift the vail and look into the most holy place. Even Aaron, himself was specially warned to "come not at all times into the holy place within the vail before the mercy seat, which is upon the ark; that he die not." Lev. xvi. 2.

We now have our type sufficiently before us to see the application of it in the antitype. The court or yard was a place where all the people had a right to enter, and fitly represents that state called the world. The place where the seed of the kingdom was sown, in the parable of the tares. Matt. xiii: 38. That state which distinguished the people from the disciples. "These things I command you, that ye love one another. If the world hate you, ye know that it hated me before it hated you. If ye were of the world, the world would love his own; but because ye are not of the world, but I have chosen you out of the world, therefore the world hateth you." John xv: 17-19. From this state the people must be converted or they never can be saved.

But what will they be when converted? In our type the sons of Aaron of the tribe of Levi only, could be priests; but under the more perfect system *all Christians are priests;* and how men and women are *converted from the world into priests* is the great feature of our lesson.

But is it true that all Christians are priests? "Ye also, as lively stones, are built up a spiritual house, a holy priesthood, to offer up spiritual sacrifices, acceptable to God by Jesus Christ." 1 Pet. ii: 5. Verse 9: "But ye are a chosen generation, a royal priesthood, a holy nation. a peculiar people; that ye should show forth the praises of Him who hath called you out of darkness into his marvelous light." Surely all Christians should do this. Again: "I beseech you therefore, brethren, by the mercies of God, that ye present your bodies a living sacrifice, holy, acceptable unto God, which is your reasonable service." Rom. xii: 1. It was the business of the priests to offer sacrifice, and here Paul admonishes the brethren at Rome to offer their bodies as *living* sacrifices in contrast with the animals slain in sacrifice under the law.

Other Scriptures might be quoted, but these are enough to show that *all Christians are priests under the gospel*, and sustain the same relation that priests did under the law. Hence the importance of our inquiry—how do we come to the priesthood? or, *how are we made priests* under the gospel? There must be some resemblance between type and antitype.

First then, there was a sin offering made—our sin offering has been made. Jesus Christ is our high priest and as such made our sin offering for us. "For such a high priest became us, who is holy, harmless, undefiled, separate from sinners, and made higher than the heavens; who needeth not daily, as those high priests, to offer up sacrifice, first for his own sins, and then for the people's; for this he did once, when he offered up himself." Heb. vii: 26, 27. Again: "But Christ being come an high priest of good things to come, by a greater and more perfect tabernacle, not made with hands, that is to say, not of this building; neither by the blood of goats and calves, but by his own blood he entered in once into the holy place, having obtained eternal redemption for us; for if the blood of bulls and of goats, and the ashes of an heifer sprinkling the unclean, sanctifieth to the purifying of the flesh, how much more shall the blood of Christ, who through the eternal Spirit offered himself without spot to God, purge your conscience from dead works to serve the living God." Heb. ix: 11-16. Once more: "For Christ is not entered into the holy places made with hands, *which are the figures of the true*; but into heaven itself, now to appear in the presence of God for us: Nor yet that he should offer himself often, as the high priest entereth into the holy place every year with the blood of others; for then must he often have suffered since the foundation of the world: but now once in the end of the world hath he appeared to put away sin by the sacrifice of himself. And as it is appointed unto men once to die, but after this the judgment: So Christ was once offered to bear the sins of many." Heb. ix: 24–28. Finally on this point: "By the which will we are sanctified through the offering of the body of Jesus Christ once *for all.* And every priest standeth daily ministering and offering oftentimes the same sacrifices, which can never take away sins: But this man, after he had offered one sacrifice for sins for ever, sat down on the right hand of God." Heb. x: 10–12.

Many other Scriptures bearing on this subject could be produced, but these are quite enough to show that Christ is our high priest, and that he offered himself without spot to God, and that he entered heaven with his own blood having obtained eternal redemption for us. The candidate for the Jewish priesthood accepted his offering at the brazen altar, but our offering thus made by Christ we accept by faith in him. "Being justified freely by his grace through the redemption that is in Christ Jesus; whom God has set forth to be a propitiation through faith in his blood, to declare his righteousness for the remission of sins that are past, through the forbearance of God." Rom. iii:24, 25.

But the candidate next went to the laver at the door of the tabernacle and had his flesh washed in water, so Jesus says: "He that believeth and is baptized shall be saved," and speaking of this typical lesson the Hebrew letter says: "Having therefore, brethren, boldness to enter into the holiest by the blood of Jesus, by a new and living way, which he hath consecrated for us, through the vail, that is to say, his flesh; and *having* an high priest over the house of God; Let us draw near with a true heart in full assurance of faith, having our hearts sprinkled from an evil conscience, and our bodies washed with pure water." Heb. x: 19-22.

Having received the propitiatory sacrifice of Christ by faith in his blood, and having our bodies washed with pure water, what next? What did the Levite do next? We have seen that he next put on the holy garments. So we must put on the Christian character. "Our old man is crucified with him that the body of sin might be destroyed." Rom. vi: 6. "That ye put off, concerning the former conversation, the old man, which is corrupt according to the deceitful lusts; and be renewed in the spirit of your mind; and that ye put on the new man, which after God is created in righteousness and true holiness." Eph. iv: 22-24. "Seeing that ye have put off the old man with his deeds; and have put on the new man, which is renewed in knowledge after the image of him that created him." Col. iii: 9, 10.

When a Levite put on the priestly garments he entered the tabernacle—so we are delivered from the power of darkness, and translated into the kingdom of God's dear son; in whom we have redemption through his blood, even the forgiveness of sins. Col. i: 13, 14.

The order of worship in the tabernacle is nowhere given that I remember, but we know something of what was done. The priest waited upon the golden candlestick, the seven lamps which furnished all the light in the holy place, which we have already seen was a figure of the church or kingdom of God's dear Son. We have found our high priest ruling over the house of God (Heb. x: 21) and Paul tells us this is the church of God. (1 Tim. iii: 15).

As the seven lamps on the candlestick furnished a perfect light to the holy place, so the word of God furnishes a perfect light for the church of God. David said: " Thy word is a lamp unto my feet, and a light unto my path." Ps. cxix: 105. Verse 130: " The entrance of thy words giveth light; it giveth understanding unto the simple." " We have also a more sure word of prophecy whereunto ye do well that ye take heed as unto a light that shineth in a dark place." 2 Pet. i: 19. We read of certain characters who believed not, " lest the light of the glorious gospel of Christ, who is the image of God, should shine unto them." 2 Cor. iv: 4. " All Scripture *is* given by inspiration of God, and is profitable for doctrine, for reproof, for correction, for instruction in righteousness; that the man of God may be perfect, thoroughly furnished unto all good works." 2 Tim. iii: 16, 17. The perfection of this light precludes the necessity for more; and as it is our only light it is unquestionably the antitype of that which gave the only light in the type.

The priests ate of the shew-bread every Sabbath day. There is a striking analogy between this and the Lord's supper in the more perfect tabernacle. It was set in order every Sabbath day, and the priests ate of it on every Sabbath, which was the day devoted to the service of God during that typical age. The disciples met together on the *first day of the week* to break bread. When the Jew was required to observe the Sabbath day he understood that to be *every Sabbath* day. Then when we learn that the disciples met together on the first day of the week to break bread shall we not understand that to mean *every first day of the week?* The observance of the Sabbath day passed away with the law written on tables of stone.—2 Cor. iii : 3–11. The first day of the week Christ rose from the dead and brought life and immortality to light through the gospel, and the disciples kept this day as regularly as the Jew kept the Sabbath day. The shew-bread was lawfully eaten only by the priests. The Lord's supper was for the Lord's people only. But it was for all of them.

The priests offered, or burned incense on the golden altar morning and evening. This incense was typical of the prayers of the saints which should be offered also morning and evening. "Let my prayer be set forth before thee as incense; and the lifting up of my hands as the evening sacrifice." Ps. cxli : 2. "And when he had taken the book, the four beasts and four and twenty elders fell down before the Lamb, having, every one of them, harps and golden vials full of odours, which are the prayers of saints." Rev. v : 8. And another angel came and stood at the altar, having a golden censer; and there was given unto him much incense, that he should offer it with the prayers of all saints upon the golden altar which was before the throne." Rev. viii : 3.

It will be remembered that this altar was before the vail and the nearest approach to the mercy seat that the priest could make. Let us learn, therefore, that when the Christian is pouring out the earnest prayer of a devoted heart he is as near God as he can get in this life. And if we would make the nearest approach to God that is allowed to mortals on earth, we must make that approach in prayer.

The vail separated between the holy and most holy

place, and this vail is the *flesh*, (Heb. x : 20) the confines of mortality. "We are confident, I say, and willing rather to be absent from the body, and to be present with the Lord." 2 Cor. v: 8. When we pass through the flesh, or out of the body, we pass out of the holy place, or church on earth into the Most Holy Place, where God is on the mercy seat, and angelic guards are anxiously looking at the glory of his countenance, and ready to bear the messages of his love.

A few plain questions and we are done, for we have already extended this discourse beyond reasonable limits. Please turn and look on the ground plan while we consider the questions proposed. It is said that a man can go to heaven just as well out of the church as in it. Please notice that all the entrances are from the east, and that there is no way into the most holy place only through the holy place. To enter it at all you must pass into the holy place and through the vail which is the flesh. Now then, as the holy place was a type of the church, and the most holy place a type of heaven, how are you going to heaven only through the church?

The first thing in order was a sin offering made at the brazen altar, then wash at the laver. Now, suppose we go by the altar and begin with the laver, what then? Does any one do this way? How is it in baptizing a babe? Does this not begin with the laver?

But they always washed before putting on the holy garments; suppose we go to the brazen altar and accept Christ, the sin offering, by faith, and put on the holy garments *before* we wash—perhaps not wash at all—will this do? Does any one do this? This is a very general practice—get religion—become a Christian by faith in

Christ. This puts on the priestly garments or Christian character before washing.

But suppose they go to the brazen altar, accept Christ by faith, put on the holy garments, or Christian character, and are received into the church by vote, given the hand of fellowship, and baptized afteward! This takes the laver from the outer court where God put it, into the tabernacle or holy place, that is, takes baptism from the door into the church. No one in the church was ever baptized by divine authority.

But the golden altar was in the holy place hard by the vail and on this altar the priests offered incense. We have found this a type of the prayers of the saints. Now suppose we take the golden altar (of prayer) out of the church and give it to the world, what then? As the Lord commanded Moses so did he—*as God commands us so ought we*. If any disregard of God's order was punished with death what will be our fate if we disregard God's law and substitute our own will? "If ye love me keep my commandments." John xiv: 15.

Thus we see a most perfect fitness of this type to the system of salvation taught by Christ and the apostles in the New Testament; but if we attempt to fit it to modern theories, the furniture has to be removed from the positions in which God located it, and re-arranged; or, rather, scattered around promiscuously. When each piece was located it was emphasized by, "as the Lord commanded Moses." But when taken out of the positions in which God placed them and located elsewhere, it cannot be said, "as the Lord commanded Moses," but as commanded by men. "If the Lord be God follow him; but if Baal then follow him." "Why call ye me Lord, Lord, and do not the things which I say?" We have seen that any departure from God's order in the tabernacle was punishable with death; would it not be well for us to take heed how we set at naught the counsels of God; and set up our own altars, and walk in our own ways? Though the punishment come not as speedily as in olden times, it will none the less surely come; and be none the less terrible when it does come.

CHAPTER VIII.

FREEDOM FROM SIN.

"Know ye not, that to whom ye yield yourselves servants to obey, his servants ye are to whom ye obey; whether of sin unto death, or of obedience. unto righteousness? But God be thanked, that ye were the servants of sin, but ye have obeyed from the heart that form of doctrine which was delivered you. Being then made free from sin, ye became the servants of righteousness." Rom. vi: 16–18.

THOUGH the epistles were written to Christians, there are allusions, in most of them, to the way those to whom they were written had become Christians; a careful examination of which will exhibit the plan of salvation very perfectly. One such allusion we find in our text.

The church at Rome was composed of Jews and Greeks, or Gentiles; and the chief object of the Roman letter seems to have been to show that they were emancipated from the law of Moses, and were under the gospel of Jesus Christ. In the first chapter, he says: "I am not ashamed of the gospel of Christ: for it is the power of God unto salvation to every one that believeth; to the Jew first, and also to the Greek. For therein is the righteousness of God revealed from faith to faith: as it is written, The just shall live by faith." Rom. i: 16, 17.

Again he says: "But now the righteousness of God without the law is manifested, being witnessed by the law and the prophets; even the righteousness of God *which is* by faith of Jesus Christ unto all and upon all them that believe: for there is no difference: for all have sinned, and come short of the glory of God." Rom. iii : 21–23. The law of Moses and the prophets of the Old Testament bore witness to the righteousness of God through the system of faith revealed in the gospel through Jesus Christ, unto all and upon all who will believe. While the gospel is the power of God unto salvation, it has no power to save them who will not believe it. Hence the apostle goes on to contrast the system of works in the law of Moses with the system of faith revealed in the gospel, showing that by the former there is no justification, but by the latter there is not only justification, but peace with God through our Lord Jesus Christ. Pursuing this line of thought he comes to the way they were made free from sin, and the time when it was accomplished. This prepares us for the analysis of our text.

We note first that they became *free* by becoming *servants;* and they became servants by *obedience.* This was a *voluntary* servitude. They were the servants of that to which they *yielded* themselves servants to obey. This shows us that man is perfectly free to yield to the allurements of sin and die, or turn to the service of God and live. God invites man to him, but he will not compel him to heed the invitation. He is as free to serve sin as he is to serve God; but he is plainly shown that the service of sin brings death. This he makes still more prominent in the closing verses of the chapter. "For the end of those things *is* death. But now being made free from sin, and become servants to God, ye have your fruit unto holiness, and the end everlasting life. For the wages of sin *is* death; but the gift of God *is* eternal life through Jesus Christ our Lord." What a contrast! sin and death—servants of God, the end everlasting life. Shall we not turn away from the former and yield ourselves, heart and life, to the latter? There can be no such thing as a servant without obedience; hence if we would become the servants of righteousness we must obey God; and by becoming his servants we are made free from sin—free from one master by becoming the servant of another.

But we next notice that the obedience which frees us from sin is an *obedience from the heart*. Though we do the very thing God requires of us, if we do it not with a sincere desire to honor God, the service is worth nothing to us. God is not mocked; and he looks to the motive prompting the service rendered him. If a man obeys God to please his wife, or the wife to please her husband, the service is not from the heart. If a young man obeys God to please a young lady whose hand he hopes to win, or a professional man obeys God to secure professional patronage, such service is a foul stench in the nostrils of Jehovah, and he will spew them out of his mouth.

Suppose a farmer has a good farm in this country, but he has more children than he can hope to be able to settle, or furnish with homes at the price land sells for in his neighborhood. He therefore determines to sell his land here and go to a new country where lands are new and productive, and so cheap that with what he can get for his land here he can secure as much as will be quite sufficient to make himself a good home, and furnish a home for each of his children. Acting upon these reflections he sells his farm and goes to the Western frontier; and after looking for a time, he finds a large body of fertile land, well-tim-bered, with plenty of good water, in a genial and pleasant climate, with all the prospective conveniences desirable to make him a satisfactory settlement for himself and children. He purchases and secures title to as much as he desires, and draws a plot of it on paper that will enable any one to find it without trouble. He looks out a beautiful eminence that affords a commanding view of the landscape for miles around. Hard by there is a beautiful spring, furnishing an abundant and perpetual supply of clear, cool and pure water; and he determines that on this eminence shall be erected the buildings that are necessary to make his future home. After determining the precise location, shape and size of his dwelling, he marks it off on the ground and makes corresponding signs on his plot, with ample directions concerning it. He next determines the location of his meat house—marks it off on the ground and on his plot. Next he selects a suitable place for his barns and cribs, and marks them off, giving distance and degree from the site of the dwelling, and then transfers the corresponding marks to his plot. But he remembers that barns, cribs, stables, etc., are very liable to be burned, either by incendiaries or accident, and he determines that he will have his stables for the protection of his stock isolated from his barns and cribs; so that if he should lose part he may not lose all; and he selects, as he thinks, a suitable location for stables, and marks them off on the ground and on his plot.

All things completed, he comes home, gladly meets his family, and reports his success. He has a son about grown to whom he shows his plot, and fully explains every thing; and tells him to take the plot, and go to the land, and erect the buildings just as indicated on the plot and bill of directions; and by the time he can get the buildings ready for their reception he will have wound up his business and be there with the family.

The son goes as directed and finds the land without trouble. Before going to work, however, he rides over the land, looks at the lines and the soil, and in short makes a general survey of the whole prospect. He is wonderfully pleased with his father's purchase; and especially is he pleased with the beautiful eminence selected for the dwelling house. It gives a beautiful view of the whole country for miles, and his heart swells with admiration as he contemplates the Eden home they will have in that beautiful place.

Thus delighted he goes to work and erects just such a dwelling as his father directed, on the very spot designated for it. He next finds the place selected for the meat house, and after careful consideration he thinks the place well chosen, and he erects the meat house just where his father had directed. Next he looks for the location selected for the barn and cribs. He thinks the place well chosen in the back ground, and a suitable distance from the dwelling, and feeling sure that a more suitable location could not be found, he builds them there just as instructed in the bill of directions given by his father. Finally he looks for and finds the place for the stables, and on looking around he concludes that his father has made a wonderful mistake here. "The food for the stock will have to be carried quite a distance; and the stables are to be on one side of the branch and the cribs on the other; and I shall have to cross the branch, and perhaps get my feet wet, every time I feed; and when there comes a freshet I may fall in and get wet all over. It is just terrible, and I will not put it in that inconvenient place, I am sure. It must be over here on the same side of the branch the barns and cribs are on," and he goes to work and puts it there.

Now, I submit that that boy has not obeyed his father in any thing he did, and in place of deserving his father's blessing, he deserves the severest censure his father can give him. "Did he not locate the other buildings where his father directed they should be built?"

Yes, but he did it because his own judgment approved it, and not because his father commanded it. Whenever his judgment ceased to accord with that of his father, he left his father's will and went his own way; showing that he would have gone his own way at first, had not his father's way been his way.

The obedient child, wishing to honor the father, only wishes to know the father's will, in order to know the line of his duty. When God commanded Abraham to leave his native country and go into a land that he would show him, *he went*, not knowing whither he went. This was an exhibition of faith that met God's approval, and it is recorded for our imitation. Until we can feel a disposition to know God's will and do it, and to want to do it *because it is his will*, we are not in a fit frame of mind to acceptably obey God in any thing.

But we cannot *obey from the heart* without first *believing with the heart*. This is self-evident. Obeying from the heart implies an obedience springing from the heart, from the will or inclination of the heart. The heart must approve the service before we can heartily render it. We cannot obey Jesus Christ from the heart until we first believe in him with the heart. Until we believe him clothed with authority to command us, we cannot render hearty obedience to him. This is so very evident that all will agree to it without a dissenting voice. Are we entirely sure of this? Let me admonish you to be sure it is right before you agree to it; for when you agree to it you make a full surrender of the whole doctrine of justification by faith only. Paul says that it was when the Romans *obeyed* from the heart that they were made free from sin, hence if they had to *first believe* with the heart *before* they could do that which brought freedom from sin, then it is certain that *believing* did not reach the freedom, but only prepared them to do that which did reach it. Do you see, now, what the concession does for you? But it is too late to take it back now. It is true—evidently true, and we should not want to take it back simply because it comes in contact with our peculiar views.

Once more: He who is in love with sin—yielding himself to the service of sin; delighting in sin; working all uncleanness with greediness—cannot obey from the heart without a changed heart.* In order to obey God from the heart he must love God, and sin is opposed to God. We cannot love God and love sin at the same time. "If any man love the world, the love of the Father is not in him. For all that *is* in the world, the lust of the flesh and the lust of the eyes, and the pride of life, is not of the Father, but it is of the world. And the world passeth away, and the lust thereof: but he that doeth the will of God abideth for ever." 1 John ii: 15–17.

This Scripture needs no explanation. While the heart is filled with love of the world, with its sinful lusts, appetites and passions, there is no place for that love of God that prompts acceptable obedience to him. But when these carnal desires are subjugated to the will

---

*For a full examination of the subject of a change of heart see Gospel Plan of Salvation, pages 222 to 232.

of God until we cease to love them, and love him instead; then we have all the change of heart that is necessary. When we really and truly cease to love sin and love holiness, when we cease to love the company of the wicked, and desire the company of the pure and righteous, then we have the change of heart that enables us to obey from the heart. This change in our affections is the happy result of *believing with the heart* as already seen. We love God because he first loved us; and God commendeth his love to us in that while we were yet sinners Christ died for the ungodly God's love revealed to us, and believed by us, is certainly sufficient to cause us to love him and desire to serve him. This faith gives us proper conceptions of our unworthiness and sinfulness, and makes us realize our need of a Savior. Now, what hinders obedience from the heart?

Just here is the great mistake by the religious world of to-day. In place of telling the sinner what God requires him to do that he may obey it, and rejoice in the pardon of his sins, and in a Savior's love, he is kept praying for, and expecting something, he knows not what; and with a heart bowed in bitterest grief he goes from day to day, week to week, month to month, and often year to year as honest and as truly penitent as ever he can get to be; and as willing and anxious to do any thing and every thing that he believes to be his duty as was Saul when Ananias went to and instructed him. And if, unbiased by any previous teaching, the same instructions were given such a man he would gladly accept and obey them without a moment's delay—even in the same hour of the night, if it were in the night. We dare not pray that an Ananias may be sent to such, since the law of the Lord has been written, and is open to them; but we may pray that they may give heed to what Ananias did say to one in their condition : " Arise and be baptized and wash away your sins calling on the name of the Lord." Acts xxii : 16.

But we are ready now, to look for the *form of doctrine* which the Romans obeyed, in doing of which they were made free from sin. And while we look for it you will please bear in mind that we have found that *no one can obey from the heart without first believing with the heart*; and hence when we speak of obedience from the heart, we mean an obedience rendered by one who has earnestly and Scripturally believed with the heart *before* rendering the obedience of which we are speaking—such obedience as freed the Romans from sin.

In what sense are we to understand the word *form*, in connection with the word *doctrine*, in our text? The *form* of a thing is not the thing of which it is a form. Usually it is construed to mean *mould* or form of teaching. Then the apostle meant to say that the Romans obeyed the *doctrine itself* in some particular *arrangement* of it. Is this the thought? What is the doctrine? Paul says : " Moreover, brethren, I declare unto you the gospel which I preached unto you, which also ye have received, and wherein ye stand ; by which also ye are saved, if ye keep in memory what I preached unto you, unless ye have believed in vain." You preached the *gospel* to them Paul? Yes, for it is the power of God unto salvation to every one that believes it; and these Corinthians were saved by it too, if saved at all. Now Paul, what was the gospel you preached at Corinth? " For I delivered unto you first of all that which I also received, how that Christ died for our sins according to the Scriptures ; and that he was buried, and that he rose again the third day according to the Scriptures." 1 Cor. xv : 1–4.

Now Paul, did you preach the same gospel at Rome that you preached at Corinth? Yes; "if we or an angel from heaven, preach any other gospel unto you than that which we have preached unto you, let him be accursed. As we said before, so say I now again, if any man preach any other gospel unto you than that ye have received, let him be accursed." Gal. i: 8, 9.

Certainly Paul did not so anathematize any one for preaching another gospel and preach another himself. Then these *three facts* were the facts of the gospel, and was the *doctrine* preached at Rome as well as at Corinth, the form of which the Romans obeyed, in doing of which they were made free from sin. Now let us look at these items separately. That Christ died for our sins according to the Scriptures—can we obey this? No, there is nothing in it to obey. And that he was buried —can we obey this? We can see nothing here to obey. And that he rose again the third day according to the Scriptures—can we obey this? We cannot see how. *Mould* these items as we may, or arrange them any way we can there is no way by which to obey them. This *doctrine* consisted of *facts* and could not be obeyed. We may obey something symbolizing, or resembling it, but the facts themselves we cannot obey. Then the apostle did not mean that the Romans obeyed some special arrangement of the doctrine itself. This is not the thought exactly. We have the gospel in *facts, commands and promises*. The facts may be *believed*, the commands may be *obeyed*, the promises may be *enjoyed;* but neither *facts* nor *promises* can be *obeyed*. There can be no obedience to them.

The word *form* in Romans vi: 17, is from the original word *tupon*, usually rendered *type;* but it is not again used in the Greek Testament in the same form it here appears; hence we can get but little assistance from analogy. The word *type*, however, implies an antitype, or something made by the type and answering to it. That which is made by, and answers to the type must and will resemble the type. The apostle uses the word *likeness* in the fifth verse of this chapter, conveying a somewhat similar idea to the word *form* in the seventeenth verse; and the word *likeness* may assist us in catching the meaning he gave to the word *form*. The *form* of the doctrine was that which the Romans obeyed, and not the doctrine itself. The doctrine, we have seen, could not be obeyed, but they could obey the *likeness* or *form* of it—something symbolizing, representing or figuratively exhibiting it.

But to *recognize* the form or likeness of a thing we must be acquainted with the thing of which it is a form. Were we to present you a most perfect likeness or form of some person entirely unknown to you, you could not recognize the likeness, picture, or form, because you have no acquaintance with the person of which it is a form. On the contrary, were we to present you a form, picture, or likeness of some one you see every day, you would recognize it at once. So in order to recognize the *form of doctrine* obeyed by the Romans we must familiarize ourselves with the doctrine *itself*, of which they obeyed the form.

We have seen that the first fact mentioned by Paul as the gospel, was "that Christ died for our sins according to the Scriptures." Then there must be something in the *form* resembling this. In the second verse of this chapter the apostle asks: "How shall we, that are dead to sin live any longer therein." Then as Christ died FOR sin, the sinner must die to sin.

Second item: "And that he was buried." Then there

is something in the form resembling *burial;* hence we read again: "Know ye not that so many of us as were baptized into Jesus Christ were baptized into his death?" Being dead to sin we are ready to be baptized into the benefits of the death of Him who died for us. "Therefore we were buried with him by baptism into death." v. 4. Here, then, we see that as Christ was buried, so we are buried with him in baptism.

Third item: "And that he rose again the third day according to the Scriptures." Then in the *form* there must be something resembling a resurrection; hence we read: "That like [yes like—this is the word] as Christ was raised up from the dead by the glory of the Father, even so we also [having been raised] should walk in newness of life." Here we see that in baptism there is not only a burial but also a resurrection. "For if we have been planted together in the likeness of his death, we shall be also in the likeness of his resurrection." And again: "Buried with him in baptism wherein also ye are risen with him." Col. ii: 12. Then we see that in baptism we are both buried and raised with Christ.

Posting up, then, we find that Christ died for our sins according to the Scriptures, and the Romans died to sin as required by the Scriptures. Christ was buried, and the Romans were buried with him in baptism—planted in the likeness of his death. And that Christ arose again the third day according to the Scriptures; and the Romans were raised from their burial in baptism to walk in newness of life. Thus they obeyed from the heart the form of doctrine delivered them, in doing of which they were made free from sin. And Paul says: "Now being made free from sin, and become servants to God, ye have your fruit unto holiness, and the end everlasting life. For the wages of sin is death; but the gift of God is eternal life through Jesus Christ our Lord." Rom. vi: 22, 23. Glorious end—*everlasting life*. End that never ends. Priceless gift—*eternal life*. Life that knows no death.

But before leaving these items of the gospel we would call attention to a very loose way of quoting them. When preachers attempt to tell what the gospel is, they say it is the death, burial, and resurrection of Christ. Now we respectfully suggest that there is not a particle of gospel in that. No more than in the death of Washington or any other man.

What is gospel? It is *good news—glad tidings*. What good news could there be in the death, burial, and resurrection of Christ? Quoted in that way, none whatever. Does not Paul say these are the gospel? No, not exactly. The first item he gives is that Christ died for our sins according to the Scriptures. Not that Christ died; but that Christ died for our sins. This is gospel or good news. Good news to me—that Christ died for me. We are interested in his death and may be benefited by it. Quoted as Paul gave it, it is good news; but the vitality is all cut out of it by the loose habit of quoting it.

"But the Baptism reported in the sixth of Romans is Holy Ghost baptism." Is it indeed? Take care lest you spoil the *pouring* in Holy Ghost baptism. The baptism in the sixth of Romans was a *burial;* and if that was Holy Ghost baptism then Holy Ghost baptism was a burial; and hence the *pouring* of the Holy Ghost was an insignificant circumstance, but not the baptism at all.

But was this Holy Ghost baptism? We have seen that it was obedience to a form of doctrine that freed the Romans from sin. Was there any obedience in Holy Ghost baptism? "Being assembled together with them, commanded them that they should not depart from Jerusalem, but wait for the promise of the Father, which, saith he, ye have heard of me." Wait for the *promise of the Father?* what promise? "For John truly baptized with water; but ye shall be baptized with the Holy Ghost not many days hence." Acts i: 4, 5. Here we see that the baptism of the Holy Spirit was a promise, and could not be obeyed. It never was a command to any one, nor was there ever any obedience on the part of any one in being baptized with it. Then as the baptism recorded in the sixth of Romans *was obedience*, it is certain it was not Holy Spirit baptism. This ought to put that matter forever at rest, it seems to us.

A few questions and we shall have done. If the facts of the gospel be the *doctrine* of which the Romans obeyed the *form* or likeness, can any one tell what likeness there is to a *burial* and *resurrection* in sprinkling or pouring a few drops of water on the head of the subject? While the subject may have died to sin, surely the *form or likeness of burial and resurrection* must both be wanting in such procedure as that. And worse still. If the subject be an infant it could not have died to sin; and in its so-called baptism every element of the form of doctrine obeyed by the Romans is wanting—every one.

Lives there a man on the earth to-day, who has only had a few drops of water sprinkled or poured upon him, who can put his hand on his breast and lift his eyes to heaven and say, I have been buried and raised with Christ in baptism?

Will every one ask himself the question: "Have I obeyed from the heart the form of doctrine obeyed by the Romans? If not, have I been made free from sin as they were? If not, will the end of my course be everlasting life, as Paul said theirs would be? Remember that the wages of sin is death; but the gift of God is eternal life through Jesus Christ our Lord. This is a matter so important that you cannot afford to trifle with it. There is too much at stake on the decision you make concerning it. This may be the last time you will ever have an opportunity to decide the question. Certainly you will decide it for the last time ere long, how soon you cannot tell. Hence the decision you make *now* may settle your final destiny. Then let me beg you to decide wisely, and decide now, for *now* is all the time you can certainly claim. The past is gone—the future may never come to you. Now is your time. Then come now.

CHAPTER IX.

JUSTIFICATION.

TO justify means to declare *innocent*, or *blameless*. In this sense the term *justification* may apply to such as are accused of crime of which they have never been guilty. But it also means to *acquit*, to *absolve* from guilt where guilt has really and justly been incurred—to declare innocent after actual violation of the law—to declare *blameless* where blame has justly attached. In this sense it is applied in the *justification of sinners*, and in this sense we propose to employ it in this chapter.

As all men sin and come short of the glory of God, we want to find a *system* of justification, if there be one, by which the *guilty* may become *innocent*, in the sight of God. In this sense justification must include the idea of *pardon of sin—remission of sin—salvation from sin—blotting out of sin*, so that the party may stand before God as though he had never sinned—as a new born babe, beginning a new life in the family of God—in the kingdom of God's dear Son. Surely, then, the subject of *justification* is second in importance to nothing that has ever engaged the attention of men. Let us, therefore, open the Divine Volume and examine the subject with that care and attention which its importance demands.

On this, as on most other subjects connected with the salvation of man, there are different and conflicting theories, each having its advocates claiming support from the word of God. Before Luther's day the theory of Romanism was *all works*—doing penance; and he, very naturally, vibrated to the other extreme, rejecting all works, and adopting a theory of *all faith*, or justification by *faith only*. Out of these two have grown other theories. One that justification grows out of "God's free grace and love without any foresight of faith, good works, or any other thing in the creature as causes or conditions moving Him thereto." And closely akin to this is another theory that justification grows out of an eternal covenant made between God and his Son, in which the salvation of the elect was unconditionally secured by Christ, who in due time gave his life for them, and none others were at all interested in or benefitted by his death, as God never loved them or made any provision for them.

It is not our purpose to enter upon an examination of these theories, or still others which we might mention; sufficient it is to say that they cannot ALL be true; and we think it will abundantly appear, in this investigation, that they are all wrong. If we examine the word of God closely we will find a number of items in the system of justification revealed in the gospel, each one filling an important place; and hence it cannot be true that man is justified by any one thing alone. To find these several items, and the God-appointed place and office of each, is the object of this investigation.

We suppose it is scarcely necessary to offer proof that remission or pardon of sin is embraced in the idea of justification. If any are troubled at this point, however, we refer such to the following Scriptures as proof:

" Be it known unto you therefore, men and brethren, that through this man is preached unto you the forgiveness of sins; and by him all that believe are justified from all things, from which ye could not be justified by the law of Moses." Acts xiii : 38, 39. Here we see that forgiveness of sins was preached through Jesus Christ, and that those who believed were justified or forgiven.

And again : "Being justified freely by his grace through the redemption that is in Christ Jesus ; whom God hath set forth to be a propitiation through faith in his blood, to declare his righteousness [righteous method of remission] for the remission of sins that are passed, through' the forbearance of God ; to declare, I say, at this time his righteousness [God's righteous method of justification] that he might be just and the justifier of him which believeth in Jesus." Rom. iii : 24–26. Here the remission of sins and the justification of the believer must mean the same thing.

Finally : "But to him that worketh not, [the works of the law of Moses] but believeth on him that justifieth the ungodly, his faith is counted for righteousness. Even as David also describeth the blessedness of the man, unto whom God imputeth righteousness without works, saying, blessed are they whose iniquities are forgiven, and whose sins are covered ; blessed is the man to whom the Lord will not impute sin.' Rom. iv: 5–8. This illustration drawn from David, by Paul, shows that the justification of the ungodly and forgiving iniquity are one and the same thing. If a man is justified, his sins are pardoned, forgiven or remitted ; and if his sins are pardoned, forgiven, remitted, he is justified. Assuming, now, that this point is conceded, we wish next to look for the

PARDONING POWER.

We have already quoted : "That he [God] might be just and the justifier of him which believeth in Jesus."

Rom. iii : 26. This shows that God justifies the believer, and as none others are justified at all, it follows that the pardoning power is alone in Him. But Paul says: "Who shall lay any thing to the charge of God's elect? It is God that justifieth." Rom. viii: 32.

Seeing then that in God alone is power to justify or pardon, it follows that pardon takes place in the mind of God and not in the heart of the sinner. Man has no power to pardon himself, nor has he wisdom sufficient to enable him to devise a plan by which to obtain pardon of another. God is the offended party, and from Him pardon must come, or the guilty can never stand justified in his sight. As God is the offended party, in whom is lodged all pardoning power, it follows that he alone has the right to suggest terms of reconciliation; and it is the duty of him who wishes forgiveness to accept the terms imposed without effort to change or supplement them in any way—indeed this he must do if the priceless boon is ever enjoyed by him. We cannot see why any one should wish to be pardoned otherwise than as suggested by God against whom he has sinned, and from whom must come the mercy sought. Rejoicing in his love he should gladly accept salvation on any terms, and comply with any conditions upon which he may stand justified before God, and be re-instated in his favor. Speak, Lord, thy servant heareth. But are not all willing to do this? Perhaps they are willing, but for want of proper instruction they sometimes fail to do it. When the blind lead the blind, they both fall into the ditch. They are like the Jews who "being ignorant of God's righteousness, and going about to establish their own righteousness, have not submitted themselves to the righteousness of God." Rom. x : 2, 3.

Seeing, then, that it is God that justifieth the ungodly, and showeth mercy to the guilty, we come next to inquire for the

AGENCIES, MEANS AND CONDITIONS

upon which justification may be extended to guilty sinners by a merciful God. And first we may remark that God has done for man what he was unable to do for himself; but what he was able to do for himself God has required of him, and *will not do* for him. Man could not devise a system of justification for himself; divine wisdom has done this. Man could not consummate the system when conceived; God sent his Son to do this. Man could not provide himself an offering that could take away sin, but " we are sanctified through the offering of the body of Jesus Christ, once for all." All things being thus provided, we *can believe and obey God*, and we will be lost if we refuse to do this.

Man having alienated himself from God by wicked works, could not re-instate himself in the favor of God, or do any thing to *merit* the forgiveness of his sins; but God loved him still; not only did he love him, but he *so loved him* as to provide a way by which to save him. This unmerited love or favor which moved the Heavenly Father to offer terms of salvation to man makes the salvation or justification

BY GRACE.

Hence says the apostle: " Being justified freely by his grace through the redemption that is in Christ Jesus, whom God has set forth to be a propitiation through faith in his blood, to declare his righteousness [righteous method] for the remission of sins that are passed, through the forbearance of God." Rom. iii; 24, 25.

And again: "But after that the kindness and love of God our Savior toward man appeared, not by works of righteousness which we have done, but according to his mercy he saved us, by the washing of regeneration, and renewing of the Holy Ghost, which he shed on us abundantly through Jesus Christ our Savior; that being justified by his grace, we should be made heirs according to the hope of eternal life." Titus iii: 4–7.

We are, then, justified freely by his grace—how? Through the redemption that is in Christ Jesus. That is, the grace of God caused him to give the world the redemption, or rather the PLAN of redemption that is in Christ Jesus, and those who accept it have the remission of their past sins and are thus justified by grace, for they did not, nor could they *merit* the salvation thus provided for them. And we could only be thus saved or justified by grace, after that the kindness and love of God appeared in the gift of Jesus Christ.

Before leaving the Scriptures quoted we would call attention to the fact that both passages show that justification or salvation is not secured by grace alone without any conditions to be complied with by man. Note first that we are only justified by grace through the redemption that is in Christ Jesus; and he is a propitiation only through faith in his blood. Hence, no faith, no propitiation; and no propitiation, no redemption in Christ Jesus; and no redemption, no justification by grace. "Therefore it is of faith that it might be by grace." Rom. iv: 16. Hence, after the grace of God has perfected the plan of justification in the gospel, it is only the power of God to the salvation of him who believes it. Rom. i: 16.

But again, Paul says: "God, who is rich in mercy, for his great love wherewith he loved us, even when we were dead in sins, hath quickened us together with Christ, (by grace ye are saved) and hath raised us up together, and made us sit together in heavenly places in Christ Jesus; that in the ages to come he might show the exceeding riches of his grace, in his kindness toward us, through Christ Jesus; for by grace are ye saved through faith; and that not of yourselves; it is the gift of God." Eph. ii: 4–8.

Here we learn that the riches of God's mercy and his great love for his creature man, are at the very foundation of the system of salvation; hence truly may it be said, "by grace ye are saved." But it is through *faith;* hence, no faith, no salvation by grace, or otherwise; for without faith it is impossible to please God." Heb. xi: 6.

But we are told that "faith is the gift of God and not the act of the creature." Surely the apostle does not mean this. What does he say? *That* not of yourselves, it is the gift of God. What is the gift of God? When the last thought in a sentence is referred to, the *demonstrative* THIS is used to designate it; but when the word *that* is used it cannot refer to the last thought presented, but must refer to something beyond it. To what then does it refer? "By grace are ye saved through faith, and that *salvation*, not of yourselves, it is the gift of God." To this agrees the language of the same writer when he says: "The wages of sin is death; but the gift of God is eternal life through Jesus Christ our Lord." The gift of God, then, is not faith, but salvation which ends in eternal life." Rom. vi: 23.

But it is "not of works, lest any man should boast." v. 9. Certainly this is true. As stated before, we could not save ourselves, nor could any works of our own *merit* salvation; if so, then salvation would be an equivalent for our works, and hence salvation would be of *debt* and not of *grace* at all. But are we to understand this as excluding all acts of obedience to the gospel, under the head of works? Surely not; for this would damn the last one of the human race. To believe on Jesus is a *work;* not only so, but is the work of God, because it is commanded of God to be done by man. (John vi: 29.) Yet *it* is excluded if *all works* are excluded; still, Jesus says, "he that believeth not shall be damned." Mark xvi: 15. Hence if all works done in obedience to the gospel are excluded, then the last ray of hope for the salvation of man is swept away. Of course the apostle meant nothing like this; but when he said "not of works lest any man should boast," he meant that *salvation* is not of works done by man, but is of God, just as Paul said, "*it is God that justifieth*," and the means of salvation was His free gift to man.

That we may see further that obedience to the gospel was not the works referred to by Paul, as excluded, we quote again his language to Titus: "Not by works of righteousness which we have done, but according to his mercy he saved us, by the washing of regeneration and renewing of the Holy Ghost." Titus iii: 5.

Here it is distinctly stated that God saves us according to his mercy: and he *does not save us by works* of righteousness which we have done. But he *does save us* in some other way. How? By the washing of regeneration and renewing of the Holy Ghost. By the washing of regeneration here is meant *baptism* as every commentator of note agrees. It could not mean spiritual washing, for the renewing of the Holy Spirit is mentioned specifically as an additional item. This being so it follows that baptism or the washing of regeneration *by which we are saved, is not included in the works of righteousness by which we are not saved.* Surely this is plain enough.

By the grace of God we have bread to eat. In the production of bread God has done for us that which we could not do for ourselves. We could not provide the soil—God has done this. We could not provide the sun to give light, and heat the earth—God has furnished this. We could not furnish the atmosphere, the carbon of which is the necessary food of vegetation—God has furnished this. We could not provide the rain to moisten the earth—God has provided this. We could not furnish the seasons—spring-time to plant, summer to cultivate, autumn to gather, and winter to recuperate the soil, but God has arranged all this. We can, however, prepare the soil, plant the seed, cultivate and gather the crop and have it converted into bread; and God requires us to do this, and if we do not use the means thus provided for the production of bread, we will surely perish, and ought to perish; but he that uses the means, graciously provided, will, *by the grace of God*, have bread. So in justification by grace. God has provided the means and we must use them—believe and obey him, or we will as surely be lost as will the man perish for bread, who refuses to use the means for its production.

But are the means of grace provided only for the *elect?* Paul says: "The grace of God that bringeth salvation hath appeared to all men." Titus ii: 11. Thus we see that the grace of God that brought salvation, brought it to all men; yet all men will not be saved by it. "Grace and truth came by Jesus Christ." John i: 17. "He became the author of eternal salvation unto all them that obey him." Heb. v: 9. Thus we see that the grace of God has brought salvation within the reach of all men and *all who obey him will be saved;* but those who refuse to obey him will be lost, however ample the provisions made for them.

WE ARE JUSTIFIED BY CHRIST.

Speaking of Jesus Christ Paul said; " Be it known unto you, therefore, men and brethren, that through this man is preached unto you the forgiveness of sins; and by him all that believe are justified from all things, from which ye could not be justified by the law of Moses." Acts xiii: 38, 39.

Here *forgiveness of sins* through Christ and *justification* by him seem to indicate the same thing. Again Paul says: "Knowing that a man is not justified by the works of the law, [of Moses] but by the faith [gospel] of Jesus Christ, even we have believed in Jesus Christ, that we might be justified by the faith [gospel] of Christ and not by the works of the law, [of Moses] for by the works of the law [of Moses] shall no flesh be justified. But if, while we seek to be justified by Christ, we ourselves also are found sinners, is therefore Christ the minister of sin? God forbid." Gal. ii: 16, 17.

Here justification by Christ through the gospel is contrasted with the law of Moses by which none can be justified. But the point to which we invite attention at present is that we are justified by Christ. The grace of God was manifested to the world in the gift of his Son. This we have already seen. When the plan of salvation was conceived by Divine Wisdom, it was necessary that it be revealed to his Son, through whom it should be set up and carried out on earth. Hence Jesus said, "I do nothing of myself; but as my Father hath taught me, I speak these things. And he that sent me is with me, the Father hath not left me alone; for I do always those things that please him." John viii: 28, 29. "I have not spoken of myself; but the Father which sent me, he gave me commandment, what I should say, and what I should speak; and I know that his commandment is life everlasting; whatsoever I speak therefore, even as the Father said unto me, so I speak." John xii: 49, 50. Hence, "by his knowledge shall my righteous servant justify many."

But it pleased God by the foolishness of *preaching* to save them that believe; hence it was not only necessary that the Father should give his Son the words of eternal life, but he must reveal them to those whose duty it would be to preach them to others. In his prayer to his Father he said: "I have manifested thy name unto the men which thou gavest me out of the world; thine they were, and thou gavest them me, and they have kept thy word. Now they have known that all things whatsoever thou hast given me, are of thee; for I have given unto them the words which thou gavest me; and they have received them, and have known surely that I came out from thee, and they have believed that thou didst send me." John xvii: 6–8.

Jesus is the center of the Christian system, the object of the Christian's faith, the anchor of his hopes; and in him are centered all the blessings of the gospel. Well may we say with the apostle that we are justified by Christ, for he is the author and finisher of the faith.

WE ARE JUSTIFIED BY THE BLOOD OF CHRIST.

"Without the shedding of blood is no remission." Heb. ix: 22. But the blood of animals could never take away sins. (Heb. ix: 4). "Neither by the blood of goats and calves, but by his own blood he entered in once into the holy place, having obtained eternal redemption for us." Heb. ix : 12. But God commendeth his love toward us, in that, while we were yet sinners, Christ died for us; much more then being now justified by his blood we shall be saved from wrath through him." Rom. v : 9.

"Whom God hath set forth to be a propitiation through faith in his blood to declare [reveal] his righteousness [righteous method] for the remission of sins that are past, through the forbearance of God." Rom. iii : 25. "In this was manifested the love of God toward us, because that God sent his only begotten Son into the world that we might live through him. Herein is love—not that we loved God, but that he loved us, and sent his Son to be the propitiation for our sins." 1 John iv : 9, 10. "And he is the propitiation for our sins; and not for our sins only, but also for the sins of the whole world." 1 John ii : 2.

"If we walk in the light as he is in the light, we have fellowship one with another, and the blood of Jesus Christ his Son cleanseth us from all sin." 1 John i : 7. "In whom we have redemption through his blood, the forgiveness of sins, according to the riches of his grace." Eph. i: 7. "In whom we have redemption through his blood even the forgiveness of sins." Col. i : 14. "For a testament is of force after men are dead, otherwise it is of no strength at all while the testator liveth." Heb. ix : 17. We have not space for a comment on each of the foregoing Scriptures having reference to the blood of Christ, nor is it at all necessary—they explain themselves. Sufficient it is to say that man by sin forfeited his right to live, and God graciously permitted him to substitute the life of animals for his own life.

But this blood could not take away sin; it could only lay them over for a year at a time until Christ perfected these offerings, giving his life for the redemption of the transgressions that were under the first testament. (Heb. ix: 15). He also, by his death, sealed and ratified the New Testament, "by the which will we are sanctified by the offering of the body of Jesus Christ once for all." Heb. x. 10. We therefore have redemption through his blood even the forgiveness of sins according to the riches of God's grace. The blood of Jesus was unlike the blood offered under the Old Testament in that sins forgiven through his blood were forever gone—*blotted out—remembered no more.* How grateful we should be that we are permitted to live under a *better covenant* founded upon *better promises* than that dedicated only by blood that could never take away the sins of those for whom it was offered. Strange that the Jews, after they had been emancipated from the law under which they had been held for ages, and were introduced to the superior privileges of the new covenant should want to return again to the bondage of the old covenant. But as the bird that has been raised in confinement, when set at liberty is not content, but wishes to re-enter its cage, so the Jews after they were set at liberty, were not content, but continually clamored for a return to the old covenant and the bondage of the law of Moses. When freed from Egyptian bondage they longed for a return to the flesh-pots of Egypt and the slavery in which they had been held; so when freed from the bondage of Judaism and introduced to the glorious light and liberty of the gospel, they were not content to remain free, unless the gospel could be engrafted upon the Jewish law. But we need not marvel at this, for there are many to-day who wish to amalgamate the law of Moses and the gospel of Jesus Christ. Having never been under the law, it is strange indeed that they want to be entangled with it. Surely it must be that they have never clearly seen the perfection and beauty of the system presented in the gospel or they would not wish to adulterate it with defunct law or human tradition. But we have not space to pursue this thought further here.

WE ARE JUSTIFIED IN THE NAME OF THE LORD JESUS.

Paul says: "And such were some of you; but ye are washed, but ye are sanctified, but ye are justified in the name of the Lord Jesus, and by the Spirit of our God." 1 Cor. vi: 11.

And what has his name to do with the justification of the sinner? As the blood of Christ sealed and ratified the new covenant that took the place of, or succeeded the old covenant, so that the name of Jesus Christ gives *authority* to the new covenant and every feature of it, his name gives authority to every command in it; and assures the fulfillment of every promise contained in it. "Whatsoever ye do in word or deed, do all in the name of the Lord Jesus, giving thanks to God and the Father by him." Col. iii: 17. "For there is none other name under heaven given among men, whereby we must be saved." Acts iv. 12. "To him give all the prophets witness that through his name whosoever believeth on him shall receive remission of sins." Acts x: 43. Thus Peter instructed the Gentiles at the house of Cornelius; and that they might have the promised remission of sins, "he commanded them to be baptized in the name of the Lord." v. 15. Thus they were washed, sanctified, and justified in the name of the Lord Jesus.

When the believing Jews were cut to the heart on the day of Pentecost and asked what to do, Peter answered. "Repent and be baptized every one of you in the name of Jesus Christ for the remission of sins." Acts ii: 38. When the disciples found by Paul at Ephesus were properly instructed, "They were baptized in the name of the Lord Jesus." Acts xix: 5. Peter said to the cripple found at the gate of the temple, "in the name of Jesus Christ of Nazareth rise up and walk." Acts iii: 6. When Paul was grieved by the spirit of divination in the damsel at Philippi he said to the spirit "I command thee in the name of Jesus Christ to come out of her. And he came out the same hour." Acts xvi: 18.

Other Scriptures might be quoted, but these are sufficient to show that the name of Jesus Christ is the source of all authority in heaven above and on the earth beneath. Every command given, every promise made, and every punishment threatened in the gospel, derive authority, validity and force from the name of Jesus Christ, the ever blessed Son of God.

JUSTIFIED BY THE SPIRIT.

In the passage already quoted it is said: "But ye are washed, but ye are sanctified, but ye are justified in the name of the Lord Jesus and by the Spirit of our God." 1 Cor. vi: 11.

By the *Spirit of our God* we suppose is meant the Holy Spirit. Before leaving the world Jesus said to the disciples: "I have yet many things to say unto you, but ye cannot bear them now; howbeit when he the Spirit of truth is come he will guide you into all truth; for he shall not speak of himself; but whatsoever he shall hear, that shall he speak; and he will show you things to come." John xvi: 12, 13. Thus we learn that whatever was lacking to perfect the plan of salvation the Holy Spirit would furnish. Jesus assured them that the "Holy Ghost, whom the Father will send in my name, he shall teach you all things, and bring all things to your remembrance, whatsoever I have said unto you." John xiv: 26. Thus the frailty of human memory was provided for by the Holy Spirit which was to be sent them from the Father, after Jesus should leave the world.

Jesus said to his disciples: "I will pray the Father and he shall give you another comforter that he may abide with you forever; even the Spirit of truth whom the world cannot receive, because it seeth him not, neither knoweth him; but ye know him for he dwelleth with you, and shall be in you." John xiv: 16, 17.

Here we learn that the Holy Spirit was promised to the disciples and was to dwell with and be in them forever; hence, after it came it is scarcely necessary for us to pray to the Lord to send down the Holy Spirit, unless we can show that it has left the disciples and gone back to heaven.

But from this quotation we learn another thing, which is, that the world cannot receive the Spirit. By the term *world* here we understand the *unconverted* portion of the race. But we hear Jesus saying of the Holy Spirit, that "when he is come, he will reprove the world of sin, and of righteousness, and of judgment." John xvi: 8.

We learn then that while the *world cannot receive the Spirit yet it may be operated on or reproved by it*. It was promised to the disciples—came to them on the day of Pentecost, and took up its abode in them, and through Peter's words dictated by the Spirit, cut the hearers (who as yet were of the world) to the heart—reproved them of sin, righteousness, and judgment. Seeing their lost and ruined condition they cry out, "Men and brethren what shall we do?" Peter was inspired by the Holy Spirit and spake as it gave him utterance. Surely he knew what to say and how to say it; and he knew well that what he said would be a rule of action for others in all time to come. If there was ever a time and place to invite inquirers to the anxious seat or mourner's bench that the apostles might engage in prayer to God for them, this was the time; and had such procedure been in harmony with God's will, surely such would have been the instructions given. But the inspiring Spirit put a different answer into Peter's mouth, and he spake it in burning words fresh from the court of heaven: "Repent and be baptized, every one of you, in the name of Jesus Christ for the remission of sins." Was this answer *correct* and *appropriate?* And if we, to-day, give a similar answer, under similar circumstances, to a similar question, can we be wrong? What was the effect of this teaching upon those who had made the inquiry? As many as gladly received his word were baptized; and thus they were justified in the name of the Lord Jesus and by the Spirit of our God, because the command was given in the *name of Jesus Christ* as guided by the *Holy Spirit.* This must be infallibly correct.

But we are a little ahead of our lesson. In getting a brief view of the Spirit's relation to the plan of justification we have been precipitated into the obedience rendered by man. Let us go back and post up a little.

(1) We have seen the *grace, love* and *mercy* of God at work in providing a system of justification for man by which he might be reinstated in the favor of God.

(2) We have seen Jesus Christ the ever blessed Son

of God, leave the realms of bliss and come to the world to *execute* the scheme of redemption conceived in infinite wisdom and given to him by his Father for the salvation of man.

(3) We have seen Jesus execute his *will* or testament containing ample provisions for the salvation of sinners; and seal and ratify it with *his blood*—die that his will might go into effect—enter heaven with his own *blood* to make an atonement for the sins of the world; that we might have redemption through his blood even the forgiveness of sins.

(4) We have seen the *name* of Christ so connected with the new covenant as to give force, authority and validity to every command, promise and threat contained in it.

(5) We have seen the Holy Spirit come to and take up its abode in the disciples, to bring to their recollection all things Jesus had taught them, and perfect any thing that might be wanting, enabling them to preach the word of life in all languages spoken by man, so that every one might hear and understand the terms upon which God proposed to save him. And finally, we learn that the gospel preached was confirmed by signs and wonders, and with divers miracles, and gifts of the Holy Ghost. Heb. ii: 4.

Thus we find the scheme of redemption complete—the plan of salvation perfected—all things necessary to a system of justification provided, which man was unable to provide for himself. But there are duties assigned to man which he can do, and is required to do—conditions to be complied with by man with which he can and must comply—terms to be accepted by man which are every way reasonable and just. Will he accept the terms, comply with the conditions, and perform the duties assigned him that he may be justified?

We have seen that in the production of bread God has provided the soil, the light, the heat, the moisture, the atmosphere, and the seasons which man could not have provided for himself; but he can prepare the soil, plant the seed, cultivate and gather the crop, and if he refuses to do this he will most certainly starve. So we have seen the plan of justification prepared and placed before man for his reception, and if he refuses to accept the terms offered him he will as surely be lost as the earth will fail to produce bread without effort on the part of man.

What, then, is left for man to do? What are the conditions of acceptance on his part with which he must comply in order to be pardoned—saved—justified?

WE ARE JUSTIFIED BY FAITH.

"Therefore being justified by faith we have peace with God through our Lord Jesus Christ; by whom also we have access by faith into this grace wherein we stand, and rejoice in hope of the glory of God." Rom. v: 1, 2.

By this quotation we see that we are justified by faith and being justified we have peace with God, and that this peace comes through our Lord Jesus Christ, and that through our Lord Jesus Christ we have access into the grace wherein we now stand, and rejoice in hope of the glory of God. Thus we are by faith connected with the grace of God, the Son of God, and the glory of God, and being so connected we have peace with God. "Therefore we conclude that a man is justified by faith without the deeds of the law." *i. e.* the law of Moses. Rom. iii: 28.

Seeing that we are justified by faith, it is pertinent to inquire what faith is; for unless we know what it is we cannot tell when we have it, or exercise it.

When contrasting the gospel with the law of Moses, the apostle uses the word faith as the synonym of gospel, meaning a system of faith. "Knowing that a man is not justified by the works of the law [of Moses] but by the faith of Jesus Christ [the gospel of Jesus Christ] even we have believed in Jesus Christ, that we might be justified by the faith of Christ, [gospel of Christ] and not by the works of the law [of Moses]; for by the works of the law [of Moses] shall no flesh be justified." Gal. ii: 16. "And the Scripture, foreseeing that God would justify the heathen through faith [through the gospel] preached before the gospel unto Abraham." Gal. iii: 8. "After that faith [the gospel] is come we are no longer under a schoolmaster." v. 25.

Again Paul addressed Titus as his own son "after the common faith." Titus i: 4. This shows that at that time there was, or had been, an uncommon faith. This uncommon faith was enumerated among the spiritual gifts, (1 Cor. xii: 9) and was imparted by imposition of apostolic hands, and enabled those who had it to perform miracles. It was doubtless the same kind of faith to which Jesus referred when he said, "If ye had faith as a grain of mustard seed, ye might say to this sycamine tree, be thou plucked up by the roots and be thou planted in the sea; and it should obey you." Luke xvi: 17. We suppose no one claims to have this faith now. If he does let him remove a mountain or a tree by his word, and thereby establish his claim. This faith was purely miraculous and passed away with the age of miracles.

But Titus was Paul's son after the common faith,

that is, Paul had preached the gospel to Titus and he had believed it. Then the common faith is the belief of the gospel without which none can come to God or be saved; for Jesus said he that believeth not shall be damned. Mark xvi: 16.

A few quotations will make this point clear enough. The Centurion went to Jesus and reported his servant sick. Jesus proposed to go and heal him. The Centurion said he was not worthy that the Master should come under his roof; but he requested that he speak the word only, and his servant should be healed. Jesus said to those about him: "I have not found so great *faith*, no not in Israel." And to the Centurion he said, "Go thy way, as thou hast *believed* so be it done unto thee; and his servant was healed in the self same hour." Matt. viii: 5–13. Here the belief of the Centurion is called faith, hence belief is faith.

Again: "Abraham believed God and it was counted unto him for righteousness." Rom. iv: 3. What was counted unto Abraham for righteousness? Believing God. "But to him that worketh not, but believeth on him that justifieth the ungodly, his faith is counted for righteousness." Here *believing* God and *faith* are clearly the same thing, and counted for the same thing. After telling us in the third verse that Abraham believed God and it was counted unto him for righteousness, Paul tells us in the ninth verse that "faith was reckoned to Abraham for righteousness." This clearly shows that believing God was the faith that was reckoned to him for righteousness.

Once more: "But without faith it is impossible to please him; for he that cometh to God must believe that he is, and that he is a rewarder of them that diligently seek him." Heb. xi: 6. Here *faith* and *belief* are used interchangeably, and surely mean the same thing. Other Scriptures might be quoted, but these are enough. When a man believes all God has said, and believes it *because* he has said it, he has all the faith that God requires of any one, and he has all the faith any one can have.

Since the uncommon or miraculous faith passed away with the miracles connected with it, there has been but *one faith* (Eph. iv : 5), and this is the belief of testimony. It may differ in degree but not in kind. It may be weak or strong, dead or alive, fruitful or barren, but in kind it is one. It is the belief of testimony and can be nothing else.

There is no power in the English language to convert faith into a verb or into a participle. We cannot say, Abraham *faithed* God, but we can say Abraham *believed* God and his *faith* was counted unto him for righteousness. We cannot command any one to *faith* on the Lord Jesus Christ and thou shalt be saved; but we can command any one *to believe* on the Lord Jesus Christ and thou shalt be saved. We cannot say he that *faitheth* not shall be damned, but we can say he that *believeth* not shall be damned. We cannot say, and that *faithing* ye may have life through his name, but we can say, and that *believing* ye may have life through his name. When the thought is expressed in the *noun* form we use the word *faith*, but if in the *verbal* or *participial* form, it is of necessity expressed by *believe*, in the form adapted to the construction of the sentence.

Thus it is easy to see that faith is the belief of testimony, and without testimony there can be no faith. A fact must exist, then there must be testimony sufficiently clear to be understood, and sufficiently strong to be convincing or conclusive; then when parties are sufficiently interested to take hold of the testimony there may be faith, but beyond the testimony faith cannot go.

To make this clear to the satisfaction of all, let us consider some of the points established in the testimony concerning Jesus the Christ. He was born in Bethlehem, of the Virgin Mary—grew up to manhood, was baptized by John in the river Jordan—did many miracles in confirmation of his claim to be the Son of God—was betrayed by Judas—condemned by Pilate—crucified on Calvary, and buried in Joseph's tomb. Now had the testimony stopped here, how much faith would any one have to-day in his resurrection from the dead? Just none at all. Our faith would end in the tomb just where the testimony left him. Beyond this it could not go. Faith must end with the testimony.

From this view of the subject it is quite easy to see what Paul meant when he said: "So then faith cometh by hearing, and hearing by the word of God." Rom. x: 17.

Faith comes by hearing the word of God which contains the testimony necessary to produce faith; and faith that does not come in this way is not the faith of which Paul wrote, for it did come by hearing; nor is faith of any other kind, the faith that justifies; for by Christ all that *believe* are justified from all things from which they could not be justified by the law of Moses.

Jesus understood the subject just as Paul here taught it; for in his ever memorable prayer to his Father he prayed for them that should believe on him through the words of the apostles. If your faith came by visions, dreams or mystical operations of the Spirit, then Jesus did not pray for you to be one with him and such as did believe through the apostles' words.

JUSTIFICATION.

That we are justified by *faith*, has, we think, been made plain enough. But it is claimed that we are justified *by faith only*, or by faith alone. *Faith only, or alone* means faith by itself, to the exclusion of every thing else. Surely no one really believes this. The objector does not mean that we can be justified without the grace of God, the mission of Jesus, the blood of Christ, and the Holy Spirit. Certainly not. Then the language is unfortunate, for faith only or alone would exclude all these.

Then what does he mean? We suppose he must mean that faith is the only condition of justification *to be complied with by man.* Well, is this true? Will any one say that we can, as sinners, be justified without repentance? Jesus said: "Except ye repent ye shall all likewise perish." Luke xiii: 3. "The times of this ignorance God winked at; but now commandeth all men every where to repent:" Acts xvii: 30. So the sinner can no more be justified without *repentance* than without the grace of God or the blood of Christ.

But says the objector: "When I say a man is justified by faith only, I do not mean to exclude repentance." Then you ought not to say we are justified by *faith only*, for this does exclude repentance. But he explains: "Repentance is before faith, therefore the moment a man believes, he is justified, hence it is by faith only." This is not quite satisfactory. If faith and repentance are both necessary, changing places and putting repentance before faith, does not make it any the less important to justification, or any the less a condition of pardon. When a blessing is promised on compliance with a given number of conditions, it is reached on compliance with the last condition, but this can be reached only through compliance with all conditions preceding the last. Hence when there are a number of conditions indispensable to justification, it cannot be true that justification is by the last condition *only;* and it cannot, therefore, be true that sinners are justified by *faith only,* though it were true that repentance precedes faith; which, however, is by no means true. Repentance is *produced* by faith, and never exists without it.

There is but one verse in the Bible that speaks of justification by faith only; and that says: "Ye see, then, how that BY WORKS A MAN IS JUSTIFIED, and not by faith only." James ii: 24. Here the phrase *not by faith only* shows that faith and works are connected in the system of justification; and each fills its own place, and can not be dispensed with. Faith is the cause of every act of obedience to God; for without faith it is impossible to please God in any thing. Heb. xi: 6. Hence were it possible to repent without faith, such repentance would not be pleasing to God.

We know of but one verse in the Bible that speaks of *faith alone.* That verse says: "Even so faith, if it hath not works, is dead, being alone." James ii: 17. Thus we see that James puts it in both forms—*faith alone,* and *faith only. Faith alone is dead,* and we are *justified by works and not by faith only.* Can dead faith save or justify any one? "But wilt thou know, O vain man, that faith without works is dead." Verse 20. And still again: "For as the body without the spirit is dead so faith without works is dead also." Verse 26. It occurs to us that argument ought to stop, on this subject, just here.

James' teaching on the subject of justification is in exact harmony with the commission under which he acted. He associated faith and works in justification. So in the commission given by Christ to the apostles, after he arose from the dead, and before he ascended to heaven, he said: "Go ye into all the world, and preach the gospel to every creature. He that believeth and is baptized shall be saved; but he that believeth not shall be damned." Mark xvi: 15, 16.

Here belief or faith and baptism are both made conditions on which salvation depends. By works we understand James to mean just whatever is commanded in order to the perfection of faith; for "by works is faith made perfect." Repentance is not here specifically mentioned, nor was it necessary that it should be, for repentance being the necessary *result* of a God-approved *belief* or *faith*, wherever faith is mentioned its necessary result is presumed to be present whether mentioned or not.

Let it be observed that Jesus does not say "*He that believeth and is saved may or should be baptized if convenient;*" but he does say: "He that believeth and is baptized shall be saved." Salvation is promised on compliance with all the conditions stipulated. Was ever language more plain than this? It could not be misunderstood in every-day affairs of business life. Suppose I say to a business man: "Dig me a cistern and wall it up with brick and you shall have one hundred dollars." He accepts the proposition, the specifications are all made out and reduced to writing. The man digs the cistern, just as he agreed to dig it, and demands full pay for the job, though he has not put a brick in it—is he entitled to the one hundred dollars? Certainly not. He was to dig the cistern and wall it up with brick. He has dug the cistern, but not having walled it up with brick, he has not brought himself within the range of my promise, and cannot recover the pay. The commission says: "He that believeth *and* is baptized shall be saved." The man believes—has not been baptized—is he saved? Surely not. He has not brought himself within the range of the Savior's promise. He has not put a brick in the cistern. If he wants salvation let him obey the commands given; then, and not till then, he will get salvation, or the promise of Jesus fails. But his faith must be alive to the performance of the work commanded, otherwise it is dead, being alone. Thus we see that James and Jesus agree most perfectly.

Before leaving the commission we want to try it by the same logic that is used to prove justification by faith only, because, says the theory, repentance precedes faith. Faith comes after repentance, therefore justification is by faith only. Well, in the commission the style is "He that believeth and is baptized shall be saved." Baptism comes after faith, therefore salvation is by *baptism only.* This is *your* logic—how do you like it? Oh, circumstances alter cases, we suppose! Of course they do!!

But we are told that Paul taught justification by faith only. Surely he did not. He taught justification by faith, and so do we. There is no controversy about this. It is by adding the word *only* to Paul's teaching that the trouble comes. While his language is allowed to remain as he used it, there is no controversy whatever. Suppose I say I live by *eating*—that is true, for if I do not eat I shall die. But if I say I live by eating *only*, then it is false; for I live by *breathing* as well as by eating. I live by *sleeping*, I live by *exercise;* but it is not true that I live by any one thing *only*. A place for every thing, and every thing in its place, is the order of life, and it is the order of justification as well.

Paul and James both refer to Abraham's faith as the faith of which God approves. But we are told that Paul refers to Abraham's justification in the sense of *pardon* of sins, and James refers to it in the sense of *approval* of a righteous man, hence the apparent difference in their teaching. Here again the theory is wrong. *No man knows when Abraham was pardoned.* He was just as good a man the first we know of him as he ever got to be. Never was there a more faithful exhibition of obedience to God than he gave, when first we hear of him. He was in Ur of the Chaldees, surrounded by idolaters, and God told him to leave there; and so strong was his faith that he went out not knowing whither he went; and yet we are asked to believe that he was an *unpardoned sinner* then, and so remained for twenty-five years, until the time when Paul speaks of his faith as counted unto him for righteousness. Certainly nothing could be more foreign from the truth. Paul and James both refer to Abraham as furnishing an example of the faith that is well pleasing to God—faith strong enough to take God at His word and go right along in obedience to what He commanded. This is the argument they both draw from Abraham's faith; and *God never approved any other kind or degree of faith in saint or sinner.* When God told Abraham to do any thing he staggered not, in unbelief, but *obeyed* at all times and under all circumstances. When God promised him any thing he believed and *trusted* Him; and this he did from the very *first mention* of him in Bible history—*would an unconverted sinner have done so?* If the theory of justification or pardon *by faith only*, be true, then as Abraham had the faith, how can it be that he was an unpardoned man up to the time of which Paul speaks of him as justified? Surely it cannot be. Then the theory, that Paul alludes to Abraham's faith at the *time of his pardon* is an unscriptural and illogical effort to make him prove a doctrine different from that taught so clearly by James, that a *man is not justified by faith only*. There is not the slightest difference in their teaching. If we remember that Paul never used the word *only* in connection with justification by faith, the trouble is all gone, and surely he never did so use it.

There is not an example of approved faith recorded in the Bible, that was not perfected by *doing* whatever was commanded to be done by the party mentioned, and that before it was recorded for our imitation. The great cloud of witnesses mentioned in the eleventh chapter of the epistle to the Hebrews furnishes abundant evidence of this fact. And if we supply the word *only* after the word *faith* in the examples there given we shall make a palpable absurdity of every one of them.

We have only room to examine a single case, but this will serve as an example of all. "By faith Abraham, when he was tried, offered up Isaac: and he that had received the promises offered up his only begotten son, of whom it was said, That in Isaac shall thy seed be called." Heb. xi: 17, 18.

Now, the theory is that when Paul says we are justified by *faith*, that means that we are justified by faith only. Then when it is said: by faith Abraham, when he was tried offered up Isaac, it is meant that by *faith only* he offered him up. Now imagine the old Patriarch sitting in his tent, and by *faith only* going three days journey, attended by his servants and his son. By *faith only* his servants are left at the foot of the mountain, while he by *faith only* ascends the mountain, builds an altar, binds his son thereon, and lifts his knife to slay him. This is all done by *faith only*, while Abraham is resting quietly in his tent, and has not moved hand or foot in the whole matter. Is this ridiculous enough? Not a particle more absurd is it than it is to assume that we are justified by *faith only*, because it is said that we are justified by faith.

Paul says: "For ye are all the children of God by faith in Christ Jesus." Now Paul, how is it that we are all the children of God by faith in Christ Jesus? "For as many of you as have been baptized into Christ have put on Christ." Then by being baptized into Christ and thus putting him on in faith we become the children of God by faith in Christ Jesus, who said in the commission, "He that believeth and is baptized shall be saved;" and in whose name and by whose authority we are commanded to be baptized. Then in him, "there is neither Jew nor Greek, there is neither bond nor free, there is neither male nor female; for ye are all one in Christ Jesus; and if ye be Christ's then are ye Abraham's seed, and heirs according to the promise." Gal. iii : 26–29.

Then when, in faith we are baptized into Christ and thus put him on, we not only become the children of God by faith, but we become the seed of Abraham and heirs according to the promise God made to him. Is this plain enough?

Now, friendly sinner, when Jesus says: "He that believeth and is baptized shall be saved;" and Peter, to whom this commission was given, commanded believers to repent and be baptized for the remission of sins, and said to the saints scattered abroad, baptism now saves us; and James says we are justified by works and not by faith only, *is it safe to adopt and act upon a theory of justification by faith only?* Is it not infinitely more safe to let the word of God be the guiding star of our lives? When the Bible says we are justified by *grace*, believe it, for it is true. When it says we are justified by *Christ*, believe it. When it says we are justified by his *blood*, believe it. When it says we are justified in the *name* of Christ, believe it. When it says we are justified by the *Spirit*, believe it. When it says we are justified by *faith*, believe it; but add not the word *only*, nor any thing else, to it, for it is dangerous to add to the word of the Lord. When the Bible says we are justified by *works, believe this also,* for the Bible is the same inspired book when it says that, that it is when it says we are justified by faith. Seek to know what is required of you in order to the perfection of your faith, and when you have learned what the Lord requires of you, go and do it without delay, trusting in God to verify his promises to you, and you will not trust in vain. His word cannot fail.

When God says *believe*, do it. When God says *repent*, do it. When God says be baptized and wash away your sins, (Acts xxii: 16) do that too. No matter who says no, it God says do it, why tarriest thou? Obey God and let events take care of themselves. When God says go to the mourner's bench, go there; but if man, and not God, tells you to go there, you will do well to pause before going. When God says go, you may go, but when the light of his word ceases to shine on your pathway, it is dangerous to proceed.

Let us beware lest we make void the command of God by our traditions; for in vain do we worship him teaching for doctrines the commandments of men.

CHAPTER X.

REGENERATION.

"But after that the kindness and love of God, our Savior, toward man appeared, not by works of righteousness, which we have done, but according to his mercy he saved us, by the washing of regeneration and renewing of the Holy Ghost, which he shed on us abundantly through Jesus Christ our Savior; that being justified by his grace we should be made heirs according to the hope of eternal life." Titus iii: 4--7.

WE think it likely that as much has been spoken and written on the subject of *regeneration* as on any other subject connected with the salvation of man; why then should any thing further be attempted? If it is fully understood in the light of what has been said, then nothing more is needed, and if it is not understood yet, is it likely that any thing we may be able to say will contribute to a more perfect understanding of that which is obscure, after so much thought has been bestowed upon it? As there are many different and conflicting theories given by those who have favored the public with their views of it, we think it certain that *all* do not understand it. The Bible is not a book of contradictions, and hence it cannot be the source of conflicting theories on this or any other subject, therefore, while such theories are taught and believed, we may feel sure that the subject needs further investigation.

It is not our purpose to attempt to harmonize these

conflicting theories—this would indeed be impossible. Truth and error cannot be made to harmonize, and it is still more difficult to harmonize a number of conflicting theories all of which have their foundation in error. This is just the case in hand. Not a single correct theory on the subject of *regeneration* has ever fallen into my hands, or saluted my ears—if I have seen or heard such a theory, then I am quite free to confess that I do not understand the subject myself, for certain it is I have not found any thing entirely satisfactory to me. It is quite probable that those from whom I differ will be just as far from believing what I am about to write. Very well—they have had their say, may I not have mine? I have read what they have written—will it be asking too much of them to hear what I have to say? If I speak not as the oracles of God, then they ought to reject it, and will be sure to do it. All I ask is a candid and respectful hearing. Hear and then decide.

Of the various theories extant, I will mention only one—viz: *Regeneration and the new birth are identical.* This is the theory of most of our brethren who have spoken out on the subject. This is not only untrue in fact, but is a pernicious and mischievous error, an error which leads to conclusions as objectionable to those who advocate it as they are to us.

John says: "Whosoever believeth that Jesus is the Christ is born of God." 1 John v: 1. It is conceded by all parties that when a man is born again he is in a saved state. Speaking of God, Paul says: "Who hath delivered us from the power of darkness and hath translated us into the kingdom of his dear Son, in whom we have redemption through his blood, even the forgiveness of sins." Col. i: 13, 14. Out of the kingdom, then, we are subject to the power of darkness

—under the dominion of Satan—in the kingdom, we are freed from this evil power, have redemption through the blood of Christ, even the forgiveness of sins, hence in a state of salvation.

Now then, whosoever believeth that Jesus is the Christ, is born of God, and if a man be born of God, he is in the kingdom, has redemption through the blood of Christ, the forgiveness of sins, and is saved, whether baptized or not. Do you see where you are? The premises conceded, the conclusion comes like a conqueror and takes possession of the field, whether we so will or not. This looks to me like a clear, unequivocal, unconditional surrender to the doctrine of justification by faith only. I know that those who believe regeneration and the new birth to be identical are as far from accepting the conclusion as I am, but it seems to me they must have trouble to keep out of it. I am not unfamiliar with the route taken to find relief, but it is not very satisfactory even to themselves, and can never satisfy those who oppose them, while the thought expressed in the passage sparkles like a gem on its very surface.

But we may be told that the phrase *born of God* in 1 John v: 1, should read, *begotten of God*, as the context clearly shows; and it is so rendered in the New Version, and by all critics of any note every where. This is true, most certainly true, and brings out the real thought in the passage most beautifully, but what relief can this bring to him who has already admitted that *regeneration and the new birth are identical?* Begetting is generation, and regeneration is simply re-begetting, and if regeneration or begetting of God and the new birth are the same, what difference can it make which you render it? You are tied hand and foot either way. "Whosoever believeth that Jesus is the Christ, is born of God, or begotten of God—regenerated; and regeneration being the new birth, whosoever thus believes is begotten of God—regenerated, born again, and saved beyond the possibility of a respectable quibble.

Believing, as we do, that there is a vast difference between generation and birth, or, if you please, between rebegetting or regeneration and the new birth, we can see a beauty and fitness in the apostle's language: " Whosoever believeth that Jesus is the Christ, is *begotten* of God, and every one that loveth him that *begat* loveth him that is *begotten* of him." Never was there a truth more beautifully expressed by the inspiring Spirit of God. It enables us to clearly see and appreciate the whole theory of regeneration as taught in the word of God.

Whosoever believeth that Jesus is the Christ is begotten of God—regenerated. But how shall they believe in him of whom they have not heard? and how shall they hear without a preacher? In order to believe they must hear, for faith cometh by hearing and hearing by the word of God; and this is the word which by the gospel is preached unto you. Hence, says Paul: "Though ye have ten thousand instructors in Christ, yet *have ye* not many fathers: for in Christ Jesus I have begotten you through the gospel." 1 Cor. iv: 15. Paul preached the gospel to the Corinthians, and when they believed it, they believed that Jesus was the Christ, for this is included in the gospel; and when they believed this they were begotten of God—regenerated. But were they born again at the time they believed? Not yet. Were they physically born, when naturally generated or begotten? Surely not. How and when were they born again? " And many of the Corinthians hearing believed and were baptized." Acts xviii : 8. Now they are both *begotten and born;* or *regenerated and born again.* Begotten or regenerated when they believed through the gospel that Jesus was the Christ; and born again of water and of the Spirit when they were baptized as required by the Spirit.

But regeneration is the subject in hand for the present. What is regeneration? Surely by this time we are prepared to define the term. Generate means to *beget.* *Re* as a prefix means *again,* hence regenerate must mean to beget again. We are generated naturally —we are regenerated spiritually. Birth means brought forth—delivered. We are born naturally, we are born again spiritually. We use the term *spiritual* in contrast with natural because the means are in both regeneration and birth appointed by the Spirit.

But is not the same Greek word translated *begotten* in some places and *born* in others? Certainly, but is this conclusive evidence that begetting and birth are the same? Surely not. The word *pneuma* is translated *wind* and *spirit*—are wind and spirit the same? A thousand examples might be given where the same word means different things in different connections. The word *gennao* may be translated *begotten* or *born* as the context may demand, but it cannot mean both begotten and born at the same time and in the same place. Well established rules of exegesis tell us that in no language can a word have more than one literal meaning at the same time and in the same place. This is true of all words every where, and hence is true of *gennao.* It may be translated *begotten* or *born,* and the context must decide which, but it cannot mean both at once, or in a single occurrence.

Now if we will keep in mind that *regeneration* is simply

re-begetting the whole subject becomes easy enough. That this is its philological import is as certain as it is that language means any thing. We take it that Jesus and the apostles, guided by the Holy Spirit, understood the figures they used and the language they employed, and if they did they never taught that generation and birth are the same, and consequently could not have meant to teach that the thoughts represented by these figures of speech are the same—never.

That God is our spiritual Father I need not stop here to prove. James says: "Of his own will begat he us with the word of truth." James i: 18. Here we learn that God our spiritual Father begets us, and that the word of truth is the instrument employed by him in this work. Peter says: "Being born [begotten certainly] again not of corruptible seed, but of incorruptible, by the word of God, which liveth and abideth forever." 1 Pet. i: 23. That the word *born*, here should read *begotten* is admitted by all scholars, and it is so rendered by the revisers in the New Version. To talk of being *born of seed* is not respectable nonsense. Here again we learn that the word of God is the incorruptible seed with which men are spiritually begotten. When this spiritual seed is deposited in a good and honest heart, and through this God-appointed means a hearty trusting faith in Jesus is secured, the subject is *begotten of God*, truly and really *regenerated*, as John says: "Whosoever believeth that Jesus is the Christ is begotten of God."

Now as nothing can be naturally born that has not been previously generated, so nothing can be born again that has not been previously regenerated. The regenerated man may be born again, no one else can be. Born again, how? Born of water and of the Spirit. "Except a man be born of water and of the Spirit, he cannot enter into the kingdom of God." John iii: 5. Water is the element appointed by the Spirit of which the regenerated man must be born, hence washing in *water* is that washing which belongs to or follows regeneration by which Paul says God saves us. Is this plain enough?*

There is no place for water in regeneration. Regeneration is the work of faith in Christ through the gospel. The inspiring Spirit said whosoever believeth that Jesus is the Christ is begotten of God, and it is true. We repeat with emphasis: as well may we talk of *natural birth without previous generation*, as to talk of the *new birth without previous regeneration*. The one is just as absurd as the other. Such a thing cannot be. What then, becomes of the oft-repeated slander of *baptismal regeneration?* Baptism has nothing to do with regeneration only as a sequence to it. But it occurs to us that the charge is not without some degree of plausibility if regeneration and the new birth are identical.

But what becomes of the well-established doctrine of baptism for remission of sins if regeneration must precede baptism? Is not a regenerated man saved the moment he is regenerated? I think not. I know this will sound strange in the ears of many. How can that be? *Regenerated and still unsaved!* Yes, unquesably *regeneration precedes salvation* if Paul understood the subject. He says: "Not by works of righteousness which we have done, but according to his mercy he saved us by the washing of regeneration and the renewing of the Holy Ghost." Titus iii: 5. He saved us

---

*For a full and thorough examination of the New Birth, see our book on the Gospel Plan of Salvation, pages 189–208.

according to his mercy. Yes, but how? By regeneration? No, he did not say so, but why did he not say it? Because it is not true. Is this a good reason? He does not leave us in the dark to guess at the matter, for had he so left us we might have guessed that we are saved by regeneration, but he tells us plainly how God does save us. Well, how is it? He saves us by the washing of regeneration and the renewing of the Holy Ghost. Then he did not save us by regeneration, but by the washing that belongs to or follows regeneration, and renewing of the Holy Ghost.

We have a very similar construction in reference to John's baptism. John preached the baptism of repentance for the remission of sins. What did John preach for remission of sins? Not repentance, but that the baptism that belonged to or followed repentance was for remission of sins. Very well, the washing of regeneration. What does this mean? Surely it must mean the washing that belongs to or follows regeneration. Certainly then, we are not saved by regeneration, but by that which belongs to or follows it. Suppose I say the house of my friend gave me shelter for the night. What gave me shelter? Not my friend, but the house that belonged to him. We are saved by the washing of regeneration. By what are we saved? Not by regeneration, but by the washing that belongs to it. Other illustrations might be given, but surely this is plain enough.

That the washing of regeneration is baptism in water is already apparent, but at the risk of being tedious, I beg permission to suggest a few additional thoughts on this feature of our text. That it cannot refer to the renewing of the Holy Spirit is evident from the fact that this is specifically mentioned as an additional item.

Paul says: "Husbands, love your wives, even as Christ also loved the church, and gave himself for it; that he might sanctify and cleanse it with the washing of water by the word." Eph. v: 25. Here I suppose the same washing is referred to, and it is a washing of *water*. And it is the washing of water by the Word. That is, the washing of water contained in or required by the Word. What other washing of water is contained in the Word beside baptism?

But it is the *church, not the sinner*, that is to be sanctified and cleansed by this washing. Ah, indeed! Then the sinner is to be put into the church uncleansed, and washed afterward, that he may be cleansed! Is this the idea? The church is cleansed by cleansing the material of which it is composed, and this is done by washing it in water as required by the Word.

"Let us draw near with a true heart in full assurance of faith, having our hearts sprinkled from an evil conscience, and our bodies washed with pure water." Heb. x: 22. Here we find what the washing is. It is a *washing of the body*, in or with water. This looks very much like what we call baptism. Peter says: "Baptism doth also now save us." 1 Pet. iii: 21. Hence the language of Paul: "According to his mercy he saved us by the *washing of regeneration* and renewing of the Holy Ghost."

All this is in perfect harmony with the commission. Jesus said: "Go ye into all the world and preach the gospel to every creature. He that believeth and is baptized shall be saved." Mark xvi: 15, 16. We have found that whosoever believeth that Jesus is the Christ is begotten of God, or regenerated. In the commission this is believing the gospel. If believing results in regeneration, then we want to find the washing of regeneration, that is, the washing that belongs to or follows this belief that produces regeneration. Very well. He that believeth and is baptized shall be saved. Believing, he is regenerated, and when baptized, he is saved with the washing of regeneration or the washing that belongs to or follows it.

Finally, this view of regeneration *buries* the doctrine of justification by faith *only*, beyond the possibility or hope of resurrection. As an abstract *condition* the work of faith ends in *regeneration*. Whosoever believeth that Jesus is the Christ is begotten of God. Then he is prepared to be born again, in other words, saved with the washing of regeneration. The regenerated man may be born again—no one else can be, but he must be born again, or into the kingdom of God he cannot go. Jesus said it and it is true, as every thing he said was true.

But we have not written this for the purpose of antagonizing this or any other doctrine, or for the purpose of coming in contact with the views of any one; but for the sole purpose of developing the truth on a subject, as we think, not well understood. If we have come in contact with the views of any one, it has been incidental to the line of thought we have sought to present.

But we are asked what we will do with the *regeneration* of Matt. xix: 28. This is not the same regeneration referred to in Titus iii: 5, of which we have been writing. This any one can see who will examine the context carefully. In Titus the word *regeneration* is connected with salvation: "He *saved* us by the washing of regeneration." This subject was not under consideration in Matt. xix: 28. This the *connection* will clearly show. Let us examine it.

"Then answered Peter and said unto him, Behold,

we have forsaken all, and followed thee; what shall we have therefore? And Jesus said unto them, Verily I say unto you, That ye which have followed me, in the regeneration when the Son of man shall sit in the throne of his glory, ye also shall sit upon twelve thrones, judging the twelve tribes of Israel. And every one that hath forsaken houses, or brethren, or sisters, or father, or mother, or wife, or children, or lands, for my name's sake, shall receive an hundred fold, and shall inherit everlasting life."

Here the word *regeneration* refers, not to salvation, as in Titus iii : 5, but to a *state* or time when certain things should be. The thought is not " ye which have followed me in the regeneration," but ye that have followed me, shall, in that state of things called the *regeneration*, have certain privileges. Salvation from sin was not the subject spoken of here at all.

We are by no means certain that the *regeneration* here spoken of has come yet. We have not yet seen the time when the apostles were sitting on the twelve thrones judging the twelve tribes of Israel. In this regeneration they were to do this; and they will do it when the regeneration here spoken of comes. We have read much that has been written to prove that they are now on their thrones judging the twelve tribes; but it has never been satisfactory or conclusive to us. In this promise of Jesus some things were to be realized in this life; others not until in the world to come. Mark and Luke both report this same conversation. Mark says:

" Then Peter began to say unto him, Lo, we have left all, and have followed thee. And Jesus answered and said, Verily I say unto you, There is no man that hath left house, or brethren, or sisters, or father, or mother, or wife, or children, or lands, for my sake, and the gospel's, but he shall receive an hundred fold now in this time, houses, and brethren, and sisters, and mothers, and children, and lands, with persecutions; and in the world to come eternal life." Mark x: 28–30.

Luke says: "Then Peter said, Lo, we have left all, and followed thee. And he said unto them, Verily I say unto you, There is no man that hath left house, or parents, or brethren, or wife, or children, for the kingdom of God's sake, who shall not receive manifold more in this present time, and in the world to come life everlasting." Luke xviii: 28–30.

Thus we quote the *three* reports of this conversation. Matthew says they shall inherit eternal life, but does not tell us *when* they will get it. He tells us that the apostles shall sit on twelve thrones in the *regeneration*, but he does not tell us *when* that will be. He speaks of the manifold things they should get, like those forsaken for His sake; but does not say when they should have them. Mark and Luke tell us we shall have these in this life, and will get the *eternal life in the world to come.* They say nothing of the *regeneration*, or thrones on which the apostles were to sit in the regeneration. Then we respectfully suggest that the *time* and *nature* of this regengeneration are not set out in Matthew's report of it; and neither of the others reports the regeneration at all. As we have never seen the apostles on such thrones yet, and know not where the twelve tribes of Israel are that are now being judged by them, we take it that the time has not yet come for the regeneration of which Jesus spake.

Jesus ought to be pretty good authority on this subject and he has clearly spoken out upon it. He says: "When the Son of man shall come in his glory, and all the holy angels with him, then shall he sit upon the throne of his glory; and before him shall be gathered all nations; and he shall separate them one from another as a shepherd divideth his sheep from the goats; and he shall set the sheep on his right hand, but the goats on his left." Matt. xxv: 31-33.

Bear in mind that he was to sit upon the throne of his glory in the regeneration, and this is here clearly connected with his coming to judge the world. The only trouble in avoiding confusion here is, (as in Matt. xxiv) that events are crowded together as though to occur simultaneously, which we learn elsewhere, are to occur after considerable intervals. But that the regeneration of Matt. xix: 28 is as far in the future as Christ's second coming, we think scarcely admits of a doubt.

But we have another pointer to the same time. After John saw Jesus come, and all the armies of heaven with him (called angels in Matthew) he says: "And I saw thrones and they sat upon them, and judgment was given unto them." Rev. xx: 4. Here we have a *plurality of thrones*, corresponding, we suppose, with the twelve thrones upon which the apostles were to sit to judge the twelve tribes. This looks clear enough to us. Certain it is that the regeneration of Titus iii: 5 is not the same regeneration recorded in Matthew. The two are perfectly consistent, but quite different.

Our work, in this effort, has been to prepare the sinner, by regeneration, for a birth of water and Spirit, that he may enter the kingdom of God and be saved. That he may be delivered from the power of darkness and translated into the kingdom of God's dear Son. We have sought to brush away the mist and fog that have beclouded the subject, so that the truth may be seen by those who wish to know it. We have said, and we wish to repeat with emphasis, that *the regenerated man may be born again—no one else can be.**

Are we able to rise above all preconceived notions, and long-cherished theories, to a reception of the truth as revealed in Holy Writ? We are bound by no creed but the Bible. Every truth taught in that book belongs to us as fast as we can learn it. If we are in error with regard to any thing, we are perfectly free to accept the truth when we see it. We never stop to inquire what is believed among us; but what does the Bible teach? This settles everything. Before a "thus saith the Lord" every one should be willing to bow at all times. We should have no wills of our own, but to know and do the Lord's will. Not my will, but thine, O Lord, be done in all things. This is the true spirit of the religion instituted by Christ. It was the spirit that actuated him, and it should control us.

> "Wide as the world is thy command,
> Vast as eternity thy love;
> Firm as a rock thy truth shall stand,
> When rolling years shall cease to move."

---

*For a thorough examination of the New Birth see Gospel Plan of Salvation, pages 189–208.

CHAPTER XI.

THE TRANSFIGURATION.

"AND after six days Jesus taketh Peter, James, and John his brother, and bringeth them up into an high mountain apart, and was transfigured before them: and his face did shine as the sun, and his raiment was white as the light. And, behold, there appeared unto them Moses and Elias talking with him. Then answered Peter, and said unto Jesus, Lord, it is good for us to be here: if thou wilt, let us make here three tabernacles; one for thee, and one for Moses, and one for Elias. While he yet spake, behold, a bright cloud overshadowed them: and behold a voice out of the cloud, which said, This is my beloved Son, in whom I am well pleased; hear ye him. And when the disciples heard it, they fell on their face, and were sore afraid. And Jesus came and touched them, and said, Arise, and be not afraid. And when they had lifted up their eyes, they saw no man, save Jesus only. And as they came down from the mountain, Jesus charged them, saying, Tell the vision to no man, until the Son of man be risen again from the dead. And his disciples asked him, saying, Why then say the scribes that Elias must first come? And Jesus answered and said unto them, Elias truly shall first come, and restore all things. But I say unto you, That Elias is come already, and they knew him not, but have done unto him whatsoever they listed. Likewise shall also the

Son of man suffer of them. Then the disciples understood that he spake unto them of John the Baptist." Matt. xvii: 1-13.

While there is great unanimity among commentators as to the *facts* connected with the transfiguration, they are not so well agreed as to the *lesson* intended to be taught by it.

(1) By some it is made to teach the *resurrection of the dead*. While we believe as firmly that the dead will be raised as we believe any other well-established fact taught in the Bible, yet it would require much clearer proof than can be found in the transfiguration to establish our faith in it. To our mind there is about as much proof in the appearance of Samuel from the dead, as in the appearance of Moses and Elias. This proof is entirely too short. Moses and Elias were both good men—who represented the wicked in the proof here furnished? The wicked must be raised as well as the righteous. When Christ taught the resurrection he did not leave out the wicked. "Marvel not at this, for the hour is coming, in the which all that are in their graves shall hear his voice, and shall come forth; they that have done good, unto the resurrection of life; and they that have done evil unto the resurrection of damnation." John v: 27, 28. This announcement was made *before the transfiguration*, and it occurs to us that Peter, James, and John did not need proof of the resurrection after this; and if they did, *they would scarcely find it where there was not a word said about it.*

(2) By others it is made to teach the doctrine of *future recognition, i. e.* that the saints will personally know each other in heaven. It is not necessary to our present purpose to inquire whether this doctrine be true or false; sufficient it is to say that *it is scarcely perceptible*

in the transfiguration. It is assumed that the saints will carry a *personal recollection* with them to heaven, and will therefore know those there, with whom they were acquainted here—husbands and wives, parents and children will remember and know each other as such; and this is all shown by the fact that Peter, James and John knew Moses and Elias. Well, but this proves too much, and that which proves too much proves nothing at all. It is certain that the apostles had never seen Moses, and if Elias of the transfiguration was the old Jewish prophet, Elijah, then it is certain they had never seen him; hence, no recollection of personality could have enabled the apostles to recognize them. If this proves any thing, it proves that if we get to heaven, we shall know every one there, whether we knew them before or not. We will know Abel, Noah, Abraham, and Lot, just as well at first sight as we will know our mothers. Does any one believe this? Hardly, we guess. The apostles heard Moses and Elias talking with Jesus. (Matt. xvii: 3. Mark ix: 4. Luke ix: 30.) They talked to him about his crucifixion at Jerusalem; and we think it much more likely that they had knowledge of them by what they heard, than by personal marks of identity which they could not have known otherwise than by inspiration.

(3) Others think the transfiguration designed to teach *three states* of existence for man—(1) the living or earthly state, (2) the dead or intermediate state, and (3) the heavenly or final state; and that the transfiguration furnished a representative of each state—viz: Jesus in the living state; Moses from the dead or intermediate state; and Elijah, who was taken alive to heaven, from the heavenly state.

I once listened to a very fine discourse by a brother

on the "Power of the Word," and after it was done he asked me what I thought of it. I told him I thought it a most excellent discourse, but I was at a loss to see any connection between the *discourse* and the *text* from which he preached it. I could not see how he got the sermon out of the text. I am inclined to admit, nay I *believe* in three such states for the *righteous*, but I am unable to see that the transfiguration was intended to teach it, or that it even incidentally does teach it.

Matthew, Mark and Luke record the transfiguration and not one of them, either directly or remotely, alludes to the *three states* of man. Is not this a little significant? Peter mentions a thrilling announcement which he heard on the "holy mount," and yet he makes no reference to the *three states* taught there. Is it not a little strange that no one of the inspired writers mentions any thing of such a lesson taught in that most wonderful vision? The conclusion comes like a conqueror, that no such thing was seen by them, or some one of them would have mentioned it some where. What right have we to come to such a conclusion when there is not an intimation of it any where?

But was the Elias of the transfiguration the Elijah of the Jewish prophets? If not, he could not have been a representative of the heavenly state in the vision. Were we to concede that he was, it would not authorize the assumption that *he was there as a representative* of the heavenly state, in the absence of any mention of it by those who record the facts concerning it. But let us see how this is:

Elias and Elijah are but different forms of the same name. We concede this to start with. The name Elias of the common version is Elijah of the new version. But this settles not our question—was the *Elijah of the vision the Elijah of the Hebrew prophets?* With one voice the commentators, preachers and writers, great and small, ancient and modern, say *yes;* and in the face of such unanimous authority we fear to say *no;* for an exegesis so hoary with years, and honored with universal acceptance, must be cautiously set aside. This is right—unquestionably right. But it stamps it not with the seal of *infallibility.* However old, and honorable a theory may be, it may still be wrong. We still have the right to think for ourselves, and it is our duty to do so. "Prove all things, and hold fast to that which is good," is still very wholesome advice.

God by the mouth of Malachi said: "Behold, I will send you Elijah the Prophet before the coming of the great and dreadful day of the Lord; and he shall turn the heart of the fathers to the children, and the heart of the children to their fathers, lest I come and smite the earth with a curse." Mal. iv: 5, 6.

Here we find that God said he would send Elijah the prophet, and this was quoted by the angel who announced the birth of John to Zacharias in the temple. "And he shall go before him in the spirit and power of Elias, to turn the hearts of the fathers to the children, and the disobedient to the wisdom of the just; to make ready a people prepared for the Lord." Luke i: 17. Thus we see that *John the Baptist* was *Elijah the prophet* who was to come. After Jesus had sent back the messengers sent to him by John, he said: "And if ye will receive it, this is Elias [new version, Elijah] which was for to come." Matt. xi: 14.

After the transfiguration, " as they came down from the mountain, Jesus charged them, saying, Tell the vision to no man till the Son of man be risen from the dead." Please note the fact that the *vision* is the subject of their conversation—" tell the vision to no man," etc. And they are coming right down the mountain from where it had occurred but a short time before. What could be more natural than that they, so soon, should think and talk of little else? " And his disciples asked him, saying, Why then say the scribes that Elias [Elijah] must first come?' And Jesus answered and said unto them, Elias [Elijah] truly shall first come, and restore all things. But I say unto you, That Elias [Elijah] is come already, and they knew him not, but have done unto him whatsoever they listed. Likewise shall also the Son of man suffer of them. Then the disciples understood that he spake unto them of John the Baptist." Matt. xvii : 10–13.

Now how are we to conclude that the Elijah of this conversation about the vision, so soon after its occurrence, was a different person from the Elijah seen in the vision, without a single intimation of any change of thought with reference to the persons spoken of? Without this conversation we might be left in doubt as to which Elijah was seen in the vision; but with this conversation it looks to us like the matter was settled —clearly settled.

Now we have learned that John the Baptist was Elijah the prophet, that God, by Malachi, said he would send—we have learned that John the Baptist was to come in the spirit and power of Elijah—we have learned that John the Baptist was the Elijah that was to come, and John the Baptist was the Elijah that had come; and we have learned that John the Baptist was the Elijah that was put to death by the wicked, as Jesus was to be put to death in the near future; and much of this we have learned from a *conversation about the vision between Christ and those who witnessed it.* Then how are we to know that John the Baptist was not the Elijah seen in the transfiguration? Is there a single intimation forbidding it? We think not. *Then why should the connection be broken to make it refer to the old Jewish prophet?* We confess we are unable to see a reason for it, and therefore cannot teach it.

We have not forgotten that when John was baptizing the people, the Jews asked him if he were Elijah and he said he was not. This, of course, was understood by him to refer to the old Jewish prophet; otherwise we bring him and Jesus into contradiction of each other, for Jesus said John was the Elijah that was to come. This shows that the prophecies concerning the coming of Elijah in the person of John the Baptist were not understood by the Jews, nor perhaps by John himself at that time.

But we are told that Moses appeared in the transfiguration as the Jewish law-giver, and Elijah as a representative of the Jewish prophets. This is pure and unadulterated *assumption*—nothing else. Where is the proof that Elijah appeared in the vision as a *representative* of the Jewish prophets? I have read nothing from any one who attempted to prove it. And had a prophet been desirable to complete the vision, Jesus said: "Among those that are born of women there is not a greater prophet than John the Baptist." Luke vii: 28. It is not necessary to tell us that his greatness was not as a prophet—Jesus said there is *not a greater prophet* than John the Baptist—that settles that point with us. If the object had been a representative prophet, would not John have filled this demand, as there had never been a greater prophet born of women than was he? He was not only a prophet, but he was greater than a prophet. Matt. ii: 9. He was to prepare the way of the Lord before him. He was to give knowledge of salvation to his people by the remission of their sins. Hence he was the law-giver through whom the law of pardon was proclaimed in that preparatory work. His conception was as much a miracle as was that of Jesus himself. But it is denied that he was a law-giver, because we no where read of the *law of John.* What constitutes a law-giver? What made Moses a law-giver? Did he proclaim his own laws, or God's laws? He was a law-giver only in that he was the person through whom God gave laws to be observed by the people. Did not John give the law of pardon to those to whom he gave knowledge of salvation by the remission of their sins? It was not his law, but God's law given through him. He preached faith, repentance, and baptism; and the baptism he preached was for the remission of sins, and *he was the first that ever did preach it on this earth* of whom we know any thing, or can know any thing.

But it is said, "His preaching of repentance and its consequents were substantially Old Testament ideas." By this we suppose we are to understand that John learned what he preached from the Old Testament, perhaps the law of Moses. We respectfully suggest that *John's ministry was no part of Judaism.* Why bring John into the world by special miracle, of parents who were past age, and fill him with the Holy Spirit from birth, and send him forth on *a special God-appointed mission* to preach "Old Testament ideas" that any Jewish priest would have been abundantly competent to do? John was directly sent of God. John i: 6, 33. Mal. iii: 1. iv: 5.

But our reviewer says: "He could not have been preeminent in this office, certainly, without a hint, at least, of it in the gospels." O yes, my brother, that is the easiest thing imaginable. Don't you see how easy it is to break the connection between *Elijah in the conversation about the vision, and Elijah in the vision* right in the same chapter without even a hint or intimation about it in the whole connection? Not even one hint.

But our reviewer speaking of John says: "He truly added baptism; but it may be questioned whether this was not in too close a connection with the coming Lord, to whom he pointed, to distinguish John as a lawgiver." Now we are not very sure we catch the thought here. Does he mean that John was in close connection with the coming Lord and therefore got what he preached from him, hence was not a law-giver himself? If this is not the thought in it, we can see no point in it at all. If this is the thought, we suggest that John was sent *before the L*ord to prepare a people for him —to make his paths straight—to bear witness of the light that all men through him might believe.

But so far as my point is concerned, it matters not whether we call John a *law-giver or a teacher.* One thing is certain: Peter wanted to stay there and take lessons from them or be instructed by them, and this called forth the exaltation of the Son—*hear him.*

Then may not this be the thought? In the vision the three great law givers: Moses, the giver of the Jewish law; John, the Elijah that was to come, through whom the law of pardon, or remission of sins was given in preparing a people for the Lord; and Jesus, the great law-giver under the new and better covenant. Peter proposed to make tents and stay there to take lessons of, or be instructed by all of them; but God lets him know that the time to hear Moses and John has passed —this is my Son, honor him. He it is that was to be raised up like unto Moses, to whom all should hearken—"*hear him.*"

This certainly was the leading thought in the lesson. It was certainly not to convince Peter, James and John that Jesus was the Son of God, for they knew this before. In answer to a question put by Jesus to the disciples, six days before the transfiguration, Peter said: "Thou art the Christ, the Son of the living God." Matt. xvi: 16. And Jesus said this had been revealed to them by the Father in heaven. When the Father made him manifest to Israel at his baptism, he said: "This is my beloved Son in whom I am well pleased."

At the transfiguration he used the same words: "This is my beloved Son, in whom I am well pleased;" adding, "hear ye him." Why was this supplement made to the words used before? If the announcement had been made to confirm his divine character only, surely the language used at his baptism would have been quite sufficient. Is there not significance in the fact that this announcement was not made until Peter proposed to make three tents—one each for the three distinguished persons seen in the vision? Does it not seem that Peter reasoned something like we suggested before: "Lord, how fortunate it is to be here under such favorable circumstances; if it please thee, let us make tents and stay here, that we may sit at the feet of these great lawgivers, or teachers, and take lessons of heavenly wisdom from all ot them?" This proposition called forth the wonderful announcement: "This is my beloved Son, in whom I am well pleased; hear ye him." The language used at his baptism would not have conveyed the lesson intended here. It would have given assurance of his divine character, but this the disciples had before. Peter had proposed to stay there and take lessons from these three great teachers—Moses, Elijah, and Jesus. God answered: "This is my beloved Son, in whom I am well pleased; hear ye him." As much as to say, Moses and Elijah were persons through whom I gave law to the people in time past, and it was right to hear them then; but my Son is the law-giver now—*hear him.* Thus God honored his Son above Moses and Elijah, and being above *them,* it may be assumed that he was honored above all through whom God had ever spoken to man before.

Peter says: "For we have not followed cunningly devised fables, when we made known unto you the power and coming of our Lord Jesus Christ, but were eye witnesses of his majesty. For he received from God the Father honor and glory, when there came such a voice to him from the excellent glory, This is my beloved Son, in whom I am well pleased. And this voice which came from heaven we heard, when we were with him in the holy mount." 2 Pet. i: 16–18.

Perhaps there was never a grander exhibition of majesty, glory, and honor bestowed by the Father on the Son than was connected with this transfiguration. His raiment was as white as snow, whiter than any fuller on earth could make it, and his face shone as the sun in the glory of its light at mid-day. No human face ever glowed in light sublime as that which sat on the face of Jesus as it reflected the glory of the ever blessed Father in that transfiguration. A bright cloud overshadowed them. Not a cloud like that which enveloped Mount Sinai in fire, which burned in blackness, darkness, and a tempest, until even Moses feared and quaked exceedingly; but it was a *bright cloud,* lighted up by the glory of God, from the midst of which he proclaimed the majesty of his Son, and the supremacy of his law, even over those who were permitted to appear with him in this most wonderful transfiguration. This was the grandest trio ever seen by mortal eyes on this earth; but God declared the right of his Son to reign above the other two—"*hear ye him.*" This is *the* lesson of the transfiguration. What else may be incidentally taught in it matters not. *This is taught beyond dispute.* We are not dependent on far-fetched inference, and imaginary platitudes, but we have it coming in clear and unmistakable utterances fresh from heaven—*hear ye him.*

Though we were to admit a thousand times that the Elijah of the vision was the old Jewish prophet it would not hush to silence the voice that came from heaven, saying, "This is my beloved Son, in whom I am well pleased—*hear ye him.*"

Now, are we ready to hear him? Or are we ready to follow him as long as he *leads where we want to go?* We cannot go with him in that way. We must hear him all the way of our journey through life. There are no collisions when he conducts the train. The waves of life's tempestuous ocean are harmless when he commands the ship on which we sail. He is our all in all. Without him we can do nothing; with him we can do much. Let us hear him. Let us obey every command coming from him. This is hearing him— less than this is not hearing him. When temptations, trials, and troubles come, let us lay our hand in his, and trust his gentle care, and all will be well. He never forsakes those who confidingly put their trust in him.

"By and by we shall meet him,
By and by we shall greet him,
And with Jesus reign in glory by and by."

Some suppose that the transfiguration was designed

to give us an idea of the grandeur and glory that will characterize the person of the redeemed in heaven. It is not easy to see how persons can believe this, and at the same time believe that Elijah of the transfiguration was the old Jewish prophet. If their theory be true, *he* was fresh from heaven and *his appearance* might have been expected to represent the appearance of those in that state: and yet there was nothing unusual in his appearance at all. If Moses or Elijah was transfigured or in any way changed in appearance, the record fails to give an account of it; hence their appearance can furnish no idea of the appearance of the immortalized in heaven or elsewhere.

But is this taught in the transfiguration? If so, the apostles who witnessed it failed to find it out. John says: "Beloved, now are we the sons of God, and it doth not yet appear what we shall be; but we know that, when he shall appear, we shall be like him, for we shall see him as he is." 1 John iii: 2. How could John have said this if the transfiguration had shown him what we shall be? If the appearance of Jesus in the transfiguration was to be the appearance of the redeemed in heaven, it would be quite as easy to describe what that appearance will be as to describe the appearance of Jesus in the vision; hence as John did not know what likeness the saints would wear in heaven, it is certain that no such lesson was taught in the transfiguration witnessed by him. This is plain enough.

In the vanity of poor fallen humanity we can scarcely restrain the wish that such a lesson were taught, but when we realize our unworthiness, we feel that *if we may but get there*, we would be willing to sit in ashes at the feet of the dear Savior, clothed in sack cloth for ever. Oh, let us get there! Dear, blessed Savior, may we be among the redeemed, to see and live with thee in glory on any terms. Grand and sublime thought—we shall see Jesus as he is, and be like him; be among those who have washed their robes and made them white in his most precious blood. This will be glory enough for us.

> "I am weary, I'm fainting, my day's work is done,
> I am watching, I'm waiting for life's setting sun,
> The shadows are stretching far o'er the lea;
> Then, oh, let me anchor beyond the dark sea!"

CHAPTER XII.

PAUL'S CHARGE TO TIMOTHY.

"I charge thee therefore before God, and the Lord Jesus Christ, who shall judge the quick and the dead at his appearing and his kingdom; preach the word; be instant in season, out of season; reprove, rebuke, exhort with all longsuffering and doctrine. For the time will come when they will not endure sound doctrine; but after their own lusts shall they heap to themselves teachers, having itching ears; and they shall turn away their ears from the truth, and shall be turned unto fables." 2 Tim. iv: 1-4.

IS it possible that the time of which Paul spoke has come, as he said it would? Is it true that in this boasted age of enlightenment, men will not endure sound doctrine? Do you not often hear men say, "I do wish he would quit preaching about baptism. I never go to preaching without hearing baptism! baptism!! baptism!!! I am sick and tired of hearing it?" Well, my brother, you would best not read the New Testament, for if you do you might find Jesus saying: "He that believeth and is baptized shall be saved." And you might find where Peter, in his very first discourse under the great commission, commanded the people to "repent and be baptized in the name of Jesus Christ for the remission of sins;" and it would be awful if you should open his letter to his brethren and find him saying "baptism doth also now save us." And you might find where Paul says, "as many of you as have been baptized into Christ have put on Christ." Or, "buried with him in baptism wherein ye are also risen with him." Thus you see, my dear sir, the only safe way is to not read the New Testament at all; for if you do, you may blunder right on the nauseating word and be kept sick all the time. And you must lecture your preachers until they learn better manners, and can quote the commission in good modern style: "He that believeth, etc., shall be saved;" or, "he that believes and obeys the gospel shall be saved." Many preachers have learned this style already, and if you will let your preacher know that you cannot endure sound doctrine, he may learn to feed you on fables, and tickle your itching ears with nice little half-hour speeches exactly suited to your taste.

Preachers are not so dull as to be unable to learn that half-hour discourses are much more easily prepared and delivered than discourses of an hour or more in length. There is not a field hand in all the country that does not know that a half hour's work is more easily done than an hour's work. There is another advantage, too, in half-hour sermons. When a preacher has to preach to the same congregation for a number of years, if he cuts up what he knows into small sermons, having only one or two thoughts in each, the balance in nice filling, he will be able to make his stock go much further than if he prunes out all surplus drapery and puts in discourses of an hour or more, filled with solid shot throughout. Oh, but he who makes short discourses learns to consolidate his thoughts and say more in less time. Such has not been our observation. These half-hour speeches are made up of flowers designed to tickle the itching ear, and, as a rule, have nothing solid in them. The man who has something to say is the one who consolidates. He knows he can discuss no important subject thoroughly in half an hour, and if he wishes to teach the people he selects subjects that have something in them worth preaching, and he has no use for surplus words, or redundant verbiage just to fill up, or embellish his sermons. We have no objection to elegance of style, but we are more concerned about *what* is said than about elegance of expression. We would rather have *sound doctrine* plainly and forcibly expressed, than to have the ears tickled with a straw.

"But we are tired of so much doctrine. I do wish you would quit preaching doctrinal sermons and give us something pretty." Well, dessert is very nice with which to close out a meal, but it does not do very well to live on, or even to make one entire meal. The most substantial food is very nice when well served up; so the most substantial doctrine may be beautifully told; and viewed from different standpoints, may furnish very great variety, too. And what is more touchingly sublime than the melting story of the cross? It is ever new, and never grows old. It is food on which the hungry soul never cloys—food of which it never gets enough. As the poet has well said, so the hungry soul ever says,

"Sing them over again to me,
Wonderful words of life;
Let me more of their beauty see,
Wonderful words of life.
Words of life and beauty,
Teach me faith and duty,
Beautiful words, wonderful words,
Wonderful words of life."

Paul told Timothy to "take heed to thyself and unto the doctrine, continue in them; for in doing this thou shalt both save thyself, and them that hear thee." 1 Tim. iv: 16. The inference is very clear that if he failed to thus take heed, he would neither save himself nor those who heard him. But my brother, will you remember that while you understand the gospel, and need not that it be preached to you, there was a time when you did not understand it; and had it not been preached to you, it is possible you might not have understood it yet. Thousands of your neighbors and neighbors' children are just in the condition you were in before you learned it; and if they are ever saved by it, they will have to learn it as you did. Those who heard it before you, were anxious that you should hear it, and be saved by it, as they had been. Then as you have heard it, and been saved by it, you should never grow weary in hearing it proclaimed to others. Should you not rather

> "Shout the tidings of salvation,
> To the aged and the young;
> 'Till the precious invitation
> Waken ev'ry heart and tongue.
> Send the sound, the earth around,
> From the rising to the setting of the sun;
> 'Till each gathering crowd, shall proclaim aloud,
> The glorious work is done."

Never was there a more solemn charge clothed in human language, or uttered by mortal tongue, than Paul gave Timothy in the opening of our text. "I charge thee therefore before God, and the Lord Jesus Christ, who shall judge the quick and the dead at his appearing and his kingdom; preach the word." And why preach the word? Because in so doing he might both save himself and those that heard him. "And this is the word which by the gospel is preached unto you." 1 Pet. i: 25. Then when the word is preached, the gospel is preached; and when the gospel is preached the word is preached. We cannot believe in him of whom we have not heard; and we cannot hear without a preacher; "so then faith cometh by hearing, and hearing by the word of God." Rom. x: 17. "Without faith it is impossible to please him." Heb. xi: 6. As we cannot please God in any thing without faith; and as faith comes by hearing the word of God, we see the importance of Paul's charge to Timothy to preach the word. If it was so important to preach *the word* then, is it any less important to preach *the word* now? Again Paul said: "The things that thou hast heard of me among many witnesses, the same commit thou to faithful men, who shall be able to teach others also." 2 Tim. ii: 2. This shows that the things taught by Paul to Timothy were to be perpetuated through all time; hence it is as important that the word be preached to-day as it was when Paul so solemnly charged Timothy to preach it.

Paul says: "I am ready to preach the gospel to you that are at Rome also; for I am not ashamed of the gospel of Christ; for it is the power of God unto salvation to every one that believeth." Rom. i: 15, 16. So then the gospel is the power of God unto salvation! Yes *the* power, not *a* power, *one* of the powers, or *some* power, but *the* power. This implies that there is no power *beside, above, or beyond* the gospel by which God proposes to save man. But ample as may be the power which God has placed in the gospel, he proposes to save only those who believe it. "He that believeth not shall be damned." If he will not believe the gospel he cannot be saved by it; and as it is *the* power of God to salvation, if he is not saved by it, he cannot be saved at all, and will be lost without remedy.

In the parable of the sower we learn that if any casualty happened to the seed there was no crop produced. We learn also that the sower sowed the word, and that the word was the seed of the kingdom. And as the farmer can have no crop without seed are sown, so there can be no spiritual crop without the word, or seed of the kingdom in the hearts of men; hence the necessity of *preaching the word.* No seed, no crop—no word preached, no Christians made. One result is just as certain as the other.

In no land on which the sun shines to-day, can a Christian be found where the word of God has not gone. Where the rays of gospel light have never shone, there ignorance and superstition cover the earth, and gross spiritual darkness hangs like a black pall of night over the people. Were it possible to banish the word of God, and every recollection of every thing learned from it, from this fair land of ours, as complete spiritual darkness would envelop our country as physical darkness would cover the earth were the sun, our only source of physical light, blown out of existence, as we extinguish a candle or a lamp. Well hath David said: "Thy testimonies are wonderful; therefore doth my soul keep them. The entrance of thy words giveth light; it giveth understanding unto the simple." Ps. cxix: 129, 130. "Thy word is a lamp unto my feet, and a light unto my path." verse 105.

Jesus said: "As long as I am in the world, I am the light of the world." John ix: 5. Again: "I am the light of the world; he that followeth me shall not walk in darkness, but shall have the light of life." John viii: 12. If Jesus is the light of the world, where he is not preached there is no light. He that followed him had the light of life. But how can we follow him? Thy word is a lamp to my feet, and a light unto my path.

But he said he was the light of the world as long as he was in the world. Yes, and while in the world he prepared a light to shine after he left it. Addressing his disciples he said: "Ye are the light of the world." Matt. v: 14. In his prayer to his Father he said: "I have given unto them the words which thou gavest me, and they have received them." John xvii: 8. "Neither pray I for these alone, but for them also which shall believe on me through their word." verse 20. Thus we see that Jesus gave the words he received of his Father, to the apostles, and he prayed for those who believed on him through their words. On one occasion when many of the disciples had left the Master, he said to the twelve: "Will ye also go away? Then Simon Peter answered him, Lord to whom shall we go? Thou hast the words of eternal life." John vi: 67, 68.

The words that Jesus had, were the *words of eternal life*. He received them of his Father, and gave them to his apostles, and commissioned them to preach these *words of eternal life* to every creature in all the world. Thus Jesus was the light of the world, and the disciples were the light of the world as they proclaimed the *words of eternal life* to the world. Before leaving the world, Jesus perfected every thing, and charged the apostles to *preach the word;* and Paul charged Timothy to *preach the word*, and commit it to faithful men who might be able to teach others; and so the charge comes to us, *preach the word*, and this is the word which by the gospel is preached unto you.

But we are told that no country has ever been found where the people did not worship something; and hence no country can be found where the Holy Spirit has not taught the people the necessity of worship. Without stopping, for the present, to deny that the idea of worship exists every where, let us ask; if the Holy Spirit taught them the necessity of worship why did it fail to teach them *what* to worship, and how to worship him? Why did the Holy Spirit teach them the *necessity* or duty of worship and leave them in *idolatry* to worship any and every thing of which their imagination could conceive? This is not like the Holy Spirit of which we read in the New Testament. Here we find that the comforter was to guide the taught into *all truth*; but there the heathens were only taught the duty of worshiping without a knowledge of *whom* to worship or *how* to worship him. Now I respectfully suggest that the Holy Spirit does *no such imperfect work as this*. It is all a myth. There is not a word of truth in it. *No word of God—no spiritual light*, is just as certain as it is that the farmer can have no crop where he sows no seed. If the Holy Spirit operates on the heart of men and women *without the word*, where the word is in every house, why does it not make Christians in heathen lands where the word has never gone? And if the Holy Spirit does so operate without the word here, or there; then of what use is the word? Why shall we worry ourselves to preach it where it is, or send it where it is not, if men and women may be converted without it as well as with it?

But is there not a more rational way of accounting for a disposition in heathen lands to worship something, than by supposing that the Holy Spirit taught them the necessity of worship, and then left them without teaching them *how*, and *what* to worship? Paul says. "Have they not all heard? Yes verily, their sound went into all the earth, and their words unto the ends of the world." Rom. x: 18. And again: "If ye continue in the faith grounded and settled, and be not moved away from the hope of the gospel, which was preached to every creature under heaven." Col. i: 23. Here we learn that there was a time when all nations had the gospel; and hence not only knew the necessity of worship, but they knew the true God, and *how* to worship him according to the gospel.

Why, then, are they now without a knowledge of God and the true worship? "Because that, when they knew God, they glorified him not as God, neither were thankful; but became vain in their imaginations, and their foolish heart was darkened. Professing themselves to be wise, they became fools, and changed the glory of the uncorruptible God into an image made like to corruptible man, and to birds, and fourfooted beasts, and creeping things." Rom. i: 21-23.

Here we find that when they knew God, they glorified him not as God, but voluntarily went into idolatry, worshiping images of men, birds, and beasts. In the course of ages they forgot God and the true worship. Those who had the knowledge of God, all ceased to worship him in some countries; and their children and grand children, seeing nothing but *image worship*, naturally enough fell into that kind of worship; and hence the idea of their worship came, not from the Holy Spirit, but from the *tradition of the fathers*, first derived from the true worship, then corrupted as we have seen, and perpetuated through tradition. David says: "The wicked shall be turned into hell, and all the nations that forget God." Ps. ix: 17. Here David speaks of nations *forgetting God;* and they could not forget that which they never knew. Hence only such nations as once had a knowledge of God, could forget him. Thus we account for a disposition to worship among the heathens.

The word of the Lord, or gospel of Jesus Christ, is able to do for man every thing necessary to his conversion, sanctification, and final happiness that he can desire. Does the sinner need conversion? "The law of the Lord is perfect, converting the soul." Ps. xix: 7. The soul is that which needs conversion; and the law of the Lord is perfect in the performance of this very work. That which is *perfect* cannot be improved. If the law of the Lord needs any outside touch, or additional influence to apply it, or make it effective then it is not perfect. David said it was *perfect*, and not only perfect, but perfect in this matter of converting the soul. In this work then, it needs no supplement—none whatever.

If the sinner needs *faith*, the word of the Lord tells him what it is, how it comes, and what it does. If he has not repented, it tells him to *repent*, and if he fails to repent, he will surely perish. If he has not *confessed* his faith in Christ, from the word of the Lord he can learn what to confess, and how to confess it. If he has not been *baptized*, the word of the Lord tells him how he must be baptized, and what he must be baptized for. If he has arisen to walk in the newness of life, the word of the Lord meets his wants in all the relations and conditions of life, and thoroughly furnishes him to every good work.

If he has a hard and unfeeling heart: "Is not my word like as a fire? saith the Lord; and like as a hammer that breaketh the rock in pieces." Jer. xxiii: 29. As the *fire* and the *hammer* break the hardest rock in pieces, so will the word of the Lord mellow, subdue, and subjugate the hardest heart that listens to its teaching; and he who will not hear, cannot believe, and therefore cannot be saved.

Do you want *sanctification*? Jesus prayed to his Father for the sanctification of his disciples; and how did he pray that it be done? "Sanctify them through thy truth; thy word is truth. As thou hast sent me into the world, even so have I sent them into the world; and for their sakes I sanctify myself, that they also might be sanctified through the truth." John xvii: 17–19. The *word* was the *truth* through which he expected the Father to sanctify his disciples. Paul says: "Husbands love your wives even as Christ also loved the church, and gave himself for it; that he might sanctify and cleanse it with the washing of water by the word." Eph. v: 25, 26. Sanctification and cleansing are here connected, and are accomplished as taught by the word. Jesus said: "Ye are clean through the word which I have spoken unto you." John xv: 3. Then both sanctification and cleansing are to be accomplished by the word, and this simply means as taught in or by the word. Thus we see how the gospel saves men.

If you want *salvation* Jesus tells you in the commission how to be saved; and the angel told Cornelius to "send for Simon whose surname is Peter, who shall tell thee words whereby thou and all thy house shall be saved." Acts xi: 13, 14. "Men and brethren, children of the stock of Abraham, and whosoever among you feareth God, to you is the word of this salvation sent." Acts xiii: 26. And James exhorts his brethren to "receive with meekness the engrafted word which is able to save your souls." Jas. i: 21. Other passages might be quoted, but these are enough to show that the way of salvation is clearly revealed in the word of the Lord, and by its teaching we must be saved, if saved at all.

If you are hungering for the grace of God, "I commend you to God and to the *word of his grace*, which is able to build you up, and to give you an inheritance among all them which are sanctified." Acts xx: 32.

If you want to be reconciled to God, you must remember that *you are the party* to be reconciled. "And all things are of God, who hath reconciled us to himself by Jesus Christ, and hath given to us the ministry of reconciliation: to wit, that God was in Christ, reconciling the world unto himself, not imputing their trespasses unto them; and hath committed unto us the word of reconciliation." 2 Cor. v: 18, 19. There is no use of begging God to be reconciled to you. The *word of reconciliation* was given to the apostles, and when you will comply with the terms of reconciliation you will be reconciled.

If you would make good soldiers of the cross you must " put on the whole armor of God, that ye may be able to stand against the wiles of the devil. For we wrestle not against flesh and blood, but against principalities, against powers, against the rulers of the darkness of this world, against spiritual wickedness in high places. Wherefore take unto you the whole armor of God, that ye may be able to withstand in the evil day, and having done all, to stand. Stand therefore, having your loins girt about with truth, and having on the breastplate of righteousness; and your feet shod with the preparation of the gospel of peace; Above all, taking the shield of faith, wherewith ye shall be able to quench all the fiery darts of the wicked. And take the helmet of salvation, and the sword of the Spirit, which is the word of God." Eph. vi: 11–17.

By close observation you will find that every part of this armor of God is provided in his word; and the sword of the Spirit with which the Christian soldier is to fight the battles of the Lord, is the *word of God itself.* Please notice that while this is the sword of the Spirit, the Christian soldier is the party that is to use it. You need not wait for the Spirit to use it, but use it yourself. My Christian brother, are you clad in God's armor? and are you using the sword of the Spirit in fighting the battles of the Lord? If not, are you doing your duty in the cause of the Master? If you cannot preach the word yourself, can you not support some one else who can? How do you expect to pass roll-call in the great day, having done nothing? The most worthless soldier of whom we can conceive is the mere hanger-on, who does nothing but *eat the rations* of those who do the fighting. Better that such were in the camp of the enemy subsisting on his commissaries, than be doing nothing for the Master but consume his substance. Go over and draw rations from the stores of the devil, and leave your rations for your brethren, who are doing service for the Lord. You will weaken the enemy that much and do less harm at home.

"According as his divine power hath given unto us all things that pertain unto life and godliness through the [revealed] knowledge of him that hath called us to glory and virtue." 2 Pet. i: 3. *God's revealed knowledge constitutes his word,* in which are given to us all things that pertain to life and godliness. Then what more can we ask or desire? Not *some things,* but *all things* which pertain to life and godliness are given to us through God's revelation, or word. Surely this is enough.

But Timothy was not only to preach the *word* to the sinner, but he was to *reprove* the wayward, *rebuke* the persistently rebellious, and *exhort* the negligent. It is not enough to become Christians, but we must live so that our natures will be so transformed as to be assimilated to the pure and holy with whom we are to associate in heaven. The church is a school in which we are to be trained and fitted for association with God, angels, and purified spirits in a higher state of existence than this.

Many seem to be going through this life as though they believed it to be the end of existence. They seem to dream of nothing beyond the grave; and hence they seek to make the most of this life, which its opportunities afford, in order to promote carnal pleasures only.

> "This world can never give,
> The bliss for which we sigh;
> 'Tis not the whole of life to live,
> Nor all of death to die.
> Beyond this vale of tears,
> There is a life above;
> Unmeasured by the flight of years,
> And all that life is love."

The religion of the Bible was intended to prune off the excrescences of our nature, and develop those Godlike attributes that make us partakers of the *divine nature*, so that we shall be prepared to enjoy heaven when we get there. If a man, fresh from the haunts of wickedness, be placed in the company of the pure and holy of earth, where their habits of thought and subjects of conversation are wholly unlike those with whom he has been accustomed to associate, he cannot be happy, because he cannot partake of their spirit, nor enter into their sources of enjoyment; hence he will withdraw at the earliest practicable moment, and seek company congenial to his feelings and habits of life. So if it were possible to transfer the wicked from earth to heaven, with all his depraved appetites and passions clinging to him, it would be a place of misery, rather than a place of happiness to him. His nature is not assimilated to the nature of those with whom he would have to associate, and he could not be happy. To enjoy heaven, then, we must be made partakers of the *divine nature,* like the nature of those with whom we must associate when we get there.

In the revealed knowledge of God " are given unto us exceeding great and precious promises; that by these ye might be partakers of the divine nature." 2 Pet. i: 4. Who can contemplate the exceeding great and precious promises made by our Father in his ever blessed word without partaking of the nature of him who made the promises? We are promised remission of sins and the gift of the Holy Spirit in obedience to the gospel. He has promised to be with us in our temptations and trials, and that he will not allow us to be tempted beyond our ability to bear; but in every trial he will make a way for our escape, and bring us off more than conquerors through him that loved us and gave himself for us. He has promised to go with us through the dark valley and shadow of death; and that he will not forget us in the tomb, but will bring us up to live again, if worthy, in the glorified image of his Son. He has promised that if we are faithful and do his commandments, we shall at last enter through the gates into the city, where God is, where Jesus is, where angels are, and where the spirits of just men made perfect will ever be, and that we shall there be permitted to bask in the sunny smiles of his love for ever and ever. Nor is this all : he has promised that we shall there be restored to the tree of life from which our parents were driven; and that we shall be permitted to pluck and eat of its lifegiving fruit, beyond the reach of temptation, disease and death ; hat we shall there be permitted to drink of the stream of life that gurgles from beneath the throne, of which he that drinks shall thirst no more; and that there we shall, with tongues immortal, engage in singing a new song to God and to the Lamb, with angels around the eternal throne, in sweeter strains than mortal tongues have ever made. Well hath the poet said:

> "The Bible reveals a glorious land,
> Where angels and purified spirits dwell,
> Where pleasures ne'er end, at God's right hand,
> And anthems of praises for ever swell.
> Outgushing beneath the throne of God,
> And of the blest Lamb at his right hand,
> Thence runneth the crystal stream of life,
> A fountain of joy in that glorious land.
> In th' midst of the street on either side,
> The tree of life, arching the way, o'ershades,
> With health-giving foliage far and wide,
> No sickness this glorious land invades.
> Twelve manner of fruits hang pendent there,
> And they who partake shall never die:
> With Jesus they dwell, and ever share
> The joys of that glorious land on high."

CHAPTER XIII.

A REASON FOR THE CHRISTIAN'S HOPE.

"But sanctify the Lord God in your hearts: and be ready always to give an answer to every man that asketh you a reason of the hope that is in you with meekness and fear." 1 Pet. iii: 15.

ALL Christians are expected to have a hope, and they should be able to give a reason for it when asked to do so. They are not expected to proclaim it on the house top and from the street corners as a thing of which to boast; but when respectfully asked for it, they are expected to be able to give a reason for the hope that is in them, in that spirit of humility that should ever characterize the meek and humble followers of the Lord.

It is true they are admonished to "earnestly contend for the faith which was once delivered to the saints;" (Jude 3.) but there is a *time*, *place*, and *manner* of doing this, so as to have a salutary influence upon those to whom the reason is given; and if not given in this way and under proper circumstances, our reason may do more harm than good, however scriptural the matter of it may be. Arrogant street-corner disputations on religious subjects, are always of doubtful propriety, to say the least of them. But while this is true, it is also true that we are to be always ready to give a reason for the hope within us, when asked for it. And please note the fact that we are not only to *be ready*, but we are to *be always ready* to give every man—yes, not some men, but *every man that asks us.* To do this requires intelligence, and more thought than is sometimes given to this very important subject. We think it likely that the word *hope* is about as badly abused by unscriptural usage as any word in the Bible. If a man be asked whether or not he is a Christian, he is likely to answer, "I *hope* I am." Have you got religion? "I *hope* I have." Such expressions are very often heard; but they betray an inexcusable ignorance of Bible teaching on the whole subject. And this ignorance is frequently seen as plainly in the one who asks the question, as in those who answer it.

A man cannot hope he *has* any thing, or that he *is* any thing. *Hope* always looks ahead to something future. It includes both *desire* and *expectation*. We cannot hope for any thing unless we both *desire* and *expect* that thing. The apostle says. "For we are saved by hope; but hope that is seen is not hope; for what a man seeth why doth he yet hope for? but if we hope for that we see not, then do we with patience wait for it." Rom. viii : 24, 25.

Desire looks ahead, so does *expectation*. We do not either *desire* or *expect* that which we already have. We must both *desire* and *expect* a thing before we can *hope* for it. We all expect to die, but *we do not hope to die*, because we do not *desire* to die. Most persons cling to life as long as they can. While we may hope to go to heaven when we die, yet we do not *hope* to die at all; but would linger on the shores of time, in vigorous manhood, forever if we could.

All good men desire the salvation and final happiness of *all men*; but we do not *hope* for the salvation of all men, because we do not *expect* it. Believing the Bible, we cannot expect it; therefore, however much we may desire it, we cannot hope for it. Expectation is *absent*, and without it there cannot be hope.

While the *elements* of hope (desire and expectation) are ever the same, the objects of hope may be very different. The sick may hope for health. The poor may hope for wealth. The obscure may hope for fame. Even the wicked may hope to be saved; for they think they will quit their wickedness after awhile, and as they desire salvation they hope to be saved at last. Job said: "What is the hope of the hypocrite when God taketh away his soul." Job xxvii : 8. Solomon says: "When a wicked man dieth his expectation shall perish; and the hope of unjust men perisheth." Prov. xi : 7. But no one of these is the hope for which the Christian is to give a reason.

Our text was addressed to such as had been begotten again unto a lively hope by the resurrection of Jesus Christ from the dead, to an inheritance incorruptible and undefiled, and that fadeth not away, reserved in heaven for them. 1 Pet. i : 3, 4. Their hopes were *not that they were Christians—not that they had religion*, but that they should finally come to the enjoyment of an eternal inheritance which was reserved in heaven for them. This they both *expected* and *desired*, and hence it was truly said they *hoped* for it. This is plain enough.

The writer of the letter to the Hebrews said: "And we desire that every one of you do show the same diligence to the full assurance of hope unto the end; that ye be not slothful, but followers of them who through faith and patience inherit the promises. * * * That by two immutable things, in which it was impossible for God to lie, we might have a strong consolation, who have fled for refuge to lay hold on the hope set before us : which hope we have as an anchor of the soul, both sure and steadfast, and which entereth into that within the veil." Heb. vi : 11-19.

Amid our labors, toils, trials, temptations, vexations, disappointments and persecutions, our hope anchors the soul securely in heaven, where Jesus, our forerunner, has gone to prepare a home for us " if we hold fast the confidence and the rejoicing of the hope firm unto the end."

This is the Christian's hope for which he should always be ready to give a reason in meekness and fear, to every man who respectfully asks him for such a reason. My brother have you this hope? and are you always ready to give a satisfactory reason for it?

But in order to give a reason for the Christian's hope within him with meekness and fear, a man must, himself, be a Christian; and we have seen that it is a mistaken use of terms to say " he hopes he is a Christian;" for he cannot hope for that which he has, or is; but if he hopes for that which he has not, then he can with patience wait for it. If he is a Christian he cannot hope to be one, for he is one; and there can be no hoping for what he is; nor can he hope for that which he already has. If he is a Christian, he knows it, and there is no place for hope in that. He cannot expect to be what he already is, and he must both *expect* and *desire* that for which he hopes, otherwise he cannot hope at all; therefore he cannot hope he is a Christian.

He is a Christian or he is not. If he is a Christian, he cannot hope he is one; and if he is not a Christian, he cannot have the Christian's hope within him, and cannot give a reason for a hope within him that is not in him. If he is a Christian, he may hope to remain one, for he may both expect and desire to hold out faithful to the end, " laying up in store for himself a good foundation against the time to come, that he may lay hold on eternal life." 1 Tim. vi : 19.

But we have said that if a man is a Christian, he knows it—how does he know it? This question has been so thoroughly examined in other parts of our work that it need not detain us long here.

To be a Christian we must be *in Christ*. Paul says: "Therefore if any man be in Christ, he is a new creature; old things are passed away; behold, all things are become new." 2 Cor. v : 17. As any one in Christ is a new creature, it follows that those out of Christ are not new creatures. Old things have not all passed away to them; nor have all things to them become new.

Once more: "There is, therefore, now no condemnation to them which are in Christ Jesus, who walk not after the flesh but after the Spirit; for the law of the Spirit of life in Christ Jesus hath made me free from the law of sin and death." Rom. viii : 1, 2. The language, "there is no condemnation to them who are in Christ Jesus," implies that there *is condemnation* to such as are *not in* Christ Jesus. If a man is free from condemnation, he is a pardoned man—a saved man—a justified man—a Christian. He does not *desire*, or *expect*, or *hope* to be free from condemnation, for *there is no condemnation to such a man*. His hopes reach ahead to things future. They never fasten upon old things that have passed away.

Then how do we get into Christ? We will let Paul answer: "Or, are ye ignorant that all we who were baptized into Jesus Christ were baptized into his death? We were buried therefore with him through baptism into death; that like as Christ was raised from the dead through the glory of the Father, so we also might walk in newness of life." Rom. vi : 3, 4. [*New Version.*]

Then when the Romans were baptized they were baptized into Jesus Christ. Their baptism put them into Jesus Christ, and into his death, that is, into the benefits of his death; "in whom we have redemption through his blood, even the forgiveness of sins." Col. i: 14. "Buried with him in baptism, wherein also ye are risen with him through the faith of the operation of God, who hath raised him from the dead. And you, being dead in your sins and the uncircumcision of your flesh, hath he quickened together with him, having forgiven you all trespasses." Col. ii: 12, 13.

They were baptized into Christ, and when raised from their burial with him in baptism they had redemption through his blood, even the forgiveness of sins. They were quickened together with him, and all their trespasses were forgiven. They were new creatures in him, and had the Christian's hope, for which they were always ready to give a reason to every man that asked them for it. Being in Christ, they were new creatures, and could walk in newness of life, for indeed it was a new life to them. Old things had passed away. Their old life was done. They had put off the old man with his deeds, and had put on the new man which was renewed in righteousness; hence to such all things had become new. If you want to be a Christian, and have the Christian's hope, would it not be safe to do as these did who were guided by inspired teachers?

But how did the Galatians get into Christ? "For ye are all the children of God by faith in Christ Jesus." How were they the children of God by faith? "For as many of you as have been baptized into Christ have put on Christ." Then the Galatians got into Christ the same way the Romans did. They were baptized into Christ, and so put him on. If you want all the blessings of the gospel, they are in Christ; hence when you are in him, you are where *every thing is.* You cannot be at a loss to know how to enter into, or put on Christ. Paul wrote to the Romans, Galatians, and Colossians as to what they had done; and he wrote of it as though it was right. If it was right then, is it not right yet? If it saved them, will it not save you, if you do as they did under the same law? If what they did put them into Christ, would it not put you in, if you were to submit to it just as they did? If not, why not? Is there any other way of entering him and being made new creatures? If so, what is it?

But the baptism of the Galatians put them where "there is neither Jew nor Greek, there is neither bond nor free, there is neither male nor female; for ye are all one in Christ Jesus. And if ye be Christ's, then are ye Abraham's seed, and heirs according to the promise." Gal. iii : 28, 29.

Thus we see how the Galatians became children of God by faith. They acted out their faith—perfected it by obedience. Christ said in the commission: "He that believeth and is baptized shall be saved." The Galatians believed, hence had faith; and when they were baptized into Christ, they were baptized into his teaching; and hence put him on, where there was no distinction of classes, but perfect equality among all. By being baptized into Christ, and putting him on, they became his, and Paul says: "If ye be Christ's, then are ye Abraham's seed, and heirs according to the promise." What promise? Certainly the promise which God made to Abraham concerning Christ, in whom all the families of the earth were to be blessed. Is this plain enough?

Now, you are in Christ, or you are not. If you are

in Christ you know it, and know how and when you entered him. There is no place for hope in that part of it. You can likely explain it, and tell all about how you put on Christ. But the hope that is in you goes not backward to that matter, but it goes within the heavenly city. For this hope you can give a reason, if you have the hope.

Though your entrance into Christ, or becoming a Christian, may be the *foundation* of your hope, and must be understood before you can have the hope, *yet it is not the hope* that the Christian has, and for which he is at all times to be ready to give a reason. The hope is one thing and the reason for it quite another thing. Hope rests upon faith in, and obedience to God. These two pillars must rest under and support our hope through life; and if at any time one or both of them be withdrawn, the hope that rested upon them will be destroyed.

We have stated already that in the commission under which the apostles were to operate in converting the nations to God, Jesus said: "He that believeth and is baptized shall be saved." Mark xvi: 16. If you have believed the gospel, you know it. If you have believed in Christ through the gospel, you know it. And if, believing, you were baptized, you know it; unless you have been fearfully deceived by the teaching of men. And if you have believed and been baptized, you know you are saved; for Jesus said, in terms too plain to be misunderstood, that he that believeth and is baptized shall be saved. Now then, if asked whether or not you are a Christian, will you reply "I hope I am?" No sir, where is any room for hope in this process? You are saved, or you are not saved; and you know on which side of the line to place yourself. If you have believed and been baptized, you know you are saved; and if you have believed, but have not been baptized, you know equally well that you *are not saved according to the terms of this commission.*

There is no middle ground about it. You are saved or not saved, and you know very well which. If you are saved, you have the Christian's hope. You do not hope you are a Christian, for this you know, if you have obeyed the gospel. There is no room to hope about that. But if you have obeyed from the heart that form of doctrine which was delivered you, and been made free from sin, then as a Christian, you hope to persevere until death, and be saved in heaven at last. This is the Christian's hope. Paul says: "If in this life only we have hope in Christ, we are of all men most miserable." 1 Cor. xv: 19. Then the Christian's hope reaches beyond this life, in the direction of the future state.

"Then Peter began to say unto him, Lo, we have left all and have followed thee. And Jesus answered and said: verily I say unto you, There is no man that hath left house, or brethren, or sisters, or father, or mother, or wife, or children, or lands, for my sake, and the gospel's, but he shall receive an hundredfold now in this time, houses, and brethren, and sisters, and mothers, and children, and lands, with persecutions, and in the world to come eternal life." Mark x: 28–30.

Now we cannot say we hope for the *persecutions* here promised, for we scarcely *desire* them; and as desire is an indispensable element of hope, we cannot hope without it. But we can hope for eternal life in the world to come. Paul says: "But now being made free from sin, and become servants to God, ye have your fruit unto holiness, and the end everlasting life; for the wages of sin is death: but the gift of God is eternal life through Jesus Christ our Lord." Rom. vi: 22, 23.

There is no looking backward to the time of pardon in the Christian's hope. Though based on pardon, it looks to eternal life.

For this *eternal life* the Christian hopes. Paul clearly intimated as much in his letter to Titus. He says: " Paul, a servant of God, and an apostle of Jesus Christ, according to the faith of God's elect, and the acknowledging of the truth which is after godliness; in hope of eternal life." Titus i: 1, 2.

And again: " For the grace of God that bringeth salvation hath appeared unto all men, teaching us that, denying ungodliness and worldly lusts, we should live soberly, righteously, and godly, in this present world; looking for that blessed hope, and the glorious appearing of the great God and our Savior Jesus Christ; who gave himself for us, that he might redeem us from all iniquity, and purify unto himself a peculiar people, zealous of good works." Titus ii: 11–14. And once more: " That being justified by his grace, we should be made heirs, according to the hope of eternal life." Tit. iii: 7.

These Scriptures teach, very clearly, that *eternal life* is the great object of the Christian's hope. He may hope for other things, but they are all subordinate to, and centered in *eternal life* at last. And we are taught how to live that we may confidently look for a realization of that blessed hope. Being Christians, if we live according to the laws laid down, there need be no fears as to what the end will be. If we deny ourselves of all things wrong, and cultivate only that which is good, the end will be eternal life in heaven.

Jesus says: "Ye shall know them by their fruits." Matt. vii: 16. "I am the vine, ye are the branches.

He that abideth in me, and I in him, the same bringeth forth much fruit, for without me ye can do nothing." John xv : 5.

Here is the rule by which we may know others, and we see not why we may not apply it to ourselves. Paul classifies the fruit for us that we may know the good from the bad fruit. "Now the works of the flesh are manifest, which are these: Adultery, fornication, uncleanness, lasciviousness, idolatry, witchcraft, hatred, variance, emulations, wrath, strife, seditions, heresies, envyings, murders, drunkenness, revelings, and such like." Are you doing these things? Is this the kind of fruit you are bearing? If so, here is what he says of you : " Of the which I forewarn you, even as I did forewarn you, that they which practice such things shall not inherit the kingdom of God." [*Revision.*] This is plain enough; no comment is needed to simplify it. Then he gives the good fruit: "But the fruit of the Spirit is love, joy, peace, longsuffering, gentleness, goodness, faith, meekness, temperance : against such there is no law. And they that are Christ's have crucified the flesh with the affections and lusts. If we live in the Spirit, let us also walk in the Spirit." Gal. v : 19–25. Being in Christ, are you bearing this fruit ? If so, you know it, and if not, you know it. We have already found Paul saying that the servant of God has his fruit unto holiness and the end everlasting life. If you are a child of God, bringing this fruit, you have good reason to hope for eternal life " in the sweet fields of Eden where the tree of life is blooming."

HOW DOES HOPE COME?

On this division of our subject we must be brief—indeed there is no need that we should be otherwise than brief. "For whatsoever things were written aforetime were written for our learning, that we through patience and comfort of the Scriptures might have hope." Rom. xv: 4. The Scriptures were written for our learning, but how much of the Scriptures will he learn who never studies them? By patient study of the Scriptures we learn what God *has done for us*, and what he *proposes to do for us*, and what he *requires of us* in order that we may enjoy the blessings he has *promised* us. When we learn what he requires of us, it is quite easy to decide for ourselves whether we are doing it or not. And if we are doing what he requires us to do, surely we may most confidently hope to enjoy what he has promised us. "We give thanks to God and the Father of our Lord Jesus Christ, praying always for you, since we heard of your faith in Christ Jesus, and of the love which ye have to all the saints, for the hope which is laid up for you in heaven, whereof ye heard before in the word of the truth of the gospel." Col. i: 3–5. "If ye continue in the faith grounded and settled, and be not moved away from the hope of the gospel which ye have heard, and which was preached to every creature which is under heaven." Col. i: 23.

These Scriptures clearly show that the *object* of the Christian's hope is laid up for him in heaven, that is, the realization of things hoped for is future—not past, and that those having the hope, learned of the things for which they hope through the gospel. When we have a firm faith in Jesus Christ through the gospel, and know that we have done, and are still doing, that which is required of us in the gospel, we have *a good reason to hope* to enjoy that which is *promised* us in the gospel. Thus we see that our hope comes through, and is predicated upon the gospel; and hence we see that he who would be always ready to give a reason, when asked, for the hope that is in him must study the gospel, or a scriptural and intelligent reason for his hope he cannot give.

Finally, these Scriptures teach that while we may have a well-grounded hope of heaven, and be able to give a good reason for it, still we may forfeit our inheritance and blast our hopes. We have no room to discuss this thought here, but only call attention to the fact that it is quite apparent in the Scriptures already quoted. "And you, that were some time alienated and enemies in your mind by wicked works, yet now hath he reconciled in the body of his flesh through death, to present you holy and unblameable and unreproveable in his sight; if ye continue in the faith grounded and settled, and be not moved away from the hope of the gospel, which ye have heard." Col. i : 21–23.

Here were persons once alienated by wicked works, as all other sinners are, who had become reconciled with a purpose of presentation to the Father, holy, unblameable, and unreproveable in his sight, if they continued in the faith, and were not moved away from the hope of the gospel. Yes, but what if they do not continue in the faith, and *are moved away from the hope* of the gospel? It would be folly to talk about *continuing* in the faith if *not in the faith*. This could not be; and it would be absurd to talk of being *moved away from the hope* of the gospel, if they *did not have the hope* of the gospel. And it would be equally absurd to talk of making their presentation to the Father *contingent* on their continuing in the faith, if they could not depart from it. And it would be ridiculous to make their presentation to the Father contingent on not being moved away from the *hope* of the gospel, if they could not be moved away from it. But Christ was a son over his own house; "whose house are we, if we hold fast the confidence and the rejoicing of the hope firm unto the end." Heb. iii : 6. But if we do not hold fast, firm, unto the end what then ? "Let us hold fast the profession of our faith without wavering for he is faithful that promised." Heb. x : 23.

Blessed thought—*he is faithful that promised.* Men may prove unfaithful, and their promises may fail. They may deceive and disappoint us, but he who has promised to save the obedient believer is faithful, and cannot disappoint those who trust in him to the end.

"Looking for that blessed *hope*, and the glorious appearing of the great God and our Savior Jesus Christ." Yes, that blessed *hope!* How could we live without it? Beset with trials, vexations, disappointments, and sore persecutions at every step, our spirits would sink within us were it not for the *glorious hope* that our troubles will end in an eternity of bliss by and by. "For our light affliction, which is but for a moment, worketh for us a far more exceeding and eternal weight of glory, while we look not at the things which are seen, but at the things which are not seen, for the things which are seen are temporal, but the things which are not seen are eternal." 2 Cor. iv : 17, 18. These are the things for which we *hope—not temporal, but eternal.* We can scarcely see how Paul could call such affliction as he endured *light affliction.* But they were of short duration, while the weight of glory, wrought out by them, was *eternal.* Says he: "We know, that if our earthly house of this tabernacle were dissolved, we have a building of God, a house not made with hands, eternal in the heavens." 2 Cor. v : 1. This enabled him to look with indifference, even, on the dissolution of the body, in the *hope* of being clothed in another one not made with hands, which would last while the eternal years of God should roll their endless cycles on. *Blessed hope! glorious hope!* Who could weather the storms incident to a pilgrimage through this life without *such a hope?*

Who of us could bear patiently Paul's afflictions now and think them light? "In stripes above measure, in prisons more frequent, in deaths oft. Of the Jews five times received I forty stripes save one. Thrice was I beaten with rods, once was I stoned, thrice I suffered shipwreck, a night and a day have I been in the deep; in journeyings often, in perils of waters, in perils of robbers, in perils by mine own countrymen, in perils by the heathen, in perils in the city, in perils in the wilderness, in perils in the sea, in perils among false brethren. In weariness and painfulness, in watchings often, in hunger and thirst, in fastings often, in cold and nakedness." 2 Cor. xi: 23-27. And yet in this same letter he speaks of our *light affliction!* Surely it took a *faith* that never knew a doubt, and a *hope that knew no fear* to rise above such furiously mad cyclones of persecution as this. His *hope* was anchored firmly within the vail and sustained him to the end. He says: "I am now ready to be offered, and the time of my departure is at hand. I have fought a good fight, I have finished my course, I have kept the faith; henceforth there is laid up for me a crown of righteousness, which the Lord, the righteous judge, shall give me at that day; and not to me only, but unto all them also that love his appearing." 2 Tim. iv: 6-8.

Here is a grand summing up of his life—the *ground of his hope*, and the *crown for which he hoped*, and there was consolation enough in it to compensate for all the suffering he had borne. He might well call the momentary affliction light compared with an eternity of bliss like this. Even death itself has no terrors for him who had such a hope as he had.

His hope rested upon his knowledge of what awaited him in the future. "For we know that if our earthly house of this tabernacle were dissolved, we have a building of God, a house not made with hands, eternal in the heavens. For in this we groan, earnestly desiring to be clothed upon with our house which is from heaven; if so be that being clothed we shall not be found naked." 2 Cor. v: 1-3. His hope robbed death of its sting, and this grand victory may be ours, if we live as **he did.**

CHAPTER XIV.

ZEAL WITHOUT KNOWLEDGE.

"Brethren, my heart's desire and prayer to God for Israel is, that they might be saved; for I bear them record that they have a zeal of God, but not according to knowledge; for they, being ignorant of God's righteousness, and going about to establish their own righteousness, have not submitted themselves unto the righteousness of God." Rom. x: 1-3.

ZEAL is defined: "Energetic pursuit; passionate ardor; fervent earnestness." It is commendable when properly directed, but misguided zeal becomes fanaticism. No one knew better how to sympathize with the religious intolerance of the Jews than did Paul. He had been the very impersonation of religious madness. He verily thought he ought to do many things contrary to the name of Jesus, and he did them. He gave his voice against those put to death for their devotion to the Christian religion. He held the clothes of those who stoned the devoted Stephen. Even women escaped not the fierceness of his wrath. Not content with persecuting them in Jerusalem, he pursued them into strange cities. He was, as he says, "exceedingly mad against them." *He lived in all good conscience while pursuing this mad career,* and could concede honesty of purpose to those who were doing as he had done. After his conversion to the Christian religion, and he had seen the error of his way, he realized that he would have been lost, notwithstanding all his honesty of purpose, had he died while persecuting the church of God. Knowing well the ignorance that beclouded the mind of the Jews, and caused them to substitute their own righteousness for the righteousness of God, his great desire was that they might come to a knowledge of the truth and be saved.

But why should Paul have been so deeply concerned about the salvation of these Jews? We are told that *whatever a man believes to be right is right to him.* These Jews had a zeal of God. True, it was not according to knowledge, but they thought it was. It was what they believed to be right—was it not right to them? If not, why not? In their ignorance they had substituted their own plan of salvation for God's plan; but are there not religious parties doing the same thing to-day? They think they are right, so did the Jews. If one can be saved, why not the other? But the parties of to-day think they are right and we are wrong. Yes, there is no doubt about their thinking so. The Jews just as certainly thought they were right and Paul wrong. Did they not? They thought they were right in rejecting the Lord Jesus Christ and having him crucified—did that make it right? Peter says: "But ye denied the Holy One, and the Just, and desired a murderer to be granted unto you; and killed the Prince of Life, whom God hath raised from the dead: whereof we are witnesses." "But they knew better." Peter did not think so. He says: "And now, brethren, I wot [know] that through ignorance ye did it, as did also your rulers." Acts iii: 14, 15, 17.

Did their ignorance even *excuse* them? He did not think so. He says: "Repent ye therefore, and be converted, that your sins may be blotted out, when the times of refreshing shall come from the presence of the

Lord." v. 19. Killing the Lord, believing it to be right, did not make it right; nor did it excuse those who did it. They had to repent of what they ignorantly did that was wrong, and turn away from it, or perish for having done it, however honest they had been in doing it. Does this mean any thing?

We think it likely that there was never a man on the earth that had a more profound sympathy for any people than Paul had for the Jews, yet he did not feel authorized to *expand* the plan of salvation in order to save them, however honest and zealous they were in devotion to their law, while they rejected the gospel. He says: "I say the truth in Christ, I lie not, my conscience also bearing me witness in the Holy Ghost, that I have great heaviness and continual sorrow in my heart; for I could wish that myself were accursed from Christ for my brethren, my kinsmen according to the flesh." Rom. ix: 1-3.

What could indicate a higher degree of sympathy than this? That he should be willing to forfeit his own salvation to save them! He exerted all his great powers in trying to convince them of their wrong, and turn them from the law to the gospel; but he never once intimated that their ignorance would excuse them, in rejecting the gospel, or that they could be saved without obedience to it.

Had Jesus proposed to *supplement* Judaism with Christianity, they most likely would have accepted his teaching without a murmur; but when he came proposing to cut up the Jewish religion, root and branch, and substitute an entirely new one, they revolted at it. They knew their religion was from God. They had seen too many evidences of this to be mistaken about it. Knowing this, they were not prepared to submit to its removal without a struggle. Many there are now who know how hard it is to give up a theory in which they have lived all their lives. When they have imbibed it from their parents, and have been taught from the cradle to manhood that it was *true* and *sacred*, they have found it very hard to give it up. The Jews had seen many miraculous evidences of God's approval of their religion. This is more than any man can say of his religion now. If persons are so slow to give up religious theories in which they have been trained from childhood, why should we be astonished that the Jews were unwilling to give up a religion in which they had been brought up, and of which they had seen very many evidences of God's approval?

But Paul knew that give it up they must, or saved they could not be; hence his great concern for them. The Jewish law had been taken out of the way by the death of Christ, after which they had to be saved by the gospel of Christ, or they could not be saved at all. He greatly desired their salvation, and it grieved him much to see them still clinging to the carcass of the law which could do them no good.

Being ignorant of God's righteousness and going about to establish their own righteousness, they had not submitted themselves unto the righteousness of God. The word *righteousness* sometimes has only a personal application, but in passages like this it has a much wider signification, embracing the whole plan of salvation, or God's plan of making men righteous.

All unrighteousness is sin. No one having the smallest taint of sin upon him can enter heaven. The Jews, as all other men, were sinners. They could not go to heaven in their sins. Their good resolves for the future could not cancel the sins of the past. A distinguished evangelist has preached all over the United States, that if a man wanted to be a Christian, all he had to do was "to quit sinning, join the church of his choice, and live right." But what is to be done with the dark mantle of sin covering the past life of the sinner? He must get rid of the sins of the past or be eternally lost. He cannot atone for them himself. The blood of Jesus Christ alone can take away sins. That can only be reached through the gospel; for it is the power of God unto salvation. It is God's righteousness —God's only way of making sinners righteous. Ignorant of this, Paul's kindred sought relief in a system of their own—the law of Moses, or the Jewish law. There was no pardon for them in this. They did not submit themselves to the gospel—how, then, could they be saved? Had Paul wept tears of blood over them, he could not have saved them without submission, on their part, to God's plan of salvation. He could not obey the gospel for them. There is an *individuality* in religion that cannot be dispensed with. No one can obey the gospel by proxy. Each one must obey it for himself. This obedience the Jews refused to render; therefore they could not be saved. But was there not as much chance for their salvation as for any one else who does *now*, as they did *then*? They were zealous; and their zeal was a zeal of God—religious zeal. They were as honest as any are now; but they would not obey the gospel. It was the power of God to salvation, but they did not obey it. They tried a plan of their own, but that could not save them. Can the systems of men save now? If not, why adhere to them?

Paul said his heart's desire and prayer to God for Israel was that they might be saved; so our heart's desire and prayer to God for *every honest man* is that he may be saved. But Paul's desire and prayer for Israel could not change the law of God concerning them. They had to abandon their own righteousness, and submit themselves to God's righteousness, or be lost. So now we must give up the doctrines and commandments of men, and believe and obey the gospel, or we shall be lost. "This is a hard saying—who can bear it?"

But we are told that this is religious *intolerance*. That it is *uncharitable*, and *unkind*. That it is *religious bigotry* and *egotism*. Were we to admit, at every breath, that we are wrong and others right, it would not change a single principle in God's government—not one. We only claim that *the Bible is right*—unquestionably right; and every thing antagonistic to it is wrong to the full extent of that antagonism. Is there any thing wrong in this? Surely not.

How intolerant it was to reject Saul from being king over Israel because he spared Agag alive, and brought him back as evidence of his victory, and saved the best of the flocks and herds to sacrifice to God in Gilgal. He doubtless thought God would be pleased at this. He had commanded sacrifice to be made to him of such animals. Saul did not propose to sell them and pocket the money, but he proposed to offer them to the Lord. We suppose he was *honest*, for he withstood Samuel to the face, affirming that he *had obeyed the commandment of the Lord*. How exceedingly intolerant in God to reject him for a matter so small, and apparently, unimportant done with an honest purpose!

Was it not a little unkind to slay the young prophet for going back to Bethel and refreshing himself after having faithfully done every thing for which God sent him there? God paralyzed the arm of Jeroboam when he sought to lay violent hands on him while in the discharge of his duty, thus showing that God was with him, and protected him while he obeyed him. When the king offered to reward him if he would go in and refresh himself with him, he told him he would not do it for half his kingdom; because God had commanded otherwise. Though he could not be *bribed*, he could be *deceived*. An old man lied to him and made him believe that God, through a prophet, had ordered him to return. So he went and was slain for it. Was this not a small matter to kill a man for? Just went back and *ate his dinner*, honestly believing that God had so ordered! Was not this bordering on *cruelty*?

Was it not *downright cruelty* to kill old Uzzah for putting his hand on the ark of the covenant when he thought it was in danger of falling? In all the devotion of his soul he did it. He loved that sacred ark and did not want to see it injured by falling; hence he *inadvertently* put his hand on it to stay it, but it was a violation of God's law, for which he was smitten with instant death. Even David did not like this breach upon Uzzah. But God's law had to be honored; hence Uzzah suffered the penalty for its violation, however pure his motives.

Once more; Was it not *cruel* to slay all the Amalekites, *men, women* and *children,* for a crime committed by their ancestors *four hundred years before they were born?* You would scarcely have done that, would you? "For my thoughts are not your thoughts, neither are your ways my ways, saith the Lord; for as the heavens are higher than the earth, so are my ways higher than your ways, and my thoughts than your thoughts." Isa. lv: 8, 9.

But we are told that all religious parties believe the Bible. Not only do they believe it, but they believe it to be an *infallible* standard of right. Every man believes that his party faithfully teaches what is taught in the Bible. And the denominations, one and all, just as firmly and honestly believe us to be wrong as we believe them to be wrong. All this we freely concede; but we cannot concede that all the conflicting and contradictory doctrines taught by the denominations are taught in the Bible, and are, therefore from God. What then is to be done with them? Some tell us to just let them alone. Will this ever heal the breaches in the walls of Zion? Hardly, we suppose. No one will ever be moved from any position, however dangerous it may be, by telling him that he is all right—that he is as safe where he is as he would be any where else. We can scarcely regard him as our friend who sees us believing and practicing grievous error, and yet fails to warn us of our danger.

Jesus prayed to his Father that all who should believe in him through the words of the apostles might be one; and it occurs to us that every true and devoted Christian should earnestly labor to bring about the state of things for which Jesus prayed.

We make no quarrel with any one for teaching what he honestly believes. This is right. All true men will teach just that. He would be a hypocritical deceiver were he to teach otherwise. We have no respect for him who caters to public opinion, especially in matters of religion. "Preach the truth if the heavens fall." *Preach it in love, but preach it.* Of course we mean that you preach it as you understand it. You cannot preach it as others understand it, unless you understand it as they do. Stop not to inquire whether it is popular or unpopular, or whether it will be accepted or rejected by those for whom you preach. Preach the truth, and leave results to God and those who hear and read. Let every one take what he hears and reads to the Bible; and, for himself, diligently try it by that infallible standard. That which cannot abide this test should be rejected, no matter how high the source from which it comes. If it is in harmony with that standard, it cannot be wrong, and should be accepted, whether our parents believe it or not. Were this course pursued, *all* differences might not disappear; but we are fully persuaded that many of them would. God will settle the others in the great day of accounts, if not before, as may be pleasing to him. Here we are content to leave this issue. There is no dogmatism in this. We want every one to have the utmost liberty of thought, feeling, and action. This is a God-given liberty. We are glad that no man can take it away if he would. We are sure that we would not if we could; but God said: "The prophet that hath a dream, let him tell a dream, and he that hath my word, let him speak my word faithfully. What is the chaff to the wheat? saith the Lord." Jer. xxiii: 28. We can not see why this should not apply to preachers as well as prophets. "When I say unto the wicked, Thou shalt surely die; and thou givest him not warning, nor speakest to warn the wicked from his wicked way, to save his life; the same wicked man shall die in his iniquity; but his blood will I require at thine hand. Yet if thou warn the wicked, and he turn not from his wickedness, nor from his wicked way, he shall die in his iniquity; but thou hast delivered thy soul." Again: "When a righteous man doth turn from his righteousness, and commit iniquity, and I lay a stumblingblock before him, he shall die; because thou hast not given him warning, he shall die in his sin, and his righteousness which he hath done shall not be remembered; but his blood will I require at thine hand." Ez. iii: 18–20.

GOD'S RIGHTEOUSNESS.

We have already quoted John saying: "All unrighteousness is sin." 1 John v: 17. "Sin is the transgression of the law." 1 John iii: 4. Therefore unrighteousness is the transgression of the law; and the transgression of the law is unrighteousness. "He that doeth righteousness is righteous, even as he is righteous." 1 John iii: 7. To be fit for companionship with Jesus we must be perfectly righteous as he is, for no one defiled by sin can enter heaven.

> "No cloud those blissful regions know,
>   For ever bright and fair;
> For sin, the source of every woe,
>   Can never enter there."

Jesus, himself was the only sinless one that ever lived on this earth. "If we say that we have no sin, we deceive ourselves, and the truth is not in us." And again: "If we say that we have not sinned, we make him a liar, and his word is not in us." 1 John i: 8, 10. Then as all men sin, and one defiled by sin cannot enter heaven; it follows that all must become righteous, in some way, or be lost.

He that doeth righteousness is righteous even as Jesus is righteous. He that is thus perfectly righteous stands before God as guiltless as though he had never sinned. "He that doeth righteousness is righteous." When Peter went with the message of life to the Gentiles, he said: "Of a truth I perceive that God is no respecter of persons; but in every nation he that feareth him, and worketh righteousness, is accepted with him." Acts x: 34, 35. When we speak of obeying God, our friends quote Paul, "not of works—not of works," without stopping to enquire what Paul meant by the expression, "not of works." Peter here says: he that feareth God and *worketh* righteousness is accepted with him. Will the objector say, "stop Peter, there *must be no works* about it, lest there be room for boasting?" But Peter is sustained by John. There is no difference in doing righteousness, and working righteousness. He that accepts *God's righteousness becomes personally righteous.* That is, he that believes and obeys the gospel, wherein God's righteousness is revealed, is saved—made righteous. "If we walk in the light, as he is in the light, we have fellowship one with another, and the blood of Jesus Christ his Son cleanseth us from all sin." 1 John i: 7. The blood of Jesus is the only thing which can cleanse from sin. It can only cleanse those who come in contact with it. This can only be done through the means which God has appointed for that purpose. Hence Paul said: "For I am not ashamed of the gospel of Christ, for it is the power of God unto salvation to every one that believeth; to the Jew first, and also to the Greek; for therein is the righteousness of God revealed from faith to faith; as it is written, The just shall live by faith." Rom. i: 16, 17.

The gospel of Christ is the power of God to the salvation of no one who fails to believe it. It is the power of God to the salvation of the believer, because God's righteousness is revealed in it from faith to faith. That is, God's righteous plan of saving men by a *system of faith,* is revealed in the gospel in order to *personal faith.* From faith to faith; *i. e., from a system of faith to personal faith.* Therefore Paul says: Faith cometh by hearing, and hearing by the word of God." Rom. x: 17.

But faith has nothing meritorious in it, more than any other act of obedience to God. Its value consists in bringing us to Christ. "He is the propitiation for our sins; and not for ours only, but also for the sins of the whole world." 1 John ii: 2. He is the great Physician who has power to cure the sin-sick soul. Faith moves the sinner to him; but it must do more than this—it must induce him to take the remedies prescribed. Faith that does not do this, is worthless. The power of the Physician is in his remedies, and his skill consists in his ability to adapt his remedies to the condition of his patient. The patient may have all faith in the skill of the Physician, and in the potency of his remedial agents; but if he refuse to submit to his treatment, the Physician can do him no good. So the sinner may believe in Christ, but if he refuse to obey him, he will be lost. As the patient could not be cured by the doctor until he took his remedies, neither can the believing sinner be saved by Christ, until he complies with the conditions on which Christ proposes to save him.

When the dying Israelite was commanded to *look* on the brazen serpent placed on a pole, and reared in the camp, he was not healed *until he looked as required.* Had he believed, ever so earnestly, that the brazen serpent was on the pole, and that God was able to cure him when he should look upon it, and still refused to look as commanded, he would have died, notwithstanding his *faith* in the means prepared for his cure. The remedy was, *believe* and *look,* (of course he would not look until he did believe, hence belief was implied.) Now it is *believe* and be *baptized,* with the promise that salvation will be the result. "Well, but I think God will save me without baptism." Perhaps he will, but it occurs to us that a very important question for your consideration is, *has he promised to save you without it ?* He could have cured the dying Israelite without his looking on that brazen serpent; but did he promise to do it that way?

"But Paul told the jailer to believe on the Lord Jesus Christ, and he should be saved." Yes, but did he say "believe on the Lord Jesus Christ and you shall be saved without baptism?" Had he thus spoken it would have been in direct antagonism to the commission given by the Lord Jesus, saying, "He that believeth and is baptized shall be saved." Surely Paul did not command belief in the Lord Jesus Christ and in the same moment antagonize his teaching. We can scarcely believe he did this, at the jail, or any where else.

Suppose we visit our neighbor and find him very sick. We urge him to send for the doctor. He has no confidence in the doctor suggested, and declines to send for him. Knowing the doctor better than the sick man, we say to him: "*Believe in the doctor and he will cure you.*" Would any one understand us to mean that if the sick man would believe in the doctor, he would be cured without the means prescribed by the doctor? Surely not. We suppose all would understand us to mean that the sick man should believe in the doctor strong enough to send for him, and submit to his treatment when he should come. So when Paul told the jailer to believe on the Lord Jesus Christ and he should be saved, he did not mean that he should be saved without compliance with the commission. The obvious design was that he should believe on the Lord Jesus Christ so that he might be willing to do what the Lord Jesus Christ required of him. Hence he spake unto him the word of the Lord, and to all that were in his house, and they obeyed it the same hour of the night. The jailer abandoned his own righteousness, if he had any, and promptly submitted to God's righteousness and was saved. Those who will do now as he did, may be saved as he was. This no one who is loyal to the Bible will deny. Then will all persons wishing to be saved, accept salvation on the same terms proposed to, and accepted by him? If not, why not?

The sinner has no righteousness of his own to commend him to the favor of God. There is nothing he can do that will pay God an equivalent for his salvation. No wisdom of his can devise a plan by which to save himself. Through Christ alone is there hope of salvation for any son of Adam. Hence there is no place for boasting. It is excluded by the law of faith. Christ is made unto us wisdom, and righteousness, and sanctification, and redemption. So then let him that glorieth, glory in the Lord. "Unto him that loved us, and washed us from our sins in his own blood, and hath made us kings and priests unto God and his Father; to him be glory and dominion for ever." Rev. i: 5, 6.

"Should my tears forever flow,
　Should my zeal no languor know,
This for sin could not atone;
　Thou must save, and thou alone:
In my hand no price I bring
　Simply to thy cross I cling.

While I draw this fleeting breath,
　When my eyelids close in death,
When I rise to worlds unknown,
　And behold thee on thy throne;
Rock of ages, cleft for me,
　Let me hide myself in thee!"

CHAPTER XV.

PAUL'S NATURAL MAN.

> "But the natural man receiveth not the things of the Spirit of God: for they are foolishness unto him: neither can he know them, because they are spiritually discerned." 1 Cor. ii: 14.

THIS Scripture is used by many to show that man is incapable of understanding the Bible without supernatural aid. The Catholic expositors take the Bible from the people because they cannot understand it. The advocates of direct spiritual influences invoke the aid of this passage as conclusive proof of their position. Both classes start out with quite a number of unsupported

ASSUMPTIONS.

(1) "The *natural man* is the sinner—the unconverted, and includes all the unconverted in contrast with the converted man, which includes all Christians."

(2) "The Bible, or Word of God, if not the *things* of the Spirit, is at least a thing of the Spirit."

(3) "Therefore the word of God will not be received by the sinner, for it is foolishness to him; neither can he know or understand it because it is spiritually discerned. Until God spiritually illuminates his understanding—converts him—makes a Christian of him, he can know nothing about the Scriptures."

Then of what use is the Bible? If God must illuminate the mind of the unregenerate sinner by a direct operation of the Holy Spirit before he can understand what is revealed in the Bible concerning him, why not make the revelation without the Bible? If the Bible cannot be understood by the unconverted man, then we respectfully submit that it is no revelation until he is converted. Indeed, a revelation which cannot be understood by those for whom the revelation is made, is simply no revelation at all. Such a thought is a most ridiculous absurdity.

David says: "The law of the Lord is perfect, converting the soul." In the very matter of converting the soul, the law of the Lord is perfect; and yet the man to be converted by it cannot understand a word of it, or get a thought out of it, or from it, until he is converted. "The testimony of the Lord is sure making wise the simple." Ps. xix: 7. How could it make a man wise who could not understand a word of it? How any one can grow wise by reading and studying that which he cannot understand, is a matter incomprehensible to us.

But if the sinner cannot understand the revelation until God converts him from a natural to a spiritual man, and the good Lord fails to convert him, whose fault will it be, should he fail of conversion entirely? The gospel is the power of God unto salvation, (Rom. i: 16) and therefore, without it, there can be no salvation, and the gospel is all foolishness to the natural man or sinner—he cannot know any thing about it until God illuminates him by conversion—he waits for the illumination and it never comes, who is responsible for the failure? Certainly not the natural man or sinner, for he can do nothing. All God's power to save him is in the gospel, and it is utterly incomprehensible to him, and he has no more power to understand and believe it than he has to make a world; and yet God will damn him if he does not believe it. "He that believeth not shall be damned." Mark xvi: 16. And from this stand-point it looks a little like God is about as powerless to save as the sinner is to be saved. The gospel is the power of God unto salvation—not a power—some power—one of the powers, but *the* power, and the sinner cannot receive that, how then, can he be saved by this arrangement? The God of the Bible that made the heavens and the earth, and all things that in them are, did not fix up such a system of salvation as this. It is man's work, surely.

"For the word of the cross is to them that are perishing foolishness; but unto us which are being saved it is the power of God; for it is written, I will destroy the wisdom of the wise; and the prudence of the prudent will I reject. Where is the wise? Where is the scribe? Where is the disputer of this world? Hath not God made foolish the wisdom of the world? For seeing that in the wisdom of God the world through its wisdom knew not God, it was God's good pleasure through the foolishness of the thing preached to save them that believe." 1 Cor. i: 18-21. [*N. V., margin.*]

While the preaching of the cross of Christ seemed to be foolishness to them who were trying to find out God by their own wisdom, it was the power of God to the salvation of those who were being saved by it. While the world through its wisdom knew not God, it pleased God to save, through the gospel, them who believed it, though it seemed only foolishness to them who were relying on their own wisdom. The Epicurian philosophers and Stoics of Athens thought Paul a setter forth of strange gods, because he preached unto them Jesus and the resurrection. Acts xvii: 18.

Jesus said: "I thank thee, O Father, Lord of heaven

and earth, that thou hast hid these things from the wise and prudent, and hast revealed them unto babes: even so, Father; for so it seemed good in thy sight. All things are delivered to me of my Father: and no man knoweth who the Son is, but the Father; and who the Father is, but the Son, and he to whom the Son will reveal him." Luke x: 21, 22.

These Scriptures show the utter impossibility of knowing or finding out God but by revelation. and surely these revelations were intended to be understood by those to whom and for whom they were made, otherwise they could have furnished no assistance in coming to a knowledge of God, and would have left the world to the wisdom of man at last.

Let us next see *how* God made revelations for the benefit of his creature man. " Knowing this first, that no prophecy of the scripture is of any private interpretation. For the prophecy came not in old time by the will of man: but holy men of God spake as they were moved by the Holy Ghost.' 2 Pet. i: 20, 21.

David said: "The Spirit of the Lord spake by me, and his word was in my tongue." 2 Sam. xxiii: 2.

Thus we see that holy men of God spake as they were moved or inspired by the Holy Spirit, and that the tongues of inspired men were used to reveal or make known God's will to other men, or, if you please, natural men. These spiritual men were not always under the spirit of inspiration, nor was every thing revealed at once; but when God saw fit to reveal any thing, he put his words into their mouths and caused them to speak them, not for their own benefit exclusively, but for the benefit of such as were intended to be affected by the revelation. This has ever been God's method of communicating his will to the race of man;

and this was the subject under consideration when the apostle used the language of our *text*, as an examination of the context will clearly show.

He says: "And my speech and my preaching was not with enticing words of man's wisdom, but in demonstration of the Spirit and of power; that your faith should not stand in the wisdom of men, but in the power of God." 1 Cor. ii: 4, 5. Paul, as an apostle, had power to confirm and to demonstrate what he preached; and at no place did he more freely confer these gifts of the Spirit than at Corinth, so that no congregation excelled the Corinthians in the exercise of these supernatural powers.

"Howbeit," says he, "we speak wisdom among them that are perfect: yet not the wisdom of this world, nor of the princes of this world, that come to nought: but we speak the wisdom of God in a mystery, even the hidden wisdom, which God ordained before the world unto our glory: which none of the princes of this world knew: for had they known it, they would not have crucified the Lord of glory." v. 6–8. No, if they had been inspired or spiritual men, as Paul was, they would have known the Lord and would not have put him to death. This is clear enough.

"But as it is written, Eye hath not seen, nor ear heard, neither have entered into the heart of man, the things which God hath prepared for them that love him; but God hath revealed them unto us by his Spirit; for the Spirit searcheth all things." Yes, God has revealed these things unto us. Us whom? We will see directly.

"For this cause I Paul, the prisoner of Jesus Christ for you Gentiles, if ye have heard of the dispensation of the grace of God which is given me to you-ward:

How that by revelation he made known unto me the mystery; (as I wrote afore in few words, whereby, when ye read, ye may understand my knowledge in the mystery of Christ) which in other ages was not made known unto the sons of men, as it is now revealed unto his holy apostles and prophets by the Spirit." Eph. iii: 1–5.

Here were things that had been hidden from the world for ages, which God had now revealed to his holy apostles and prophets by his Spirit; and Paul wrote them to the Ephesians that they might understand that which had hitherto been a mystery. However profound and long concealed this mystery, when it was revealed to Paul, and he wrote it to them, it was a mystery no longer; for the very object of writing it to them was that they might understand his knowledge in the mystery.

Then we see that God, by his Spirit, revealed these things unto *us holy apostles and prophets.* Having seen this, we resume our examination of the context.

"For what man knoweth the things of a man, save the spirit of man which is in him? even so the things of God knoweth no man, but the Spirit of God [knows]." Until the spirit of man reveals what is in him, no other man can know it, even so no man can know the things of God until he by his Spirit reveals them.

"Now we have received, not the spirit of the world, but the spirit which is of God; that we might know the things that are freely given to us of God. Which things also we speak, not in the words which man's wisdom teacheth, but which the Holy Ghost teacheth; comparing spiritual things with spiritual." v. 12, 13.

The apostles had received the Spirit of God that they might know the things freely given to them of God; and the things thus received by them they spoke in words furnished by the Spirit, and the object was that those to be benefitted might receive and understand the revelation thus made.

"But the natural man recciveth not the things of the Spirit of God: for they are foolishness unto him: neither can he know them, because they are spiritually discerned." v. 14. Natural men not having the Spirit of God by which inspired men knew things freely given to them, could not receive spiritual communications, for they were foolishness to them until spiritual men received them, and wrote, or spoke them, in words which natural men could understand.

Thus God made known spiritual things through spiritual men to natural men; not that the things revealed might remain in mystery, but that they might be enveloped in mystery no longer.

All men are natural men in the sense in which Paul used the phrase. He meant *uninspired* men who could not receive spiritual communications directly from God; hence, whether saint or sinner, as there are no *inspired* men, *all are natural men* now, and will so remain, whether converted or not.

The same thought in our text may be seen by an examination of examples, showing that God put his Spirit into men to reveal things of which *natural men* could know nothing until spiritual men revealed them—then they were plain enough to be understood by all. We have room for a very few only, of the many examples which might be given in illustration of this fact.

When Joseph was a slave in Egypt, for no fault of his own, he was put into prison; and after a time the king's chief butler and baker were put into the same prison.

"And they dreamed a dream both of them, each man

his dream in one night, each man according to the interpretation of his dream, the butler and the baker of the king of Egypt, which were bound in the prison. And Joseph came in unto them in the morning, and looked upon them, and, behold, they were sad. And he asked Pharaoh's officers that were with him in the ward of his lord's house, saying, Wherefore look ye so sadly to-day? And they said unto him, We have dreamed a dream, and there is no interpreter of it. And Joseph said unto them, Do not interpretations belong to God? tell me them, I pray you." Gen. xl : 5-8.

Each one told Joseph his dream, and Joseph, or rather God through Joseph, gave the interpretations. He informed the butler that in three days he would be restored to his office, and bear the king's wine as before he was put in prison; and he told the baker that in three days he would be hanged on a tree and the birds would eat his flesh.

"And it came to pass the third day, which was Phaoh's birthday, that he made a feast unto all his servants: and he lifted up the head of the chief butler and of the chief baker among his servants. And he restored the chief butler unto his butlership again; and he gave the cup into Pharaoh's hand; but he hanged the chief baker: as Joseph had interpreted to them. Yet did not the chief butler remember Joseph, but forgat him." Gen. xl. 20-23.

Now, why could not the baker and butler interpret their own dreams? Simply because they were *natural men*—not discerners of spiritual things. Why could Joseph interpret and make plain that which was foolishness to them until revealed? Because he was a man in whom the Spirit of God dwelt, and through whom God made revelations to natural men. We suppose the baker and butler understood the interpretation of their dreams quite well as soon as Joseph gave it to them, even before it was verified on the third day.

When Joseph saw that the butler was to be set at liberty, he made a request of him in his own behalf. "But think on me when it shall be well with thee, and shew kindness, I pray thee, unto me, and make mention of me unto Pharaoh, and bring me out of this house: for indeed I was stolen away out of the land of the Hebrews: and here also have I done nothing that they should put me into the dungeon." Gen. xl: 14, 15.

"And it came to pass at the end of two full years, that Pharaoh dreamed: and, behold, he stood by the river. And, behold, there came up out of the river seven well-favored kine and fatfleshed; and they fed in a meadow. And, behold, seven other kine came up after them out of the river, ill-favored and leanfleshed; and stood by the other kine upon the brink of the river. And the ill favored and leanfleshed kine did eat up the seven well-favored and fat kine. So Pharaoh awoke. And he slept and dreamed the second time: and, behold, seven ears of corn came up upon one stalk, rank and good. And, behold, seven thin ears and blasted with the east wind sprung up after them. And the seven thin ears devoured the seven rank and full ears. And Pharaoh awoke, and, behold, it was a dream. And it came to pass in the morning that his spirit was troubled; and he sent and called for all the magicians of Egypt, and all the wise men thereof: and Pharaoh told them his dream; but there was none that could interpret them unto Pharaoh."

Ah, indeed! why not? Here are wise men and magicians, doubtless learned in all the wisdom of Egypt, why did they fail? Because they were *natural men*, not discerners of spiritual things; hence these dreams were foolishness to them. By the wisdom of men they could not know them.

"Then spake the chief butler unto Pharaoh, saying, I do remember my faults this day: Pharaoh was wroth with his servants, and put me in ward in the captain of the guard's house, both me and the chief baker: and we dreamed a dream in one night, I and he; we dreamed each man according to the interpretation of his dream. And there was there with us a young man, an Hebrew, servant to the captain of the guard; and we told him, and he interpreted to us our dreams; to each man according to his dream he did interpret. And it came to pass, as he interpreted to us, so it was: me he restored unto mine office, and him he hanged."

Yes, poor, frail, ungrateful humanity. At liberty himself he thought no more of his friend, and allowed him to languish in prison for two full years, until his services were needed to do that which none of them could do, then his memory was quickened into a confession of his fault. Are there not many *butlers* to-day? Devoted to a friend as long as they can use him to their own advantage, but forget him in his distress, when they need him no longer.

"Then Pharaoh sent and called Joseph, and they brought him hastily out of the dungeon: and he shaved himself, and changed his raiment, and came in unto Pharaoh. And Pharaoh said unto Joseph, I have dreamed a dream, and there is none that can interpret it: and I have heard say of thee, that thou canst understand a dream to interpret it. And Joseph answered Pharaoh, saying, It is not in me: God shall give Pharaoh an answer of peace."

Unaided of God, Joseph would have been as other

men, but God, through him, made revelations which natural men could understand well enough after the revelation was made.

"And Joseph said unto Pharaoh, The dream of Pharaoh is one; God hath shewed Pharaoh what he is about to do. The seven good kine are seven years; and the seven good ears are seven years: the dream is one. And the seven thin and ill-favored kine that came up after them are seven years; and the seven empty ears blasted with the east wind shall be seven years of famine. This is the thing which I have spoken unto Pharaoh: What God is about to do he sheweth unto Pharaoh. Behold, there come seven years of great plenty throughout all the land of Egypt: And there shall arise after them seven years of famine; and all the plenty shall be forgotten in the land of Egypt; and the famine shall consume the land; and the plenty shall not be known in the land by reason of that famine following; for it shall be very grievous. And for that the dream was doubled unto Pharaoh twice; it is because the thing is established by God, and God will shortly bring it to pass." Gen. xli: 25–32.

Here were things revealed by God through Joseph, and they did come to pass. The seven years of plenty did come, and the seven years of famine did follow. And the king understood the interpretation very well, for he took Joseph's advice and went to laying up food during the seven years of plenty to supply the wants of the people during the seven years of famine.

Now, this exactly illustrates the natural man of our text. Paul's natural man could not receive the things of the Spirit of God, neither could the wise men and magicians of Egypt. Pharaoh's dreams were just as foolish to the wise men of Egypt as was any thing to the natural men of Corinth; and the things which Paul spake in words furnished him by the Holy Spirit were just as easily understood after he spoke them, as were the words of Joseph, in which Pharaoh's dreams were interpreted to him. Let us examine another case.

While many of the Jews were held captive in Babylon, the king "Nebuchadnezzar dreamed dreams, wherewith his Spirit was troubled, and his sleep brake from him. Then the king commanded to call the magicians, and the astrologers, and the sorcerers, and the Chaldeans, for to shew the king his dreams. So they came and stood before the king." Dan. ii: 1, 2.

Surely if man's wisdom could reveal the things of God, here is enough of it to accomplish the work. But they were *natural men*, not discerners of spiritual things; hence the king's dream was nought but foolishness to them, and he issued a decree that they should all be slain as pretenders.

"Therefore Daniel went in unto Arioch, whom the king had ordained to destroy the wise men of Babylon: he went and said thus unto him; Destroy not the wise men of Babylon: bring me in before the king and I will shew unto the king the interpretation. Then Arioch brought in Daniel before the king in haste, and said thus unto him, I have found a man of the captives of Judah that will make known unto the king the interpretation. The king answered and said to Daniel, whose name was Belteshazzar, Art thou able to make known unto me the dream which I have seen, and the interpretation thereof? Daniel answered in the presence of the king, and said, The secret which the king hath demanded cannot the wise men, the astrologers, the magicians, the soothsayers, shew unto the king; but there is a God in heaven that revealeth secrets, and maketh known to the king Nebuchadnezzar what shall be in the latter days. Thy dream, and the visions of thy head upon thy bed, are these; As for thee, O king, thy thoughts came into thy mind upon thy bed, what should come to pass hereafter: and he that revealeth secrets maketh known to thee what shall come to pass.* But as for me, this secret is not revealed to me for any wisdom that I have more than any living, but for their sakes that shall make known the interpretation to the king, and that thou mightest know the thoughts of thy heart. Thou, O king, sawest, and behold a great image. This great image, whose brightness was excellent, stood before thee; and the form thereof was terrible. This image's head was of fine gold, his breast and his arms of silver, his belly and his thighs of brass, his legs of iron, his feet part of iron and part of clay. Thou sawest till that a stone was cut out without hands, which smote the image upon his feet that were of iron and clay, and brake them to pieces." Dan. ii: 24-34.

Without stopping to quote all the interpretation of this dream, it is sufficient to state that Daniel, by the Spirit of God, did interpret it, and show that each of these parts of the image represented a government that should arise, and in the time of the last one the God of heaven would set up a kingdom which should never be destroyed. Thus we see that the Spirit of God, through Daniel, made clear what the combined wisdom of Babylon failed to explain. "The Chaldeans answered before the king and said, There is not a man upon the earth that can shew the king's matter." And this was true of *natural men*, who, without inspiration, were not able to discern spiritual things. Take another example.

Belshazzar, the king, made a great feast, and "In

the same hour came forth fingers of a man's hand, and wrote over against the candlestick upon the plaster of the wall of the king's palace: and the king saw the part of the hand that wrote. Then the king's countenance was changed, and his thoughts troubled him, so that the joints of his loins were loosed, and his knees smote one against another. The king cried aloud to bring in the astrologers, the Chaldeans, and the soothsayers. And the king spake, and said to the wise men of Babylon, Whosoever shall read this writing, and shew me the interpretation thereof, shall be clothed with scarlet, and have a chain of gold about his neck, and shall be the third ruler in the kingdom. Then came in all the king's wise men: but they could not read the writing, nor make known to the king the interpretation thereof." Dan. v: 5–8.

Here is another failure of the wisest of *natural* men to comprehend the things of the Spirit; but Daniel, aided by the Spirit of interpretation, did read the writing on the wall, and revealed the doom of the king, and the division of his kingdom between the Medes and Persians. "In that night was Belshazzar the king of the Chaldeans slain." v. 30.

Thus we see that God has always made revelations through spiritual men for the benefit of *natural men*, who could know nothing of spiritual things until revealed by the Holy Spirit that they might understand them. "And he gave some, apostles; and some, prophets; and some, evangelists; and some, pastors and teachers; for the perfecting of the saints, for the work of the ministry, for the edifying of the body of Christ: till we all come in the unity of the faith, and of the knowledge of the Son of God, unto a perfect man, unto the measure of the stature of the fullness of Christ." Eph. iv: 11–13.

All these spiritual gifts and revelations were given through God's appointed agencies with a view to the salvation of the world; and if any are not saved, it is not because they cannot understand the revelation made concerning their duty, but because they will not avail themselves of the means provided for their salvation that they may be saved.

"Come unto me, all ye that labor and are heavy laden, and I will give you rest. Take my yoke upon you, and learn of me, for I am meek and lowly in heart: and ye shall find rest unto your souls. For my yoke is easy, and my burden is light." Matt. xi : 28–30.

Jesus would not mock the sinner by inviting him to come to him if he could not come. The very fact that Jesus invites him is proof enough that he *can come*, if he will. But he invites only him who *labors* and is *heavy laden*. He who is not weary of sin and feels not his need of a Savior *will not come*. All overtures of mercy are made in vain to him. The cross of Christ is planted in vain before him. He will look with perfect indifference on his quivering flesh as the rusty spikes make him fast to the wood. He can look upon the mangled body of the ever blessed Son of God, as his blood flows for the sins of men, without a blush or a tremor of a nerve. He must realize that he is lost without Jesus, before he will accept salvation through him on any terms. It is idle to talk of the sinner's *inability to understand the gospel*. It is quite easy to teach him what God requires of him when he wants to know it. It is much more difficult to awaken the sinner to a sense of his danger, and get him to *want to be saved*, than it is to tell him *how to be saved*, provided, always, that *the preacher understands the gospel himself*. The heavy laden sinner who comes to Christ will always find the promised rest; but he must come trusting in the shed blood of Jesus and the promises of God. And he must come in the way marked out by the Savior. In this way "the Spirit and the bride say, come. And let him that heareth say, come. And let him that is athirst, come. And whosoever will, let him take the water of life freely." Rev. xxii: 17. Yes, *whosoever will!* Thank God, whosoever will, may come. If the sinner is not saved it is because he will not be saved. God loved him—Jesus died for him—the Spirit invites him—the church or bride invites him—angels are concerned for him. "But ye will not come unto me." This is the trouble.

> "What could your Redeemer do,
>   More than he has done for you?
> To procure your peace with God,
>   Could he more than shed his blood?"

CHAPTER XVII.

THE DIVINE NATURE IN THE CHRISTIAN.

"Grace and peace be multiplied unto you through the knowledge of God, and of Jesus our Lord. According as his divine power hath given unto us all things that pertain unto life and godliness, through the knowledge of him that hath called us to glory and virtue: whereby are given unto us exceeding great and precious promises: that by these ye might be partakers of the divine nature, having escaped the corruption that is in the world through lust." 2 Pet. i: 2–4.

WE inherit human nature from our parents; but we must be partakers of the *divine nature* before we can be fit for divine society. To enjoy the society of God, Jesus, angels, and purified spirits in heaven, our natures must be assimilated to theirs; and the Christian religion is calculated to effect this transformation. We think it likely that this life was given us in which to prepare for another—a higher, purer, and more perfect state of existence, of which God is the center, and where angels and purified spirits make up the society. This would not be a state of happiness to the wicked and vicious even if it were possible for them to be placed in it. They cannot be happy in good society here; how, then, could they enjoy the society of heaven? Take a man who has grown up in the constant practice of vice and wickedness—who has visited places of riotry and dissipation much more frequently than he has gone to church—who has gone where profanity and vulgarity were indulged in by his daily associates—where dishonesty and fraud were studied as an occupation—where theft is dishonorable only when exposed; and where murder is so common that there is no more respect for the life of a man than for the life of a good clever bird-dog; and place him in a company wholly made up of Christian men and women, who are talking about the deplorable consequences of sin, or the glorious success of a protracted meeting that is going on in the neighborhood—could he enjoy such company, and with pleasure participate in the conversation? He would be quite miserable, and would withdraw at the earliest practicable moment, and seek company more congenial to him. If it were possible to place such a man in heaven, he would abscond to hell as soon as he could get away. Heaven would be a place of indescribable horror and awful misery to such a character. The purer the association of such men, the more miserable they are. What a picture for the contemplation of a Universalist!

Heaven can be entered by only the pure and holy. None others could enjoy it, if there. It requires assimilation of nature to the nature of those who will make up, and constitute the society of heaven to enable the saints to be happy in heaven. The Christian religion was designed to mould the affections, and so control the life of man as to plant and develop the *divine nature* in him who is in the daily practice of it.

Jesus said: "Love your enemies, bless them that curse you, do good to them that hate you, and pray for them which despitefully use you and persecute you." Matt. v: 44. An objector says: "It is impossible for me to do this. I cannot love that man that cursed and abused me—that slandered me and my family—that swindled me out of my property—that tried to kill me when I had done him no harm—I cannot love him. It is contrary to *human nature* to love such a man." Yes, it is certainly contrary to human nature to love him; but is it contrary to the *divine nature* to love him? If you will bring yourself under the control of the *divine nature*, perhaps you might find it quite easy to do that which seems so revolting to human nature. Jesus prayed for those who crucified him: "Father forgive them, they know not what they do." If you possessed the same nature which he had, could you not pray for your enemies as he did? God loved the world, when it was in rebellion against him. "For when we were yet without strength, in due time Christ died for the ungodly. For scarcely for a righteous man will one die: yet peradventure for a good man some would even dare to die. But God commendeth his love toward us, in that, while we were yet sinners, Christ died for us." Rom. v: 6-8.

Had the divine nature acted from the impulses of human nature, when would the scheme of human redemption have been wrought out? Never. The world was lost, and lost it would have remained without the very love which Jesus requires of us. The divine nature is equal to this—human nature is not. Oh, but you say: "I have not this nature, and never can have it, for I cannot love my enemies. If God requires this of me, I am lost, for I never can do it." Peter thought it possible for those to whom he wrote to be partakers of the divine nature, and if they could partake of this nature, why may we not become partakers of it as they did? We have the same religion they had, and can read the same instructions given to them—why may we not partake of the same nature which they had?

This nature is not to be put on in full development

at once, as a man may put on his coat, but it is to be cultivated and progressively developed by a system of means given for that purpose. The character that is void of love is wholly unlike God, and cannot enjoy him; for so prominent is love in the attributes of God that the apostle says: "He that loveth not, knoweth not God; for God is love." 1 John iv: 8. There can be no congeniality between the "God of love" and a character without love.

"In this was manifested the love of God toward us, because that God sent his only begotten Son into the world, that we might live through him. Herein is love, not that we loved God, but that he loved us, and sent his Son to be the propitiation for our sins. Beloved, if God so loved us, we ought also to love one another. No man hath seen God at any time. If we love one another, God dwelleth in us, and his love is perfected in us." 1 John iv: 9–12.

Thus we see that it is not enough that we love God, but we must love one another. "We love him because he first loved us." But this would seem to be an interested love—we love because we are loved. Our love must go beyond this. "If a man say, I love God, and hateth his brother, he is a liar: for he that loveth not his brother whom he hath seen, how can he love God whom he hath not seen? And this commandment have we from him, that he who loveth God, love his brother also." 1 John iv: 20, 21.

From these Scriptures we see that *love* is a prominent element in the *divine nature*, and if we would be partakers of the divine nature we must cultivate the spirit of love—love for God, love for the brethren, love for our enemies, love for all men. Our love must be as broad as the universe of God, and the race of man.

"Owe no man any thing, but to love one another: for he that loveth another hath fulfilled the law. For this, Thou shalt not commit adultery, Thou shalt not kill, Thou shalt not steal, Thou shalt not bear false witness, Thou shalt not covet; and if there be any other commandment, it is briefly comprehended in this saying, namely, Thou shalt love thy neighbor as thyself. Love worketh no ill to his neighbor: therefore love is the fulfilling of the law." Rom. xiii : 8–10.

Thus we see that the law of love not only cultivates that God-like principle, but restrains vicious propensities and evil desires. It prunes off redundancies, rounds off the angles, and smooths over the rough places of our nature, and cultivates purity of heart and holiness of life, until we are brought to that standard of perfection that makes us ever anxious to do good, and tremble at the thought of offending God by doing evil. It embodies the golden rule, "Do unto others as you would have them do unto you." "Love worketh no ill to his neighbor." When we see a man seeking to injure his neighbor in order to profit himself, we may feel sure that he has not partaken of the divine nature, and is a stranger to that love which fits men for the society of heaven. If he would swindle his neighbor or his brother here, he would seek to swindle Gabriel out of his position in the presence of God, if he could get there and make it profitable for him to occupy it. Such men are wholly unfit for the climes of bliss, however long their faces, or sanctimonious their pretensions.

"Though I speak with the tongues of men and of angels and have not love, I am become as sounding brass or a tinkling cymbal. And though I have the gift of prophecy, and understand all mysteries, and all knowledge; and though I have all faith, so that I could remove mountains, and have not love, I am nothing. And though I bestow all my goods to feed the poor, and though I give my body to be burned and have not love, it profiteth me nothing. Love suffereth long, and is kind; love envieth not; love vaunteth not itself, is not puffed up, doth not behave itself unseemly, seeketh not her own, is not easily provoked, thinketh no evil; rejoiceth not in iniquity, but rejoiceth in the truth; beareth all things, believeth all things, hopeth all things, endureth all things." 1 Cor. xiii: 1–7.

By this we learn that it matters not what amount of knowledge we have, what the strength of our faith, or what the extent of the sacrifices we make, if we have not *love*, nothing we are, have, or do, will avail us any thing. Thus the apostle sums up the grand achievements of love, in moulding human character in accordance with the *divine nature.*

After thus impressing the Corinthians with the utter barrenness of Christian character without *love*, and the glorious achievements of it, the apostle winds up his most impressive lesson on the importance and supremacy of *love* in the following words: "But now abideth faith, hope, love, these three; and the greatest of these is love." 1 Cor. xiii: 13. When we rightly consider the importance of *faith* and *hope* with which *love* is here compared, we may the better appreciate the value of the latter. Let us look at them a little.

Faith is the main-spring of all acceptable obedience to God—without it we cannot please him in any thing. It purifies the heart, and works by love. It is the first condition of salvation, and produces repentance; and, perfected by obedience, secures eternal life; yet love is greater than faith. The apostle says so, and so it is.

Hope is the anchor of the soul, and enters within the

vail where Jesus has for us entered. It sustains the drooping spirits of the wayworn pilgrim amid the persecutions, trials, vexations, and disappointments incident to his journey through life, insomuch that the apostle says "we are saved by hope," for without it we would sink into despondency and die in despair; yet *love* is greater than *hope*.

Faith and hope end with this life. They cannot cross the chilly waters of death and enter into the home beyond. Faith will be lost in sight. Our feet will walk the golden streets of the celestial city, and we shall see Jesus as he is. Hope will be swallowed up in *realization*. Here we hope for glory, honor, and eternal life—in heaven these will be enjoyed, and for them we shall hope no more. There will be neither *faith* nor *hope* in heaven. But *love* will continue to bind us to God and humanity through this life, and its golden cords will perhaps grow stronger in the life which is to come. Love will live in immortal vigor while eternal years roll on. Love will have no end, but will go on while God and immortality endure.

> "Love is the golden chain that binds,
> The happy souls above;
> And he's an heir of heaven who finds,
> His bosom glow with love."

There are other elements in the divine nature, but they are subordinate to and measured by love. Every thing required by God of his creature, man, was intended to be conducive to the highest happiness of man. Nothing can add to the glory of God. The earth is filled with the glory of the Lord, (Num. xiv: 21. Ps. lxxii: 19.) and the very heavens declare the glory of God. (Ps. xix: 1.) All our efforts to glorify God is but a recognition of the glory which already belongs to him. There can be no such thing as *selfishness* in God. He requires no service at our hands to enrich him, or add to his glory. Such a thought is ridiculously absurd. Jesus told the Jews that what they did to benefit others they did to and for him. We honor the Bridegroom by partaking of the supper prepared for us at his own expense. We give glory to God when we wash our own robes in the blood of his Son. Obedience to the gospel secures eternal life to us through the grace of God manifested to the world in the gift of his Son. My dear friend, have you ever considered the depth of your ingratitude to the Bridegroom, in refusing to go in with him to the supper prepared for you at such fearful cost? Your acceptance of the invitation would add nothing to the richness of the feast. The fatlings are killed and the feast is prepared whether you go or not. Your presence would add nothing to the happiness of the guests at the supper. They will be quite as happy whether you are present or absent. Perhaps they will not miss you if you stay away. Their great love for you interests them for you now; but when the door is shut, closing them in, and you out, they will weep for you no more. Their cup of bliss will be unmixed and full. The loss will be entirely yours. God can do without you—can you do without him? Jesus Christ will be entirely happy, whether you are saved or lost. If you think he cannot administer the affairs of heaven without you, you are mistaken. He will allow you to be lost, if you are determined not to be saved. That is a matter about which every one is entirely free to decide for himself. One thing is certain, however, if you go to heaven, Jesus Christ intends to conduct the train on which you go. If you take passage with any other conductor, you will get side-tracked, ditched, or wrecked most certainly. To speak without a figure, Jesus proposes to save only those who come to God by him. While there is the slightest disposition to *go to heaven in our own way* we cannot be saved. There must be an unreserved and entire surrender to the Lord's will, or there is no salvation for any one.

How are Christians made partakers of the divine nature? Peter says that in the revealed knowledge of God " are given unto us exceeding great and precious promises; that by these ye might be partakers of the divine nature." By a proper consideration of the great and precious promises revealed in the word of the Lord, we are drawn to God, and made partakers of his nature, seen in the promises. Of these promises, there are so many that we can only present a few of them.

(1) He has promised that he will never leave nor forsake us while we walk uprightly before him. He will, in nothing, allow us to be tempted beyond our ability to bear, but in every trial he will be near us, to deliver us and make a way for our escape. If we put our hand in his, and allow him to lead us, he will keep our feet from sliding, and conduct us in the way of life everlasting. What a blessed and precious promise is this! How often do we feel our great weakness, and the need of a Father's care!

> " Guide me, O thou great Jehovah,
> Pilgrim through this barren land;
> I am weak but thou art mighty,
> Hold me with thy powerful hand."

Martha said to Jesus: "Lord, if thou hadst been here, my brother had not died." John xi: 21. Like Martha, we feel safe when in company with, and led by the Savior. When the light of his word shines upon our pathway, we feel sure that we cannot fall. When going by his direction, we feel sure that we are in his company.

> "I need thee every hour—teach me thy will,
> And thy rich promises, in me fulfill.
> I need thee, O, I need thee; every hour I need thee,
> O, bless me now my Savior, I come to thee."

O, Lord make us equal to the trials awaiting us, and all the duties assigned us. Thy will in all things be done.

(2) "Yea, though I walk through the valley of the shadow of death, I will fear no evil: for thou art with me; thy rod and thy staff they comfort me." Ps. xxiii: 4. The decree has gone forth, and is irrepealable, that dust we are and unto dust we must return; but "as in Adam all die even so in Christ shall all be made alive." 1 Cor. xv: 22. God has promised that he will not forget us in the tomb, but he will awaken our sleeping dust to live again, if worthy, in the glorified image of his Son. "For if we believe that Jesus died and rose again, even so them also which sleep in Jesus will God bring with him." 1 Thess. iv: 14.

> "Asleep in Jesus! blessed sleep,
> From which none ever wake to weep,
> A calm and undisturbed repose,
> Unbroken by the last of foes."

Blessed promise—we shall live again. If this life were all there is for man, it would scarcely be worth the living. In many cases it were far better never to have lived. Life to many is a grievous misfortune, if there is nothing beyond death. Suffering, misery, vexation, and disappointment, with an *intellect* capable of appreciating his condition, without a ray of light, or a gleam of hope coming from beyond the grave! *Better have been a brute*, without intelligent appreciation to augment his suffering and intensify his miserable condition. Begone from me, thou most unwelcome thought. We have no time, space nor inclination to pursue the vile intrusion further here.

(3) "Blessed are they that do his commandments, that they may have right to the tree of life, and may enter in through the gates into the city." Rev. xxii: 14. Our parents were driven from the presence of God, away from the tree of life, and out of the garden of Eden.

Here, those who are faithfully obedient to the commandments of the Lord, are promised an entrance into the city of God, where God is—where Jesus is—where angels are—where the spirits of just men made perfect will ever be. They are promised a right to the tree of life from which our parents were driven, where they may pluck and eat of its life-giving fruit, and live forever, beyond the reach of pain, sickness, disease, and death; *provided,* that a restoration to the tree of life means a restoration to the privileges possessed by Adam and Eve before they were driven from it; and we cannot see how such a privilege could mean less. They will be permitted to drink of the stream of life, which gurgles from beneath the throne of God, of which he that drinks will thirst no more. They will, with tongues immortal, engage with angels around the eternal throne in a new song of glory to God and to the Lamb forever and ever.

Who has not felt his soul swell within him when listening to the songs of praise made by mortal tongues in the house of God on the Lord's day. If such be the effect of songs sung by mortal tongues on earth, what must be the character and effect of the sweeter strains made by tongues immortal, when singing the new song in the city of God? Human imagination is lost in attempting to contemplate it. Are not these "exceeding great and precious promises?" They are given to us in the revealed knowledge of God; and by them Peter says we are made partakers of the *divine nature*. Is it not true that in feasting the soul on such promises, we drink copious drafts of the *divine nature* which streams through them? Can we fail to gather spiritual strength as our hearts run out in gratitude to God for such manifestations of his love? Can we not love our worst enemy in view of what God has done for man, when man was an enemy to God? What human nature refuses to do, the divine nature can do.

These may well be called exceeding great and precious promises; and by great and precious promises Peter says the disciples are made partakers of the divine nature; but he does not say they are made partakers of the divine nature by *promises only*. Every principle in the government of God which tends to restrain evil propensities, control appetites, moderate inordinate desires, subjugate angry passions and vicious inclinations on the one side, and cultivate love, mercy, kindness, gentleness, goodness, benevolence, holiness, and purity of heart on the other, is calculated to develop the divine nature in the Christian. The Christian religion is intended to make men and women like God; and just as they are brought under the divine influence they are made partakers of the divine nature. "For as many as are led by the Spirit of God, they are the sons of God." Rom. viii: 14.

"This I say then, Walk in the Spirit, and ye shall not fulfill the lust of the flesh. For the flesh lusteth against the Spirit, and the Spirit against the flesh: and these are contrary the one to the other: so that ye cannot do the things that ye would. But if ye be led of the Spirit, ye are not under the law. Now the works of the flesh are manifest, which are these; Adultery, fornication, uncleanness, lasciviousness, idolatry, witchcraft, hatred, variance, emulations, wrath, strife, seditions, heresies, envyings, murders, drunkenness, revelings, and such like: of the which I tell you before, as I have also told you in time past, that they which do such things shall not inherit the kingdom of God. But the fruit of the Spirit is love, joy, peace, longsuffering, gentleness, goodness, faith, meekness, temperance: against such there is no law. And they that are Christ's have crucified the flesh with the affections and lusts. If we live in the Spirit, let us also walk in the Spirit." Gal. v: 16-25.

Quite a number of Scriptures might be cited, showing things to be avoided, and others to be cultivated; but this is sufficient to give the thought we are seeking to bring out—viz: That we become partakers of the divine nature by moulding our hearts, and controlling our actions in harmony with the divine will—by avoiding that which is wrong, till the disposition to do such things is crucified—banished from the heart, and we have no inclination to do that in which we once delighted; and by faithfully doing that which the Lord requires, until the Lord's will becomes part of our nature; and it becomes a pleasure to do that which was once repulsive to us. We can love to do things because we know it to be the Lord's will that we shall do them. We can love our enemies because it gives us pleasure to do any thing that is well pleasing to God. Once it may have required constant watch care for one to avoid the use of profane language; but he has cultivated himself under the divine Spirit, ever present in the word of the Lord, until profanity is repulsive to his very nature.

Has he not partaken of the divine nature on this subject? and can we not see how he did it? It was by training and educating himself on the subject of profanity in harmony with the divine will; and God has *promised* to bless those who trust in, and obey him on this, as in every thing else. Thus the promises of the Lord, relied upon, make us partakers of the divine nature, having escaped the corruption that is in the world through lust.

"Therefore if any man be in Christ, he is a new creature: old things are passed away; behold, all things are become new." 2 Cor. v: 17. "And be renewed in the Spirit of your mind; and that ye put on the new man, which after God is created in righteousness and true holiness." Eph. iv: 23, 24. "But now ye also put off all these; anger, wrath, malice, blasphemy, filthy communication out of your mouth. Lie not one to another, seeing that ye have put off the old man with his deeds; and have put on the new man, which is renewed in knowledge after the image of him that created him." Col. iii: 8–10.

These Scriptures show that the Christian is in Christ, and is a new creature. He has put off the old man or character, and has put on the new man, which is renewed in knowledge after the image of his Creator. He has put off the old behavior, and has been created in righteousness and true holiness. The elements of the divine nature have been planted in his heart, and if cultivated and developed to perfection, he will be so completely like God as to be happy in his presence, and fit for association with the redeemed in heaven. The Christian religion is intended to bring about this transformation, and without it man is wholly unfit for association with God, angels, and purified spirits above.

Oh, what a world we should have if every one in it were a partaker of the divine nature, and guided wholly by the word of the Lord. All jails and penitentiaries would be pulled down and thrown away, and the praises of God would resound from pole to pole; and love would fill every heart, and the glory of God would be sung by every tongue, and universal peace and happiness would fill the world. Why will not every man and every woman co-operate in bringing about such a glorious state of things on the earth? God speed the day when even the church, in all its members, shall so appreciate the promises of God as to be made partakers of the divine nature, and be brought fully under its influence. We are persuaded that the world would feel its power as it has never felt tt before.

"Precious promise God hath given,
To the weary passer by;
On the way from earth to heaven,
I will guide thee with mine eye."

CHAPTER XVII.

EXCUSES.

> "Then said he unto him, A certain man made a great supper, and bade many : and sent his servant at supper time to say to them that were bidden, Come; for all things are now ready. And they all with one consent began to make excuse. The first said unto him, I have bought a piece of ground, and I must needs go and see it: I pray thee have me excused. And another said, I have bought five yoke of oxen, and I go to prove them : I pray thee have me excused. And another said, I have married a wife, and therefore I cannot come. So that servant came, and shewed his lord these things." Luke xiv: 16-24.

IT is not our purpose to dwell upon the first invitation of the Jews to the privileges of the gospel, and the subsequent invitation of the long outcast Gentiles, compelled by earnest argument and entreaty to accept the salvation spurned by those so highly favored of God, as had been the Jews; but we desire to draw a more practical lesson from the *excuses* rendered by those invited, for the benefit of those who are doing now as they did then—rendering frivolous excuses for not obeying the gospel, and accepting salvation under very favorable circumstances, when the dearest friends they have on earth so earnestly importune them to be saved.

The excuses show very plainly that they were founded in hypocrisy, and prompted in an utter want of interest in the feast prepared for their entertainment. The first had bought a piece of ground and had to go and see it. Did he buy a piece of ground without seeing it before he bought it? It being real estate, it would hardly have run away until the next day. He could have gone to the supper if he had been anxious to honor the master by going.

The next one had bought five yoke of oxen and had to go to prove them. Strange that he bought them without trying them before buying them. If he had been anxious to go to the supper to which he had been invited, he could have put off proving his oxen for another day. When persons do not wish to do a thing, it is quite easy to find some excuse for not doing it.

But the next one had married a wife, and of course he could not go. He did not even ask to be excused; he could not go, and that was enough. He was newly married and could not, so soon, leave his wife long enough to go to a supper. But could he not have taken his wife with him? From the general character of the invitation, we suppose the presence of ladies was not prohibited; and the application of the lesson would show that the supper was for *men and women*. True, the narrative says, "That none of those men which were bidden shall taste of my supper;" but this only shows that the men were to blame for the non-attendance. There is nothing showing that this man might not have taken his wife with him to the supper. Had he been very anxious to go he could have gone. He felt no interest in honoring the master of the supper, and the master knew it, and was very angry. These flimsy excuses did not satisfy him.

The excuses made by men to-day are no better than those made by the Jews. We will examine a few of them and see whether or not they are valid.

(1) "There are so many different doctrines preached

that I do not know which is right. If wise men differ, how am I to decide which is right?" The Bible is right, infallibly right. Have you ever taken that infallible standard and carefully examined it to see what is taught in it, that you might know who preached the truth? We guess not. Is it not likely that you could live in any of the churches around you and do as well as you are doing now? While it is a great misfortune that the religious world is split up into parties, and preaching different doctrines, that will scarcely justify you in refusing to read and study the Bible for yourself. There was never a counterfeit piece of money that was not an imitation of something genuine. So there may be many spurious religions in the world, but that very fact is evidence that there is something pure some where; and if you will study the great counterfeit detecter, you will be very apt to find what is spurious, and what is genuine. Generally those who render this excuse do not care which is right. They are not anxious to know about it, and hence, do not try to know.

(2) "If baptism is for the remission of sins, as you teach, then my parents are lost, for they were not baptized. My mother was a good woman, and I know she went to heaven without baptism. For me to be baptized for the remission of sins would be to say that my mother has gone to hell. I am not going to do that, sure. That settles it with me."

Do you suppose that any thing you can do will change the condition of your dead mother one way or the other? Suppose your mother did the best she knew, and God saved her because she did so, will he save you in neglect of your duty when you know it to be your duty? Perhaps you have light that she never had. Perhaps she thought non-essential that which you know to be a solemn command of God. Will he save you in known and willful neglect of duty, because your mother did not know it to be her duty? If your mother did the best she knew, would it not be well for you to do the best you know? Whether your mother was lost or saved is not a matter regulating your duty. If you know your duty and do it not, you will be beaten with many stripes, while few may be the stripes coming to the lot of such as come short of their duty because they knew not what duty was. Do your own duty and let God attend to others. He will manage that matter as may be pleasing to him.

(3) "I am better now than many who are in the church." Well, suppose you are; perhaps you might improve on that a little. But why compare yourself with the worst in the church? Suppose you put it this way: "I am better than any in the church." Do you think you could, in truth, say this? If every one in the church goes to hell for neglect of duty, is that any reason why you should want to go? Will that excuse you for neglect of duty? If every man in the church goes to hell, *if you will, in good faith, do your duty, you will be saved.* But " you cannot live in the church with those *bad men* who are in it." Well, the Lord will take those wicked fellows out of the church after a while, and he will put them right into your company; and you will have to spend eternity with them, if eternity may be spent. 'Twere better to come into the church and help to put those bad fellows out, then they will be out, and you in, and thus you will get rid of them. Now, we respectfully suggest that the wickedness of others is no excuse for you. Do your own duty faithfully and you will be saved, whatever may be the end

of the wicked. "The wickedness of the wicked be upon him," is God's law.

But are you not just a little inconsistent in rendering this excuse? There are but two classes—those in the church, and those out of it. You belong to the class on the outside. Do you not think there are as bad men out of the church as can be found in it? There are murderers, thieves, robbers, liars, gamblers, whoremongers, sorcerers, and all other classes engaged in the whole dark catalogue of sin, among those out of the church; and you can be quite contented to live with them out of the church, but you cannot afford to live with a *few bad men in the church!* Do you not feel ashamed of such an excuse as this? Better do your own duty, and let the Lord attend to the *tares* that the devil sowed among the wheat. This is safe—nothing else is.

(4) "Well, I am a moral man. I use no profane language. I pay my debts promptly. I speak the truth always. I am as liberal in relieving the poor as any one in the church. I do not swindle, cheat, or steal. I try to make a good neighbor and a good citizen; and I see no use in joining the church. I cannot see that that would make me any better." Have you a firmly fixed and trusting faith in Jesus Christ as your Savior? Jesus said, "he that believeth and is baptized shall be saved; but he that believeth not shall be damned." If you have not been baptized you are not within range of the Savior's promise: and if you do not believe in Christ, through the gospel, the anathemas of heaven will rest upon you if Jesus told the truth.

Again Jesus said: "Except a man be born again he cannot enter the kingdom of God." Have you been born again? "Except a man be born of water and of the Spirit he cannot enter into the kingdom of God." Have you been born of water and of the Spirit? If not, into the kingdom of God you cannot go. Jesus said this, and it must be true. In this kingdom is a state of safety—can a man be saved out of it? If so, how? Why did not Nicodemus say: " Master, there is no necessity of entering the kingdom, seeing a man can be saved out of it as well as in it." If a man can get to heaven out of the kingdom he will be saved on a plan of his own, and he may give the glory to himself, and not to God. The blood of Christ had nothing to do with it, and therefore the blood of Christ was shed for nothing. If you can be saved without it, all others can. Cornelius was a devout man, and one that feared God with all his house, who gave much alms to the people and prayed to God always. Are you better than he was? He had to hear words from Peter by which to be saved. (Acts xi: 14.) Jesus requires you to believe and obey him; you live every day in rebellion against him while you fail to obey him. Do you think it safe to live in rebellion against God?

(5) "I am not good enough to obey the gospel and be a Christian." Well, how long do you think it will require for you to get to be good enough while you spend your time in serving the devil? Is that not rather a slow way of improving much? Jesus came not to call the righteous, but sinners to repentance. If you are a sinner you are among the class he came to save. Are you worse than the murderers of Jesus Christ? If they could be saved, why may not you? On the day of Pentecost Peter told the Jews that they had, with wicked hands crucified and slain the Lord Jesus Christ; and yet many of them obeyed the Lord and were saved that day. It is difficult to conceive of any worse than

they were; and yet they were not required to mourn and weep, and wrestle with the Lord like Jacob did; but when they believed on the Lord Jesus Christ through Peter's preaching, and were cut to the heart by it, and cried out to know what to do, Peter told them to repent and be baptized, in the name of Jesus Christ, for the remission of sins; and as many as gladly received his word were baptized and the same day added to the saved. Now, if they could do this, why may not you do as they did, and be saved as they were?

"I want to feel like I am pardoned—my sins forgiven, before I am baptized." Will you be sure you are pardoned when you feel like you are pardoned? Such feelings are the result of your faith. When you believe you are pardoned, you will feel like you are pardoned, whether you are pardoned or not. If you could be made believe, without a doubt, that when you shall have *counted ten*, you will be pardoned, when you have *counted ten*, you will feel just like you are pardoned. In other words, *whenever a man does that which he believes will secure his pardon, he will feel like he is pardoned.* Jacob believed Joseph was dead, when he was alive and governor of Egypt; and while he believed his son to be dead, he felt just like he was really dead. *A falsehood believed, will produce the same feelings that would follow from the belief of the same thing if it were true.* When, therefore, you believe you are pardoned, you will feel like you are pardoned, whether you are pardoned or unpardoned. When the Catholic pays his money to the priest to absolve him from guilt, or secure his pardon, he *feels* like he is pardoned; and *he feels like it because he believes it.* So the heathen man, who bows before his idol god, feels like he is pardoned for the very same reason. *Are not his feelings as reliable as yours?* Why not? We confess we can see no reason why.

But you say: "He is deceived, for his idol god has no power to pardon him." Very true indeed; but he thinks his god has the power, and believing this, he feels just as happy as you do. *If his feelings deceive him, may not your feelings deceive you?* Jesus said: "He that believeth and is baptized shall be saved." If you are saved before you are baptized, for what will you then be baptized? Jesus did not say: "He that believeth and is saved, may, or should be baptized." Had he said this, your position might have been plausible; but as he did not say it, your position is unreasonable and absurd. Better accept salvation as it is offered to you by him who has the power to save you.

Since the last will went into force on the day of Pentecost, there is not a case of conversion recorded, where the *converted rejoiced in his pardon before he was baptized* —not one. The Eunuch went on his way rejoicing after he was baptized. Acts viii: 39. The jailer rejoiced in his salvation after his baptism. Acts xvi: 34. A man may well feel like he is pardoned when he knows he has complied with all the conditions upon which Jesus said he should be saved; but until then his feelings may deceive him, however honest he may be in relying upon them.

We feel good because we know we are pardoned; and we know we are pardoned because we know we have obeyed the Lord. You want your good feelings as evidence of your pardon *before obedience*, when in truth good feelings should spring from a knowledge of pardon, *based upon obedience* to the commands, and a firm *reliance on the promises* contained in the word of the Lord. The child feels good when it knows it has obeyed its parents, so we feel good when we know we have obeyed the Lord; and, as his children, may call him "our Father." *We feel good because we know we are pardoned—you know you are pardoned because you feel good.* This is the real difference. We submit the two positions for your very careful consideration. One, or the other, may be true—both cannot be. You can decide which.

(6) "I don't know enough yet." How much do you know? Do you know that you are a sinner, and in need of a Savior? Do you know that Jesus died to save sinners, and that he proposes to save all who come to God by him? Do you know what he requires you to do in order that he may save you? If you do, you know enough to be saved: and you will be lost if you fail to do that which you know to be your duty. You are required to *grow* in grace and in knowledge; and there could be no growth in knowledge if you knew every thing at the beginning.

There is no age specified in the Bible at which children may obey the gospel. This very much depends on their general intelligence and their opportunities of obtaining a knowledge of the Lord's will. Some children at ten years old know more of the Bible than some men ever learn. As soon as they know their duty they are old enough to obey the Lord, and they will be lost if they fail to render the obedience which the gospel requires. They can then render the *obedience of faith*, and until this can be done no obedience is worth any thing.

(7) "I am afraid I cannot hold out faithful, and I do not want to bring reproach upon the cause of Christ." This is a laudable feeling. Surely no one desires to bring reproach upon the cause of the Master, but we think it likely that those most fearful of bringing reproach are most secure against it. They will be

more careful in exercising a watch-care over themselves, and will therefore be less liable to fall than the self-confident, who will be more reckless and less safe. With faith and trust in God, and constant prayer for success, the humble soul will not fail.

(8) "There is time enough yet. I am young and have not enjoyed myself enough. By and by, when my cup of pleasure is full, I will obey the Lord." A wise man said: "Remember now thy Creator in the days of thy youth, while the evil days come not, nor the years draw nigh, when thou shalt say, I have no pleasure in them." Eccl. xii: 1. It is not the cross, nor does it cost the struggle to surrender to the Lord in youth that it costs those who have been hardened in sin. In youth, as a rule, vicious habits have not been formed, and there is but little reformation to make; the heart is not all scarred up by indulgence in crime. The affections are tender and readily moulded in love for a crucified Savior. But how hard it is to turn back from a life of indulgence in sin; and alas! how few there are who ever come to Jesus in old age. It is hard to give up habits so long indulged. How ungrateful it is to give the strength of manhood to the devil, and blow the ashes from the candle of life into the face of the Lord when the hardened old wretch can serve the devil no longer! But my young friend, while you are indulging in your career of pleasure, suppose death should knock at your door! You are expecting to live a long time, but you may die to-day. Though your cheeks may bloom in the rose tints of health and youthful vigor, death may already have marked you as his own. To-day is the day of salvation. Now is the accepted time. To-morrow to you may never come. And if you knew

you would live to be old, you owe all to the service of God. You can never repay God for what he has done for you. You will never regret an early obedience to God—you may have eternity in which to regret that you did not honor God when you had an opportunity to do so. Don't delay—come to Jesus and come now.

(9) "Well, but I have not made money enough yet. I know that my business is contrary to the spirit and genius of the Christian religion, and I am in debt, and cannot give up my business yet. Or, I have not as much land as I want, and I cannot afford to give up my business until I make my contemplated purchase. When I make enough I will consider the subject of religion." In the first place, you should not want to make money by such immoral business. No man should want money made by dishonest or immoral means. We know nothing about *repentance* that does not repair damages done, or restore all ill-gotten gains to the full extent of his ability. We cannot see how a man can truly repent with money in his pocket obtained in this way. It is unsafe to risk it.

We can readily conceive it possible for a man to *inconsiderately* pursue an immoral calling and truly repent and come to Christ for pardon; but for him to *deliberately* resolve to indulge in wrong-doing in the hope of washing out the stains in the blood of a crucified Savior, and keep what he has made in his unholy calling, is putting the grace and mercy of God to a strain that is extremely dangerous, to say the least of it. We dare not say that all possibility of repentance is gone; but such deliberate resolve is infinitely worse than the overt acts committed in pursuance of the resolve. We earnestly hope that few have reached the degree of depravity capable of such a resolve. The risk is surely a fearful one. There is little chance for him to be saved.

(10) "But another says; "I am waiting for others. I want my friend to go with me. I want my wife to go with me, or, I want my husband to go with me when I go to the Savior." This is a mistaken policy. If you wish your friend to obey the Lord through your influence, it is better to set him an example worthy of his imitation. This is far better. It shows that you are in earnest—that you intend to be honest with your God, yourself, and your friend. We have often seen wives who seemed to be more concerned for their husbands than for themselves; and in the hope of inducing them to obey the Lord they have lived in disobedience themselves, when if they had gone along and met their own obligations to God, their influence would have been much more potent in bringing their husbands to a discharge of their duty. And the same is true of husbands with regard to their wives. But the whole procedure is wrong. No one should trifle with his salvation in that way. He should do his own duty and let consequences take care of themselves. He cannot afford to risk his own salvation to save any one, even though it be the dearest friend he has on earth. Suppose the person should die while waiting for a companion, would waiting for a companion be a valid excuse in the day of judgment? It looks a little like the man who had married a wife and could not go to the supper. But there is a principle behind all this. You owe the service of your *whole life* to God; and you have no right to withhold any part of that service in waiting on any one; nor have you any right to contract with any one about your duty to your God. "I will go if you will." If you love your friend better than your God, you are unworthy of him, and you are not in a suitable frame of

mind to obey God in anything. Better stay away until you can rise above this. Were you to go to the Lord in such a frame of mind as this, you might find yourself in the attitude of the man who went in to the marriage supper not having on a wedding garment.

(11) "My parents and friends are all opposed to that church. I believe it right myself, but I ought to obey my parents, and they would be greatly offended were I to join the Campbellites." Well, suppose you simply obey the gospel without joining the Campbellites. We know but little about these Campbellites any way. They must be very bad people, for we have never heard any thing good of them. All the reports that come to us concerning them are decidedly unfavorable, and we would not encourage an alliance with them, unless an earnest and hearty obedience to God should put you in company with them. This could not be unless they are doing the same thing; and if they are thus faithfully obedient to God, they are not quite so bad as reported. If you will faithfully obey the Lord, these unworthy Campbellites cannot hurt you, however bad they may be. It is true that you should obey your parents; but only when parental authority is in harmony with the law of God. If parental authority comes in conflict with God's authority, then obey God rather than the parents. Suppose your parents should command you to steal, when God says, "thou shalt not steal," what then? Will you steal in obedience to your parents, or refuse to steal in obedience to God? "But my parents will not require me to steal." Very well, this settles the principle.

You will obey your parents until their will comes in conflict with the Lord's will. If your parents undertake to control your obedience to God, you will obey

God and take the consequences. They cannot obey God for you. You are responsible for yourself, and will be judged for yourself. Jesus said: "He that loveth father or mother more than me is unworthy of me." If it becomes necessary to forsake all for Jesus' sake, then the sacrifice must be made. All things will work together for your good, if you will do your duty faithfully. Your obedience may lead your obdurate parents to repentance. If not, you will at least save yourself.

(12) "This religion is unpopular. The people are not fashionable. It will injure me in my business." Yes, the preaching of Noah was very unpopular. Only his own family gave attention to it in one hundred and twenty years. Yet, of all the world, only these eight souls were saved. Would you have preferred the fate of the popular world rather than the salvation of Noah? Jesus was exceedingly unpopular. He consorted with the poor. The aristocracy would have nothing to do with him. He preached to the poor and the illiterate, and of them selected his apostles; yet they were able to confound and put to silence the wisdom of the wise. The poor and despised Lazarus was carried by angels to the bosom of Abraham, while the rich man opened his eyes in the flames of hell. Who would you rather be, the rich man, or the poor Lazarus?

Paul said: "The fashion of this world passeth away." 1 Cor. vii: 31. And James said: "Let the brother of low degree rejoice in that he is exalted: but the rich, in that he is made low: because as the flower of the grass he shall pass away. For the sun is no sooner risen with a burning heat, but it withereth the grass, and the flower thereof falleth, and the grace of the fashion of it perisheth: so also shall the rich man fade away in his ways." James i: 9–11.

Let us not seek the fashion of the world that passeth away like the grace of the flower under the burning heat of the mid-day sun; so also shall the rich man fade away in his ways. Let us not be conformed to this world, but be clothed with that humility that characterized the meek and lowly Son of God. No matter what the world may say of us, if God be for us, who can be against us? "I will not be afraid of ten thousands of people, that have set themselves against me round about." Ps. iii: 6. "Better is little with the fear of the Lord than great treasure and trouble therewith." Prov. xv: 16.

Suppose that obedience to the gospel does injure you in your business; then let your business go. Obey God and let business take care of itself. There are very few that do not prefer to do business with an honest Christian man. Some customers may withdraw their patronage on account of your religion, but you will gain two more for every one you lose. And if you do not, you cannot afford to barter your soul for business. If you gain the whole world and lose your soul, what will you give in exchange for it? "Because thou sayest, I am rich, and increased with goods, and have need of nothing; and knowest not that thou art wretched, and miserable, and poor, and blind, and naked: I counsel thee to buy of me gold tried in the fire, that thou mayest be rich." Rev. iii: 17, 18.

Paul told Timothy to "charge them that are rich in this world, that they be not highminded, nor trust in uncertain riches, but in the living God, who giveth us richly all things to enjoy; that they do good, that they be rich in good works, ready to distribute, willing to communicate; laying up in store for themselves a good foundation against the time to come, that they may lay hold on eternal life." 1 Tim. vi: 17-19. This is safe.

The riches of this world are uncertain. They are liable to be blown away by the first adverse wind that comes; but God gives us the true riches that endure unto eternal life. "He that oppresseth the poor to increase his riches, and he that giveth to the rich shall surely come to want." Prov. xxii: 16.

(13) "I have not time to be a Christian now—I am too busy. When I have leisure, I will consider the subject of religion." Yes, you are very busy—do you think you can take time to die when death comes? You are like Martha, cumbered about with many things; but Jesus said that Mary had chosen the good part that should never be taken away from her. The seed that fell among thorns were choked out by the cares of the world and the deceitfulness of riches, and they brought no fruit to perfection. Jesus told the Jews to seek first the kingdom of God and his righteousness, and other things should be added; but you propose to reverse his rule and begin at the other end, leaving the kingdom of God to be sought at the last. Yes, you propose to serve the devil as long as you can, and when you can serve him no longer, then you will say: "Here Lord, take me. I am very busy, it is true, but I can do no more just now, so I guess I will surrender. Here I am, take me." Of course, no one says this in words, but the *lives of many do say it.* Oh, the depth of such ingratitude! God loved them, and Jesus died for them, and yet they expect to be saved after spending their manhood in rebellion against God! Can this be? If so, they may, every one, sing,

"Amazing grace, how sweet the sound,
That saved a wretch like me."

We think it likely that procrastination has sent more

souls to hell than any other one thing that has ever cursed the race. Few men have ever gone down to the grave unprepared, who had not intended at some time to be Christians; but from one cause and another have put it off and neglected it till too late. In full view of all their responsibility they have drifted down the stream of life to the end, until the harvest was passed, the summer ended, opportunities all gone, and nothing done. All acknowledge such a course unwise, and unsafe, but thousands go through life just this way. They take the risk, and a fearful risk it is. Whenever a man has opportunity to obey the gospel and he fails to do it, he takes his salvation in his own hands, with all the risk attaching to it. If he lives to have other opportunities, he is fortunate if he accepts them; but if he falls into conditions which put it out of his power to obey, he can scarcely hope that God will excuse him for slighting the opportunities of the past. When he had the privilege, then was the time he should have accepted it; and as he did not, in vain may he call for mercy when the time has been passed in rebellion against his Maker. The eternal principles of justice can only be vindicated in his punishment, and punished he will surely be. In the Hebrew letter the soul-stirring question is asked: "How shall we escape if we neglect so great salvation." Neglect may make escape impossible. Oh, then, do not neglect your duty another day. Remember that the lord of the supper said that not one of those who made excuse should taste of his supper, for they were unworthy. Will you not be unworthy to go into the marriage supper of the lamb? And think you that your excuses will be worth any more than theirs? "Where there is a will there is a way." They who want to come to Christ always find a way to come.

CHAPTER XVIII.

THE ORIGIN, MISSION, AND DESTINY OF ANGELS.

For this cause I bow my knees unto the Father of our Lord Jesus Christ, of whom the whole family in heaven and earth is named." Eph. iii: 14, 15.

BY this text we clearly learn two things—(1) that God has a family; (2) that part of them are on this earth and part in heaven, and this was true at the time the apostle wrote this letter to the Ephesians. That living Christians are God's family on the earth is so very generally admitted as to scarcely need proof. John says: "Behold, what manner of love the Father hath bestowed upon us, that we should be called the sons of God: therefore the world knoweth us not, because it knew him not. Beloved, now are we the sons of God, and it doth not yet appear what we shall be: but we know that, when he shall appear, we shall be like him; for we shall see him as he is." 1 John iii: 1, 2. "Blessed are the peacemakers: for they shall be called the children of God." Matt. v: 9. "For as many as are led by the Spirit of God, they are the sons of God." "The Spirit itself beareth witness with our spirit, that we are the children of God." Rom. viii: 14, 16. "For ye are all the children of God by faith in Christ Jesus." Gal. iii: 26. These Scriptures, with many others which might be given, so clearly identify that portion of God's family which is on the earth, that we need not spend more time looking for them. We propose to seek an acquaintance with that part of the family which were in heaven at the time the apostles wrote, whence they came, how long they had been there, and what they were doing—in a word, every thing we may know of them.

First, then, was that portion of God's family which were in heaven at the time the apostle wrote, made up of the saints who had lived, died. been judged and glorified before then? We think not. "Because he hath appointed a day, in the which he will judge the world in righteousness by that man whom he hath ordained; whereof he hath given assurance unto all men, in that he hath raised him from the dead." Acts xvii: 31.

We take it that this day was appointed as a time for the judgment of *all men*, without regard to the *time* in which they lived. That it was not appointed as a day in which to judge *only* those who might be living at that time, is evident from the language of Jesus himself. He says: "Marvel not at this: for the hour is coming, in the which all that are in the graves shall hear his voice, and shall come forth; they that have done good, unto the resurrection of life; and they that have done evil, unto the resurrection of damnation." John v: 28, 29. This resurrection reaches those who are *in their graves*, and brings them up for judgment.

Again: "And I saw a great white throne, and him that sat on it, from whose face the earth and the heaven fled away; and there was found no place for them. And I saw the dead, small and great, stand before God; and the books were opened: and another book was opened, which is the book of life: and the dead were judged out of those things which were written in the books, according to their works. And the sea gave up the dead which were in it: and death and hell delivered up the dead which were in them: and they were judged every man according to their works." Rev. xx: 11–13. This brings the dead—*all the dead*, to judgment. Then the family was not composed of those who had lived and died on the earth, for *they had not been judged* when Paul wrote.

That all men do not immediately go to heaven or hell at death, is further evident from the fact that David had been dead and buried more than a thousand years before the day of Pentecost; yet, on that day, Peter said: " David is not ascended into the heavens." Acts ii: 34. If David, a man after God's own heart, did not go direct to heaven at death, who else may expect to go?

But let us hear Peter further on this subject. He says: " The day of the Lord will come as a thief in the night; in the which the heavens shall pass away with a great noise, and the elements shall melt with fervent heat, the earth also and the works that are therein shall be burned up. Seeing then that all these things shall be dissolved, what manner of persons ought ye to be in all holy conversation and godliness, looking for and hasting unto the coming of the day of God, wherein the heavens being on fire shall be dissolved, and the elements shall melt with fervent heat?" 2 Peter iii: 10–12. The day of the Lord—what day? "But the heavens and the earth, which are now, by the same word are kept in store, reserved unto fire against the day of judgment and perdition of ungodly men." v. 7. This *day*, to which the heavens and the earth are reserved, is here called the " day of the Lord," " day of God," " day of judgment and perdition of ungodly men." Hence the apostle says: " The Lord knoweth how to deliver the godly out of temptation, and to reserve the unjust unto the day of judgment to be punished." 2 Pet. ii: 9.

This settles the question. There is awaiting all men a day of judgment, when the final doom of the wicked will come upon them, and the righteous will receive their reward. But a general day of judgment would be a most ridiculous farce if men should have to be brought back from heaven and hell to be re-sentenced to the same positions in which they have been before.

Enoch and Elijah were taken alive to heaven, and many of the saints were raised when Christ arose, but these were exceptions—not the rule. The rich man and Lazarus are supposed to show a different theory. The only thing necessary in understanding *that case*, is to learn whether that was a *literal past event*, or was it a *parable*. If it was a literal description of a literal past event, then the whole doctrine of a general day of judgment for all men is false; for the judgment was passed as to them, certainly. And worse still, heaven and hell will be in sight of each other, and the wicked and righteous will be talking across the line; and heaven will be made vocal with the cries and groans of the damned in hell, which may be heard across the line. There is no escape from this if the case of the rich man and Lazarus was a literal description of a literal past event. That *it was a parable*, we think is beyond dispute; and hence, like all other parables, it was intended to illustrate a single thought; and must not be strained beyond the one thing taught in it. Then it cannot apply to the case in hand at all, unless that be shown to be the point in the parable. This will scarcely be attempted by any one.

But we have not yet found that portion of God's family who were in heaven at the time Paul wrote. Let us try again. "Take heed that ye despise not one of these little ones; for I say unto you, That in heaven their angels do always behold the face of my Father which is in heaven." Matt xviii : 10.

And again: "But of that day and hour knoweth no man, no, not the angels of heaven, but my Father only." Matt. xxiv : 36.

These Scriptures, with many others which might be given, show that there are *angels* in heaven, and of them we shall learn more as we proceed. We think it likely that they were the chief portion of the family in heaven at the time the apostle wrote. Of this, however, each one will think for himself. We are now fully introduced to the subject of

ANGELS,

and with them we propose to cultivate an acquaintance for a time.

Besides the heavenly or celestial angels already seen, there are also *earthly,* or *terrestrial* angels, which are simply messengers; examples of which we have in the angels of the seven churches of Asia. Rev. ii : 8, 12, 18. iii : 1, 7, 14. And there are also *infernal* angels, or such as wait upon and serve the devil. Those infernal angels were once in heaven. "And there was war in heaven: Michael and his angels fought against the dragon; and the dragon fought and his angels, and prevailed not; neither was their place found any more in heaven. And the great dragon was cast out, that old serpent, called the Devil, and Satan, which deceiveth the whole world : he was cast out into the earth, and his angels were cast out with him." After describing the means by which the devil was overcome and cast out of heaven into the earth, with all his angels, the result is indicated. "Therefore rejoice, ye heavens, and ye that dwell in them. Woe to the inhabitants of the earth, and of the sea! for the devil is come down unto you." Rev. xii : 7–9, 12. Jesus said to his disciples : " I beheld Satan as lightning fall from heaven." Luke x : 18.

We propose to dismiss the devil and his angels here, at least for the present—indeed, we do not care to cultivate a very intimate acquaintance with them. We wish to know more of the angels of heaven, believing, as we do, that they constitute the major part of the *heavenly family*.

WERE THEY CREATED, OR WERE THEY ETERNAL?

"For by him were all things created, that are in heaven, and that are in earth, visible and invisible, whether they be thrones, or dominions, or principalities, or powers : all things were created by him, and for him." Col. i : 16. See also Eph. iii : 9. Heb. i : 2. John i : 3.

This is certainly broad enough to include angels, for it includes every thing in the heavens above, or on the earth beneath; visible or invisible, dominions, principalities, or powers, all things were *created*, hence God only was eternal. This shows that *angels were created*, whether they be in heaven, earth, or hell.

WHEN WERE THEY CREATED?

Not in the six days of creation; for every thing is mentioned that was created on each day, and yet we have no account of the creation of angels or devils. As soon as God left man in the garden, under law, we find the devil there, and at work; and we know that there were good angels as soon as there were bad ones; for we have already seen that there was war in heaven, between the good and the bad angels, which resulted in casting out the devil and his angels to the earth; hence unless the devil, by some strategy, got back into heaven, that war was anterior to the devil's operations in the garden of Eden. Therefore we conclude that the creation of angels, good and bad, must have been before the creation recorded by Moses.

God said to Job: "Where wast thou when I laid the foundations of the earth? declare, if thou hast understanding. Who hath laid the measures thereof, if thou knowest? or who hath stretched the line upon it? Whereupon are the foundations thereof fastened? or who laid the corner stone thereof; when the morning stars sang together, and all the sons of God shouted for joy." Job xxxviii: 4-7.

Who were the *sons of God* who shouted for joy when God laid the foundations of the earth? Those who deny angelic existence before the creation of Adam are at sea here, without chart or compass. They are hopelessly engulfed in the Stygian waters of infidelity. The truth gets into no such trouble, as we will see directly.

We have spoken of *good* and *bad* angels as *created* beings. By this we would not be understood to say that bad angels were bad when created; on the contrary all were good when created; but they were placed under law, which some kept and remained good, while others rebelled against God and violated his law, thereby making themselves bad. This we now propose to prove.

"And the angels which kept not their first estate, but left their own habitation, he hath reserved in everlasting chains under darkness unto the judgment of the great day." Jude 6. These angels had an estate and a habitation, else God would scarcely punish them for leaving the one, and failing to keep the other.

Peter is equally clear on this subject. He says: "For

if God spared not the angels that sinned, but cast them down to hell, and delivered them into chains of darkness, to be reserved unto judgment." This hypothetical case is so put as to assume it to be true. 2 Pet. ii: 4. Peter assumes that they *were not spared because they sinned.* Sin is the transgression of the law. 1 John iii: 4. Where there is no law there is no transgression. Rom. iv: 15. Hence, these angels that sinned were under law and violated it, thereby making themselves bad, and subject to punishment.

But we have said others obeyed the law and remained good. David says: "Bless the Lord, ye his angels, that excel in strength, that do his commandments, hearkening unto the voice of his word. Bless ye the Lord, all ye his hosts, ye ministers of his, that do his pleasure." Ps. ciii: 20, 21.

John says: "And I John am he that heard and saw these things. And when I heard and saw, I fell down to worship before the feet of the angel which showed me these things. And he saith unto me, See thou do it not. I am a fellow servant with thee, and with thy brethren the prophets, and with them which keep the words of this book. Worship God." Rev. xxii: 8, 9. *New Version.*

These quotations show that angels were under law in the days of David and John; and there was, perhaps, never a time when they were without law. We presume they are under law now, and will ever be. We have seen that some sinned in violating the law, and others were obedient to it. This, we think, the proofs cited clearly show.

But our question is not yet answered. *When were angels created?* We reply that we do not certainly know We can only reason about it—that is all. We have found that *they were created—not eternal*. We think we may feel pretty sure that they were created before the fall of Adam, for the devil was there, an active agent in that event; and the sons of God shouted for joy when the foundations of the earth were laid, before there was a man on the earth. We think we may feel pretty sure that they were not created in the six days of creation, for we have every thing mentioned that filled up the work of each day. Then we repeat our question—when were they created?

We have seen that a day will come, in which the heavens will pass away with a great noise, and the elements will melt with fervent heat, the earth also, and the works that are therein shall be burned up. "Nevertheless, we, according to his promise, look for a new heavens and a new earth, wherein dwelleth righteousness." 2 Pet. iii: 13.

Now, as *this state* of existence will fill its God-appointed mission and come to an end, to be *succeeded* by another, may we not justly conclude that it was *preceded* by another, perhaps by others May it not be true that a state analogous to the present state preceded our creation, in which intelligent beings existed under law, as we exist under law—that that state filled its mission, was brought to a close, and was succeeded by the present state; as the present state will be brought to a close and be succeeded by the new heavens and the new earth? The angels of the present state were perhaps the inhabitants of the previous state, and were ready for service *before* the creation described by Moses. The *holy* were the sons of God "who rejoiced when the works of God were complete in the creation; and the devil was the leading spirit among the wicked, ready to deceive our parents in the garden of Eden as soon as they were left under law, as he had been. This theory is plausible—we do not claim it to be *certainly true*. We only say we believe it is true.

It is sometimes claimed that *angels are the spirits of those who have lived and died* in the present state; but this theory breaks down in the operations of the devil in the garden *before the death of any one* whose spirit he could have been. And this theory is unable to account for the *sons of God* spoken of by God to Job, who rejoiced when the foundations of the earth were laid. A theory so manifestly defective can scarcely be true.

We cannot very readily conclude that the devil existed as a fallen angel before there were any other angels. We very soon find the angels of the Lord engaged in his service, and the Bible is as silent as to their creation, as it is with reference to the creation of the devil. And as he existed before the death of any human being, we think it likely that good angels were at least co-existent with him. Hence, we are not prepared to believe that angels are the spirits of those who have lived and died on this earth as it now is. We cannot resist, therefore, the conclusion that angels, good and bad, existed in some form anterior to the creation of Adam. One thing is certain, *they are here;* and have been here from a period more remote than any record we have. It becomes us as students of the Bible to learn what is revealed concerning them: We think they will be found very important agents in conducting the affairs of God's universe, perhaps both spiritual and physical.

In their usual, or, if you please, normal state, they are

INVISIBLE TO UNAIDED HUMAN VISION.

A few examples illustrative of this are all for which

we have room. The beast on which Balaam rode was permitted to see the angel that stood in the way, but Balaam could not see him without divine aid. "Then the Lord opened the eyes of Balaam, and he saw the angel of the Lord standing in the way, and his sword drawn in his hand." Num. xxii: 31. Balaam's unaided human eye could not see the angel, though it was in the way before him, and even visible to the beast on which he rode. Whether the beast was aided by divine power in seeing the angel or not, we cannot know certainly.

When Elisha was in Dothan the king of Syria sent a great army to take him. "And when the servant of the man of God was risen early, and gone forth, behold, an host compassed the city both with horses and chariots. And his servant said unto him, Alas, my master! how shall we do? And he answered, Fear not: for they that be with us are more than they that be with them. And Elisha prayed, and said, Lord, I pray thee, open his eyes, that he may see. And the Lord opened the eyes of the young man; and he saw: and, behold, the mountain was full of horses and chariots of fire round about Elisha." 2 Kings vi: 15-17. That these horses and chariots of fire were angelic, would seem scarcely to admit of doubt; and the young man's natural eyes, unaided by divine power, could not see them, though the mountain was full of them, all around him.

"The angel of the Lord encampeth round about them that fear him, and delivereth them." Psa. xxxiv: 9. Though the Psalmist may have had direct reference to the deliverance of Elisha seen above, yet he makes a general statement without specifications, leaving us to infer that the rule would apply to all who fear the

Lord. They are constantly surrounded by angels invisible to them. What a consolation to know that God has made such wonderful provisions for the protection and deliverance of his children in times of danger and trouble.

WHAT IS THEIR FORM?

Angels are capable of assuming any form in which God is pleased to employ them. We have just seen them as *horses* and *chariots of fire*, encamped around about Elisha. Another example similar, may be found in the account of Elijah's ascent to heaven. 2 Kings ii: 11. Another example was witnessed by Moses. "And the angel of the Lord appeared unto him in a flame of fire out of the midst of the bush; and he looked, and behold, the bush burned with fire, and the bush was not consumed." Ex. iii: 2. Here the angel appeared in a flame of fire.

"And of the angels he saith, Who maketh his angels spirits, and his ministers a flame of fire." Heb. i: 7. These Scriptures show that God employed his angels in the appearance of fire when he saw fit to do so.

THEY OFTEN APPEARED AS MEN.

We think it likely that angels more frequently appeared as men than in any other form. "And the Lord appeared unto him in the plains of Mamre: and he sat in the tent door in the heat of the day; and he lifted up his eyes and looked, and, lo, three men stood by him: and when he saw them, he ran to meet them from the tent door, and bowed himself toward the ground." Gen. xviii: 1, 2. These three angels, in the appearance of men, refreshed themselves with Abraham as men, they detected Sarah's falsehood, they gave assurance to Abraham that his wife should have a son, and they also made known to him God's purpose to visit and destroy the cities of Sodom and Gomorrah. Two of these men, as they seemed to be, went on to Sodom and were entertained by Lot. "And there came two angels to Sodom at even; and Lot sat in the gate of Sodom; and Lot seeing them rose up to meet them; and he bowed himself with his face toward the ground." Gen. xix: 1, 2. In verses ten and twelve these angels are called *men*.

The angel that appeared to Manoah's wife, and then to him, announcing the birth of Samson, was in the appearance of a man. Judge xiii: 6–13. The angel that made known to the women at the sepulchre the resurrection of Jesus, was a young man. Mark xvi: 5. Matt. xxviii: 5. The two angels who proclaimed the return of Jesus to the disciples, who witnessed his ascension from the summit of Mount Olivet, were in the appearance of men, clothed in white apparel. Acts i: 10, 11.

ANGELIC ATTRIBUTES.

They were *wise*, but not *omniscient*. The destroying angel that smote, with death, the first born of every family in Egypt, save the Hebrews, on the night of the departure of the children of Israel, had to have, or did have, a sign by which to know the houses of the Hebrews from those of the Egyptians. Had they been *omniscient*, they would have known the houses of the Hebrews without the blood on the door-posts and lintels to assure them that a Hebrew lived there.

When the Jews wanted to know the time of Christ's second coming, he said: "But of that day and hour knoweth no man, no not the angels in heaven, but my Father only." Matt. xxiv: 36. Here is a specification of one thing which angels did not know. We are not left to inferential reasoning about this, but the fact is plainly stated that the angels in heaven know nothing about when the Savior will come again to the earth. This settles the question of angelic omniscience. Much more proof might be furnished, but we have not room for it, nor do we deem it at all necessary. They know what God reveals to them—no more.

THEY ARE NOT OMNIPRESENT.

They were capable of rapid motion, capable of passing over any space in an inconceivably short time, but they *had to go to a place* when it was necessary for them to be there. They *went* to visit Abraham. They *went* down to Sodom and Gomorrah to destroy them and save Lot. The angel of death passed through the whole land of Egypt, so as to smite with death at midnight the first born in every house. " There was not a house in which there was not one dead." Ex. xii : 29, 30.

" And while I was speaking, and praying, and confessing my sin and the sin of my people Israel, and presenting my supplication before the Lord my God for the holy mountain of my God; yea, while I was speaking in prayer, even the man Gabriel, whom I had seen in the beginning, being caused to fly swiftly, touched me about the time of the evening oblation. And he informed me, and said, O Daniel, I am now come forth to give thee skill and understanding. At the beginning of thy supplication the commandment came forth, and I am come to show thee; for thou art greatly beloved: therefore understand the matter, and consider the vision." Dan, ix: 20–23.

Here we find the angel Gabriel is called the "man Gabriel." In appearing to Zacharias he is called "the angel Gabriel." Luke i: 26. By the appearing of Gabriel to Daniel, we learn that he was caused to *fly swiftly*, starting from the presence of God (Gabriel stands in the presence of God. Luke i : 9.) at the beginning of Daniel's prayer, and reaching him before his prayer ended. He came in obedience to command—was sent. Hence the fitness of David's remark—the angels that do his commandments. He came to bring information to Daniel. Daniel was an inspired man—could not God have given this message to him without the agency of an angel? We know not what God *could* have done, but of one thing we are sure; he did employ an angel to carry and deliver the message. He did send this same messenger to Zacharias. And the angel answering said unto him, I am Gabriel, that stand in the presence of God; and am sent to speak unto thee, and to show you these glad tidings." Luke i : 19. Thus we see that Gabriel's place was in the presence of God, and *he was sent—had to go* to parties with communications from God. *He was not*, therefore, *omnipresent*. Let us not forget this. We may have use for it again.

"And I saw another angel fly in the midst of heaven, having the everlasting gospel to preach unto them that dwell on the earth, and to every nation, and kindred, and tongue, and people. Rev. xiv : 6. Here we find another angel flying in the midst of heaven, showing that though capable of rapid motion, he was *not omnipresent*.

THEY ARE NOT OMNIPOTENT.

"So the Lord sent a pestilence upon Israel from the morning even to the time appointed: and there died of the people from Dan even to Beersheba seventy thousand men. And when the angel stretched out his hand upon Jerusalem to destroy it, the Lord repented him of the evil, and said to the angel that destroyed the people, It is enough : stay now thine hand." 2 Sam. xxiv :

15, 16. Here were seventy thousand people of Israel slain by an angel; but when God said it is enough, stay now thy hand, the power of the angel was gone. The angel was simply the agent through whom the power of God was put forth. The angel had no power only as God gave it to him.

"And the Lord sent an angel, which cut off all the mighty men of valor, and the leaders and captains in the camp of the king of Assyria. So he returned with shame of face to his own land. And when he was come into the house of his god, they that came forth of his own bowels slew him there with the sword. Thus the Lord saved Hezekiah and the inhabitants of Jerusalem from the hand of Sennacherib the king of Assyria, and from the hand of all other, and guided them on every side." 2 Chron. xxxii : 21, 22.

Thus Sennacherib's army was destroyed by the Lord, through an angel, who had no power only as the Lord exerted his power through the angel.

"And, behold, there was a great earthquake: for the angel of the Lord descended from heaven, and came and rolled back the stone from the door, and sat upon it. His countenance was like lightning, and his raiment white as snow. And for fear of him the keepers did shake and became as dead men." Matt. xxviii: 2–4.

This angel came from heaven to roll away the great stone from the door of the sepulchre that held the Son of God. The power that could make the earth quake, could, of course, roll away the stone however great. But his countenance struck terror to the hearts of the Roman soldiery until they were frightened nigh unto death. No face ever seen on this earth glowed in light like this, save that of the ever blessed Son of God when transfigured on the holy mount.

When Peter was bound with two chains and made to sleep between two soldiers, and keepers were placed before the doors of Herod's prison, secured by iron gates, bolts, bars, locks, and doors, an angel entered the prison and led Peter out as though nothing had been in the way. "When they were past the first and second ward, they came unto the iron gate that leadeth unto the city; which opened to them of his own accord; and they went out." Acts xii : 10. No keys were necessary to open doors, or gates, or shake off chains where the angel of the Lord was desiring to pass through. They opened and closed in obedience to his will.

THEIR NUMBER.

The first announcement of a Savior born was by an angel to the shepherds, who watched their flocks in the plains of Bethlehem by night. And after this angel had given such directions as would enable them to find the infant Jesus, " suddenly there was with the angel a multitude of the heavenly host praising God, and saying, Glory to God in the highest, and on earth peace, good will toward men.' Luke ii : 13, 14.

How many of this grand company there were we know not, but there was a *multitude*—a vast number.

When Peter smote off the ear of the high priest's servant the Lord rebuked him, saying : " Thinkest thou that I cannot now pray to my Father, and he shall presently give me more than twelve legions of angels." Matt. xxvi. 53. This word *legion* may have referred to a division of the Roman army called a *legion*, and numbered from five to six thousand men. Taking this as true, then more than twelve legion would be more than *sixty thousand* angels.

Of many places which might be referred to in this

connection, we will mention only one more. "But ye are come unto Mount Sion, and unto the city of the living God, the heavenly Jerusalem, and to an innumerable company of angels." Heb. xii: 22. Here we find that the science of numbers is unable to furnish figures to express the number of this company. Figures can express millions, billions, trillions, and on until the mind reels and staggers under the contemplation of their power; and yet they are incapable of expressing that which is *innumerable;* hence there is no power to compute the number of angels connected with God's mighty universe. As well may we attempt the computation of the grains of sand upon the seashore, or the stars that glitter in the heavens, as to attempt to compute the number of angels at this moment engaged in the service of God.

THEY ARE INTERESTED IN THE SALVATION OF MEN.

We have already witnessed the rejoicing of the angelic multitude at the birth of the Savior. "Glory to God in the highest, and on earth peace, good will toward men." Luke ii: 14. What but an interest in man's redemption could have brought such joy on account of the Savior's birth?

When the devil ceased to tempt the Savior, "angels came and ministered unto him." Matt. iv: 11. When Jesus was borne down by the prospects of coming death, "there appeared an angel unto him, strengthening him." Luke xxii: 43.

Once more: "What man of you, having a hundred sheep, if he lose one of them, doth not leave the ninety and nine in the wilderness, and go after that which is lost, until he find it? And when he hath found it, he layeth it on his shoulders, rejoicing. And when he cometh home, he calleth together his friends and neighbors, saying unto them, Rejoice with me; for I have found my sheep which was lost. I say unto you, that likewise joy shall be in heaven over one sinner that repenteth, more than over ninety and nine just persons, which need no repentance." Among whom was this rejoicing in heaven on account of the repentance of one sinner? We will see. "Either what woman having ten pieces of silver, if she lose one piece, doth not light a candle, and sweep the house, and seek diligently till she find it? And when she hath found it, she calleth her friends and her neighbors together, saying, Rejoice with me; for I have found the piece which I had lost. Likewise, I say unto you, there is joy in the presence of the angels of God over one sinner that repenteth." Luke xv: 4-10. Thus we learn that angels watch with anxious solicitude for the salvation of sinners, and when one repents they have a season of rejoicing in heaven.

One other thought is apparent in this connection. We know there is rejoicing in the family of God on earth when a sinner is converted, is not the rejoicing in heaven among the heavenly family when a sinner is converted? We think so. Who rejoices in heaven over the repentance of a sinner? The angels of God. Then the angels of God are the heavenly portion of God's family. This seems clear enough. Did any one ever read in the Bible where one or more of the apostles rejoiced *in heaven* over the conversion or repentance of a sinner? Though they may be in a perfectly conscious state of existence, they are scarcely in heaven yet. "For we must all stand before the judgment seat of Christ." Rom. xiv: 10. And again: "For we must all appear before the judgment seat of Christ;

that every one may receive the things done in his body, whether it be good or bad." 2 Cor. v : 10. This " we " includes Paul. When shall we all appear before the judgment seat of Christ? " Because he hath appointed a day, in the which he will judge the world in rightness by that man whom he hath ordained; whereof he hath given assurance unto all men, in that he hath raised him from the dead." Acts xvii : 31. When this day comes Christ will be on the judgment seat, and *we* shall all appear before him—not before.

We return to the consideration of angels. Their services have been rendered *in answer to prayer*. A few examples must suffice. Manoah prayed for a return of the angel who had appeared to his wife. "And God hearkened to the voice of Manoah: and the angel of God came again to the woman as she sat in the field." Judges xiii : 9.

Again : " And for this cause Hezekiah the king, and the prophet Isaiah, the son of Amoz, prayed and cried to heaven. And the Lord sent an angel, which cut off all the mighty men of valor, and the leaders and captains in the camp of the king of Assyria." 2 Chron. xxxii : 20, 21.

We have already seen an account of the angel Gabriel coming to Daniel while he was praying, an account of which may be found in Daniel ix : 3–23.

Peter was arrested by order of Herod, and put in prison, " but prayer was made without ceasing of the church unto God for him." Acts xii : 5. We have already seen an account of his delivery by an angel, in answer to the prayers of the church, unceasingly made in his behalf. That they are engaged for God's children, in some way, is as certain as it is that the Bible is true. " Are they not all ministering spirits sent forth to minister for them who shall be heirs of salvation?" Heb. i: 14. "The angel of the Lord encampeth round about them that fear him." Ps. xxxiv: 7. "For he shall give his angels charge over thee, to keep thee in all thy ways." Ps. xci: 11. "Take heed that ye despise not one of these little ones; for I say unto you, that in heaven their angels do always behold the face of my Father which is in heaven." Matt. xviii: 11. If these passages do not prove the active agency of angels in the salvation of man, then we confess our inability to tell what they do mean, or to prove any thing by the language of Holy Writ.

When God would comfort Hagar, he sent an angel to her; he sent angels to Abraham to give him promise of a son in his old age; he sent an angel to stay his hand to save the life of Isaac; he sent an angel to Manoah to give him the promise of the birth of Samson; he sent an angel to Zachariah to give him the promise of the birth of John the Baptist; he sent an angel to Mary to assure her that she should be the mother of the Son of God; he sent an angel to warn Joseph that Herod sought the life of the infant Jesus; and what has the Lord not done through angelic agency? From the burning bush an angel revealed to Moses God's purpose to deliver the Hebrews from Egyptian bondage. Through an angel God gave to Moses the law from Sinai's burning top, (Acts vii: 53. Gal. iii: 19.) and time would fail us to give even *a tithe* of what God has done through angelic agency. One thought more and we shall have done.

THEY WILL BE EMPLOYED IN THE JUDGMENT.

In explanation to the parable of the tares, Jesus said: "The enemy that sowed them is the devil; the harvest is the end of the world; and the reapers are the angels. As therefore the tares are gathered and burned in the fire; so shall it be in the end of this world. The Son of man shall send forth his angels, and they shall gather out of his kingdom all things that offend, and them which do iniquity; and shall cast them into a furnace of fire: there shall be wailing and gnashing of teeth." Matt. xiii: 39-41.

"And he shall send his angels with a great sound of a trumpet, and they shall gather together his elect from the four winds, from one end of heaven to the other." Matt. xxiv: 31.

"When the Son of man shall come in his glory, and all the holy angels with him, then shall he sit upon the throne of his glory: and before him shall be gathered all nations; and he shall separate them one from the other, as a shepherd divideth his sheep from the goats; and he shall set the sheep on his right hand, but the goats on the left." Matt. xxv: 31-33.

"And to you who are troubled rest with us, when the Lord Jesus shall be revealed from heaven with his mighty angels, in flaming fire taking vengeance on them that know not God, and that obey not the gospel of our Lord Jesus Christ." 2 Thess. i: 7, 8.

These Scriptures (and many others might be quoted to the same import) show clearly that angels will be actively engaged in the final winding up of this world. They were in existence from the very dawn of creation, and we think they existed *before time began.* We have seen them active agents in God's work in all ages of the world. Who can measure the extent of their operations in all the universe of God? Of course God could have administered the affairs of his government without them, but it is certain he did not see fit to do so. Having been created, they will never cease to be; and is it not likely that God administers the affairs of the universe through their agency? Surely this is possible.

THEIR DESTNIY.

We have already seen that angels were under law in the time of David. He says: "Bless the Lord, ye his angels, that excel in strength, that do his commandments, hearkening unto the voice of his word." Ps. ciii: 20. This shows that there were angels that obeyed the commandments of the Lord in the time of David. Had they no commandments from the Lord they could not have obeyed any. They also hearkened to the voice of his word. His word was addressed to them, or they could not have hearkened to it.

John says: "When I had heard and saw, I fell down to worship before the feet of the angel which shewed me these things. And he saith unto me, See thou do it not: I am a fellow servant with thee, and with thy brethren the prophets, and with them which keep the words of this book. Worship God." Rev. xxii: 8, 9. *New Version.*

This shows that in John's day this angel was a servant of God with John and the prophets, and kept the sayings of that book. This would seem to indicate that he was under the same law which applied to John. Certain it is that he was obedient to law; hence he had a law; and if he had, all others had. They were the innumerable company to whom allusion is made in the letter to the Hebrews, unto whom the saints had come. Hence, the obedient angels will be the eternal companions of the redeemed in the new heavens and new earth.

But what will be the destiny of wicked angels? Jude says: "The angels which kept not their first estate, but left their own habitation, he hath reserved under chains of darkness unto the judgment of the great day to be punished.

These angels were wicked, or they would not be held for punishment. This shows also, that they were under law, and violated it in *this state* of the world's existence; for had they violated law in a state anterior to this, they would have met their doom in the winding up of that state. There can be no doubt that angels are under law now, just as they have always been. This being so, they are free to keep or violate their law, for God never put man or angel under a law which he was compelled to keep, whether he willed so or not. Men and angels must be free when under law, in order that they may be responsible for violating law. Hence, the destiny of angels will not be unlike the destiny of men. Jesus will say to the wicked: "Depart from me, ye cursed, into everlasting fire, prepared for the devil and his angels." Matt. xxv: 41. As wicked men will be placed *with the devil and his angels*, it follows that wicked men and wicked angels will be together, and their punishment will be of the same kind, yet, perhaps, not of the same intensity. The pure and the holy will be eternally happy, while the rebellious and disobedient will be eternally miserable. We think this most certainly true. This will be the fate of wicked men—why not of wicked angels? What wonderful incentives are these to prompt us all to live lives of purity and holiness, that we may have association with angels and purified spirits for ever. As the holy angels were most likely the spirits of those who lived in a state anterior to this state of being, is it not likely that the immortalized spirits of those who have lived in this world will swell the number of the angelic hosts in the new heavens and the new earth that will succeed the heavens and the earth that now are? And thus angels will be the eternal companions of the redeemed, over whom they have watched, and for whom they have ministered in the ages and dispensations of the past. Do you tell us this is all speculation? then we derive comfort from the speculation. It is a source of great joy to contemplate even the *possibility* of being forever associated with angels in giving glory to God and to the Lamb that was slain to redeem us. God help us to be worthy of such honor.

"When the angel of the Lord proclaims that time shall be no more,
  We shall gather, and the saved and ransom'd see,
Then to meet again together, on the bright celestial shore,
  What a gathering of the faithful that will be!

" At the great and final judgment, when the hidden comes to light,
  When the Lord in all his glory we shall see;
At the bidding of our Savior, 'Come, ye blessed to my right,'
  What a gathering of the faithful that will be!

"When the golden harps are sounding, and the angel bands proclaim,
  In triumphant strains the glorious jubilee;
Then to meet and join to sing the song of Moses and the Lamb,
  What a gathering of the faithful that will be!"

CHAPTER XIX.

THE MILLENNIUM.

"And I saw thrones, and they sat upon them, and judgment was given unto them: and I saw the souls of them that were beheaded for the witness of Jesus, and for the word of God, and which had not worshiped the beast, neither his image, neither had received his mark upon their foreheads, or in their hands; and they lived and reigned with Christ a thousand years. But the rest of the dead lived not again until the thousand years were finished. This is the first resurrection. Blessed and holy is he that hath part in the first resurrection: on such the second death hath no power, but they shall be priests of God, and of Christ, and shall reign with him a thousand years." Rev. xx: 4-6.

THE revised or new version is a manifest improvement on the above, so much so, that we propose to insert and use it as the *text* for this discourse, rather than the old version. Indeed, we treat the new version just as we do any other version, receive and adopt its *improvements*, but continue to use the old, and more familiar version where it is not improved in the new.

"And I saw thrones, and they sat upon them, and judgment was given unto them; and I saw the souls of them that had been beheaded for the testimony of Jesus, and for the word of God, and such as worshiped not the beast, neither his image, and received not the mark upon their forehead and upon their hand; and they lived, and reigned with Christ a thousand years. The rest of the dead lived not until the thousand years should be finished. This is is the first resurrection.

Blessed and holy is he that hath part in the first resurrection; over these the second death hath no power, but they shall be priests of God and of Christ, and shall reign with him a thousand years." Rev. xx: 4-6.

Time, the great prover of all things, has shown much of what has been written on the millennium to be false; and public sentiment has about settled down to the conviction that there is nothing clearly taught in the Bible concerning it; hence, those who propose to speak or write about it, are judged and condemned without a hearing. The verdict is that it will be all speculation, and so the matter is settled in advance. We have never manufactured much reputation as a *speculator* on theological questions, and we are a little too old to begin that kind of work now. Hear us before passing sentence upon us.

There is surely something taught in the Bible on the subject, and it can do us no harm to study it. While it is *vastly interesting*, it is not so important as that any one's salvation depends upon a knowledge of it. A mistake concerning it, therefore, would be entirely harmless. Hence, we do not see cause for alarm, even were we to indulge a little speculation about it, so long as we make no effort to force our speculations on any one else.

We have read much of what has been written on the subject, and Bro. M. E. Lard is the only man whose writings have fallen under our notice, who seemed to have a tangible theory as to *what the millennium really will be*. On this point we believe his theory is correct, but we shall write as though he had not written.

Some writers boldly deny that there is any such thing taught in the Bible as a *thousand years' reign* with Christ by any class, at any time, any where, in any way. With this class we propose no argument. Our text says, as plainly as words can express any thing, that *there shall be such a reign*, and this ought to settle it with those who believe the Bible; and we propose no argument with those who do not believe it. All such labor is worse than thrown away.

Others admit that there will be a thousand years' reign with Christ, but they insist that it will be some sort of a *figurative* affair, and they figure it all away, until there is nothing left that they can describe, or that we can see. We know not how to reason with this class, for they give us nothing on which to reason.

Others think that it will consist in the breaking down of denominationalism; and the universal acceptance of the pure gospel of Christ, as taught by Mr. Campbell and his co-workers. However desirable this may be, we see no prospect of it; nor can we find satisfactory evidence on which to base such a belief. Denominationalism is here, and it is here to stay. It will be here when Jesus comes, perhaps about as it is now. Some of the denominations that are here now will doubtless pass away. Some are dying, and have been struggling in the throes of death for a number of years. The hand-writing is on the wall, and they must go; and he is but a poor reader of the signs of the times who does not already see this; but perhaps other parties will rise up and take their place, and thus denominations will continue as long as time endures. All the world has never accepted the pure word of God, and never will. He is dreaming who expects the millennium to come about in this way.

Still others believe that the millennium will consist in the return of the Jews to Jerusalem as a nation, and their conversion to the Christian religion; and that

Christ will literally come to Jerusalem and reign among them in person. Some go so far on this line as to assume that after the Jews shall be converted, they will go out as missionaries to convert the world, and that through their agency the world is yet to be converted to Christ—that the nation that rejected and crucified the Lord of glory, is to be the means of converting the world to him. This may be all true, but it is, to our mind, not only unscriptural, but wholly unreasonable. We have two good reasons for not believing it—(1) the Bible does not teach it, (2) the Bible teaches just the opposite.

"Thus saith the Lord, go and get a potter's earthen bottle, and take of the ancients of the people, and of the ancients of the priests; and go forth unto the valley of the son of Hinnom, which is by the entry of the east gate, and proclaim there the words that I shall tell thee, and say, Hear ye the word of the Lord, O kings of Judah and inhabitants of Jerusalem; Thus saith the Lord of hosts, the God of Israel; Behold, I will bring evil upon this place, the which whosoever heareth his ears shall tingle." Jer. xix: 1-3.

The prophet then goes on to recount the wickedness to which they would be parties, as though it were accomplished. This is prophetic style. Looking down the stream of time into the future, *he sees things as they will be when completed* long before they transpire. Take an example of this style: "He was led as a sheep to the slaughter; and like a lamb dumb before his shearer, so opened he not his mouth: In his humiliation his judgment was taken away: and who shall declare his generation? for his life is taken from the earth." Acts viii: 32, 33.

This is a quotation from Isaiah, which was predicted

more than seven hundred years before the events transpired, and yet the verbs are in the *past tense*, as though expressive of events completed when the prophet used the language. So in describing the wickedness of the Jews, the prophet speaks of things as already done, which were long future: "Because they have forsaken me, and have estranged this place, and have burned incense in it unto other gods," etc., etc. Then he describes the calamities that were brought upon the Jews at the destruction of Jerusalem, by the Roman army under Titus, as perfectly as Josephus, who was there, an eye witness to the awful siege. " And I will make void the counsel of Judah and Jerusalem in this place; and I will cause them to fall by the sword before their enemies, and by the hands of them that seek their lives: and their carcasses will I give to be meat for the fowls of heaven, and for the beasts of the earth. And I will make this city desolate, and an hissing; every one that passeth thereby shall be astonished and hiss because of all the plagues thereof. And I will cause them to eat the flesh of their sons and the flesh of their daughters, and they shall eat every one the flesh of his friend in the siege and straitness, wherewith their enemies, and they that seek their lives, shall straiten them." Josephus says these things literally occurred as here described by the prophet. "Then shalt thou break the bottle in the sight of the men that go with thee, and shalt say unto them, Thus saith the Lord of hosts; even so will I break this people and this city, as one breaketh a potter's vessel, that cannot be made whole again; and they shall bury them in Tophet, till there be no place to bury." Jer. xix: 4–11.

God here describes the terrible condition to which the

Jews would be reduced in that siege, and that very condition of things did come. He said he would break and scatter them as a potter's vessel, that cannot be made whole again. He did break up and scatter them, until there is not a place on the face of the earth where straggling Jews may not be found; and they have been scattered as he said he would scatter them, from then until now. Then how dare any one say they will be gathered up again, when God has said it never can be done? While that earthen bottle was clay it could be worked over; if it would not make one vessel it might make another; but when it became an earthen vessel, and was broken, the wreck was complete and final. From this there is no appeal. If the Jews are ever gathered up, and, as a nation, made whole again, then God's positive utterance by Jeremiah, as enforced by the breaking of that earthen jug, will have failed. There has not been a war in the eastern hemisphere in the last fifty years that has failed to induce the belief that the Jews would go back to Palestine as a result of it. Still, wars have ceased, peace has followed, but the Jews are scattered as before. But are there not Scriptures that speak of the return of the Jews to Jerusalem? Yes, many of them; but most of them were written either before, or during the captivity, and had their fulfillment in the return of the Jews to Babylon. We think it likely that many of the Jews will become weary of waiting for their long-looked for Savior, and will accept the Christian religion, but *as a nation*, never. This is not only unreasonable, but impossible. There is an *individuality* about the Christian religion that cannot be dispensed with. Those who accept Christ must do it as individuals, not as a nation. Each one must come to Christ *on his own individual faith.* *He can come in no other way.* In this way he can come now; and this is the only way a Gentile, or any one else can come. The Jews were broken off for unbelief, and they must come in faith. This opportunity they have now, and have always had—they need not expect, or wait for any thing more.

But suppose large numbers of the Jews were to accept the Christian religion, why should they want to go back to Jerusalem? And suppose they were to go back to Jerusalem, how would that bring about the millennium? "Oh, Jesus is coming to Jerusalem, to live among and reign over the Jews." Is he, indeed? It occurs to us that God has pretty thoroughly tested that people. He delivered them from Egyptian bondage, fought their battles, and drove out their enemies, made them the custodians of his law, raised up the prophets among them, and in a thousand ways gave them evidences of his power and goodness, clothed his Son in Jewish humanity, who performed his wonderful miracles in their presence, attesting the divine character of his mission, and yet they rejected and persecuted him, even unto death. When he came forth from the grave it was in despite of every thing they could do to keep him there. He selected his apostles of them, and established his kingdom among them, and gave them the first chances of salvation; and after all this they forsook him, and went back into Judaism; and yet we expect him to make his home among them when he comes to be admired in his saints—we suppose illustrative of the principle of doing good for evil. It requires a greater degree of credulity than we can command to believe this will ever occur.

In our opinion, the Jews will never want to return to Palestine. They are peculiarly a money-loving people. They will never wish to go to a country where opportunities for making money are no better than where they are; and certainly such facilities are not very inviting in that country. For this reason they will not likely wish to go there.

JESUS WILL COME AGAIN.

"And I saw heaven opened, and behold a white horse; and he that sat upon him was called Faithful and True, and in righteousness he doth judge and make war. His eyes were as a flame of fire, and on his head were many crowns; and he had a name written, that no man knew but he himself. And he was clothed with a vesture dipped in blood: and his name is called the Word of God." Rev. xix: 11-13.

That this had reference to Jesus is evident from the fact that his name is called The Word of God, and the fact that he is coming as a *judge* and a *warrior*. Then Jesus will come to the earth again. But we are told that the book of Revelation is so highly symbolic that we cannot know what it means. Well, let us see if the same thing is not taught elsewhere. "For the Lord himself shall descend from heaven with a shout, with the voice of the archangel, and with the trump of God." 1 Thess. iv: 16.

"When the Son of man shall come in his glory, and all the holy angels with him, then shall he sit upon the throne of his glory." Matt. xxv: 31.

"And when he had spoken these things, while they beheld, he was taken up; and a cloud received him out of their sight. And while they looked stedfastly toward heaven as he went up, behold, two men stood by them in white apparel; which also said, Ye men of Galilee, why stand ye gazing up into heaven? this same Jesus, which is taken up from you into heaven, shall so come in like manner as ye have seen him go into heaven." Acts i: 9–11.

There is no symbolism in this; but a plain statement of a literal fact. These witnesses are assured that as they had seen Jesus ascend into heaven, he would in like manner come again. They saw him ascend literally—then he will as literally come as he went. Of this there can be no mistake.

"And the armies which were in heaven followed him upon white horses, clothed in fine linen, white and clean." Rev. xix: 14. Who were the armies of heaven that followed him? "When the Son of man shall come in his glory, and all the holy angels with him." Matt. xxv: 31. Then the *armies of heaven that followed him were the holy angels that came with him.* See also Matt. xvi: 27.

We have seen that while the disciples beheld him going, or ascending up, a cloud received him out of their sight. He shall so come as they saw him go into heaven. Then he will come in the clouds." "And they shall see the Son of man coming in the clouds of heaven with power and great glory." Matt. xxiv: 30. "And then shall they see the Son of man coming in the clouds with great power and glory." Mark xiii: 26. "Behold, he cometh with clouds; and every eye shall see him, and they also which pierced him." Rev. i: 7.

Then if authority can establish any thing, the statement in the vision of John, relative to the coming of Christ, is made out. He will come; and the armies, or angels of heaven, will come with him. And he was received by, and went up in a *cloud*, and he will come in the clouds. We have these things in Revelation fully corroborated by other witnesses. Then they are true—literally true.

WHEN WILL HE COME?

Many have been the calculations made on this subject. Some have set the very day for his coming. But time has shown that these calculations were wrong. The days set have passed and he has not come yet. We think we can give all the information attainable on this subject. We feel sure that we have reached the truth in the premises. Then when will he come? *We do not know any thing about it.* Not one thing. Nor do we think it at all possible for any one else to know. "But of that day and that hour knoweth no man, no, not the angels which are in heaven, neither the Son, but the Father. Take ye heed, watch and pray; for ye know not when the time is." Mark xiii: 32, 33. Now, why should we worry ourselves in seeking to know that which no man knew—no angel knew—that which not even the Son of God himself knew. We should so live as not to be taken by surprise when he comes: hence the admonition: "Watch therefore; for you know not what hour your Lord doth come. But know this, that if the goodman of the house had known in what watch the thief would come, he would have watched, and would not have suffered his house to be broken up. Therefore be ye also ready; for in such an hour as ye think not the Son of man cometh." Matt. xxiv: 42–44. While we may not know *when* the Lord is coming, of one thing we may be sure—he is not coming when all the world is looking for him. "For yourselves know perfectly that the day of the Lord so cometh as a thief in the night; for when they shall say, Peace and safety; then sudden destruction cometh upon them." 1 Thess. v: 2, 3. When the Lord shall come, the world will be moving on about as it is now. We see no prospect of much improvement, and we most earnestly pray it may get no worse. The farmer will be going to his plow, the mechanic to his shop, the merchant to his counter, the accountant to his desk, the editor to his sanctum, the banker to his vaults, the doctor to his pills, the lawyer to his office, the miser to his gold. "As the days of Noah were, so shall also the coming of the Son of man be; for as in the days that were before the flood they were eating and drinking, marrying and giving in marriage, until the day that Noah entered into the ark, and knew not until the flood came, and took them all away; so shall also the coming of the Son of man be. Then shall two be in the field; the one shall be taken, and the other left; two women shall be grinding at the mill; the one shall be taken, and the other left." Matt. xxiv: 37–41.

These Scriptures show that the world will be drifting along as usual, without any visible change in the vocations of men, just as if the Lord were not coming at all. Of this there can be no doubt. That the people will all be converted to the Christian religion, there is not the slightest probability. We have seen that Jesus is coming as a *warrior* and a *judge*. "In righteousness he doth judge and make war." On whom will he make war? Not on the righteous, surely; for in righteousness he doth judge and make war, not upon the righteous, but the wicked. He will not fight against his friends, but his enemies.

"But this is from that symbolic book." Then we will see what Paul says about it. "And to you who are troubled, rest with us, when the Lord Jesus shall be revealed from heaven with his mighty angels, in flaming fire taking vengeance." Vengeance? Yes. Vengeance on whom? "On them that know not God, and that obey not the gospel of our Lord Jesus Christ; who shall be punished with everlasting destruction from the presence of the Lord, and from the glory of his power; when he shall come to be glorified in his saints, and to be admired in all them that believe (because our testimony among you was believed) in that day." 2 Thess. i : 7-10.

While there is no intimation as to *how* the events here alluded to will be brought about, it is clearly seen that Jesus will take vengeance on the wicked—them that refused to obey him; and this fact is made, if possible, more plain by the fact that he will be glorified in, and admired by his saints. The two classes are clearly seen in this quotation, and the contrast is well drawn. No one need be mistaken as to the parties against whom Jesus will fight in this war. No plea of "symbolic language" can be made to cover them up—*them that know not God and obey not the gospel.*

WITH WHAT WILL HE FIGHT?

"And out of his mouth goeth a sharp sword that with it he should smite the nations; and he shall rule them with a rod of iron; and he treadeth the winepress of the fierceness and wrath of Almighty God." "And the remnant were slain with the sword of him that sat upon the horse, which sword proceeded out of his mouth; and all the fowls were filled with their flesh." Rev. xix: 15, 21. "This is more from that *symbolic* book." Who can be at a loss to know that the sword which proceeded out of his mouth *was his word?* This is by no means the first use of such a style. Paul says: "And take the helmet of salvation, and the sword of the Spirit which is the word of God." Eph. vi: 17. This book of Revelation was the "Revelation of Jesus Christ," which God gave unto him * * * and he sent and signified it by his angel unto his servant John. To the angel of the church in Pergamos he said: "Repent; or else I will come unto thee quickly, and will fight against them with the sword of my mouth." Rev. ii: 16. "We understand that the worlds were framed by the word of God." Heb. ii: 3. God spake and things were. He upholds "all things by the word of his power." Heb. i: 3. He who spake the world into existence, and upholds all things by the word of his power, *will speak the word*, and the wicked will be slain, in a moment they will die—be dead—slain by the sword which proceedeth out of his mouth.

"And I saw an angel standing in the sun; and he cried with a loud voice, saying to all the fowls that fly in the midst of heaven, Come, and gather yourselves together unto the supper of the great God; that ye may eat the flesh of kings, and the flesh of captains, and the flesh of mighty men, and the flesh of horses, and of them that sit on them, and the flesh of all men, both free and bond, both small and great." Rev. xix: 17, 18. "And the remnant were slain with the sword of him that sat upon the horse, which sword proceeded out of his mouth; and all the fowls were filled with their flesh." v. 21.

This shows that the wicked who are slain will not be buried, but will be devoured by the fowls of heaven just where they chance to be when slain. Is this symbolic, or is it a literal description of what will happen? We think it must be understood literally—why not? A very similar account of what came upon the Jews at Jerusalem is given by Jeremiah, and Josephus tells us that it was literally fulfilled. Then why not this? He says: "I will cause them to fall by the sword before their enemies, and by the hands of them that seek their lives; and their carcasses will I give to be meat for the fowls of heaven and for the beasts of the earth." Jer. xix: 7. Josephus was in Jerusalem, and he says they buried the dead until there was no place to bury, and they could bury no more, and the dead were consumed by the vultures and dogs where they lay in the streets. Now, when Jeremiah made this prediction, was it not just as improbable as that the fowls should feed upon the slain at the coming of Christ? This is a very natural and plausible result, and we think it will take place just that way. Why not?

"But they are to be burned up, destroyed, judged, and sent to hell the very day that Christ comes." Let us not crowd things too close together. They are to be *destroyed*, but that does not imply *annihilation*, surely. "Likewise also as it was in the days of Lot; they did eat, they drank, they bought, they sold, they planted, they builded; but the same day that Lot went out of Sodom it rained fire and brimstone from heaven, and destroyed them all. Even thus shall it be in the day when the Son of man is revealed." Luke xvii: 28–30.

This was intended to illustrate the condition of things at the coming of Christ by the condition of things in Sodom. As the people then went on in the usual pursuits of life, thinking nothing of danger until they were destroyed, so it will be when Jesus comes to the earth again. The people will be going on as usual until he comes and destroys them. But what is meant by the phrase, "destroyed them all?" Does it mean damned in hell forever? We suppose not. What then? They were going on, thinking of no danger, until God instantly killed them—destroyed their lives. So when the Son of man comes, they will be going on until, like the Sodomites, they will be instantly destroyed. Destroyed how? In hell forever? Then there is no fitness in this wonderful Bible illustration. The Sodomites *were not thus destroyed*, but their *lives* were destroyed. They were *destroyed as living creatures*. Then the wicked will be destroyed in the same way when Jesus comes. They will be slain by the sword that will proceed out of his mouth. And *that destruction* will be *everlasting*, too. They will never live again *as they lived before*. The question of a final resurrection and judgment is not involved *in this destruction*. These will come in due time. We will see them directly.

Will there be any *righteous* living on the earth when Jesus comes? Most certainly there will. What will be done with them? Paul says: "We shall not all sleep, but we shall all be changed, in a moment, in the twinkling of an eye, at the last trump, for the trumpet shall sound, and the dead shall be raised incorruptible, and we shall be changed. For this corruptible must put on incorruption, and this mortal must put on immortality." 1 Cor. xv: 51-53.

This shows that there will be righteous persons living on the earth when Jesus comes. We shall not all sleep, that is, all will not be dead. They will be changed—they will exchange their mortal for immortal bodies. The dead will be raised incorruptible. At the same moment when the living saints will be changed, the dead saints will be raised incorruptible; that is, *they will come forth with the same kind of body that the living will get by the change.*

"But we would not have you ignorant, brethren, concerning them that fall asleep, that ye sorrow not, even as the rest, which have no hope. For if we believe that Jesus died and rose again, even so them also that are fallen asleep in Jesus will God bring with him. For this we say unto you by the word of the Lord, that we that are alive, that are left unto the coming of the Lord, shall in no wise precede them that are fallen asleep. For the Lord himself shall descend from heaven, with a shout, with the voice of the archangel, and with the trump of God; and the dead in Christ shall rise first; then we that are alive, that are left, shall together with them be caught up in the clouds, to meet the Lord in the air; and so shall we ever be with the Lord." 1 Thess. iv: 13–17. [*New Version.*]

This quotation is full, clear, and specific. We learn that there will be righteous persons living when the Lord comes, but they will not go before those who sleep in Jesus. The dead in Christ shall rise first. This is *generic*, and includes *all* the dead in him. We are now prepared to read our *text*. "And I saw thrones, and they sat upon them, and judgment was given unto them; and I saw the souls of them that had been beheaded for the testimony of Jesus, and for the word of God, and such as worshiped not the beast, neither his image, and received not the mark upon their forehead and upon their hand; and they lived, and reigned with Christ a thousand years." *This is the millennium.* If this does not express a literal reign with Christ for a literal thousand years, we know not what assemblage of words would be capable of expressing that thought.

With the old version before them, many have concluded that this was a sort of pre-eminence, given to the martyrs, and that they are all who are included in this reign. This would exclude even the beloved apostle John himself. Holding, as he did, the most sacred place in the affections of the Savior, he could have no share in this reign with him, because he died a natural death, and was not among the martyrs. Besides this, it seems to flatly contradict what we have already quoted from the apostle Paul, that the dead in Christ shall rise first. This is without restriction, and certainly includes *all the dead in Christ.* But the new version clears up all the fog from the passage. After giving the characteristics of the martyrs, it takes in other classes. And such as worshiped not the beast, etc., showing that others were included. It clearly means all the righteous, living and dead, at the time Jesus comes. It can mean no less, when construed with the other passages cited.

The dead in Christ shall rise first. "This is the first resurrection. Blessed and holy is he that hath part in the first resurrection; on such the second death hath no power, but they shall be priests of God and of Christ, and shall reign with him a thousand years." None but the pure and holy have part in this resurrection; because none but the saints will come forth in it. This is corroborated by Paul to the Corinthians: "For as in Adam all die, even so in Christ shall all be made alive. But every man in his own order; Christ the first fruits; afterward they that are Christ's at his coming." 1 Cor. xv: 22, 23.

The resurrection will be in orders or ranks. Christ has already been raised, afterward, or in the first rank, they who are his at his coming. This is in exact accord with what he said to the Thessalonians: The dead in Christ shall rise first, for they will be his at his coming.

But Satan is to be bound during this thousand years. The wicked will be all dead, the righteous clad in the habiliments of immortality, and under the protection of their Master, there will be none subject to the machinations of the devil, and hence he will be completely shorn of his power. This will be a glorious period. No wicked living—the saints all immortalized, hence, free from pain, sickness and death. No sorrowing, no sighing, no tears, no sad farewells, and no temptations, consequently no sin. All will be joy, peace, and love. Not a ripple in the ocean of bliss for a thousand years. Then will be fulfilled the benediction of the Savior: "Blessed are the meek; for they shall inherit the earth." Matt. v: 5. Then the earth will belong to the meek—the saints; and it will be theirs by inheritance, but never before. They get very little of it now, and pay very dearly for that.

With this theory another curious saying of the Savior becomes plain enough. "Then shall two be in the field ; the one shall be taken, and the other left." One shall be slain, the other left alive, to be glorified and to reign with Christ a thousand years. Without this theory of the millennium the import of this Scripture is difficult to see.

THE SECOND RESURRECTION.

We have seen that the dead in Christ rise first, and that this is the first resurrection in which none but the blessed and holy will have part. " On such the second death hath no power, but they shall be priests of God, and of Christ, and shall reign with him a thousand years." The phrase, *first resurrection*, clearly implies a *second resurrection*, for there cannot be a *first* without a *second*. So does the phrase, dead in Christ, imply that there are dead who are not in Christ; and the sentence, the dead in Christ shall rise first, implies that the dead out of Christ will rise afterward. How long afterward?

"But the rest of the dead lived not again until the thousand years were finished." Rev. xx: 5. This clearly implies that the rest of the dead *will live again* when the thousand years shall be finished. We see not how to resist these conclusions from the premises, or from the Scriptures quoted. They are plain statements of Holy Writ, which seem to admit of no other interpretation. It seems to us that the conclusions must be admitted, or the truth of the Scriptures denied.

That "the rest of the dead" that lived not again until the thousand years were finished, are the *wicked* dead, is evident from at least two considerations. First, all the righteous dead were raised in the first resurrection, and hence the wicked must be *the rest* of the dead. Second, as the dead in Christ wll rise first, it follows that the dead out of Christ will rise next or afterward. Then at the expiration of the thousand years, the wicked will all be raised—will live again. Not as they live now, but they will have bodies as indestructible as the righteous, but capable of enduring the endless punishment awaiting them according to their works.

God will give to every one a body, just such a body as will be pleasing to him; doubtless to each one such a body as may be capable of enduring that *degree* of punishment which their works may deserve. The punishment of all will be eternal—endless; but this by no means implies that it will be to all of the same degree of intensity. "And that servant, which knew his lord's will, and prepared not himself, neither did according to his will, shall be beaten with many stripes; but he that knew not, and did commit things worthy of stripes, shall be beaten with few stripes. For unto whomsoever much is given, of him shall much be required; and to whom men have committed much, of him they will ask the more." Luke xii: 47, 48. This seems to teach clearly that the intelligence and opportunities of men, as well as their evil deeds, will have much to do with the punishment inflicted upon them; sufficient it is to our present purpose, however, to show that the punishment of all the wicked *will not be of the same degree of intensity.* This the above quotation clearly proves. That the punishment of all will be of the same kind, and of endless duration we will see as we proceed.

"And when the thousand years are expired Satan shall be loosed out of his prison, and shall go out to deceive the nations which are in the four quarters of the earth." Having always deceived the wicked, and they being now raised, will be deceived by him again. They will encompass the camp of the saints about, and the beloved city; and fire will come down from God out of heaven and devour them. And the devil that deceived them will be cast into the lake of fire and brimstone, where the beast and the false prophet will be, and they will be tormented day and night for ever and ever. Having made this general statement, the writer goes back and gives the particulars in detail. This style is common among divine writers, a sample of which may be found in the Mosaic account of creation. For John's specifications see Rev. xx: 11–15.

The fifteenth verse is: "And whosoever was not found written in the book of life was cast into the lake of fire."

This is an awful thought. A *lake* is suggestive of a *fluid*—we could not have a lake of solids. This is not a lake of water, but of brimstone in a *melted* or *fluid* state, else it could not be a lake. It is on fire—burning.

Oh the stifling fumes of burning brimstone! how intolerable the thought! But in it is to be the home of the wicked for ever. See that poor creature as he is plunged into that awful place, perhaps carried by the waves out of sight for a time, and again thrown to the surface; boiling, stewing, seething, broiling, frying; writhing, groaning, crying, and weeping. And how long is this to continue? For ever and ever. And how long is for ever and ever? Ten thousand times ten thousand years may have come and gone, and yet for ever and ever will have just begun. Ten million times ten million years may come and go, and yet forever and ever will have just begun. And thus the punishment of the wicked will go on and on—always dying, yet never dead. "Oh, this is too intolerable to contemplate." True, indeed it is; but it is the sure destiny of the wicked; and he is not their friend who fails to warn them of it.

Horrible as this picture may make hell appear, we can conceive that it originated in the *goodness* and *mercy* of God. Man can be moved by *attractive* influences and *repelling* forces. Appealing to man's love of the *enjoyable*, God has made for man a home in heaven, with all its eternal joys, and he invites him to it. Opening its beauties and pleasures before him, he seeks to attract man to him—to win him to the paths of righteousness, and keep him in the way of life everlasting. This attractive force is sufficient to save some men. They will serve God because they love him for what he has done for them, and loving him they delight in his service, and joyfully look to the reward at the end.

These attractive forces affect all men more or less; but by far the larger portion of men are so much under the control of appetite, passion, lust, ambition, pride—

in short the pleasures of sin, that attractive influences alone will not save them. Before these God has prepared, and opened up a yawning hell, with all its horrors, to deter them from rebellion against him. Thus the joys of heaven attracting, and the awful punishment of hell repelling, *both conspire to save man.* He may be lost in despite of all the means provided for his salvation; but if he is lost it will be because he *will* not be saved—because he will give up to appetite, passion, lust, and sinful desires, rather than deny himself of these, and serve God that he may be saved. We are fully persuaded that the great majority of men are influenced much more by the fear of hell, than by love for God. This should not be so, but it is so. Men should love and serve God *if there was no hell.* But they will not serve him any too well with the fear of hell ever before them. Alas! many cannot be induced to serve God, when all the joys of heaven, and the terrors of hell combine to influence them. Indeed, it sometimes seems that were hell blotted out, there would be but little religion in the world. It is right that there should be a hell, or God would not have made it. If we will obey God and do right hell will not hurt us. We do not propose to take any stock in it—why should we be terrorized by the severity of its punishment? Let us repeat, then, with emphasis—God did not institute hell from a spirit of *revenge,* or *hatred* toward those who *will go there;* but from a spirit of *love* and *mercy,* to prevent them from going there, that they might be induced to serve God and be saved.

But we are told that this is only figurative—not literal fire. Well, what relief would this bring to the wicked? If it be a figure, it must be a figure of something real; and figures always fall short of realities; hence the reality will be worse than the figure—better that it should be literal. But let us see if it is not corroborated by other Scriptures against which the plea of *symbolism* cannot be entered.

"Then shall he say also unto them on the left hand, Depart from me, ye cursed, into everlasting fire prepared for the devil and his angels." Matt. xxv: 41. Does not this look like the same fire described by John in Revelation? Is it figurative also?

Once more: Of the tares Jesus said: "The enemy that sowed them is the devil; the harvest is the end of the world; and the reapers are the angels. As therefore the tares are gathered and burned in the fire; so shall it be in the end of this world. The Son of man shall send forth his angels, and they shall gather out of his kingdom all things that offend, and them which do iniquity: and shall cast them into a furnace of fire: there shall be wailing and gnashing of teeth." Matt. xiii: 39–42. Would it require literal fire to burn up the tares? Then will it not be literal fire in this furnace into which the wicked are to be cast?

Finally on this subject we quote the language of John: "I indeed baptize you with water unto repentance; but he that cometh after me is mightier than I, whose shoes I am not worthy to bear; he shall baptize you with the Holy Ghost, and with fire; whose fan is in his hand, and he will thoroughly purge his floor, and gather his wheat into the garner; but he will burn up the chaff with unquenchable fire." Matt. iii: 11, 12. There were two classes in John's audience, one very good, comparable to wheat, who were to be baptized in the Holy Spirit; the other was composed of wicked men, comparable to chaff, who were to be baptized in unquenchable fire. As it requires literal fire to burn chaff, so literal fire will be that into which the wicked will be baptized. Is this plain enough?

Note the fact, too, that this is to be *unquenchable* fire. What other than hell fire is *unquenchable?*

A few passages of Holy Writ supposed to contradict what we have here taught, must now be noticed.

"And these shall go away into everlasting punishment; but the righteous into eternal life." Matt. xxv: 46. This does indeed show that the punishment of the wicked will be as endless as the life of the righteous. They are both qualified by the same word in the original, hence if the punishment of the wicked will have an end, so will the life of the righteous. But the passage has no bearing on any question we have raised—none whatever.

"Marvel not at this: for the hour is coming, in the which all that are in their graves shall hear his voice, and shall come forth; they that have done good, unto the resurrection of life; and they that have done evil, unto the resurrection of damnation." John v: 28, 29.

This passage does show that there will be a resurrection, both of the just, and of the unjust; but that both classes will come forth in the same moment is *assumption*—nothing less. There is not an intimation in it as to the *order* of the resurrection. The *fact* is stated, the *order* is not. It is certainly unsafe to bring this passage (where not one word is said about the order of the resurrection) into contradiction of a number of passages in which the order is clearly and plainly stated. It were better to take up such passages as speak of the order and show, if such be the fact, that they are not correctly construed, than to seek to contradict them by remote inferences. Such a method of meeting an argument, though often resorted to, is not very satisfactory to those who think for themselves. As this is the strongest passage relied on, we need not pursue the weaker ones, most of which have been already noticed in other connections.

AFTER THE JUDGMENT.

"And I saw a new heaven and a new earth: for the first heaven and the first earth were passed away; and there was no more sea. And I John saw the holy city, new Jerusalem, coming down from God out of heaven, prepared as a bride adorned for her husband. And I heard a great voice out of heaven saying, Behold, the tabernacle of God is with men, and he will dwell with them, and they shall be his people, and God himself shall be with them, and be their God. And God shall wipe away all tears from their eyes; and there shall be no more death, neither sorrow, nor crying, neither shall there be any more pain: for the former things are passed away. And he that sat upon the throne said, Behold, I make all things new. And he said unto me, Write: for these words are true and faithful." Rev. xxi: 1-5.

In connection with this we beg permission to quote from Peter: "But the day of the Lord will come as a thief in the night; in the which the heavens shall pass away with a great noise, and the elements shall melt with fervent heat, the earth also and the works that are therein shall be burned up. Seeing then that all these things shall be dissolved, what manner of persons ought ye to be in all holy conversation and godliness, looking for and hasting unto the coming of the day of God, wherein the heavens being on fire shall be dissolved, and the elements shall melt with fervent heat?

Nevertheless we, according to his promise, look for a new heavens and a new earth, wherein dwelleth righteousness." 2 Pet. iii: 10–13.

Many sublime thoughts are suggested in these quotations. In the grand conflagration that will envelop the universe at the close of the millennium, the heavens will be dissolved, the elements melted, and the earth burned up—dissolved. We suppose nothing will be annihilated; indeed, we think it likely that every thing created by God will exist, in some form, as long as he will exist—eternally. We say of a house, "it was burned up." We do not mean that it was annihilated only that it ceased to exist *as a house*. The matter passed off into other forms, gas, soot, ashes, etc. So we apprehend that when all material things are dissolved, the matter of which they are composed will still exist, and of it God will create a new heavens and a new earth. Certain it is there *will be* a new heavens and a new earth, for John saw them; and Peter looked for them, and he looked for them because God had promised them. Nearly seven hundred years before Christ was born in Bethlehem, God, by the mouth of Isaiah, said: "For, behold, I create new heavens and a new earth; and the former shall not be remembered nor come into mind; but be ye glad and rejoice for ever in that which I create; for, behold, I create Jerusalem a rejoicing, and her people a joy." Isa. lxv: 17, 18.

We take it that this is the promise to which Peter refers as following the events described by him. If this was not the promise in accordance with which Peter looked for a new heavens and a new earth, then we know not where to find it. Thus we learn that the new heavens and the new earth were seen in prophecy long before John saw them. That they will come as

John saw them, we think is simply certain. We can scarcely conclude that God will create them for naught, or that the new earth will be uninhabited. Who, then, will be its inhabitants? Peter's remark, "wherein dwelleth righteousness," implies that only the righteous will be on, and occupy it. May it not be that it will be the eternal abode of the glorified saints? Of this we affirm nothing. Only this we know—free from the presence of the wicked, and the alluring temptations of the devil, with nothing but righteousness prevailing there, it will be a glorious home for those who may occupy it. Fit abode for those who have washed their robes, and made them white in the blood of the Lamb.

We love life upon the earth as it now is—how much more desirable it will then be. What a strong incentive to the saints to strive after that degree of holiness that will fit them for citizenship on the new earth. We often think of moving to new countries to improve our condition; but this earth, as it now is, can never satisfy the longings of those who seek a better country. Not so there. Those who will occupy the new earth will be entirely contented—they will want nothing better. The tree of life will flourish in eternal vigor, and the river of life will ever flow through it. Yes, and it will have a city, whose maker and builder is God; and the throne of God will be in it. Oh, what a country!

> "Celestial land, could our weak eyes,
> But half thy charms explore,
> How would our spirits long to rise,
> And dwell on earth no more."

Why any child of God should be stricken with terror and alarm at the prospect of Christ's second coming is not easy to see. For those who have oil in their vessels, with their lamps trimmed and burning, and have on the wedding garment ready to meet the Bridegroom at his coming, it should be a source of inexpressible joy. It will take away the dread of death, for to them there will be no death. They will be changed in a moment without death. But those who have no oil in their vessels, and have slumbered and slept, in neglect of duty, until their lamps have gone out, and have not on the wedding garment or Christian character, may well be alarmed, for it will be too late to buy oil then. Oh, my brother, wake up to a discharge of duty now. Watch and be ready—always ready; for you know not the time when the Son of man cometh. God help us all to be ready.

Friendly sinner, do you ever think of the fact that Jesus is coming to take vengeance on them that know not God and obey not the gospel? What have you to gain by continued rebellion against God?

> "Say, have you an arm like God,
> That you his will oppose?
> Fear you not the iron rod,
> With which he breaks his foes?"

When Jesus steps down from the mediatorial throne there will be no more pardon of sin. It will then be too late, too late. Now, mercy calls, begs, pleads, and beseeches you to stop, but you will not—then stern, unbending justice will take vengeance upon you beyond the reach of mercy. Come back! come back! Surely it is madness and folly to proceed.

> "Stop, poor sinner, stop and think,
> Before you further go;
> Why will you sport upon the brink
> Of everlasting woe?"

Note:—Many persons object to every thing written or spoken on the subject of the Millennium, because the book of Revelation is so highly *symbolic* that it cannot be understood. That *much* of the book is symbolic, we most frankly admit, but that *all of it is so* we respectfully deny. Take, for example, the letters to the seven churches of Asia. That these churches did exist, wearing the names applied to them, is simply certain; and that they were literally guilty of what is charged against them in those letters will be denied by none. In the preface to the book it is said: "Blessed is he that readeth, and they that heareth the words of this prophecy, and keep those things which are writtten therein, for the time is at hand." Rev. i: 3.

How can the book be a blessing to any one who cannot understand it? If it is so symbolic that nothing in it may be understood, how can any one be expected to keep those things which are written therein? We think it likely that those who symbolize and figure it all away will not understand much of it, while grand truths sparkle on the very surface unobserved.

But to one thing we wish to call the reader's special attention: Almost every important point made in the foregoing discourse on the Millennium is corroborated by other Scriptures which have never been regarded as symbolic. We think that Peter, Paul, and Jesus himself have pretty fully supported John in Revelation on this subject. The thousand years between the first and second resurrections is the only single point now remembered that is dependent upon John's vision alone for support. Being sustained in so many points by other witnesses, is he not worthy of credit in this?

CHAPTER XX.

CHURCH ORGANIZATION.*

IT is our settled conviction, founded upon long, careful, and extensive observation, that the greatest hindrance to the advancement of the Redeemer's Kingdom, is the want of an efficient administration of the divine government. This we never can have, while it is every one's business to administer it. Very conscientiously believing this, we propose to submit a few thoughts on the subject of Church Organization and Government, that we may contribute something, if possible, to the removal of this unfortunate disease afflicting the body of Christ. We are not vain enough to suppose that we can say any thing that will change the views of those who have written upon the subject. Our acquaintance with human nature teaches us that when men take a position before the public, and fortify themselves in it, they rarely ever recede from it. It is always unfortunate for brethren to differ on any subject; and I have no taste for controversy with brethren, but I have already been notified that when I should write on this subject, "there would be blows to take as well as blows to give." I write not for the purpose of giving "blows" to any one, but in the hope that those who are not clad in a coat of mail made of preconceived opinions, may be benefitted by an investigation of the

---

*Originally written for the *Old-Path Guide*, and afterward published in a tract. Revised for this work.

subject. Before presenting the thoughts we have in mind to write, however, we beg permission to reproduce a somewhat lengthy extract from an essay written by Bro. A. Campbell in an Extra to the *Millennial Harbinger*, for the year 1835. But very few have this essay, and it occurs to us that those interested in the examination of the subject, and who have not read it, would be profited by a perusal of it. It was written in the prime of his manhood, and in his own inimitable style; at a time which called into active exercise all the powers of his giant intellect; and when the subject enlisted all the sympathies of his pure spirit. But we will let the extract itself pronounce its own eulogy.

ORGANIZATION OF A CHURCH—BY A. CAMPBELL.

"When a society of disciples agree thus to walk as Christians under the New Testament, solemnly adopted as the rule of their piety and morality, they are not organized as a body having all the officers necessary to their furtherance in the faith, and growth in the knowledge of God, and of Jesus our Redeemer. They need bishops and deacons; but it may happen that in the meantime they have no persons qualified for these highly useful and responsible offices; yet they must go forward and grow in the knowledge of the Lord. In order to be useful to the most feeble band who have come together, we shall suppose ourselves called to counsel those who have just entered into the covenant, and have yet no persons approved to place over them in the Lord.

"There are but two cases supposable, because there are but two distinct cases which have as yet occurred. The one is a church composed of disciples who have come together without the intervention of any preacher or teacher—persons who may have migrated far from the place in which they were first converted—or who have been brought to a knowledge and belief of the truth without any other creed than the Bible. The other is the case of those who have been recently illuminated by the instrumentality of a preacher, by whose labors in their neighborhood they have been translated into the kingdom of God's beloved Son. In the latter case he should labor among them till they are able to make a Scriptural selection from among themselves. But the former case presents the greater difficulty, and to it we shall more particularly attend.

"It is obvious that churches were found in the age of the apostles that were *incomplete;* still, they were churches of Christ, and enjoyed some of the ordinances without the full order of a church. Had this not been the case, Paul could not have left Titus in Crete, "*to set in order the things wanting,* and to ordain elders in every city." Even in Christian communities that had all the ordinances of the apostles, there were some more exemplary than others in all the excellencies of good order.

"Now, as in the nature of things, there is the infancy of a community as well as its manhood, so is it in every particular church of Christ. In the case before us we have an infant church, like an infant family, without an experienced oversight. Some persons must either assume the temporary management of affairs, or be appointed to officiate for the time being. There cannot be any debate in deciding whether this responsibility ought to be granted or assumed. All will agree, in theory at least, that it ought to be granted by the voice of the community, and not assumed by any individual or individuals. Numerous and great must be the misfortunes of any community who give themselves up to the assumption of any of its members. The best qualified are always the most modest and backward; while those least qualified to preside or to lead, push themselves forward. If, then, the brethren will not give their voice in favor of those they judge best qualified, they must give themselves up into the hands of an individual more zealous than intelligent, more confident than modest, or more conceited than wise in the affairs of the kingdom of heaven.

"Good order in such a case requires that some persons, and those of the best attainments, and the best character, should be elected, for the time being, to go forward in social worship and in the edification and discipline of the infant flock. The New Testament, indeed, requires this, for the apostles would not consent to the ordination of a novice, nor one who has not been first *proved* to be competent to the duties assigned to the bishops and deacons.

"It is disorderly, in the fullest sense of the word, for any person to assume any thing in an organized community. *The voice of the church must be directly heard before any person can be acceptably heard by it.* It is conceded that in a called or accidental meeting of citizens of any country, or Christ's kingdom, some person must move an organization, or call the assembly to order, anterior to their action on any subject. But as soon as they are organized no person can open his lips but by permission of the assembly, through its approved organs. And be it observed with emphasis, once for all, *that whatever is disorderly in any community is always disorderly in the Church of God;* for the house of God necessarily is, and ought always to be, the most orderly assembly on earth. When, then, a church is formed, and persons appointed to preside over it, every one that prays, sings, exhorts, speaks, or performs any service in or for the church, does it by permission, request, or appointment of the brotherhood, through the person or persons whom they have appointed to administer the affairs of the congregation. And whoever speaks or acts in or for the community, without such request, permission, or appointment, acts out of order, and despises the whole congregation; for he that dishonors the overseers of the congregation, dishonors the congregation that has called them to this office, though it were but for a single meeting.

"So long, then, as in every community there are some more advanced in knowledge, experience, and years than others, and so long as every Christian community has the living oracles—the writings and teachings of the apostles and prophets—there is not a case likely to happen, in which it will be lawful to forsake the assembling of themselves together for all the acts of social worship, and all the means of edification and consolation in the truth, because of the want of officers or persons to serve them in any capacity. If they are all such perfect babes in Christ—*infants* unable to speak a single word to edification—let them *read*, and sing, and commemorate the Savior's death, with the Book in their hands, under the presidency of the oldest infants in the Lord among them. The senior infants, chosen and appointed to lead the way, are, to them, elders and overseers in the Lord.

"It is true that this is supposing an extreme case, merely to test a principle, or its universality; yet in this extreme case the rule will work well; for if the church is composed of such very babes, they will not require learned men to instruct them. One that is a few days in advance will be relatively a senior among them, and fit to assist them in the Lord.

"'Experience is a good teacher,' and 'practice makes perfect,' are maxims of the most Catholic orthodoxy. If, then, there is not wanting devotion to the Lord, there will be a very discernible proficiency in a short time; and their infant church will soon advance under the wholesome doctrine which is according to godliness, not only in age, but in strength. They will grow in favor as they grow in knowledge, and they will advance in usefulness in the ratio of their unfeigned devotion to the Lord. Still there is no surrendering any principle of the Christian institution before us. As we have the man in the infant, so we have in this arrangement *the Church of Christ*, with its officers growing up to manhood.

"There is no wild democracy, no despotic papacy, no self-created ministry, no *lay* administration of ordinances in this economy. It is, however, an *infant* church, and it ought soon to learn to speak for Christ, by the eloquence of both word and action, suiting the action to the word, and the word to the occasion.

"Generally it happens in the present time, as it did in the age of the apostles—most new congregations are gathered by the labors of some evangelist. In such cases it becomes not only his duty to immerse them on confession of their faith, but also to teach them how they ought to walk and please the Lord in all things, by directing their attention to the apostle's doctrine, or to such portions of it as apply to their circumstances. But constitutionally it is they themselves, and not he that chooses for them their officers.

ORDINATION OF BISHOPS.

"The right to officiate in any office in the Christian Church being derived from the head of the church alone, we must regard all constitutional officers as acting under the authority, as well as by the direction of the Great King. The long debated question about the *jus divinum*, or divine right of bishops, deacons, and their ordination, we promise not to discuss in this essay, farther than a passing remark. This much of the question only falls within our present object—Whether is the right to ordain derived directly from the Lord to the church; or, indirectly through a long succession of ordained persons, in an unbroken series from the apostles.

"The great majority of Christendom, Catholic and Protestant are on the side of an *order of bishops in succession* from the apostles, with the right to ordain vested in them by the head of the church. Their model is the Levitical Priesthood. The order of Aaron and the order of Peter are, with the majority, the same sort of an institution, only with the exception of flesh and blood lineage. Their views make the priesthood an order distinct from the church, though acknowledged to belong to it and to be a component part of it.

"The right to ordain is, then, in popular esteem, a right vested in *an order of men* now of eighteen hundred years continuance, transmitted through many hands; and is, therefore, to us, indirect from Jesus Christ. We, however, from many reasons, are constrained to reject the idea of *an elect order in succession* in the

Christian Church, possessing vested rights, derived not from the community as such, but from Jesus Christ, through a distinct class in the community as essentially papistical in its tendency, and contrary to the letter and spirit of the Christian institution.

"We expect not to find the living among the dead. We seek not authority in the church from an order distinct from the church, so liable to deterioration and abuse as what is usually called 'the Christian priesthood.' Authority from the church is much more direct than that claimed by Rome, England, and Scotland. *Theirs has passed through many hands, polluted with the blood of saints and martyrs.*

"There is not a sectarian bishop on this continent, call him Episcopal, Presbyterian, Baptist, or Methodist, who pretends to trace his descent from the apostles, through Rome, English, or Scotch bishops, who, in passing up the stream of authority, through the times of Papistical and Protestant supremacy, can find one line of clean hands, pure from the blood of the confessors of the Lord Jesus. If the hands of those that consecrated him are not dripping with the blood of those crying from under the celestial altar for vengeance on their murderers, it is impossible for him to show that those who laid their hands upon his predecessors were not stained with that blood; for the bishops of the Man of Sin are crimsoned from head to foot with the blood of slain millions, who, but for them and their orders, would have given their lives rather than deny their Lord or pollute their own consciences.

"Has the Lord Jesus, then, left his church and people to seek for authority to preach, teach, and administer ordinances from the hands of his worst enemies? or has the grace of ordination descended to us, pure and uncorrupted, through hearts and hands stained with Christian blood? It cannot be. We must look for authority from the Lord more direct and less liable to deterioration than that of which many Catholics and Protestants make their boast.

"These things premised, we hasten to state and answer the following questions:

"(1) *What is ordination* as respects the Christian Church?

"It is the solemn election and appointment of persons to the oversight and service of a Christian community. To ordain is to appoint; and all appointments, from that of a successor to Judas as a witness of the resurrection, from an apostle to the messenger of a church, or an almoner, was in the beginning *by an election of the whole community.*

"But there must be some form of setting persons apart to the work, or of inducting them into the office to which they have been elected. This is self-evident. It must be done after some form. Still, we must distinguish between the election or appointment and the mode of consecration or induction. The election or choice of the community, guided in that choice by the Living Oracles, is the essential consideration without which all forms would be unavailing. *Vox populi, vox Dei*, or, in English, 'the voice of the people,' is in this case, 'the voice of God,' calling the persons elect to the work of the Lord.

"To comprehend the meaning of the form it is necessary to regard the ordination throughout in the light of a covenant, or an agreement between the congregation that elects and the persons elected. I say a *covenant;* for, in truth, a solemn compact it is. The items of agreement are these: The church, persuaded that no society can exist comfortably without government, or the exercise of authority; that what is every person's business is no person's business; and that every society, as much as every family, has its own proper business; that the congregation, as a whole, sustains a certain relation to the world as well as that subsisting among the members themselves; that she owes many duties to her own members and to the world, which she cannot discharge faithfully and effectually in the aggregate, or as a community, but by persons authorized and directed by her to act for her and in her name— stipulates and agrees with A, B, and C, whom she has proved to be qualified by the Holy Spirit for rendering those services to the church, that they devote themselves to the work of bishops or deacons as the case may be; and in consideration of their submitting and devoting themselves to the exercise of those functions from a ready mind, she agrees to submit to them in the Lord, and to sustain them in all respects, so far as she has ability, and they require her aids.

"Such, in substance, though not in all its details, is the understanding, agreement, or compact between the electors and the elected; and on this understanding they proceed to ordination, or the consecration of those persons to the work assigned them.

"Such being the agreement, in virtue of which the forms of ordination are called for, it follows that the forms themselves must, in some way, correspond with the thing signified and necessarily the parties themselves, and not a distinct order, are to take part; *for the covenant is between the electors and the elected, and not between the elected and a distinct order of men.* The corollary from these premises is, that the

CONGREGATION HERSELF ELECTS AND ORDAINS ALL HER OFFICERS.

"No person can take any part in these forms of consecration or separation to the work of the Lord, but only so far as they are regarded as members of the congregation, and to be under the authority of those whom they invest with office, or to give directions to them as servants of the congregation.

"(2) 'What, then, may we ask in the second place, are the forms of ordination?' The answer is at hand. Imposition of hands accompanied with fasting and prayer. Thus have persons been consecrated to sacred offices in the Christian Church from the beginning. And, indeed, since ever there was an *organized assembly* of worshipers on earth, the forms of ordination to office have been substantially the same—so far at least that 'holy hands' have universally been laid upon the heads of those invested with sacred offices.

"(3) The third question is still more interesting because of the crisis in which we live, and to it more attention must be paid. It is this: *Who may, or who ought to lay hands on the bishops, or deacons, or messengers elect?* I answer, without dubiety, and in a few words, the whole community, or such elders of the community as may be approved in behalf of the congregation. I am fully aware of the objections which will arise in many minds to such an unqualified declaration. We cannot argue the question here, but we dare not leave it with a simple assertion, and shall, therefore, suggest some reasons for the answer given.

"(1) The nature of the understanding or covenant between the electors and the elected, and of the authority to be delegated to the elected by the electors, demands that they who give the power, or the grace, or the office, should *give it with their own hands,* and not by proxy. Imposition of hands in the act of ordination is simply the conferring of office, or devoting a person to the work of the Lord; and, therefore, all that is decent and comely require that those who give the office give it with their own hands.

"(2) Besides, it is more dignified on the part of the elected to receive the office from those to whom they are to minister, than from any foreign order of men. To receive a crown from a foreign prince is always indicative of vassalage on the part of the prince who receives it to him who confers it. To be ordained by the hands of those without the congregation that confers the honor, is dishonorable to both parties—the bishops elect and the electors. It argues subordination and vassalage in both the bishops and their flocks to those foreigners who impose their hands in ordination.

"(3) 'Without all contradiction,' says Paul, 'the less is blessed by the superior.' If, then, the bishops and deacons are *servants* of the church, and if the conferring of office be a blessing, or an honor to them who receive it, the church being superior to them that serve, it is more apposite that the congregation impose hands, than that a class of public servants, the equals of the elect, should do it.

"(4) But more authoritative than all, when sacred office became necessary in God's first congregation, he commanded the multitude, and not Moses nor Aaron, to impose hands on the heads of those who were to be devoted to the service of the congregation. Be it then distinctly observed, that those now called *the laity* by the Man of Sin, and those accustomed to his style, were commanded by God to consecrate the Levites and to devote them to the service of the tabernacle of the Lord. Hence ordination began with the common people. Let the reader who is sceptical turn over to the book of Numbers, chapter viii, verses 9 and 10. 'And thou shalt bring the Levites before the tabernacle of the congregation, and thou shalt gather the whole assembly of the children of Israel together, and thou shalt bring the Levites before the Lord, *and the children of Israel shall put their hands upon the Levites*. And Aaron shall offer the Levites before the Lord for an offering of the children of Israel that they may execute the service of the Lord.' It is, I believe, universally agreed that the whole 600,000 militia of Israel could not impose their hands upon 22,000 Levites; but that the heads of the people, the representatives of all the tribes, for and in behalf of all the congregation, and in the presence of the whole assembly, did actually put their hands upon the heads of the Levites. But however this may be agreed upon, one thing is certain, that those who first imposed hands were the community who had never hands imposed on themselves.

"(5) In the last place here: The idea of superiority of power in those who ordain, above the community, is without countenance in the New Testament. Nay, the contrary is taught; for when the apostle Paul and Barnabas were sojourners and members of the congregation in Antioch, at the suggestion of the Holy Spirit, the prophets and teachers, with the concurrence of the whole congregation, certainly inferior to the great apostle to the Gentiles, laid hands on Paul and Barnabas, and consecrated them to the work assigned them by the great head of the church.

"From this imposition of hands we learn first—(1) That hands were imposed, not always for conferring spiritual gifts, even in the days of the apostles, but for devoting and separating persons to the work of the Lord. (2) That persons in inferior standing in point of office laid hands of ordination on those who were their superiors in gifts and abilities, as well as in general standing in the estimation of the brethren. (3) That imposition of hands was essential to ordination, accompanied with prayer and fasting; and (4) that no excellence in the gifts of preaching, teaching, or of administering the affairs of the family of God, that no call or qualification on the part of heaven, however clear and unequivocal, was allowed, in the primitive church, to dispense with these sacred forms of ordination.

"It may not be out of order to observe, that if every particular congregation thus elect and ordain its officers by the authority of the Lord, and according to the suggestions of the Holy Spirit, then, in that case, the right and authority of such officers to administer the affairs of the church is directly derived, not by succession, through ignorant and blood-stained hands, but directly from heaven. To such elders it may in truth be said: 'Take heed to yourselves and to the flock over which the *Holy Spirit* has constituted you bishops.'

"In such a case there is no need to go out of the particular congregation to search the rolls and moth-eaten registers of an order of clergy pretending to lineal official descent from Peter, through more than three hundred popes and their clergy; which, by the way, would be on the popular hypothesis essential to the confidence of the church in the legitimacy of their succession.

"In this case the church has only to consult the sacred Scriptures, and to see that the persons whom they elect are those pointed out by the Holy Spirit speaking in the apostles. They have to take heed that they are duly elected by the voice of the congregation, and that they are devoted to the Lord by the imposition of their hands, with prayer to God and fasting. Then have they assurance that they have a divinely authorized ministry, to which it is their duty, their honor, and their happiness to submit themselves as to those who are responsible to Jesus Christ and to them for the faithful performance of the duties of their office. To them they are in duty bound to submit as 'to them that watch for their souls,' under the solemn responsibility of 'giving an account to the Lord:' 'that they may do it with joy and not with sorrowing:' for that would be to their eternal detriment and dishonor.

"Against all this we anticipate that it will be repeated the ten thousandth time, that the apostles alone laid hands on those elected by the congregation. But this cannot be sustained; for the elders of a congregation laid their hands upon the head of Timothy—for the distinguished members of the church of Antioch laid their hands upon the heads of the missionaries Paul and Barnabas—as in the antecedent house of God the elders of the whole congregation, or persons deputized by the community, who had never had hands imposed on them, laid their hands upon the Levites. And even should it be still argued that it was most usual for the apostles to lay on their hands, a question arises, which, when fairly settled, nullifies the papistical argument deduced therefrom; for it can be argued, and argued triumphantly, that the apostles, not by virtue of apostleship, but because *elders* in the congregation at Jerusalem, laid hands on the deacons elect; and as *elders* in other congregations which they planted or watered, assisted in the consecration of those appointed by the churches, by and with the advice, and according to the direction of the apostles, that persons are nominated, elected, and ordained.

"If the apostle Paul could, with propriety, while absent in the body, say that he acted with the Corinthians in the exercise of discipline, may it not, in the same license be said, that 'though absent in the body, yet present in spirit,' or by his will he acts with the church in executing the orders which he gave?

"To be still more explicit and copious on this long debated topic, we would add, that when a church is once arrived at manhood, having its bishops and deacons—that when any person is elected by the congregation to fill any vacancy, by death or resignation, then indeed the congregation will most naturally act through its own elders in laying on hands on the newly elected bishop. And is not this the reason, and a good reason, why the apostles, who were always the elders in every church where they sojourned, took so active a part in the imposition of hands on the bishops and deacons elect?

"He that concludes that ordination is a part of the apostleship, must, to be consistent, plead that the eldership and deaconate are parts of the apostolic office; for the apostles acted as elders and deacons in some churches. They all attended upon tables in Jerusalem before persons were elected to those duties; and Peter exhorts elders because he says he himself is one; and consequently it was in good order for him as a bishop, and a senior bishop, to exhort not only the Christian community, but the elders that presided over them. And be it observed, that he addresses the elders as pastors or shepherds, feeding the flock of God under the supervision of the great, the chief Shepherd and Bishop of souls. The only divinely authorized Archbishop is, then, 'the Chief Shepherd' of God's flock, the Lord Jesus, who 'purchased the flock with his own blood.'

"There is no reason for the frequency of allusion to the imposition of the apostles' hands, which merits our notice. They were entrusted with the erection of the kingdom of the Messiah in the world. This threw into their hands every sort of office and duty. They preached first, they taught first, they exhorted first—first waited upon the tables of the poor—were the first bishops and the first deacons of the churches which they planted. They appointed persons, such as Timothy, Titus, and others, to assist them in getting things in order. But that they had successors in this character is insusceptible of proof, from all that is on sacred record. Many things they taught by word, and many things by letter. Their traditions by word are sometimes alluded to, and when learned are as obligatory as what is written. They are, however, only found in an authoritative form in their epistles still extant.

"One thing is most obvious: They never appointed bishops over two or more churches; but so soon as it was expedient, ordained *bishops in every city, elders in every church.* Hence we read of the *elders*, or bishops (for these words are used interchangeably) of the church in Ephesus—of the church in Jerusalem—of elders ordained in every church, *but never of one bishop over two churches.*

"Are we not now prepared to state the order of ordination?

"(1) The congregation, after having proved the abilities and capacities to teach and rule found in its own members, and, above all, tested their character as approved by those within and without the congregation, appoints a day for the proper election of its officers.

"(2) Having agreed upon those eligible, possessing, in an acceptable measure, the qualifications commanded by the apostles, a day is appointed for their solemn consecration to the Lord.

"(3) The day arrives; the church assemble with fasting, and proceed to select members to impose hands on the officers elect in behalf of the congregation. The persons thus chosen then proceed to impose their hands on the heads of those elected, while all unite in prayer to God that those brethren chosen by them, and now devoted to the Lord as their bishops or deacons, may, feeling their responsibility, with all diligence and fidelity to the Lord, and with all humility of mind and affectionate concern for the brotherhood, exercise the office with which they are hereby invested in the name of the Lord, according to the true intent and meaning of the Christian institution, as they shall account to the Lord at his glorious appearing and kingdom. The whole congregation then lifting up their voice, say, *Amen.*

" Whether this may include all the solemnities of such an occasion may, perhaps, be questioned by some; but that it does not transcend all that is taught and applied in the ancient order of ordination, cannot, we think, be doubted by any one intelligent in the oracles of God. It will be remembered that we are writing in reference to a new church—to a congregation coming into the apostolic order; for after being once set in order, it will be unnecessary to select persons to ordain, or to introduce other seniors into a participation of the oversight or ministry of the community. Those already ordained will, for the brotherhood, always act in such matters. They are the standing presbytery or senate of the congregation. It was, however, expedient, in our judgment, to select the most difficult case, and one that will place the true fountain of all official authority in the boldest relief before the brotherhood.

"No one can say that such officers, so nominated, elected, and ordained by the people, have not full ecclesiastic authority and right to officiate in behalf of the congregation, because they are of their own choice and ordination. Neither can it be said with a due regard to what is written by the apostles, that such officers have not the authority of the head of the church, as well as of the brethren, to administer the affairs of the congregation, for they are of the Lord's choice and ordination. They are persons chosen by the Lord and the people. They are ordained by the Lord and the people; because the laws of the Lord are consulted and obeyed, in the whole affair, by the people

"The jurisdiction of such bishops is always circumscribed by the congregation which ordained them. A single church is the largest diocese known in the New Testament. Neither does his election and ordination give him an indelible character, nor a perpetual office. Should he leave the church, which, under the direction of the Holy Spirit, created him and become a member of another church, he enters it as a private member, and so continues until that church elect and ordain him, should they call for his services. The bishops and deacons of the church in Philippi were the bishops and deacons of the church in Philippi, and of no other church; and so of Ephesus, Antioch, Rome, and Jerusalem.

"Of the bishops of a large congregation it will generally, perhaps always, happen that one of them will be eminent above the others. Character, age, talent, information, will inevitably bestow superiority in some respects. Although all the presbyters or eldership are equal in authority, some one will occasionally be president of the meeting;

and, perhaps, one may become standing president. This is inevitable. Although all the apostles were equal in authority, among them there were some called *pillars;* and of these one was more influential than the others. Among the first twelve, Peter, James, and John were regarded by the whole Christian community as '*pillars*' of high reputation. In the great meeting in Jerusalem, when Paul and Silas went as delegates from the church in Antioch, in behalf of the Syrian Christians; and when a general meeting was called of all the apostles, elders, and the whole congregation; and after there had been '*much debate,*' Peter and James spoke once, and all were silent. The weight of their judgment settled the controversy. Paul became the chief of all the apostles, not in church authority, but in influence; because of his extraordinary talents, labors, and spotless reputation. If so then, amongst the ambassadors of heaven, why should we think it strange, if now, in a congregation having twelve or twenty elders, one should, by common feeling and common consent, become president of the senate* or eldership of the whole community.

"By translating this influence and presidency to mean church authority, and not distinguishing between moral influence and ecclesiastic power, before the end of the second century they called the president bishop '*the bishop,*' and the others were commonly regarded only as the eldership, and finally *the* bishop became the only bishop, and his jurisdiction was extended first over the city—then over its suburbs—then over its vicinity—then over the province—then over the kingdom—then over the empire—then over the world, until it ended in 'His Holiness, *the Father universal,*' or 'the Pope.'

"Still, it is a fact that only one person can preside at a time in one congregation; and it is unavoidable but that the most gifted and dignified will most generally preside when present, for the congregation will have it so. But confine this presidency, even though it should become stated, within its constitutional limits (a single congregation), and a pope will never be born.

"In all societies this presidency will obtain. It obtains in all republics; it obtained even in the fierce democracy of Greece—in the Roman Republic; it now obtains in the American Republics during the tenure of office. The Senate has its president; a committee has its chairman; the Supreme Court, and all the courts down to that of Common Pleas, have their president judges. It obtained in the commonwealth of Israel, in the time of Moses, in the time of Joshua, in

---

*The Greek word *presbuterion* found three times in the New Testament, may be rendered either senate, presbytery, or eldership.

the time of the Judges, in the time of the kings, in the time of the captivity, in the time when it was a Roman province.

"There are hierarchs in the skies. In heaven among angels there are thrones, dominions, principalities and powers. In the church the Lord gave first, apostles; secondly, prophets; thirdly, teachers; then various helpers. And when the church arrived at its manhood state on earth, there were private persons—deacons—bishops; and of these bishops, though alike in power, one generally presided, and to this it as naturally tends as do the waters to the sea; and it is best so, provided only, all is done with knowledge, good understanding, good spirit—without pride and lordship in him that presides—and without envy, and jealousy, and evil surmising among the bishops and in the congregation. And be it observed with all emphasis, *that there is no order of things, divine or human, that, in this earthly state, can wholly exclude occasions or opportunities for the display of these evil passions.* Moses and Aaron were envied, Joseph was envied, Jesus was envied, Paul was envied, and some of his acquaintance even preached Christ through envy. Humility, condescension, brotherly kindness, paternal solicitude for all the brotherhood, and a profound regard to the model Christ Jesus the Lord of all, are the only shield and defense against the workings of evil passions."

IN THE PRESENTATION OF OUR VIEWS

on this subject, it may not be out of place to suggest a few points in which all parties are agreed; for to us it is much more pleasant to see where brethren agree and dwell together in unity than it is to look at points of difference.

(1) It is believed, by all who accept the Bible as a revelation from God, that the church is a system of government established by God's authority on the earth.

(2) It is agreed by all parties that there can be no such thing as government without *laws* for the government, and protection of the subjects for whose benefit the government is established.

(3) It will be admitted that God has provided *laws*

for the government of his people, and that these laws are revealed in the Bible—the word of God.

(4) It will be further admitted that God has provided no laws which are worth any thing to his people unless obeyed by them.

(5) We suppose we may assume it as further agreed that in every government, whether of human or divine origin, there are things to be done which every one cannot do. While it may be admitted that every one is *authorized* to do every thing, it is certain that there are things which not every one can do, and this is one reason why organization and co-operative effort are necessary.

(6) When a congregation has been fully organized for the worship of God, we suppose that all will agree that there is some work in which all cannot engage, at least at one time, though it be granted that every one is fully authorized to do it.

(7) We suppose it will be agreed further that such work must be done by some one or more for the benefit of the congregation. There may be controversy about who should do the work, and how he or they should be selected; but that it should be done by some one or more for the congregation, is, we suppose, beyond question or doubt.

(8) Finally, it will be admitted, that in every government there will be persons negligent of duty, and still others who will violate law. To suppose that every one will be faithful in the discharge of duty, and in the observance of law, is to suppose a degree of perfection in human character not found in *every* member of *any* community; hence, the necessity for some one or more whose special business it is to execute the law—to ad-

monish and encourage the negligent, reform the wayward, and punish the persistently rebellious.

But I may be told that "it is the duty of every member of the family of God to watch over and encourage his wayward brother." So it is the duty of every good citizen of the State to use his influence in promoting peace and good will among his neighbors, and the observance of law by every citizen; still there must be persons whose *special* duty it is to execute the law, and without them the State would rapidly drift into anarchy and ruin. Is not this as true of the church as of the State? Though we were to admit at every breath that every one qualified is authorized to do it, yet the fact still remains that some by nature, and others by their own neglect to use the means of spiritual growth which God has put within their reach, are incompetent for the work, then *who shall do it?* Am I told that those best qualified for the work shall do it? I then ask, who shall judge of, and decide upon the qualifications of the party who shall undertake the work? Not every one for himself, surely; for, as Brother Campbell has well remarked, the one least qualified will likely be the first to volunteer his services. Do you say the *church* shall make the selection? So do I. Then *what shall we call these parties thus selected* to take the oversight of the flock, and do such other work as the church needs to have done by persons of its own selection for that purpose? and how shall the congregation select and consecrate them to the work?

When Paul wrote his letter to the Philippians, he addressed it "to all the saints in Christ Jesus which are at Philippi, with the bishops and deacons." Phil. i: 1. By this language we understand that there were *bishops* and *deacons* in the church at Philippi; and that these classes are not included in the idea of discipleship alone, for the phrase, "all the saints in Christ Jesus which are at Philippi," would certainly have included all the disciples who were there *as disciples* only, and the phrase, "with the *bishops* and *deacons*," would be meaningless if nothing more was meant by these titles than disciples of Jesus. The text certainly warrants the conclusion that all bishops and deacons are saints, but all the saints in Christ Jesus are not bishops and deacons. To borrow an illustration used by another, "all judges are lawyers, but all lawyers are not judges." This is plain enough; but what is implied by these terms?

A bishop is an overseer—one who takes the oversight of others. This is a part of the work which we found the church must select some one to do; hence, we call the one who does it a *bishop*. But what is an overseer? One whose duty it is to take the oversight of others—teach them what to do—how to do the work assigned them, and then see that they do it; and to so rule them as to keep good order among them while doing the will of the Master. Then this is the work of a bishop—to teach the members their duty, and see that they do it, and to rule them in accordance with the Master's will. But we find another name applied to those who do this work. Paul says: "Let the elders that rule well be counted worthy of double honor, especially they who labor in the word and doctrine." 1 Tim. v: 17. What does this word mean? Literally it is the comparative of *old;* hence, an elder is an aged person. But the elders that rule well are to be counted worthy of double honor. First, it is right to honor them on account of their age, we as should honor all old men. Secondly, it is right to honor them for their work's sake—ruling well; thus they are entitled to double honor. But only the elders who rule well are entitled to this double honor; hence, there are elders who do not rule well, perhaps do not rule at all. Then some elders rule, and we have found that *ruling* is at least a part of the bishop's work; hence, these *ruling elders* are aged persons who have been called to the work of bishops. Brother Campbell says the terms *bishop* and *elder* are sometimes used interchangeably to designate the same person. In Smith's Bible Dictionary we have the following language: " When the organization of the Christian Churches in Gentile cities involved the assignment of the work of pastoral superintendence to a distinct order, the title *episcopos* presented itself as at once convenient and familiar, and was therefore adopted as readily as the word elder (*presbuteros*) had been in the mother church at Jerusalem. That the two titles were originally equivalent, is clear from the following facts: (1) Bishops and elders are nowhere named together as being orders distinct from each other. (2) Bishops and deacons are named as apparently an exhaustive division of the officers of churches addressed by Paul. Phil. i: 1; 1 Tim. iii: 1-8. (3) The same persons are described by both names. Acts xx: 17-28. Tit. i: 5-8."

In Acts xx: 17, it is said: " And from Miletus he sent to Ephesus, and called the elders of the church, and at the twenty-eighth verse he tells them, " Take heed, therefore, unto yourselves, and to all the flock, over which the Holy Ghost hath made you overseers, to feed the church of God, which he hath purchased with his own blood." We need not tell the reader that the word *overseers* is from the plural of the same word elsewhere rendered *bishop*, and might have been here rendered *bishops* just as well as *overseers*, showing that the elders of the seventeenth verse were the overseers or bishops of the twenty-eighth verse. To Titus Paul says: "For this cause left I thee in Crete, that thou shouldest set in order the things that are wanting and ordain elders in every city, as I have appointed thee. If any be blameless, the husband of one wife, having faithful children not accused of riot or unruly—for a bishop must be blameless as the steward of God—not self-willed, not soon angry, not given to wine, no striker, not given to filthy lucre; holding fast the faithful word as he hath been taught, that he may be able, by sound doctrine, both to exhort and convince the gainsayers." Titus i: 5–9. Here Paul substantially tells Titus to ordain elders in every city if he could find any who were blameless, for a bishop must be blameless, thus clearly showing that he used the words *elder* and *bishop* interchangeably, and that the elders ordained by Titus were bishops.

There is but one other solution possible, that is that he was to ordain elders to the office of bishop. We do not think this exactly the thought intended, though *possibly* it may be. Suppose we were to say the County Court ordained judges of the election, when did the parties become judges of the election? *When they were ordained, and not before.* It was the act of the court that made them judges. Then when Titus ordained elders in every city, was it not his act that made them elders? The cases look to us exactly similar. True it is that these elders were bishops when ordained, because Paul meant the same by both terms in this connection at least. This is plain enough.

We frankly admit that the word *elder* primarily means older, but words often have an appropriated meaning, and in such cases they cannot be used in their primary signification. The word soul primarily means the immortal part of man, but it is often used to indicate the whole man, as when Adam became a living soul, that is a living man.

Again: "The soul which hath touched any such shall be unclean until even, and shall not eat of the holy things, unless he wash his flesh with water." Lev. xxii: 6. Innumerable examples might be cited in which words are used in an accommodated sense; hence as bishops were always old men, they might very naturally be called *elders* just as the word soul, primarily meaning only a part, should be used to indicate the whole man. While it is certainly true that not every *elder* is a *bishop* when the word *elder* is used in its primary sense, but it is equally true that every *bishop* is an *elder*, and may be called either *bishop* or *elder* without any violence to the common usage of language. Certainly no one will object to this thought on the ground of applying two titles to the same officer (or person if it is preferred), for it would be insulting to common sense to give examples of even a half-dozen titles to the same party when the merest tyro knows this is often done.

But we have used the word *office*, and as this word is objectionable to some, we must pause long enough to examine it a little. But really this seems to us the least important part of our investigation; for if we have the right man, scripturally selected and set apart to the work of a bishop or a deacon, as the case may be, so that he may appreciate the responsibility of his position, and promptly and efficiently perform it, it would seem to be a matter of little importance whether we call him an elder, a bishop, an overseer, an officer, or a servant. If elected or chosen by the congregation, and scripturally set apart to do the work for the congregation, he would be an officer whether we call him an officer or not. It matters not by what process he be selected by the congregation, he is still an officer in the correct use of that term; hence much of what has been said and written about *officers* and *official service* in the church, has been "much ado about nothing." The far more important matters are: (1) Has the congregation scriptural authority, either by command or example, to select any one or more of its members to do any work for the congregation or community? and (2) if the congregation has such authority, how shall the selection be made? and (3) shall he be consecrated to the work? If so, how?

But to return. Are there officers in the church of God? Paul says: "If a man desire the office of a bishop he desireth a good work." "Let these also first be proved, then let them use the office of a deacon being found blameless." "For they that have used the office of a deacon well purchase to themselves a good degree, and great boldness in the faith, which is in Christ Jesus." 1 Tim. iii: 1, 10, 13. Here we have the *offices* of bishop and deacon; and, surely, if any one fill the office by divine authority, he is an *officer*. This is plain enough, we suppose.

But while this is admitted to be the teaching of the common version of the New Testament, it is claimed that there is no word in the *original* which means either *office* or *officer*.

We suppose it will be admitted that we can know nothing of the meaning of Greek words only as lexicographers define them for us. We open our Greek New Testament at 1 Tim. iii: 1, and find the word *episkopes;* what does this word mean? Without a lexicon we do not know, but with a lexicon we may know. Pickering defines it: "An inspection, superintendence, the office of bishop, N. T." Thus the learned lexicographer tells us it *does* mean office, and not only office, but the *office of bishop*. In the next verse we find the word *episkopon* translated bishop. This word, from the same root, Pickering defines: "An inspection, the office of an inspector and overseer, a keeper, a guardian * * * a bishop." There are no lexicons known to us which do not substantially agree with the foregoing definition; and it tells us that the words found in the original *do mean a bishop*, and the *office of a bishop*. We are not able to command a sufficient amount of courage to antagonize all the lexicons with reference to the meaning of Greek words, of which we can know nothing only as defined for us by them.

But we are told that office means *work*. We suppose this notion grows out of Paul's remark, that "if a man desire the office of a bishop, he desireth a good work." 1 Tim. iii: 1. Does this prove that there is no such thing as the *office* of bishop? The manifest meaning of the passage is, that the work pertaining to the bishop's office is a good work. We suppose there is not an office on the earth, in any government, human or divine, that has not work connected with it. *Officers are made for the purpose of doing the work of the office.* Were this not true, there would be no use for officers; nor would there be any such thing as an office.

Paul says: "All members have not the same office." Rom. xii: 4. Here the word *office* is from the word *praxin*, which *does mean work, action, use*, etc. Now, if Paul had meant simply *work*, without the idea of *office* in 1 Tim. iii: 1, why did he not use the same word *praxis* in some of its forms? This would have settled the matter beyond dispute. In making the New Version the revisers retain the word office. The American revisers, in their suggested changes, offered no objection to this rendering, showing that it met their approval.

This is not conclusive, we grant, but it is a circumstance entitled to some consideration; for we suppose there is not riper scholarship on earth than was employed in that revision. We have the same word in Acts i: 20, rendered bishoprick. "His bishoprick let another take." The New Version has this *office*. "His office let another take." And this is right—unquestionably right. Then if the apostleship may be called an office, why not have the idea of office in the same word where it is used to indicate another office? We are wholly unable to see why. We are sure there is nothing in the context forbidding the common rendering, "office of a bishop."

But suppose we were to dispense with the words *office* and *officer*, what then? If we render the word *inspection*, then this would be the office, and the inspector would be the officer. Suppose we should render it superintendence, this would be the office, and the superintendent would be the officer. So if we render it oversight, this would be the office, and the overseer would be the officer. So the idea of office and officer are in any rendering which might be given in harmony with the meaning given by the lexicons, whether we call it office or not. We have no recollection to have ever heard the overseer of our public roads called an officer, yet every one knows that he *is* an officer, and clothed with authority by the State to control and direct others in the performance of work for the public good; and whether we ever call him an officer or not, changes not the nature of the fact. The same is true of every officer of the government, from president to postmaster. Indeed, we rarely call them officers, but simply president, governor, postmaster, etc., but still they are officers, whether we call them so or not; so of *bishops* and *deacons*—they are officers because ordained to the performance of work for the congregation or community; and though we were never to pronounce the word office or officer again in life, it would not change their relation to the church—they would be officers still.

Suppose a man seeking an office at the hands of the president or governor were to say to one man, "I want the office." To another, "I desire the appointment." To another, "I should be glad to get the position; would any one suppose he had *abandoned the desire for office*, because he had changed his manner of expressing the desire? Surely not. These are but different ways of expressing the same thought. The idea of office is in the mind of the speaker, whether expressed by office, appointment, or position.

HOW OFFICERS ARE MADE BY THE CHURCH.

We have seen that elders or bishops and deacons were in the church in the days of the apostles? were they to pass away with the age of miracles? or, were they to be co-existent with the church? These questions, surely, need not detain us long, for every one must see at a glance that the necessity for them has not passed away, and, in the very nature of things, never can pass away. As long as it is necessary that the affairs of the church be attended to with decency and order, so long must the necessity for bishops and deacons remain. As long as men and women enter the church babes in Christ, it will be necessary for some one to feed the flock of God, and we have seen this to be the work of the overseers or bishops; and as long as widows, orphans, and the poor shall remain, the necessity for deacons will remain; and who does not know that as long as the church shall exist on earth, these, with many other things demanding the work of bishops and deacons will remain, and the church cannot fill its God-appointed mission without them. Paul gave Timothy and Titus both, very specific directions as to the character of men to fill these offices, without any intimation that there would come a time when they might be dispensed with; on the contrary he told Timothy that he gave him these instructions in order that he might know how to behave himself in the church of God, in the event of his long absence from him. In a second letter he told Timothy to teach the things which he had heard of him among many witnesses to faithful men, that they might teach others also, showing that they were to be transmitted from generation to generation perpetually. True, he says, "the things which thou hast heard of me among many witnesses," making it probable that he may not have referred to things written; but if things spoken should be transmitted, we see not why things written to him should not be transmitted also for our learning, that we should profit by them. The epistolary writings of the apostles are replete with instructions as to the character of persons to be selected, and the work to be performed by them; and the work assigned them is as necessary to-day as it ever has been; hence, if we may dispense with them, we see not why we may not close up our Bibles and abandon their teaching entirely.

HOW SHALL BISHOPS AND DEACONS BE SELECTED?

Or, rather, how shall material be selected of which to make bishops and deacons? Or, to be more plain, *who* shall make the selection? and *how* shall they do it?

As they are to serve the *congregation*, we would very naturally conclude, even in the absence of inspired teaching on the subject, that they must be selected by the congregation in the interest of which they are to labor; but the divine volume is not a blank on this subject. It is admitted, by all students of the Bible, that *inspired example* is as much to be regarded as inspired precept; and, hence, if we can find how the inspired teachers did any thing which we are to do at all, we must do it as they did; or, if we can find where uninspired men did any thing which was approved by inspired men, this is a sufficient guide for us in the performance of the same work. We have all admitted, and all debaters and writers have admitted, that even *infant baptism* might be proved in either of these ways. Indeed, if apostolic example and approved precedent are not worthy of our imitation in the performance of the same work, then we are at sea without chart or compass to guide us in the greater part of our Christian voyage through life. All writers and public men of note admit this principle, but we are writing for the "multitude of the disciples," and some of them do not appreciate it; hence, for their benefit we would impress it.

When the seven deacons were to be selected in Jerusalem, "the twelve called the multitude of the disciples unto them, and said, It is not reason that we should leave the word of God and serve tables; wherefore, brethren, look ye out among you seven men of honest report, full of the Holy Ghost and wisdom, whom we may appoint over this business; but we will give ourselves continually to prayer, and to the ministry of the word. And the saying pleased the whole multitude and they chose Stephen," etc. Acts vi: 2–5. Here we learn that the apostles addressed the *multitude of the disciples*, and told *them* to look out the persons, and the saying pleased *the whole multitude* and *they elected the parties* to be appointed.

On general principles, then, we learn that when persons were to be selected to serve the congregation, in any capacity, the whole multitude of disciples made the selection; or, if you please, *elected* the parties, for elect simply means to choose or select.

This is all plain enough as to the deacons, why may not the same principle apply to the selection of elders or bishops? We see it did obtain in the selection of Matthias to succeed Judas in the apostleship; then if it obtained in these cases of which we have a record, why shall we not conclude that it obtained in all cases where the procedure is not recorded?

But we may be asked if Titus did not select the elders ordained in Crete? We suppose not. He was commanded to ordain them, but it is not recorded that he selected them, or that he was commanded to do so. Paul gave him the qualifications of those to be ordained; but we see no reason why he should not have instructed the multitude, and left the selection to them, as in the case of the deacons at Jerusalem. Are we not bound to conclude that had there been any departure from the example recorded, the departure or exception would have been recorded also?

A good rule of Biblical interpretation, recognized among all critics is that *obscure* passages of Scripture must be interpreted in the light of plain passages on the same subject; *i. e.* all doubtful passages and examples of action must be so construed as to harmonize with passages and examples the import of which is unambiguous and without doubt. With this rule before us we cannot leave the example given us in the selection of the seven deacons at Jerusalem, where the lesson taught is beyond the possibility of doubt, and seek for light where the method of procedure is not recorded.

If, therefore, we find that some one, or more, was selected to serve the congregation in any matter, and the manner of selection is not given, we have a right to conclude that the selection was made as in the example recorded; and the fact that a record is given elsewhere, made it unnecessary to repeat it.

HOW WAS THE WILL OF THE CONGREGATION EXPRESSED?

That the will of the congregation was consulted in the selection of its servants we have seen clearly enough, but just how their choice was expressed is a matter not so clearly revealed; and it may be that the reason for this obscurity is found in the fact that any method by which the will of the congregation can be ascertained, in harmony with that decency and good order always to be observed in the house of God, will be admissible. Had the Master intended that one particular method of expression should be adopted, it would, most likely, have been revealed in precept or example, somewhere.

Paul speaks of a brother whose praise was in all the churches, "who was also chosen of the churches to travel with us." 2 Cor. viii : 19. Here was a *choice* or *election* of a person by the churches; and while there is nothing in the English words *choose* and *chosen* to indicate the *manner* of choosing, yet in the Greek word here rendered *chosen* there may be light on this point. Chosen is here a translation of *cheirotonetheis*, which is a form of *cheirotoneo*, which Young defines, "to extend the hand (in voting)." See Young's Concordance on the word *chosen*. 2 Cor. viii : 19. While it is possible that this does not exhaust the meaning of this word, we can see no other reason for its employment here than to express the manner of electing the person chosen. Taking this as true, it is entirely scriptural for the members of the congregation to express their choice *in matters of this character* by voting with the hand.

We are fully aware of the prejudices existing in the mind of good brethren against voting in the congregation, yet we know of no better way of getting at the will of the congregation in many cases which may come before it, than to allow the members to express their choice by a vote. We are quite familiar with the objections urged against voting, but the wisdom of heaven has never been able to suggest any thing against which objections cannot be brought. We know of no congregation which does not practice voting in some form. Suppose we say, in the congregation, that "if there is no objection by any one *thus* and *so* will be done." We pause for objection—none is made, and the thing is is done; did not the congregation, by its silence, vote for the thing to be done, just as clearly as if the question had been put before it in any other form, and voted upon in any other way? Most assuredly it did; and yet this is the general practice of those who object to voting! We respectfully suggest that, in many cases, this is more objectionable than other methods of voting, for native timidity, and sometimes becoming modesty, will prevent those who really have objections from rising in the congregation and giving expression to them, when if they could vote otherwise in common with the multitude, they would not hesitate to do it.

Brother Campbell has given us some excellent thoughts in his Extra to the *Harbinger* for 1835, from which, by the reader's indulgence, we will reproduce an extract. But you will say, "Brother Campbell was not inspired." This is certainly true; but you will agree with us that he was no insignificant judge of the teaching of men who were inspired; and, hence, there are not many of us who might not profit by a perusal of what he wrote in the vigor of his manhood on any subject.

A. CAMPBELL ON VOTING IN THE CHURCH.

"Some Christians are opposed to voting in the church. They only vote against voting! They will give their *voice*, but say they will not *vote*. Now, upon a little reflection, it may, perhaps, appear to them that to vote and to give their voice, is identically one and the same thing. To express their mind or their wish on any question, is certainly to vote—whatever form may be chosen, whether standing up, stretching forth the hand, or simply saying yes or no, aye or nay.

"Wherever there is an election, or choice of persons, or measures, there must be voting, or a casting of the lot. To cast the lot is an appeal to heaven; and very extraordinary, indeed, must be the incident or the occasion that will justify such a solemn appeal, or such an irrevocable decision.

"We need not labor to show that the Christians under the very eye, and with the approbation of the apostles, voted; for the apostles commanded them to vote—to choose out persons for certain works, and with reference to certain measures. But a question arises of some consequence—nay, of great consequence—*On what occasions, and for what purposes are Christians authorized to vote?*

"They are not to vote on questions of faith, piety, or morality. Truth is not to be settled by a vote, nor is any divine institution, respecting the worship or morality of the Christian Church, to be decided by a majority. These are matters of revelation, of divine authority, and to be regulated by a '*thus saith the Lord*,' and not by thus saith the majority. But in all matters not of faith, piety, or morality; in all matters of expediency, and sometimes in questions of fact pertaining to cases of discipline, there is no other way of deciding but by vote of the brotherhood. There is no revelation that A, B, or C shall be chosen elders or deacons; that D, E, or F shall be sent on any special message; that the church shall meet in any given place at any hour, or that this or that measure is to be adopted in reference to any particular duty arising out of the internal or external relations to the church. Such matters are to be decided by the vote of the whole community or not at all.

"How that vote shall be given—whether by stretching out the

hand, as the Greek word found in Acts xiv: 13, and 2 Cor. viii: 19, literally indicates; or whether by standing up, or saying *aye*, or *nay*, may itself be a question of expediency, to be decided by a vote of the community. And certainly it matters not, in this instance, what the form be, provided only the mind of the church be clearly ascertained.

"A matter of greater importance occurs: *Must the church be always unanimous before it acts upon any question of fact or expediency?* While it is possible to be of one faith and of one hope, however desirable it may be, it is not to be expected that a congregation will always be of one mind in all questions of discipline or expediency which may occur in their earthly pilgrimage. Some, however, will insist not only upon one opinion in matters of abstract speculation, but upon one mind in all matters of expediency.

"In the New Testament we have the word which the Greeks used for *majority* sometimes translated 'the greater part.' 1 Cor. xv: 6. 'The more.' Acts xix: 32; xxvii: 11. And 'the many.' 2 Cor. ii: 6. Where the censure inflicted upon a certain individual is spoken of, it is rendered by McKnight '*the majority:*' 'Sufficient for such an one is the censure inflicted by the majority; plainly intimating that not every individual, but that a decided majority of the church had concurred in the sentence pronounced.

"True, indeed, that where there is much love and great devotion to the will of the Lord, there will be the greatest approaches to unanimity in all matters of great importance. The wisdom which comes from above, is first pure, then peaceable, gentle, and *easy to be persuaded*. Self-willedness is no ornament of Christian character, and when each esteems his brother as better than himself, there will not be much earnestness displayed in striving to carry our views of expediency over the judgment of others. Besides it is sometimes inexpedient for the majority to carry all in its power. There may be occasions when it is better for the majority to waive its privilege than to carry its point. These, however, are matters which discretion and good sense must and will decide according to the bearing of all measures upon the good order, peace, harmony, and prosperity of the brotherhood. All warmth and impassioned feeling in the house of God is disorderly; and no church, acting under the guidance of the Good Spirit, will ever attempt hastily to decide a matter in the midst of the least excitement."

ORDINATION OF DEACONS.

Having seen that bishops and deacons were in the

church by divine appointment in the days of the apostles, and that they were to be co-existent with the church, we come, now, to inquire *how* they were appointed, ordained, separated, or set apart to their work.

But we are told that the *New Version* has removed the word *ordain* from the New Testament, substituting *appoint* in its place. And what of that? Does that cut any figure in the investigation at all? We cannot see how that affects the argument in any way. We have always had the word appoint in Acts vi : 3, with reference to the seven deacons; and in their appointment the apostles prayed and laid their hands on them. They said they would appoint them, and this is what they did. Why shall we not do as they did? *This is the question.* What was done? and how was it done?

In the examination of this subject we propose to pursue the same methods of interpretation pursued on the subjects of conversion, baptism, the Holy Spirit, or any other subject of Biblical controversy. When we examine the commission we collate the conditions of pardon contained in it from *all* the reports given of it; and conclude that while there may be *more* contained in it than is given in any one report, yet *nothing* contained in *any* report can be *omitted*.

With this rule before us we get *teaching, baptism*, and the *formula* to be used, from Matthew. From Mark we get *preaching, faith, baptism* and *salvation*. From Luke we get *preaching, repentance, remission of sins*, and a place at which to begin. Now, our rule requires us to take all the reports; hence, collating the items, we have *preaching, faith, repentance, baptism*, into the names of Father, Son, and Holy Spirit for the remission of sins beginning at Jerusalem. But if we are in doubt as to the meaning of the commission we will go with the

25

the apostles, to whom it was given, and see what they did in obedience to it. Nor will we stop with the examination of a *single* case, but we will examine *all* the cases recorded, and collate, from them, all the conditions of pardon required of them who were converted by the preaching of these inspired teachers; and thus we can unmistakably learn what was meant by the commission under which they acted. We will also notice *how* they obeyed the commands given by these inspired men; and if we find that they went down into the water to be baptized, and came up out of the water after they were baptized, we will conclude that this was authorized by the commission, and we will try to do as *taught in the examples recorded*. We will not get alarmed because *inspired* men did the work, for they did many things enjoined upon us; hence, *what* they did, and *how* they did it, is just what we want to know, that we may follow the examples left by them as nearly as possible. That this is a safe rule of interpretation, leading to safe conclusions, is admitted from the rising to the setting of the sun—from the rivers to the ends of the earth; then let us keep it constantly before us while we see what was done in ordaining or appointing disciples of Jesus to the work of bishops and deacons.

Addressing the multitude of disciples the apostles said: "Wherefore, brethren, look ye out among you seven men of honest report, full of the Holy Ghost and wisdom whom we may appoint over this business." Acts vi: 3.

On another occasion, while the disciples ministered to the Lord and fasted, the Holy Ghost said, "Separate me Barnabas and Saul for the work whereunto I have called them." Acts xiii: 2.

Again it is said: "When they had ordained them elders in every church." Acts xiv: 23. Here we have the words *appoint, separate,* and *ordain,* used to indicate the consecration of persons to the work of *deacons, evangelists,* and *elders* or *bishops*—we will, therefore, use them interchangeably, supposing them, in the foregoing quotations, to mean substantially the same thing; and we admit, at the beginning, that there is nothing in either of them indicating the *manner* of appointing, separating, or ordaining the persons. This can be learned only by an examination of recorded examples left for our instruction. Webster defines the word *ordain* as meaning "to set in order; to arrange according to rule; to regulate; to set; to establish. To appoint; to decree; to enact; to institute. To set apart for an office; to constitute. Especially, to invest with ministerial or sacerdotal functions; to introduce into the office of the Christian ministry, by laying on of hands or other appropriate forms." But Mr. Webster doubtless defined the word according to modern usage; hence, the value of his definition depends upon whether or not it is sustained by the practice of inspired men. To this practice we go, then, feeling assured that the words used by divine wisdom are not meaningless, and that *something* was done as indicated by them.

When the apostles commanded the multitude of disciples to select the seven men to be appointed over the business before them, "the saying pleased the *whole multitude;* and they chose Stephen, a man full of faith and of the Holy Ghost, and Philip, and Prochorus, and Nicanor, and Timon, and Parmenas, and Nicolas, a proselyte of Antioch; whom they set before the apostles; and when they had prayed they laid their hands on them." Acts vi: 5, 6. What did the apostles propose to do? They said they would *appoint* the men when selected. When they were selected and placed before them what did they do? They *prayed and laid their hands on them.* This is what was done in appointing them, and was, therefore, the appointment. *If this was not the appointment, what was?* Certainly there was something done—what was it? Do you tell me you do not know? Then you are like the witnesses who slept over the grave of Jesus—not competent to answer the question or take position on it. We *do know* that they prayed and laid their hands on them, for the Book of God says so. More may have been done, but this was *certainly done;* are we at liberty to leave it undone? Is it not more safe to do as they did?

But we are told that the words translated "laid their hands on them," should have been translated "extended their hands to them." Then why do not those who make the objection *practice what they preach*—pray and extend their hands to them. Even this rendering cannot justify doing nothing at all. Had this been the thought, the Spirit could have said it as easily as what it did say. When the right hand of fellowship was given to Paul and Barnabas, (Gal. ii: 9) words were found with which to clearly express it; and had the same words been used in connection with ordination, there would have been no ambiguity about them; and surely they would have been employed if this had been what was done.

We have the words *laid on* from the word *epitithemi,* which is composed of a preposition *epi,* meaning on or upon, and a verb *tithemi,* to lay, place or put; hence, the word *epitithemi* literally means to lay on, place on, or put on. There is nothing in the word to determine *what* is laid on—this is determined by the noun to which reference is made in each particular case. It may be a hand, a burden, punishment, or figuratively a name, etc. Will the reader please open Young's Concordance at the word *lay*, and examine the connections in which it is from the word *epitithemi* as found in that great work? For the benefit of such readers as have not the book we will transcribe every such occurrence of the word.

Matt. ix: 18 come and *lay* thy hand *upon* her
" xix: 15 he *laid* his hands *on* them, and departed
" xxiii: 4 *lay on* men's shoulders, but they
Mark v: 23 come and *lay* thy hands *on* her
" vi: 5 save that he *laid* his hands *upon* a few
" xvi: 18 they shall *lay* hands *on* the sick
Luke iv: 40 he *laid* his hands *on* every one of them
" xiii: 13 he *laid* his hands *on* her
" xv: 5 and....he *layeth* it *on* his shoulder
" xxiii: 26 *on* him they *laid* the cross
Acts vi: 6 they had prayed they *laid* their hands *on* them
" viii: 17 then they *laid* their hands *on* them
" viii: 19 that *on* whomsoever I *lay* hands
" xiii: 3 *laid* their hands *on* them, they sent them
" xv: 28 to *lay upon* you no greater burden than
" xvi: 23 when they had *laid* many stripes *upon* them
" xix: 6 when Paul had *laid* his hands *upon* them
" xxviii: 3 had gathered a bundle of sticks and *laid* them *on* the fire
" xxviii: 8 and *laid* his hands *on* him and healed him
1 Tim. v: 22 *Lay* hands suddenly *on* no man
Rev. i: 17 he *laid* his right hand *upon* me

Will the reader carefully examine these examples of the word *epitithemi?* Was the cross extended to Simon, but not laid on him? Were the stripes extended to Paul and Silas, but not laid on them? Were the sticks extended to the fire, but not laid on it? Please note the fact that it is the same word rendered *laid on* in conferring spiritual gifts; and if it does not mean *laid on* in ordination, it does not in conferring gifts either. It occurs forty-two times in the Greek New Testament, but is never once rendered *extend* or *give* in connection with hands or any thing else. Indeed, there is no example of it which might not be rendered *put on, laid on,* or *placed on* in some of their forms.

But there has been quite a change of front on this subject in the last few years. For a time hands were not laid on the seven deacons at all; but simply extended to them as in giving the hand of fellowship; but more recently it is admitted that hands *were* laid on, but not in connection with their ordination, but for the purpose of conferring spiritual gifts. While this shifting of ground gives evidence of a want of clear and settled convictions on the subject, it still becomes us to examine the theory that we may see what claims, if any, it has to our acceptance.

That apostolic hands were laid on for the purpose of imparting spiritual gifts is certainly true; but that they were *always* laid on for this purpose is assumption wholly wanting in proof. There was a murmuring of the Grecians against the Hebrews because their widows were neglected in the daily distribution of food. The apostles ordered the multitude to select seven men to be appointed over *this business.* What business? The working of miracles? No, but to supply the tables of the Grecian widows. The persons were selected and presented to the apostles for their action. They were to appoint them; but as yet they had done nothing. True, they had given the qualifications of the parties to be selected, and had ordered the selection to be made; but they proposed to appoint *after* the selection—not before it. The selection was no part of the appointment, for the multitude was to do that. Now the subjects are ready for appointment—what was done? They *prayed and laid their hands on them.* For what? To *appoint* them. Appoint them for what? To work miracles? No, but to attend to this business. What business? To supply the tables of the Grecian widows. Then hands were not laid on them to impart spiritual gifts to them; but to separate or appoint them to this business. If this is not clear, then Holy Writ can make nothing clear. We have no evidence that the subject of spiritual gifts was before them on that occasion at all.

But we are asked: " What good can it do to lay on hands if the party is not supernaturally endowed by it?" This question has been asked about baptism until even our opponents have become ashamed of it. " If there is no efficacy in water to wash away sins, what good can it do to be baptized for the remission of sins?" What good can it do to obey God at all? If God has commanded us to do a thing, or left us such examples as clearly teach us to do it, shall we stop to debate the question with him as to what good it will do? The truly loyal servant learns the will of the master and goes about the work, whether he can see any good it will do or not. The master's will is reason enough for him who would honor the master.

But does it do no good to solemnly impress any one with the responsibility of his position, and the importance of the work assigned him? All governments, in all ages and countries, whether of human or divine origin, have had their *ceremonies of consecration, installation, coronation, inauguration, etc.*, for the purpose of solemnly impressing those inducted into office with the responsibility of the position about to be assumed; and they seek to make them so impressive as never to be forgotten. Perhaps the seven deacons ordained at Jerusalem could have supplied the Grecian widows with food before they were ordained if they would, but they *did not do it*, we suppose, because they had never been specially assigned to that work, and made to realize that the congregation expected *them* to do it; but when they were thus solemnly set apart, we hear of no more neglect or complaint about it.

So it is to-day; persons may be fully competent to do the work of bishops and deacons, but until they are set apart to the work, and solemnly impressed with the responsibility of their position, and made to feel that the congregation expects *them* to do *that* work, they will not be likely to do it; and hence it will generally go undone; or, if done at all, it will be done without that *system* and *order* that should ever characterize a government of which God is the author. This reason, if there were no others, would abundantly vindicate the wisdom of God in requiring the ordination of officers in the church.

But we are told that the "imposition of hands on the seven deacons at Jerusalem was for the impartation of spiritual gifts, because they did not possess this power before that event, and did possess it afterward." Then we would inquire of the objector how he knows that they *did not* possess supernatural power or spiritual gifts before that time? Is it because we have no account of its exercise by them before that time? This may not be quite conclusive. If any one will find a record of the miracles performed by *five* of them after hands were laid on them, he will likely find in the next verse an account of the miracles wrought by all of them before their appointment to the deacon's office.

There is no record of any miracle performed by any of the seven, except Stephen and Philip. Shall we conclude, therefore, that the other five performed none? Shall we conclude that Stephen and Philip received miraculous power when hands were laid on the seven, and that the other five did not receive it because there is no record of its exercise by them? This is unreasonable, and cannot be accepted. Then shall we conclude that all of them received and exercised spiritual gifts, but there was nothing connected with what five of them did, which was of sufficient importance to make it necessary to record it? When this position is taken the assumption falls to the ground that the seven did not possess supernatural power before ordination, because there is no record of its exercise by them.

We suppose that if all the miracles, wrought by those who were supernaturally endowed in the days of the apostles, had been recorded, " the world would not have contained the books." Were there not special reasons why the miraculous power exhibited by Stephen and Philip was recorded? Stephen was the first martyr to the faith of the gospel, and the record of his glorious death would have been incomplete without his supernatural vision of heaven. In recording the conversion of the Samaritans, it was necessary to report the miracles which Philip did in confirmation of his preaching there. But for these events we might never have known that a miracle was performed by any of the seven; hence, the silence of the Scriptures on the subject is not conclusive proof that the seven had not supernatural power before their ordination to the deacon's office. Assumptions are a cheap commodity.

What are the probabilities on the subject? That the apostles had the power to convey these spiritual gifts is very certain; and it seems to have been their *custom* to confer them, if not upon all, certainly upon a large number of the primitive disciples as soon as converted. As soon as Samaria received the word of God, Peter and John were sent there for the purpose of conferring this measure of the spirit upon the converts at that place. Then is it not entirely reasonable that the faith of the disciples, who were converted at Jerusalem when the church was in its infancy, was confirmed in the same way?

One of the first questions asked by Paul of the disciples found at Ephesus was: "Have ye received the Holy Ghost since ye believed?" This shows that the disciples generally did receive it, and were expected to have it; and, doubtless, had they been converted by an apostle instead of Apollos, who knew only the system of things taught by John, they would have received it before Paul saw them. Certain it is that Paul conferred it upon them very soon after he reached them. He longed to see his brethren at Rome, that he might impart to them some spiritual gift to the end that they might be established. Seeing, then, that it was the custom of the apostles to confer this power on the early converts as soon as they had opportunity, why should the seven have been exceptions to the custom, especially as they were daily in the company of the apostles? They were prominent men among the disciples, of honest report, full of the Holy Ghost and wisdom; hence, that they were abundantly endowed with spiritual gifts *before* their ordination is much more probable than that they received spiritual gifts by imposition of hands at the time of their appointment to the deaconship. Indeed, this is not probable at all.

By the way, we are told that Ananias conferred this supernatural power on Saul when he laid his hands on him, because he said: "Brother Saul, the Lord, even Jesus, that appeared unto thee in the way as thou camest, hath sent me, that thou mightest receive thy sight, and be filled with the Holy Ghost." Acts ix: 17. The fallacy of this conclusion will appear in due time—

for the present we only call attention to it here to show the very liberal methods of reasoning on this subject. To be *be filled with the Holy Ghost* means abundantly endowed with spiritual gifts when spoken by Ananias to Saul; but *full of the Holy Ghost and wisdom* only means earnest and intelligent Christians when spoken by the apostles concerning those of whom they proposed to make deacons; hence they never had any spiritual gifts until hands were laid on them in their ordination! The blinding influences of a false theory are truly astonishing, even on the eyes of good brethren; they ought to have great forbearance with those blinded by an entire system of error.

But an objector says: "God hath set the members in the body as it hath pleased him." Certainly he did; but he sets no one in the body, nor in any position in the body, only *in accordance with law*, administered by the body. What the body or church does according to law, he does. We have seen that it pleased him to set deacons in office by prayer and the imposition of hands, and it occurs to us that we ought to be pleased with what pleases him.

But "we are to grow up into him in all things." Certainly we are to grow from babes in Christ to the stature of men; but does this prove that competent disciples are not to be ordained to any specific office or work? James A. Garfield grew up from a common school teacher to the presidency of the United States; but does this prove that the ceremonies of *inauguration* were dispensed with when he was inducted into the office of president? Growth in grace and knowledge has nothing to do with ordination to office, only in preparing the party for it; it is no part of it.

No one believes more earnestly in spiritual growth

than we do; and for this very reason we want officers to administer the affairs of the church so that its members may grow. We want the flock watched over and fed, that the lambs may not perish, nor be devoured by the wolves. Every one knows that large numbers of those introduced into the family of God every year, go back into the world, for want of an efficient eldership to look after and care for them; and this we will never have until they are made in God's appointed way.

ELDERS, OR BISHOPS.

We have seen that when Paul called the elders of the church at Ephesus, he told them to take heed to themselves, and to all the flock over which the Holy Ghost had made them overseers. The word *overseers* is from *episkopos*, elsewhere rendered *bishops;* hence, these elders, were, by the Holy Spirit, made bishops or overseers; but when or how they had been so made is not here stated. We suppose the Holy Spirit made them overseers just like it separated Paul and Barnabas to the work to which it called them; how this was done we will see in due time. Paul left Titus in Crete to ordain elders in every city, if he could find any blameless; giving as a reason that bishops must be blameless, thus using the terms elder and bishop interchangeably to designate the same persons. But here, again, we are not told how Titus was to ordain them, or what he was to do in ordaining them.

But we are told that *tithemi*, here rendered ordain, means to lay, put, or place; hence, Titus was simply to place the seniors in their proper places in the congregations. Well, the context clearly shows that the proper place for the parties to be ordained here was in the office of bishop, and there can be no doubt that Paul intended Titus to put them there; but that Paul meant nothing more than *old men* by the term *elders* in this connection, is not only inconsistent with the context, but clearly inconsistent with the subsequent instruction given to Titus as well. In the opening of the next chapter he told him what to say to the seniors, as such; and he uses a very different style to that used to designate the parties to be ordained. He says: "But speak thou the things which become sound doctrine: that the aged men be sober, grave, temperate, sound in faith, in charity, in patience. The aged women likewise, that they be in behavior as becometh holiness, not false accusers, not given to much wine, teachers of good things." Titus ii: 1-3. Here he speaks of the seniors as such; and he calls them *aged men, aged women;* and told Titus to teach them how to live; but when speaking of the elders to be ordained, he specified the character which they must have before ordination, that they might be eligible to ordination.

Will the reader take up his New Testament and read the first chapter of Titus, from the fifth to the ninth verse inclusive; then read the first three verses of the second chapter; then in calm deliberation, ask himself the question: "Can it be possible that Paul meant the same by the word *elders* in the first chapter that he did by the words *aged men* in the second chapter?" It occurs to us that a negative answer to this question must come from every unbiased mind.

Here we get the key to Paul's style in the use of these forms of expression. When he speaks of the seniors as such, he calls them aged men, aged women; but when he calls them elders, elders of the church, bishops or overseers, he means those whose duty it is to rule in the congregation and take the oversight of the flock. That such was his use of these terms seems clear enough. But we are still without light as to what Paul expected Titus to *do* in ordaining elders or bishops. We suppose Paul did not tell him *how* he was to ordain them simply because they had been together long enough for Paul to know that Titus understood the process—perhaps had seen persons ordained frequently; but how are *we* to know what was done, that we may know what to do in the performance of this work? We can only learn by the examination of recorded cases of ordination, that we may see what was done. If this examination sheds no light on the subject, then we will be likely to remain in darkness, and may join our brethren in *doing nothing* in this direction.

With the book of God in our hands, however, we open to Acts xiv: 23, and read: "And when they had ordained them elders in every church, and prayed with fasting, they commended them to the Lord, on whom they believed." Here we learn that they *prayed* and *fasted*, but the connection in which the word *ordained* occurs here shows that something more than praying and fasting was done. True, indeed, these things were done; and in similar work, therefore, we dare not omit them, even though we should not learn what else was done; for we must certainly do what we have clearly learned to be our duty, though we should fail to learn our *whole* duty—it will be quite enough to omit what we do not learn; hence we must practice what we do learn. But we must see what more was done if we would fill the measure of the example furnished us.

The word *cheirotoneo* only occurs in two forms, and but a single occurrence of each in the Greek New

Testament. *Cheirotonetheis* is found in 2 Cor. viii : 19, where it is rendered *chosen.* Young defines it here, " to extend the hand in voting." The other example is in the case under consideration, where *cheirotonesantes* is rendered ordained. Acts xiv : 23. Here Young defines it, " to elect by stretching out the hand." These two examples exhaust the word in the original of the Bible, and we see it defined substantially the same way in both places. In the first example it is easy to see that the churches elected the party chosen by voting with the hand, and the conclusion reached is natural enough. But in the case before us the solution is not so apparent—indeed, it is confessedly difficult. That Paul and Barnabas held an election where they were the only voters, and voted for the parties elected by extending their hands, is hardly probable. It would have been more natural for them to consult together as to who should be selected, if they made the selection at all. If they could not agree upon it, neither could they decide it by a vote ; for, as there were but two voters, their difference would have made a tie vote inevitable. The premises considered, therefore, we are slow to believe that Paul and Barnabas ever conducted such a ludicrous farce. The supposition is further objectionable from the fact that it would have taken from the churches the selection of their own rulers or servants —a manifest departure from the precedent established in the selection of the seven deacons at Jerusalem. We are slow to believe that one method was adopted at one place, and a different method adopted at another place. Such want of system is not characteristic of God's order of doing things. But there was, unquestionably, something done with the hand, for the use of the hand is inherent in the word employed; how can we find what it was? But a few days before, Paul and Barnabas had been set apart to the work in which they were then engaged—is it not likely that they consecrated or set apart these elders to their work in the same way in which they had so recently been set apart to their own work? Surely this is reasonable, and we will, therefore, see what was done when they were separated to their work.

"Now there were in the church that was at Antioch certain prophets and teachers; as Barnabas, and Simeon that is called Niger, and Lucius of Cyrene, and Manaen, which had been brought up with Herod the tetrarch, and Saul. As they ministered to the Lord, and fasted, the Holy Ghost said, separate me Barnabas and Saul for the work whereunto I have called them. And when they had fasted and prayed, and laid their hands on them, they sent them away." Acts xiii: 1–3.

Now let us compare the two cases. In the consecration of the elders, they fasted and prayed; in the consecration of Barnabas and Saul they fasted and prayed. Thus far the cases are exactly similar. In the case of the elders something was done with the hand—what was it? In the case of Barnabas and Saul hands were laid on them; then, unless the Lord has two ways of doing the same thing, this is what was done in the case of the elders.

All parties agree that *cheirotoneo* means to extend the hand, and all know that the hand must be extended in laying it on; hence, the demands of *cheirotoneo* are fully satisfied in laying on hands, but the demands of *epitithemi* are not satisfied with mere extension, or any thing less than contact, when used in its literal sense as it is here; hence we regard it as a thing settled that the procedure in both cases included fasting, prayer, and laying on hands.

It is admitted, in the examination of all other Biblical questions, that obscure and difficult passages of Scripture must not be relied on to explain less obscure ones, but plain passages must be used to explain obscure and difficult ones. Applying this rule to the two cases of ordination before us, the word of God becomes its own interpreter, and all obscurity at once disappears.

Thus we see, too, how the Holy Spirit makes overseers. Indeed, the Holy Spirit makes Christians, deacons, elders or bishops, evangelists, and every thing else pertaining to the church of God, *according to law;* but the notion that the Holy Spirit makes men overseers in the church without compliance with law, is as mystical as abstract spiritual influences in making Christians without compliance with the law of pardon.

" But Paul and Barnabas were ordained by the direct authority of the Holy Spirit; we cannot have such instruction now; therefore, we are not to do that work." Certainly the persons who fasted, prayed, and laid their hands on them were directly instructed by the Holy Spirit; so was Peter on the day of Pentecost, when he told believers to repent and be baptized for the remission of sins. Shall we not preach the same thing, because he did it under direct instructions from heaven? The Holy Spirit directly instructed Philip to go to the chariot and preach Jesus to the Ethiopian nobleman. Shall we quit that as well? We have been accustomed to think the Holy Spirit a pretty safe teacher in every thing we are to do, and that we ought to follow its instructions where we have the ability to do so.

"Well, but it looks too much like the Catholics to be fasting, praying, and laying on hands in ordination." The Catholics sing and pray. Shall we not sing and pray, lest we be found imitating them? They do many things which we must do, not because they do them, but because God commanded us to do them. The demons confessed Jesus to be the Son of God. Shall *we* quit it lest we imitate them? While we are running from Rome, let us be careful that we do not continue our retreat beyond Jerusalem.

Really, we cannot very well imagine why these cases of ordination were recorded at all, if not for our imitation in the performance of similar work. We readily infer that the various examples of conversion were recorded for this purpose; and if we are not to follow the examples of ordination left on record, then it seems that this is rather a worthless piece of history.

But we are told that "hands were always laid on to communicate spiritual gifts;" for what were they laid on Barnabas and Saul? We are told that Ananias communicated this power to Saul when he laid hands on him. Then why were hands again laid on to give him that which he already had? If the phrase "filled with the Holy Ghost," proves that Ananias thus endowed Paul, then Barnabas was so endowed before his ordination, "for he was a good man, and full of the Holy Ghost and of faith." Acts xi: 24. Then if this language proves supernatural endowment, they were both so endowed before hands were laid on them at Antioch. Then we repeat the question with emphasis, *why were hands laid on them to give them that which they already had?*

But did Ananias lay hands on Saul to impart spiritual gifts to him? If so, who laid hands on the other apostles to so endow them? They had this power *by virtue of their apostolic office*; for Jesus commanded them to "heal the sick, cleanse the lepers, raise the dead, cast out devils; freely ye have received, freely give." Matt. x: 8. Paul says: "In nothing am I behind the very chiefest apostles, though I be nothing. Truly the signs of an apostle were wrought among you in all patience, in signs and wonders, and mighty deeds." 2 Cor. xii: 11, 12. Here we learn that *miracles were signs of apostleship*. In what sense were they signs of an apostle? They could not prove that every one who possessed spiritual gifts was an apostle, for many possessed them who were not apostles, but had received them by imposition of apostolic hands. Then they were signs of an apostle, because *no one could be an apostle without them*—their absence would bar the claim of any one to that office, for miraculous power belonged to the apostolic office; hence, the moment Paul became an apostle, that moment he could work miracles, or do anything else belonging to that office; not because Ananias or any one else laid hands on him, but because the power belonged to the apostleship. The other apostles had it, not by imposition of hands, but by virtue of their office, and he was not a whit behind the very chiefest of them; and hence, he had it by virtue of his office. Hence, the idea that hands were laid on him to give him spiritual gifts is all a myth. When a sheriff, or any other officer, becomes sheriff, governor, or president, he has all the authority and power which belong to his office; so when Paul became an apostle, he had the power, and *all* the power, which belonged to other apostles, *because he was an apostle;* hence, he calls these miracles the *signs of an apostle*. They belonged to the office.

But if any one still insists that Ananias did confer spiritual gifts on Paul, then let him tell us who laid hands on the other apostles, and why Paul had hands laid on him at Antioch, if hands are always laid on for that purpose. But if any one takes the position (and some do) that he was not able to work miracles until hands were laid on him at Antioch, then it follows that he was an apostle more than four years without being able to give the signs of his office, and yet not a whit behind the very chiefest apostle in any thing. Certainly he was four or five years behind them in this work, according to this theory. But if laying on hands had been necessary to his endowment with spiritual gifts, we see not why he should have been all this time without it, for he had been twice up to Jerusalem before that time—had been fifteen days with Peter (Gal. i : 18), who was abundantly able to impart that power by imposition of his hands, and had just returned from Jerusalem to Antioch when hands were laid on him there. Is it not strange, then, if he had to receive this measure of the spirit by imposition of hands, that he did not get it from Peter who had the power to give or impart it to him, but waited to get it at Antioch from the hands of those *who had no power to impart it?*

The power to impart this measure of the spirit belonged to the apostles, and to them alone. It was a matter in which they could have no successors ; hence, when it was necessary that the Samaritans should receive it, Peter and John had to go there for the purpose of imparting it to them. Philip was there, and could work the miracles, but as no one but an apostle could confer the power, he could not do it. This power was not transferable at all; hence, when the apostles all died, this power had no repository on the earth. The names of the parties who laid hands on Barnabas and Saul are given, and while they were distinguished men in the church at Antioch, they had no such power as this. They were told to separate Barnabas and Saul to the work for which the Spirit had called them; and in obedience to this command they fasted and prayed, and laid their hands on them. This is what they laid hands on them for—to separate or consecrate them to their God-appointed work. It seems to have been the purpose of the Lord from the time he appeared to Saul to make him a special apostle to the Gentiles, and though he began to preach as soon as he was made an apostle, he preached to the Jews in their synagogues (Acts ix : 20-22), and not until he was ordained at Antioch did he fully enter upon his mission to the Gentiles.

But as a proof of the fact that hands were laid on Paul at Antioch to impart spiritual gifts to him, we are reminded that there is no account of his working any miracles before that time, and we very soon find him working them after that event. Here again, as in the case of the seven deacons at Jerusalem, the *silence* of the Scriptures is given as proof of the conclusion. Will any one, who so reasons, show us the record of the miracles performed by the apostles James, Andrew, Philip, Thomas, Bartholomew, Matthew, Simon, and Matthias after the day of Pentecost? In the very same chapter he will likely find a record of the many miracles performed by Paul before he was ordained at Antioch. True, it is said that many miracles were done by the apostles, but this is not sufficiently specific. These may have been done by Peter and John, for they were there; and in the next chapter they are mentioned as the two who healed the lame man at the gate of the temple; and when spiritual gifts were to be conferred on the Samaritans, the *same two* were sent there to impart them. Then if we find no account of any miracles worked by the other *ten*, shall we conclude that they had not the power to work them? As well may we thus conclude as to assume that Paul was without power to work them for more than four years after he was an apostle, because there is no record of any miracle performed by him during that time.

There is no record of any miracle that was ever performed by Timothy; yet Paul told him to stir up the gift that was in him by the imposition of his hands. 2 Tim. i: 6. Did Timothy ever work a miracle? We do not know that he did; but Paul laid his hands on him, and he not only had the power to impart spiritual gifts, but he frequently did it. Then why should he not give them to his son Timothy, who was his fellow-laborer in the gospel? The silence of the record will not quite prove that he did not work any miracles, neither will it prove that Paul worked none before hands were laid on him at Antioch.

There was a limit to the power of Paul, and we suppose of every one else, in working miracles. He could only work them when the glory of God would be promoted by doing so; for he left Trophimus at Miletum sick (2 Tim. iv: 20), and his concern for him shows that he would have cured him if he could. He did heal many there—why not him? Simply because he did not possess unlimited power to heal. This may account, in part, for the silence of the record, even when supernatural power could have been exhibited had it been in harmony with God's will that the parties should exercise it.

But whether Timothy could or could not work miracles, we think it clear that hands were laid on him when the impartation of spiritual gifts was not the object for which it was done. Paul said to him: "Till I come, give attendance to reading to exhortation, to doctrine. Neglect not the gift that is in thee, which was given thee by prophecy, with the laying on of the hands of the presbytery. Meditate upon these things; give thyself wholly to them, that thy profiting may appear to all. Take heed unto thyself, and unto the doctrine; for in doing this thou shalt both save thyself and them that hear thee." 1 Tim. iv: 13–16. That the word *presbytery* here means *eldership* can scarcely admit of doubt; and as spiritual gifts were imparted *only by apostolic hands*, the eldership did not lay hands on him for this purpose; hence, the conclusion seems to us irresistible that this refers to the laying on of hands in his ordination to the work of the ministry, as we have seen that Paul and Barnabas were separated to their work. We can scarcely conclude that divine wisdom separated Paul and Barnabas in one way and Timothy in a different way. Whether Paul laid his hands on Timothy in connection with the eldership in the ordination, or at another time, to impart to him spiritual gifts, is not certain; but that Paul communicated some power or privilege to him not given by the eldership, is made probable by the fact that he mentions a gift imparted by his hands, without intimation that the eldership had anything to do with it; and also mentions a gift imparted by the hands of the eldership without intimating that he took part in it himself. We conclude, therefore, that whether the hands of both were laid on at the same time, or at different times, something more was given by the hands of Paul than by the hands of the eldership. This, however, is merely a probability; for it is by no means certain that Timothy ever possessed spiritual gifts; and it is certain that he was not inspired, but had to learn what he knew by diligent study.

That the laying on of hands by the presbytery had reference to his position as a preacher seems clear from the context. He is told to give attention to reading, exhortation, and doctrine; for by doing so he would both save himself and those that heard him. And this style is begun before the mention of the laying on of hands, and continued after it; thus showing that his work as a preacher was the subject under consideration.

One other thought and we shall have done for the present. We are often met with the objection that none but apostles ever laid hands on in ordination. We have seen that there was no apostle present to lay hands on Paul and Barnabas at Antioch—we have now seen that the presbytery or eldership laid hands on Timothy—we have seen that Titus was left in Crete to ordain elders or bishops there; and we have seen that this was done at other places by fasting, prayer, and laying on hands—we now propose to show that Timothy was expected to do the same thing.

Paul says: "Let the elders that rule well be counted worthy of double honor, especially they who labor in word and doctrine; for the Scripture saith, Thou shalt not muzzle the ox that treadeth out the corn; and the laborer is worthy of his reward. Against an elder receive not an accusation, but before two or three witnesses. Them that sin rebuke before all, that others also may fear. I charge thee before God, and the Lord Jesus Christ, and the elect angels, that thou observe these things without preferring one before another, doing nothing by partiality. Lay hands suddenly on no man, neither be partaker of other men's sins: keep thyself pure. Drink no longer water, but use a little wine for thy stomach's sake and thine often infirmities." 1 Tim. v: 17-23.

After speaking of the honor due to elders that rule well—their right to support—the manner of receiving accusations against them, and the treatment of those who sin—a most solemn charge against partiality and preferment of one above another, Paul told Timothy to lay hands suddenly on no man. Now, how can we conclude that this means lay on hands not at all? Or, how can we conclude that it referred to laying on hands in imparting spiritual gifts when Timothy had no such power? The manifest import of the passage is that he should not be hasty or inconsiderate in ordaining persons to the eldership or bishop's office, lest he should put an unworthy man into that important position, and thereby become partaker of his sins—in such matters "keep thyself pure." Let him be tried that he may prove himself worthy and competent for the work before you lay hands on him. Surely nothing could be made more plain.

But we are told that this was a caution against fighting—"be no striker." Timothy was a weakly, infirm man, in consequence of which he was admonished to abstain from water, and to use wine. He was proverbial for his piety and knowledge of the Scriptures, and for his zeal in the cause of the Master; and yet we are asked to believe that Paul felt it necessary to caution him against becoming a bully! "Lay hands suddenly on no man" clearly implies that he *was to do it deliberately*. Did Paul intend to tell Timothy to deliberately hit a man? "Be not hasty when you go to hit a man, but be deliberate that you may give him a jolt that will finish him!" Really we know not how to reply to such a thought with becoming gravity.

As to who shall lay on hands in ordination, and the absurdity of always requiring ordained persons to lay on hands, we refer the reader to the excellent remarks of Brother Campbell in the opening of this investigation. We need not further discuss them here.

In conclusion, we wish to say that we have no unkind feeling toward those from whom we differ on this subject. As pure and good men as are known to us take a different view of it. We have not written to provoke a controversy with them, nor do we intend to have any. Those who know us best know that we have a natural and cultivated aversion to controversy with brethren; hence, we have studiously avoided quoting the publications of any one from whom we have felt it our duty to differ. We have waited until what has been written could have time to pass from before the public, lest we might seem to be writing in opposition to it. What we have written, however, we most conscientiously believe the word of God to teach; by it we have to be judged, and by it we are willing that what we have written may be judged.

CHAPTER XXI.

CONDITIONAL SALVATION.*

PROPOSITION:—The Scriptures teach that salvation from sin is conditional. The condition, or conditions to be performed by the sinner in order to salvation or freedom from sin.

MR. PRESIDENT:

I AM happy in the privilege of meeting my distinguished opponent under circumstances favorable for the examination of the word of God pertaining to the proposition just read in your hearing. It is exceedingly plain, and but few of its terms need to be defined.

Sin is the transgression of the law—God's law. 1 John iii: 4.

Salvation or freedom from sin is a release from the punishment due the sinner for such transgression.

The same thought is substantially expressed in several other forms, as " Remission of sin," " Forgiveness of sin," " Blotting out of sin," " Ceasing to remember sin," "Justification," etc., etc., the difference being merely technical. About these I suppose we will have no controversy, as it is the great subject of *pardon* that concerns us, not the phraseology in which it is expressed. One more term, perhaps I ought to define.

" A *condition* is that which must exist as the occasion or concomitant of something else; that which is requi-

---

*Opening speech of T. W. Brents in debate with Elder E. D. Herod, Franklin, Ky., March 29, 1887.

site in order that something else should take effect; stipulation; terms specified."— *Webster*.

That God alone has power to forgive sins is well understood and admitted by all; but the issue with us, is, does he pardon the sins of men on conditions to be complied with by them?

Than this, no more important subject can be considered by the human race, provided I am correct. If, however, my proposition is not true, it may be that the importance of the subject is not very great. If God unconditionally saves men without a single *thought, word, or deed* on the part of the sinner, then he may fold his arms and go to sleep, for nothing that he can do will secure his salvation, or in any way affect his future destiny. If he must even *desire* his salvation, in order that God may save him, then that desire is a *condition*, and my proposition is true. If he must *believe* any thing, or in any person or thing, in order that God may save him, then that *belief* is a *condition*, and my proposition is true. If he must perform any physcal act, as an act of obedience to God, in order that he may be saved, then *that act* is a *condition*, and my proposition is still true.

My proposition does not require me to show *what* the conditions are—it is simply my duty to show that there are conditions with which the sinner must comply or be lost. I may incidentally do more than this.

KING JAMES' VERSION.

At the suggestion of my worthy opponent, King James' version, as it is called, is made the standard of authority in this discussion. I would have preferred this otherwise. While I believe it, on the whole, about as good as any other version, yet I know there are manifest errors in it; and in discussions like this it should be the great aim of all the parties to get at the truth; and where there are errors in the translation, known to be such, we ought to be at liberty to correct them by any light we can get, either from critics or commentators who have given us the benefit of their labors, or by an appeal to the *original* for ourselves. But with all its defects in translation, we believe it sufficiently clear to enable us to understand the will of the Lord and be saved. We have agreed to be governed by it in this discussion, and to it we go for proof of our proposition.

ARGUMENT.

Much may be learned as to what God is doing, and proposes to do, by an examination of what he has done in ages past; and I insist that the same general principle embodied in my proposition has characterized God's dealings with man from the time of his creation until now; he has blessed and prospered him while he believed and obeyed him; and he has cursed and punished him when he forsook him, rebelled against him, refused to obey him, and violated his law. This has always been, is now, and ever will be true as long as man dwells in a tenement of clay. We find an illustration of this principle in the first law given to

ADAM IN THE GARDEN OF EDEN.

When God placed him in the garden, he commanded him, saying: "Of every tree of the garden thou mayest freely eat; but of the tree of the knowldge of good and evil, thou shalt not eat of it, for in the day that thou eatest thereof thou shalt surely die." Gen. ii: 16, 17. Here is a clearly implied *condition*—if you eat of it, you shall die—if you do not eat of it, you may not die, but live.

Another illustration we find recorded in the case of

CAIN AND ABEL.

When they made their offerings God respected the offering of Abel, but did not respect the offering of Cain; and Cain was angry about it, and the Lord said: "Why art thou wroth? and why is thy countenance fallen? If thou doest well, shalt thou not be accepted? and if thou doest not well, sin lieth at the door." Gen. iv: 6, 7. Here is the spirit of my proposition—if you do well you shall be accepted, but if you do not well, sin is at the very threshold of disobedience.

Another example we have recorded in the histoy of

NOAH AND THE FLOOD.

Coming down the stream of time twenty-five hundread years, "God saw that the wickedness of man was great in the earth, and that every imagination of the thoughts of his heart was only evil continually, and it repented the Lord that he had made man on the earth, and it grieved him at his heart. And the Lord said, I will destroy man whom I have created from the face of the earth; both man and beast, and the creeping things, and the fowls of the air; for it repenteth me that I have made them." Gen. vi: 5–7. God carried out this determination, and did destroy the wicked by a deluge of water. And why did he destroy them? Was it because God had unconditionally reprobated them, and decreed the wickedness for which he destroyed them? We suppose not, for their sins grieved him at his heart. Then again, we ask why this destruction came upon them? Surely it was because they were wicked, even to every imagination of their thoughts. But Noah found grace in the eyes of the Lord. Verse 8. And why did he find grace in the eyes of the Lord? "For thee have I seen righteous before me in this generation." Thus we find the spirit of my proposition. God blessed and saved Noah and his family because he was righteous in his generation, and he destroyed the residue of the human race for their great wickedness. And be it remembered that these examples are referred to in the New Testament as instructive to us.

When God gave the law, in detail, to the Jews, through Moses, at Horeb, he most graphically set forth the importance of obedience, and the consequences of disobedience, that the people might well understand the principles upon which he proposed to govern them. In giving

THE LAW AT HOREB,

He says: "And it shall come to pass, if thou shalt hearken diligently unto the voice of the Lord thy God, to observe and to do all his commandments which I command thee this day, that the Lord thy God will set thee on high above all nations of the earth; and all these blessings shall come on thee, and overtake thee, if thou shalt hearken unto the voice of the Lord thy God." Deut. xxviii: 1, 2. Then follow in detail, the rich blessings he promised them; and to impress them with the necessity of obeying the Lord he adds: "And the Lord shall make thee the head, and not the tail; and thou shalt be above only, and thou shalt not be beneath; if that thou hearken unto the commandments of the Lord thy God, which I command thee this day, to observe and to do them; and thou shalt not go aside from any of the words which I command thee this day, to the right hand or to the left, to go after other gods to serve them." Verses 13, 14.

Then he gives the other side of the picture in the fearful fruits of disobedience. Verse fifteen he says: "But it shall come to pass, if thou wilt not hearken unto the voice of the Lord thy God, to observe and do all his commandments and his statutes which I command thee this day; that all these curses shall come upon thee, and overtake thee." Then follows a list of the curses that shall come upon them, until the heart sickens in contemplating the wretchedness to which rebellion and sin should reduce them; and then, as if to more forcibly impress them, he adds: "Moreover, all these curses shall come upon thee, and shall pursue thee, and overtake thee, till thou be destroyed; because thou hearkenedst not unto the voice of the Lord thy God, to keep his commandments and his statutes which he commanded thee." v 45.

Thus we see the principle of my proposition clearly set out in the covenant which God made with Israel at Horeb; and it characterizes God's dealings with man everywhere. He blesses, prospers, and saves him when he believes and obeys him; and fails not to punish him when he rebels, and sins against him. The conditions have been changed in different dispensations; but conditions there always have been, and always will be until the God of the Bible ceases to rule.

The same principle was re-affirmed in the covenant in the land of Moab; and it was again proclaimed to Solomon at the

DEDICATION OF THE TEMPLE.

God said to him: "If my people, which are called by my name, shall humble themselves, and pray, and seek my face, and turn from their wicked ways; then will I hear from heaven, and will forgive their sin, and heal their land. * * * And as for thee, if thou wilt walk before me, as David thy father walked, and do according to all that I have commanded thee, and shalt observe my statutes and my judgments; then will I establish the throne of thy kingdom, according as I have covenanted with David thy father, saying, there shall not fail thee a man to be ruler in Israel. But if ye turn away, and forsake my statutes and my commandments, which I have set before you, and shall go and serve other gods, and worship them; then will I pluck them up by the roots, out of my land which I have given them; and this house, which I have sanctified for my name, will I cast out of my sight, and will make it to be a proverb and a by-word among all nations. And this house, which is high, shall be an astonishment to every one that passeth by it; so that he shall say, why hath the Lord done thus unto this land, and unto this house? And it shall be answered, because they forsook the Lord God of their fathers, which brought them forth out of the land of Egypt, and laid hold on other gods, and worshiped them, and served them; therefore hath he brought all this evil upon them." 2 Chron. vii: 14–22. Therefore—yes, because they forsook the Lord.

Coming down to within six hundred years of the advent of Christ, we find God, by the mouth of Ezekiel, affirming the same great principles. Ezekiel xviii: 20–28.

"The soul that sinneth, it shall die. The son shall not bear the iniquity of the father, neither shall the father bear the iniquity of the son; the righteousness of the righteous shall be upon him, and the wickedness of the wicked shall be upon him. But if the wicked will turn from all his sins that he hath committed, and

27

keep all my statutes, and do that which is lawful and right, he shall surely live, he shall not die. All his transgressions that he hath committed, they shall not be mentioned unto him; in his righteousness that he hath done he shall live. Have I any pleasure at all that the wicked should die? saith the Lord God; and not that he should return from his ways and live? * * * When a righteous man turneth away from his righteousness, and committeth iniquity, and dieth in them; for his iniquity that he hath done shall he die. Again when the wicked man turneth away from his wickedness that he hath committed, and doeth that which is lawful and right, he shall save his soul alive; because he considereth, and turneth away from all his transgressions that he hath committed, he shall surely live, he shall not die."

Comment on such Scriptures as these is surely unnecessary. They cannot be made more plain than God has already made them. If you will not deem it *irreverent*, I will say that were God here himself this day, seeking to defend my proposition, we cannot see how language could be better selected for the purpose than is here recorded. Please note the fact that temporal blessings are not all that are here promised; for he who obeys the commandments of the Lord shall save his *soul*. Is not this conditional salvation? Note the additional fact, too, that God has no pleasure in the death of the wicked, but most earnestly entreats him to cast away his transgressions, make himself a new heart, and a new spirit—turn and live. Verses 31, 32.

God compels no man to obey him, but he sets before him motives vast in importance as is the destiny of the human soul to induce him to obedience, and faithfully warns him of the dreadful consequences of disobedience, and allows him to choose for himself.

"Behold I set before you this day a blessing and a curse; a blessing, if ye obey the commandments of the Lord, your God, which I command you this day; and a curse, if ye will not obey the commandments of the Lord, your God; but turn aside out of the way which I command you this day, to go after other gods which ye have not known." Deut. xi: 26-28. Does this not look about as conditional as my proposition? A blessing if ye obey, a curse if ye disobey.

But again: "See, I have set before you this day life and good, and death and evil; in that I command thee this day to love the Lord thy God, to walk in his ways, and to keep his commandments and his statutes and his judgments, that thou mayest live and multiply; and the Lord thy God shall bless thee in the land whither thou goest to possess it. But if thy heart turn away, and worship other gods, and serve them; I denounce unto you this day, that ye shall surely perish, and that ye shall not prolong your days upon the land, whither thou passest over Jordan to go to possess it. I call heaven and earth to record this day against you, that I have set before you life and death, blessing and cursing; therefore, choose life that both thou and thy seed may live." Deut. xxx: 15-19. Does this look like man has nothing to do? The two roads are open before him—life is at the end of one, and death is at the end of the other. Man is perfectly free to choose the road he will travel. God says to the sinner in the road to death, "Turn ye, turn ye, why will you die? I have no pleasure in your death, but rather that you turn and live."

We come now to the examination of the New Testament, and though the conditions have been changed, we shall find conditional salvation meeting us at every step of our investigation.

We will have to abridge and condense every proof we introduce as much as we can, and then we will not be able to present a tithe of the proof available in support of a proposition so universally taught as is the one under consideration at present.

We begin our investigation with a very brief examination of

THE MISSION OF JOHN THE BAPTIST.

He was to go before the Lord in the spirit and power of Elias to turn the hearts of the fathers to the children, and the disobedient to the wisdom of the just; to make ready a people prepared for the Lord. Luke i: 17. As it was John's God-appointed work to make ready a people prepared for the Lord, did he perform the work assigned him? If so, how did he prepare them? He gave them knowledge of salvation. "By the remission of their sins." Luke i: 77. But how did they get knowledge of salvation? We suppose they got it by compliance with the conditions upon which God authorized John to offer it to them.

What were the conditions of salvation preached by John? "There was a man sent from God whose name was John. The same came for a witness to bear witness of the light, that all men through him might believe." John i: 6, 7. Notice in passing that the object of John's testimony was that *all men*, yes, *all men might believe*. Then it was necessary that men believe in the days of John. But what were they to believe? John verily baptized with the baptism of repentance, saying unto the people that they should believe on him which should come after him, that is, on Christ Jesus. Acts xix: 4. Thus we see they believed on a Christ to come—we believe in a Christ already come; this is the difference, no more. Christ was the object of their faith, and he is the object of our faith to-day. But what else was necessary?

"In those days came John the Baptist, preaching in the wilderness of Judea, saying, repent ye, for the kingdom of heaven is at hand." Matt. iii: 1 Then *repentance* was necessary in the days of John. What else?

"And there went out unto him all the land of Judea, and they of Jerusalem, and were all baptized of him in the river of Jordan, confessing their sins." Mark i: 5. But *for what* did John baptize the people? He "preached the baptism of repentance for the remission of sins." Mark i: 4; Luke iii: 3. What did he preach for the remission of sins? Certainly that baptism that belonged to or followed repentance. However important faith may be, there is nothing affirmed of it here; nor is there any thing affirmed of repentance, only that it was connected with the baptism preached by John for the remission of sins. Suppose I say, "the coat of my friend kept me warm;" what do I say kept me warm? Certainly the coat that belonged to my friend kept me warm. Again: "The house of my friend gave me shelter for the night;" what do I say gave me shelter? Certainly the house that belonged to my friend gave me shelter. Very well, "The baptism of repentance for the remission of sins;" what is for the remission of sins? Certainly the *baptism* that belonged to or followed repentance was for the remission of sins. If this is not plain and conclusive, then human language, common sense, and Holy Writ can make nothing so.

Then we have found believing, or *faith, repentance,*

and *baptism* preached by John, and when the people submitted to or performed these *conditions*, they had knowledge of salvation by the remission of their sins. Then our proposition is clearly sustained in John's ministry. They were pardoned and had knowledge of it, and were fit material for position in the great spiritual temple to be erected in the near future by divine authority.

We come now to examine the personal teachings of Jesus, and we will begin with an examination of his ever memorable conversation with Nicodemus, recorded in the third chapter of the gospel by John.

"Jesus answered and said unto him, Verily, verily, I say unto thee, Except a man be born again he cannot see the kingdom of God. Nicodemus saith unto him, How can a man be born when he is old? Can he enter the second time into his mother's womb and be born? Jesus answered, Verily, verily, I say unto thee, Except a man be born of water and of the Spirit, he cannot enter into the kingdom of God." Verses 3-5.

That the word *see* is here used in the sense of *enjoy*, we suppose no one will doubt. The thought is, that without being born again no man *can enjoy* the kingdom of God. How is he to be born again? "Except a man be born of *water* and of the *Spirit* he cannot enter into the kingdom of God." The converse of the statement is clearly implied, that if he be born of water and of the Spirit he does enter the kingdom of God. In this kingdom is a state of salvation, out of it is a state of condemnation. Paul says: "Giving thanks unto the Father, which hath made us meet to be partakers of the inheritance of the saints in light; who hath delivered us from the power of darkness, and hath translated us into the kingdom of his dear Son; in whom we have redemption through his blood, even the forgiveness of sins." Col. i: 12–14.

Then outside of the kingdom we are subject to the power of darkness, and under the dominion of Satan; in the kingdom we are delivered from the power of darkness, and have redemption and forgiveness of sins through the blood of Jesus.

Now, we have a few very plain questions for our worthy opponent, to which we invite his special attention; and we promise to pay our respects to his answers when he makes them.

(1) Can the class of persons for whom the kingdom was established be saved without entering into it? If so, how?

(2) Does the phrase, *born of water*, in John iii: 5, refer to water baptism? If not, to what does it refer?

(3) Can a man enter into the kingdom without being baptized? If so, how?

Nicodemus did not understand the Savior, and hence did not believe what he said. Then said Jesus, "If I have told you earthly things and ye believe not, how shall ye believe if I tell you of heavenly things?" Verse 11. He then seeks to impress him with the importance of believing on him. Not that he intended him to stop at believing on him, but by believing he might be prepared to attend to what he had previously taught him. And he begins with an illustration drawn from Jewish history, with which Nicodemus, as a master in Israel, was presumed to be familiar. He says: "And as Moses lifted up the serpent in the wilderness, even so must the Son of man be lifted up; that whosoever believeth on him should not perish, but have eternal life." Verses 14, 15. As the dying Israelite had to look upon the brazen serpent on the pole in the camp that he might live (Num. xxi: 8, 9), so Jesus must die upon the cross, that whosoever believeth on him should not perish, but have eternal life. Now, what is the object of and necessity for believing? That the believer may not perish, but may have eternal life. What can this mean? Is believing not a condition upon which depends eternal life? Will my worthy opponent say no? Will he say that looking upon the brazen serpent was not a *condition* on which depended the life of the bitten Israelite? Was looking upon the brazen serpent any more a condition of life to the bitten Israelite than believing on Christ is to the sinner to-day? We will listen attentively to his explanation of this.

"For God so loved the world, that he gave his only begotten Son, that whosoever believeth in him should not perish, but have everlasting life." Verse 16. Whom did God love? He loved the *world*. And how *much* did he love it? He *so* loved the world that he gave his only begotten Son. For what did he give his Son? That whosoever, of the world he loved, might have everlasting life, on *condition* that they would believe on him. Is not believing on him, here made a condition on which depends the eternal life of the sinner? Will our opponent say no? Surely we are here taught that the world may be saved, if they will accept salvation on the conditions upon which it is offered to them. "For God sent not his Son into the world to condemn the world, but that the world through him might be saved." Verse 17. Here the mission of Jesus is most beautifully expressed—*might be saved*, not shall be saved whether they want to be saved or not. He came to provide a way by which men may be saved if they will believe and obey him—not to force salvation upon them. And the means of salvation are as free to *all men* as they are to any man. He came to save the world, and tasted death for every man.

Though Jesus came not to condemn the world, yet all will be condemned who refuse to believe on him. "He that believeth not is condemned already." And why is he condemned already? "Because he hath not believed on the name of the only begotten Son of God." Verse 18.

Here we find belief in Jesus to be the condition upon which men may escape condemnation, and unbelief the condition upon which men bring condemnation on themselves. Of course, we understand the Lord to be speaking of such belief as takes God at his word, and goes right along in obedience to his commands. A belief perfected as the word of God directs.

"He that believeth on the Son hath everlasting life." Yes, the obedient believer has everlasting life in promise, but what about the unbeliever? "He that believeth not the Son shall not see life; but the wrath of God abideth on him." John iii: 36.

And again: "I said therefore unto you, that ye shall die in your sins, for if ye believe not that I am he, ye shall die in your sins." John viii: 24.

And still again: "If any man hear my words and believe not, I judge him not; for I came not to judge the world, but to save the world. He that rejecteth me, and receiveth not my words, hath one that judgeth him; the word that I have spoken the same shall judge him in the last day." John xii: 47, 48. Here we learn that Jesus *came to save the world;* and we learn that the world he came to save is co-extensive with the judgment of the last day. Will all be judged? Then Jesus came to save all men. But he who *rejects* and *receives not* his words cannot be saved by him, however ample the means of salvation provided for him. The words *reject* and *receive* both imply the exercise of *will* in rejecting Christ and in refusing to receive his words.

"Many other signs truly did Jesus in the presence of his disciples, which are not written in this book, but these are written that ye might believe." Yes, these signs are written that ye *might believe*, not that you shall believe whether you are interested yourself or not. But that ye might believe, what? "That Jesus is the Christ, the Son of God." These are written as evidence to convince the world of the truth of this grand proposition, that all men might believe it. But what if they do believe this? "And that, believing, ye might have life through his name." John xx: 30, 31. Yes, *might* believe, and *might have life* by believing. This expresses the thought most beautifully. Now, I want to ask my worthy opponent this question. After all these signs are recorded, if a man refuses to believe the proposition set out here, that Jesus is the Christ, the Son of God, is there a possibility for him to get eternal life through his name? If so, how? And if not, why not? I will not anticipate his answers, but will wait until he makes them. Then I will attend to them.

Peter says: "To him give all the prophets witness, that through his name whosoever believeth in him shall receive remission of sins." Acts x: 43. Here we have the same style, except the phrase, *remission of sins*, is substituted for the word *life*, by which, doubtless, the same thought is intended; and it seems to me that in the plainest terms possible *remission of sins* in the name of Jesus Christ is made to depend upon belief in him, as a condition to be complied with by those whose sins are remitted at all. Will he who does not believe on him get remission through his name? If so, how? They are condemned already.

"Be it known unto you, therefore, men and brethren, that through this man is preached unto you the forgiveness of sins; and by him all that believe are justified from all things from which ye could not be justified by the law of Moses." Acts xiii: 38, 39. Here we have *forgiveness of sins* in place of the phrase, *remission of sins*, which means the same thing; and all that believe are justified, thus plainly making belief a condition of justification.

Paul says: "I am not ashamed of the gospel of Christ, for it is the power of God unto salvation to every one that believeth, to the Jew first and also to the Greek." Rom. i: 16. But the gospel is God's power to the salvation of no one, whether he be Jew or Greek, who does not believe it. Truly, then, salvation is conditional, as the power of God to salvation is rejected by the unbeliever.

"The word is nigh thee, even in thy mouth, and in thy heart; that is the word of faith which we preach; that if thou shalt confess with thy mouth the Lord Jesus, and shalt believe in thine heart that God hath raised him from the dead, thou shalt be saved; for with the heart man believeth unto righteousness, and with the mouth confession is made unto salvation." Rom. x: 8–10.

Here we have confession with the mouth, and belief in the heart, in the plainest terms possible, made conditions of salvation. If this language does not show these to be conditions, then I respectfully submit that human language can show nothing to be a condition of any thing. To this passage I solicit the special attention of my worthy respondent. Will he say that belief and confession are not here shown to be conditions of salvation? If he will say they are not, will he be so good as to construct a sentence that will express the thought without using the very word condition?

On one occasion a young man came to Jesus and said: "Good Master, what good thing shall I do that I may have eternal life?" Matt. xix: 16. Had my proposition been untrue at that time, it occurs to me that Jesus would have answered something after the following style: "There is nothing that you may do that you may have eternal life; for eternal life is not dependent on *conditions* to be complied with by man." Not thus understanding the subject, however, the Master told him what to do that he might have *treasures* in heaven.

On the day of Pentecost, when Peter convinced the people that God had made that same Jesus whom they had crucified, both Lord and Christ, "They were cut to the heart and said unto Peter, and the rest of the apostles, men and brethren, what shall we do?" Do for what? To obtain pardon or remission of sins, as the answer plainly shows: "Peter said unto them, Repent and be baptized, every one of you, in the name of Jesus Christ for the remission of sins." Acts ii: 38.

Here, remission of sins, in the case of these *believers*, is made to depend on the additional items of *repentance* and *baptism*. The preposition *for* unites *repent* and be *baptized* on one side, with remission of sins on the other. Remission of sins is the object for which and to which the actions expressed in both verbs point as the end in view. Connected, as they are, by the conjunction *and*, they cannot be separated. Whatever one is for the other is for. The relation of one to the remission of sins is the relation of both. Then, if we can find the relation of one, we will have found the relation of both. Peter says: "Repent and be converted that your sins may be blotted out." Acts iii: 19. Then, as repentance is required that sins may be blotted out, and as baptism sustains the same relation to remission, expressed by the one preposition, occurring but one time, it follows that baptism is to be performed in order that sins may be blotted out. From this conclusion there is no appeal. Then, as the Pentecostians believed before they asked what to do, it follows that *faith, repentance,* and *baptism* were conditions of pardon then and are so to-day.

That repentance is a condition is already plain enough, but to make assurance doubly sure, we will present further proof. Jesus said; "Except ye repent, ye shall all likewise perish." Luke xiii: 2. And Paul said: "The times of this ignorance God winked at, but now commandeth he all men every where to repent; because he hath appointed a day, in the which he will judge the world in righteousness by that man whom he hath ordained." Acts xvii: 30, 31. Then without repentance sinners will not be ready for the judgment, but will surely perish.

When the rest of the apostles heard Peter's defense for going in among the uncircumcised, "they held their peace and glorified God, saying, then hath God also to the Gentiles granted repentance unto life." Acts xi: 18. Then repentance is unto life, looking to life, in order to life, a condition on which life depends. But the people at Pentecost inquired what they must do. Peter told them what to do for remission of sins. Now we respectfully ask our esteemed opponent if he would answer the same inquiry *now* as Peter did then? If not, why not?

The Philippian jailer said to Paul and Silas: "Sirs, what must I do to be saved?" Acts xvi: 30. Now in this question we have the very *issue* presented in my proposition. *What must I do to be saved?* Will my worthy opponent say whether this question does not cover the ground in controversy here? How would he answer such a question if put to him to-day? Something after the following style, I imagine: "What must you do? Do nothing. What can you do to be saved? Just nothing at all; for your salvation is not dependent on *conditions* to be performed by you; salvation is not of works lest any man should boast." But did the inspired teachers so treat the question? No, indeed; but they answered it. "Believe on the Lord Jesus Christ, and thou shalt be saved and thy house. And they spake unto him the word of the Lord, and to all that were in his house." Thus all the conditions of salvation were presented and attended to the same hour of the night.

When the Lord appeared to Saul and convinced him that he was Jesus, Saul said: "What shall I do, Lord? And the Lord said: * * * arise and go into Damascus and there it shall be told thee of all things which are appointed for thee to do." Acts xxii. 10. And a man was sent to him who told him to arise and be baptized and wash away his sins, calling on the name of the Lord. Verse 16.

Now, here are four examples recorded, where those competent to answer were asked what the inquirers must do, and in no case were they told that *they could do nothing*. But in every instance they were told what to do in order to be saved. Now, will our esteemed opponent tell us how any man, believing in unconditional salvation, as he does, can ask such a question as what must I do to be saved? or in faith do any thing to be saved? or tell any one else what to do to be saved? We suppose he will give us an explanation of these matters, and we will await his answer. We respectfully ask that it be full and explicit.

In the commission given by Christ to his apostles after he arose from the dead, and before he ascended to heaven, he said: " Go ye into all the world, and preach the gospel to every creature. He that believeth and is baptized shall be saved, but he that believeth not shall be damned." Mark xvi: 15, 16.

Here we learn that the salvation promised in the gospel was intended for every creature in all the world who would accept it on the conditions stipulated. In the plainest terms possible, we are told that of every creature in all the world, he that would believe the gospel and be baptized should be saved. If this language does not establish my proposition, then no proposition can be established by any language that may be employed. It is not necessary that I stop to show that belief and baptism sustain the same relation to the salvation promised, for if either one is a condition necessary to the enjoyment of salvation, then *salvation is conditional*, and my proposition is established. But, suppose I say to a man, " dig me a cistern and wall it up with brick, and I will give you a hundred dollars." The specifications are all made, the proposition accepted, and reduced to writing. The man makes the excavation according to the specifications, and demands the money for the job; can he get it? Has he complied with the contract? He was to dig the cistern and wall it up with brick—he has dug the cistern, but has not put a brick in it; is he entitled to the pay? Assuredly he is not. Very well, he that believeth and is baptized shall be saved. The man believes—has not been baptized; is he saved? Is he not in the same condition of the man who had not put a brick in the cistern, when by contract he was to wall it up?

But what of those who do not believe? He that believeth not shall be damned. But why did the Lord not add, "and is not baptized shall be damned." Because if he did not believe he *would not* be baptized, nor would it do him any good if he were to be; "for without faith it is impossible to please God." Baptism without faith would be about like walling up the cistern without digging it. You say that would be impossible; so it is impossible for one who does not believe to be scripturally baptized. The style is, "He that believeth and is baptized." "If thou believest with all thine heart, thou mayest.'

One of those to whom this commission was given, said to the disciples scattered abroad: "Which sometime were disobedient, when once the longsuffering of God waited in the days of Noah, while the ark was a preparing, wherein few, that is, eight souls were saved by water; the like figure whereunto even baptism doth also now save us (not the putting away of the filth of of the flesh, but the answer of a good conscience toward God) by the resurrection of Jesus Christ." 1 Peter iii: 20, 21.

Here we are told that baptism saves us, and not only so, but it *now* saves us. In what sense does baptism save us? Surely it is not the *power* that saves us, but it is a *condition*, upon compliance with which *God saves us*. We have seen that in the commission under which Peter acted, he was charged to preach the gospel, and Jesus promised that he that would believe and be baptized, should be saved; and Peter could have meant nothing else than that baptism saves us as a *condition* in harmony with the commission given to him by the Master. And it must save us from the punishment that is due us on account of our sins, as there is nothing else from which it can or does save us. It cannot refer to a future salvation, for it *now* saves us. It does not save us from temporal calamity—as insult, persecution, sickness, death, for the baptized man is still subject to these. Then, if it does not save us from our past sins, will our opponent tell us from what it does save us?

Isaiah, through the light of prophetic vision, says: "In that day there shall be a root of Jesse, which shall stand for an ensign of the people; to it shall the Gentiles seek." Is. xi: 10.

Again: "Seek ye the Lord while he may be found, call ye upon him while he is near; let the wicked forsake his way and the unrighteous man his thoughts; and let him return unto the Lord and he will have mercy upon him; and to our God, for he will abundantly pardon.' Is. lv: 6, 7.

Jesus says: "Ask and it shall be given you; seek and ye shall find; knock and it shall be opened unto you; for every one that asketh receiveth; and he that seeketh findeth; and to him that knocketh it shall be opened." Matt. vii: 7, 8.

Here we learn that we are to seek the Lord, but we must seek after the *due order*. David said: "Ye are the chief of the fathers of the Levites; sanctify yourselves, both ye and your brethren, that ye may bring up the ark of the Lord God of Israel unto the place that I have prepared for it; for because ye did it not at the first, the Lord our God made a breach upon us, for that we sought it not after the due order." 1 Chron. xv: 12, 13. Here we learn that we must seek the Lord's favor after the *due order;* and the due order is God's order. We must seek in God's appointed way. When we ask we must ask in harmony with God's revealed will. James says, we ask and receive not, because we ask amiss. We must ask in *faith*, too; "for without faith it is impossible to please him; for he that cometh to God must believe that he is, and that he is a rewarder of them that diligently seek him." Heb. xi: 6. Belief is an indispensable condition, without which none can come to God. But we must believe that he is a rewarder of them that diligently seek him. Here we have another question for our friend. Does he believe that God will reward a man, however diligently he may seek him, unless he is one of the eternally and unconditionally elect? Will he tell us?

But we will hear Paul on this matter of seeking the Lord. He says: "God that made the world and all things therein, seeing he is Lord of heaven and earth, dwelleth not in temples made with hands; neither is worshiped with men's hands, as though he needed any thing, saying, he giveth to all life, and breath, and all things; and hath made of one blood all nations of men for to dwell on all the face of the earth; and hath determined the times before appointed, and the bounds of their habitation; that they should seek the Lord, if haply they might feel after him, and find him, though he be not far from every one of us." Acts xvii: 24–27.

Here we learn that God made of one blood, all the nations of men that dwell on all the face of the earth; and that he intended them to seek the Lord and find him. And every one that seeks him will find him if he seek in God's appointed way. But we need not *seek* him, or call on him until we are willing to obey him.

"Though he were a Son, yet learned he obedience by the things which he suffered; and being made perfect he became the author of eternal salvation unto all them that obey him." Heb. v : 8, 9. The eternal salvation, of which Jesus is the author, is for them, and only them, that obey him. And it is not for *some* of them, but it is for all of them. Every one. Obedience to him is the condition upon which all men may attain to eternal salvation, and it is attainable to no one who will not obey him. If there was not another sentence in the Bible bearing on the subject, this one is enough to establish my proposition beyond even respectable quibble. Will my worthy opponent give us a plain, unambiguous exegesis of this passage? It is surely worthy of his most serious attention.*

Jesus says : " Why call ye me Lord, Lord, and do not the things which I say." Luke vi : 46. And again : " Not every one that saith unto me, Lord, Lord, shall enter into the kingdom of heaven ; but he that doeth the will of my Father which is in heaven." Matt. vii : 21. None but the *saved* can be citizens of the kingdom of heaven ; and none but those who do the will of the Father can enter the kingdom ; hence, we conclude that doing the will of the Father is an indispensable condition of salvation. Will my worthy opponent say that a man can be saved without doing the will of the Father, either as saint or sinner ?

But we must be willing ourselves. Jesus said to the Jews : "Search the Scriptures, for in them ye think ye have eternal life, and they are they which testify of me ; and ye will not come to me that ye might have life." John v : 39, 40. Life was set before them, but they would not come to Jesus through whom they could get it. When beholding the dazzling splendor of Je-

---

*Here the hour expired. The following was presented in a subsequent speech.

rusalem, and contemplating the desolation to which it would be reduced in consequence of the wickedness of the people, Jesus said: "O, Jerusalem, Jerusalem, thou that killest the prophets, and stonest them which are sent unto thee, how often would I have gathered thy children together, even as a hen gathereth her chickens under her wings, and ye would not. Behold, your house is left unto you desolate." Matt. xxiii: 37.

Does not this show that the wickedness of the people brought destruction upon themselves and their city? And they would have been saved had they heeded the oft-repeated admonitions of the Savior. Their own obdurate *will* prevented them from accepting the salvation offered them. So it has ever been. If men have not been saved, it has not been because they *could not* be, but because they *would not* obey God, that they might be saved. If men are not saved to-day, it is not because they cannot be saved, but because they *will not* comply with the *conditions* upon which God proposes to save them.

But why are men condemned? We have already heard Jesus say in the plainest terms that "He that believeth not shall be damned," and "He that believeth not is condemned already, because he hath not believed on the name of the only begotten Son of God;" and "He that believeth not the Son shall not see life; but the wrath of God abideth on him." But we will hear him further on the subject of condemnation. "Marvel not at this; for the hour is coming in the which all that are in their graves shall hear his voice, and shall come forth; they that have done good, unto the resurrection of life, and they that have done evil, unto the resurrection of damnation." John v: 28, 29. Does this need comment or explanation? They that have *done good* shall be resurrected to life, and they that *have done evil* shall be resurrected to condemnation. Was ever language more plain? They that have *done good*, either in coming into the kingdom, or as citizens of it. Why do not all do good? Simply because they *will not*.

On this subject Jesus further says: "I was hungered, and ye gave me meat; I was thirsty, and ye gave me drink; I was a stranger, and ye took me in; naked, and ye clothed me; I was sick, and ye visited me; I was in prison, and ye came unto me. Then shall the righteous answer him, saying, Lord, when saw we thee an hungered, and fed thee? or thirsty, and gave thee drink? When saw we thee a stranger, and took thee in? or naked, and clothed thee? or when saw we thee sick, or in prison, and came unto thee? And the King shall answer, and say unto them, Verily I say unto you, Inasmuch as ye have done it unto one of the least of these, my brethren, ye have done it unto me. Then shall he say also unto them on the left hand, Depart from me, ye cursed, into everlasting fire prepared for the devil and his angels; for I was an hungered, and ye gave me no meat; I was thirsty, and ye gave me no drink; I was a stranger, and ye took me not in; naked, and ye clothed me not; sick, and in prison, and ye visited me not. Then shall they also answer him, saying: Lord when saw we thee an hungered, or athirst, or a stranger, or naked, or sick, or in prison, and did not minister unto thee? Then shall he answer them, saying, Verily I say unto you, Inasmuch as ye did it not to one of the least of these, ye did it not to me. And these shall go away into everlasting punishment; but the righteous into life eternal." Matt. xxv: 35–46. Here again we learn that obedience to the will of the Lord gives entrance into life eternal, and neglect of duty sends men into everlasting punishment, whether it be with regard to entering the kingdom, or the discharge of duty in it. Then are not rewards and punishment condiional? Surely they are.

"And to you who are troubled rest with us, when the Lord shall be revealed from heaven with his mighty angels, in flaming fire, taking vengeance on them that know not God, and that obey not the gospel of our Lord Jesus Christ; who shall be punished with everlasting destruction from the presence of the Lord, and from the glory of his power; when he shall come to be glorified in his saints, and to be admired in all them that believe." 2 Thess. i: 7–10. On whom will he take vengeance when he comes? Those who know not God and obey not the gospel. In whom will he be glorified? His saints who believe on him, and have obeyed him, and have thus escaped his vengeance.

Finally, we propose to show that the final *judgment* will be based upon the very principle contained in my proposition. Indeed, we have already seen that the *wicked* will go away into everlasting punishment, and the *righteous* into life eternal; that they that have *done good* shall be resurrected to life, and they that have *done evil* will be resurrected to damnation; and that Jesus Christ will take vengeance on them that know not God and obey not the gospel, and we insist that these Scriptures are sufficient to settle this question forever. But our resources are ample, and we can afford to be liberal. We therefore invite attention to Romans ii: 4–11: "Despisest thou the riches of his goodness and forbearance and longsuffering; not knowing that the goodness of God leadeth thee to repentance? But after thy hardness and impenitent heart treasurest up unto thyself wrath against the day of wrath and revelation of the righteous judgment of God; who will render to every man according to his deeds. To them who by patient continuance in well doing, seek for glory and honor and immortality, eternal life; but unto them that are contentious, and do not obey the truth, but obey unrighteousness, indignation and wrath, tribulation and anguish, upon every soul of man that doeth evil, of the Jew first, and also of the Gentile; but glory, honor, and peace, to every man that worketh good, to the Jew first, and also to the Gentile; for there is no respect of persons with God." This is too plain to need comment. God will render to every man according to his deeds; not according to the eternal decree of election which settled his destiny before time began. Paul enters into specifications—to them who patiently continue to do well, he will render eternal life; but unto them who are contentious, and do not obey the truth, but obey unrighteousness, he will render indignation and wrath; and it matters not whether he fails to obey the truth, in coming into the church or after he is in; the principle is the same.

John says: "I saw the dead, small and great, stand before God; and the books were opened; and another book was opened, which is the book of life, and the dead were judged out of those things which were written in the books, according to their works. And the sea gave up the dead which were in it; and death and hell delivered up the dead which were in them; and they were judged, every man, according to their works." Rev. xx: 12, 13.

Every man was judged how? According to the eternal and immutable decree of election? What a ridiculous farce such a judgment would be! But they are judged according to their works. Those who have obeyed the gospel will enter upon the enjoyment of eternal life, in a glorious immortality; but those who will not obey the gospel will go into everlasting fire, prepared for the devil and his angels.

Once more, John says: "And behold, I come quickly; and my reward is with me, to give to every man according as his work shall be. I am Alpha and Omega, the beginning and the end, the first and the last. Blessed are they that do his commandments, that they may have right to the tree of life, and may enter in through the gates into the city." Rev. xxii: 12–14. The Lord says my reward is with me to give to every man *as his work shall be.* They who do his commandments here will have right to the tree of life, and be permitted to pass through the pearly gates into the city, where God, Jesus, angels, and all will be who have washed their robes in the blood of the Lamb. Will they, who have not done his commandments, enter in as well? If not, salvation from sin is conditional, the condition, or conditions to be performed by the sinner, in order to salvation or freedom from sin.

Let us hear the conclusion of the whole matter: "Fear God and keep his commandments, for this is the whole duty of man; for God will bring every work into judgment, with every secret thing, whether it be good, or whether it be evil." Ecl. xii: 13, 14.

www.ingramcontent.com/pod-product-compliance
Lightning Source LLC
Chambersburg PA
CBHW051722300426
44115CB00007B/429